POST-9/11 CINEMA

Through a Lens Darkly

John Markert

THE SCARECROW PRESS, INC.
Lanham • Toronto • Plymouth, UK
2011

Published by Scarecrow Press, Inc.
A wholly owned subsidiary of The Rowman & Littlefield Publishing Group, Inc.
4501 Forbes Boulevard, Suite 200, Lanham, Maryland 20706
http://www.scarecrowpress.com

Estover Road, Plymouth PL6 7PY, United Kingdom

British Library Cataloguing in Publication Information Available

Library of Congress Cataloging-in-Publication Data

Markert, John, 1945–
  Post-9/11 cinema : through a lens darkly / John Markert.
    p. cm.
  Includes bibliographical references and index.
  ISBN 978-0-8108-8134-1 (cloth : alk. paper) — ISBN 978-0-8108-8135-8
(ebook)
  1. Motion pictures—United States—History—21st century. 2. Motion
pictures—Political aspects—United States. 3. War films—United States—
History and criticism. 4. September 11 Terrorist Attacks, 2001—Influence.
I. Title.
  PN1993.5.U6M263 2011 791.43'658—dc22   2011008900

∞™ The paper used in this publication meets the minimum requirements of
American National Standard for Information Sciences—Permanence of Paper
for Printed Library Materials, ANSI/NISO Z39.48-1992.

Printed in the United States of America

To those who have served,
To those who have sacrificed,
And to their families.

CONTENTS

PREFACE

The attack on the World Trade Center stunned Americans as they sat glued to their televisions and watched the repeated collapse of the twin towers. The images of devastation mesmerized Americans over the coming months as people across the country watched the heroic efforts of New York public servants swarm over the site, sorting through the debris searching for survivors, and later causalities. These images were augmented by an outpouring of support to assist those public and private agencies rendering services for those working the site. The attack and the visual carnage that Americans were exposed to on September 11, 2001, was reminiscent of those who sat glued to their radios on December 7, 1941, to hear reports about Pearl Harbor, and who later watched Movietone newsreels to view firsthand the devastation of the American fleet at Pearl. Indeed, "the day of infamy" surprise of both assaults on American soil was connected by the media in the aftermath of the World Trade Center disaster and with the expectations that the same wave of patriotism that swept across America after the December 7 attack would be witnessed again in the aftermath of September 11. The patriotic fever was certainly there in the wake of 9/11, and the undertow was sufficient to generate international support for the invasion of Afghanistan the following month (October 17, 2001) and national support for the invasion of Iraq eighteen months later (March 20, 2003). But public support began to fade in the coming years as both wars raged on with no end in sight. The patriotic parallel to World War II that marked President Bush's first term in office—which reached its zenith with the president's landing on the aircraft carrier *Abraham Lincoln* to proclaim the Iraq war won—shifted increasingly to parallels with the Vietnam debacle during the president's second term in office.

This book is not about the war itself, but about the cinematic treatment of the post-9/11 attack. These films have few cinematic parallels. In their initial stage, the current crop of war films is often dramatically different from film portrayals of World War II. This is due, at least in part, to the dearth of feature films about the current conflict. The early positive portrayals that did appear were less about the war taking place in Afghanistan and more about either (1) the tragedy that took place in New York City on 9/11, or (2) those held responsible for 9/11, Saddam Hussein and Osama bin Laden. In their latter stages, contemporary war films are markedly different because of their growing antagonism toward the war while in the midst of the conflict. The negative depiction of war-related events is something that did not occur during World War II or Korea, but was also atypical during the highly contentious debate that raged in the public arena during the Vietnam conflict. The first films to critically interpret the Vietnam experience, which officially ended in April 1975, were *The Boys in Company C* (1977) and *The Deer Hunter* (1978).

In the aftermath of Pearl Harbor, the Hollywood film industry marshaled its cinematic muscle and produced, over the next four years, a tsunami of war films that depicted the heroism of America's fighting men (and women) and the evil of the Japanese Empire and the German Reich. Between one-third and one-half of all Hollywood films between 1942 and 1945 depicted the war in some manner.[1] Numerous film historians in the immediate aftermath of 9/11 anticipated a similar cinematic onslaught.[2] This did not occur. There were only a few films released in 2002 and 2003. The first "onslaught" did not occur until 2004 when approximately two dozen war-related films were released. Since then, more than one hundred films dealing with the wars in Afghanistan and Iraq have appeared. This is a thin slice of Hollywood's annual release quantitatively, especially compared to those released during World War

II that dealt with the war. This is due, at least in part, to the different structure of the movie industry.

Hollywood during World War II was dominated by a few major studios and run with the heavy hands of moguls such as Louis B. Mayer, Jack Warner, Lewis Selznick, and Adolph Zukor. These individuals could marshal, at a moment's notice, studio contract writers, directors, and actors to start work on a picture. This, coupled with the strong sense of patriotism by those in the industry—many of whom received honorary military commission, such as Lieutenant Colonels Jack Warner and William Wyler—and the market demand for these types of movies, promoted a surge in World War II movies. The financial and moral support of the government to reinforce the patriotic fever also went a long way in promoting the surge of war-related movies. The rush to capitalize on these popular films was a critical factor in their blandness. Films made during the war, with a few notable exceptions, look childish and banal. This is because, as Thomas Doherty observes, they are little more than "stiffly staged show(s) of parading toy soldiers and tightly wound dolls" formulaically cranked out. [3]

The dominance of the studios was broken when the Supreme Court ruled in *U.S. v. Paramount Pictures* (1948) that studios had to disinvest and sever their lucrative theater ties. The House Un-American Activities Committee (HUAC) hearings in 1947 and 1951–1952 and the national scandal of the "Hollywood Ten"—ten screenwriters, directors, and producers accused of Communist leanings—further hampered the studios' market control. [4] The rapid rise of television soon followed, driving the final nail into the once powerful studio system. These days, Hollywood no longer denotes domination by a handful of key studios and studio executives, or even a geographical concentration. Today the Hollywood moniker is more often associated with films made by American filmmakers. The studio names are still on the masthead—United Artists, Paramount, Columbia, Fox—but the studios mainly rely on independent filmmakers to produce films, which gives them considerably less control over what is made. The studios may help finance these films, but their primary role is to promote and distribute the product. This heterogeneity of a previously homogenous industry means that it takes more time to assemble a movie. This is one reason why there was a lapse of some years before Hollywood turned its lens on the wars in Afghanistan and Iraq.

While the structure of the industry explains the quantitative difference between post-Pearl and post-9/11 films, it only partially explains the cinematic treatment of the ensuing hostilities. The "day of infamy" mentality that connects both events that are separated chronologically by over a half-century should result in similarly themed movies. And this does occur, at least initially.

Chapter 1 examines early post-9/11 developments. One category is reminiscent of World War II films in their focus on the "evil foreigner." This starts with *Uncle Saddam*, which precedes the assault on the World Trade Center by a year, but thematically links post-9/11 films, and harbingers early Iraq invasion films. Early post-9/11 films shift attention from Saddam's weapons program to Osama bin Laden's terrorist action. The other film category focuses on events surrounding the World Trade Center. Films made in the early period—*New York Firefighters: The Brotherhood of 9/11* (2002) and *Aftermath: Unanswered Questions from 9/11* (2005)—and those made later—*United 93* (2006) and *911: In Plane Site* (2007)—are thematically linked in their treatment of the subject: Americans are the victims, while "foreigners" are "savages." This treatment is typical: Most war-related films depict an "us" versus "them" mind-set. Those few films in this category that address the "question" of 9/11 arise later (circa 2005) and do so by challenging the ineptitude of those in power, who should have known about the attack and possibly prevented the disaster. Nevertheless, these films avoid questioning the heroism of either the victims or those rendering post-9/11 assistance. They also make little attempt to understand the point of view that predicated the attack. These later films, despite the time frame that separates them, are thematically linked in their generally positive examination of how people handled themselves in the wake of these disasters. This positive cinemagraphic assessment is not the case with many other films, beginning in the pivotal years 2004 and 2005.

The initial, generally positive, crop of films begins to change between 2004 and 2005. Chapter 2 examines films during this transitional period. This includes Michael Moore's *Fahrenheit 9/11*, which is "rebutted" by *FahrenHYPE 9/11* and *Michael Moore Hates America* made later that same year. These years are also cinematically pivotal because of the release of a number of foreign films in the United States that garnered some attention and which gave a distinctly different interpretation of the war, such as *Control Room* and *The Blood of My Brother.* There were other films, however, that continued to press a positive interpretation of the war. Because this is such a pivotal year both socially, with the presidential election in 2004, and cinematically, with an increasingly disparate view of the war, these two years are critiqued at some length in this chapter.

In 2006, and increasingly thereafter, there is a marked change in the content of films focusing on the war. A strong, caustic interpretation of the war effort begins to emerge after 2005 as the war drags on and President Bush's popularity plummets. This is due, in part, to the war but also because of other (often related) social criticisms of Bush's presidency. Chapters 3 and 4 examine the groundswell of films that turn a darker lens on American involvement in Afghanistan and Iraq. Chapter 3 examines the continued role of documentaries to interpret and disseminate information about how the war is unfolding. Chapter 4 examines the feature films that begin to appear, such as *In the Valley of Elah*, *The Kingdom*, *Rendition*, *Redacted*, *Lions for Lambs*, and *Cavite*. These chapters also assess both imported foreign documentaries, such as *Taxi to the Dark Side*, and feature films, such as *The Kite Runner*, which capture a side of the war not addressed by American filmmakers. Additionally, Chapter 4 addresses the sudden surge in feature length films after nearly seven years have lapsed, explicating both the treatment of the war in these films and the reason for their late appearance.

Chapter 5 concludes this analysis by evaluating the impact of these films on the public, as well as the public's role in shaping the films that came out of Hollywood in the wake of 9/11. Before proceeding to the films themselves, however, it is first necessary to discuss the theoretical underpinning for this analysis of films and to delve into the role of documentaries, which until recently have been the primary means used to explore the post-9/11 world.

NOTES

1. Thomas Doherty, *Projections of War: Hollywood, American Culture, and World War II* (New York: Columbia University Press, 1993); Albert Auster

and Leonard Quart, *How the War Was Remembered: Hollywood & Vietnam* (Westport, Conn.: Praeger, 1988).

2. Trevor B. McCrisken and Andrew Pepper, *American History and Contemporary Hollywood Film* (New Brunswick, N.J.: Rutgers University Press, 2005); Carl Boggs and Tony Pollard, *A World in Chaos: Social Crisis and the Rise of Postmodern Cinema* (Boulder, Colo.: Rowman & Littlefield, 2003).

3. Doherty, *Projections of War*, 2. See also Patricia R. Zimmerman, *States of Emergency: Documentaries, Wars, Democracies* (Minneapolis: University of Minnesota Press, 2000); McCrisken and Pepper, *American History and Contemporary Hollywood Film*; Auster and Quart, *How the War Was Remembered: Hollywood & Vietnam*.

4. Gerald Mast and B. F. Kawin, *A Short History of the Movies* (New York: Macmillan, 1992), 276–79.

INTRODUCTION

The media has always played a socializing role. Historically, however, the effects of the media have not been of particular concern since its consumption was limited to elites, who, it was believed, were less susceptible to any potentially "harmful" message. It became a concern when media entered the public sphere and began to disseminate information more widely. This first happened with the introduction of printed material for the masses. The novel stimulated particular concern because of the potential for the reader to identify with unsavory fictional characters. The concern was that readers would lack the ability to differentiate fact from fiction, so Dr. Samuel Johnson postulated, and thus "everyman" readers might confuse the reprehensible with the exemplary qualities of a character, and this might predispose them to favor evil over virtue.[1]

Popular novels and newspapers still garner attention, but at the advent of the twentieth century, visual portrayals have generated increased concern for their socializing affect. Initially, this concern focused on film, and it started almost immediately with the quarter-second meeting of John Rice's lips with May Irwin's in *The Kiss* (1897) and the lascivious hoochy-coochy bumps and grinds in *Fatima* (1897). The continued and increased sensuality of films during the Roaring Twenties ultimately led to the Hollywood Production Code, which ensured that films would receive "official" approval only if they met certain moralistic standards.[2] Production Code standards also encompassed restrictions on profanity and the graphic depiction of violence.

Concern about the corrupting nature of film content shifted during the second half of the twentieth century to television. It became the focal point largely because of its ubiquity: Americans watch more than four hours of prime-time programs every night.[3] Conventional wisdom held that watching this much television could have a corrupting influence. This was the rationale behind the Federal Communications Commission (FCC) regulation of early television content. FCC oversight kept the content of television fairly "respectable" in the early years and even though more profanity, sexuality, and violence have filtered onto the small screen today, it is relatively sanitized compared to the "unholy trinity" of sex, violence, profanity in contemporary film. Indeed, the socializing influence of the media has returned to the pivotal role of the cinema in the world today.

Television has become so commonplace that its role as a socializing agent is actually less pronounced than film. People might watch massive amounts of television, but it makes little impact. It has been long been recognized that few people can recall more than one or two news stories after watching the evening news.[4] One reason for this is that the news is not watched closely: less than one-quarter (22 percent) view it to "keep informed."[5] Entertainment programming is even more problematic, since few people expect to learn anything from the show and do not watch it attentively. Another reason for the failure of television programs to be remembered is that so many people watch while multitasking. A study by Mediamark Research & Intelligence found that over half (51.7 percent) of those who were watching television were consuming another media form: one-third (34.3 percent) were reading either magazines or newspapers while another one-fifth (17.4 percent) were on the Internet at the same time.[6] This number would be much higher if nonmedia activities were included: eating, carrying on a conversation with others in the room, talking on the phone, or doing other sundry activities, such as balancing a checkbook, sorting through the mail, cooking, doing homework, grading papers, or prepping for a meeting.[7]

The effects of television are also deflected by the set's size. Even large-size television sets—with the possible exception of the small percentage of "movie-sized" televisions—occupy only a small visual frame in the average-sized room. This means that our peripheral vision is constantly straying from events unfolding on television. This is why people remember movies in the theater: The film dominates the setting and our focus is not circumvented by other activities. Another factor that modifies television's effect is that the show is constantly interrupted by commercials to break the narrative flow, something that does not occur at the movies.

Selectivity is also a factor that detracts from television's socializing effects. The primary reason for selecting a television show is time availability.[8] Free time at home is most likely to result in television viewing. In other words, people with time on their hands will watch television simply because it is there and they have nothing else to do, which means that, essentially, they'll watch anything.[9] Movies, on the other hand, including rental movies shown on the small screen, are selected because of the content of the film—people *want* to watch it. And although a viewer's attention may drift when watching a movie on DVD, people are more likely to focus on the film, in part because they have actively selected the movie and desire to see it. Movies viewed in theaters obviously have even more potential for socializing viewers in the ways of the world—or in this case, informing them of how to interpret post-9/11 incursions into Afghanistan and Iraq.

THEORETICAL PERSPECTIVES

The connection between culture and society has long garnered both popular and scholarly attention. One prong of this connection is the belief that values within the wider society are reflected on the screen. This view asserts that society gives rise to certain cultural forms and themes. After all, people read books and go to the movies because they can relate to the storyline. Indeed, one of the most frequent popular critiques of a movie inevitably appraises the realistic quality of the film.[10] What is depicted in the book or on the screen is something that reflects a slice of a familiar world. Even science fiction films that are cast into the future or historical films that delve into the past are seen from a contemporary lens.[11] *Southland Tales* (2006), for example, depicts a futuristic dystopian America on the verge of collapse. A contributing cause of this apocalyptic scenario is attributed to the endless war raging in Iraq and Afghanistan, a sentiment that was gaining social currency at this time among the American populace.

Regardless of the era depicted, movies portray attitudes that pervade the social world at the time the film is made. For example, movies about World War II that were made during the war years are simplistic in their storyline and unabashedly propagandistic, casting America's fighting men as clean-cut heroes (e.g., see "Why We Fight" series, 1942–1944; *Destination Tokyo*, 1943; *Memphis Belle*, 1944; *God Is My Co-Pilot*, 1945); those made in the immediate aftermath of the war are much more nuanced and less flattering of military life (*The Story of G. I. Joe*, 1945; *From Here to Eternity*, 1953), while others cast a jaundiced look at the plight of the returning veteran (*The Blue Dahlia*, 1945; *The Best Years of Our Life*, 1946). In this same vein, *Strategic Air Command* (1955; see also *A Gathering of Eagles*, 1963), starring real-life Air Force Brigadier General James Stewart, was made during the height of the Cold War and lauds the patriotic self-sacrifices of America's fighting men who fly the skies to safeguard the United States from a possible Russian nuclear attack; a decade later, *Dr. Strangelove or: How I Learned to Stop Worrying and Love the Bomb* (1963; see also *Fail Safe*, 1964) mocks this same scenario as the mood of the country shifts into the more turbulent and cynical 1960s.

The society to culture prong is generally referred to as reflection theory. This is a rather passive view of media's effect that holds, according to Herbert Gans "the prime function of the media is to reinforce already existing behavior and attitudes rather than create them."[12] Nevertheless, this *is* a form of socialization: The cultural object reinforces existing attitudes and values, and thus serves to strengthen these same beliefs. Movies, then, serve as a window on the world that allows the viewer to gain insight into social beliefs. The content of the cultural form is viewed as a mirror into the group's values. The reflective metaphor allows the cultural object, in this case, movies, to be "read" as a sign of what people in society are thinking at any given time and to track changes in popular ideology. Early films that dealt with American involvement in Southeast Asia, such *The Steel Helmet* (1951) and *China Gate* (1957), serve to remind us that the Cold War ideology that pervaded society initially applauded America's early support of Vietnam. Even in the mid-sixties, the war was not an intense social issue, except among a small but vocal group of "radical" dissidents. The novel by Robin Moore, *The Green Berets* (1966), Staff-Sergeant Barry Sadler's widely popular song "The Ballad of the Green Berets" (1966), the movie *To the Shores of Hell* (1966), and John Wayne's later financially successful, *The Green Berets* (1968), remind us that many Americans still viewed the Vietnam experience in a positive light. Wayne's movie, much more so than the other, somewhat earlier cultural artifacts, generated public debate as it was released after the Tet Offensive in January of the same year, and Tet is widely regarded as the point when the mood of the country began to change toward Americans involved in Vietnam.[13]

Public disenchantment toward America's involvement in Vietnam, which had been percolating among young people on the streets before Tet, decidedly turned after Tet. The time when the public mood shifted is clearly demarked with Vietnam. It is not as clear with American involvement in the Middle East. After all, Bush swept the 2004 presidential race, an indication not only of his popularity at the time but a message from the American people to "stay the course." But the movies in 2004 were an early harbinger of the country's mood swing. In 2004 and 2005 the public debate over America's involvement in the Middle East began to intensify and this dissension is clearly reflected in the movies that assess America's involvement in Iraq. The ambiguity toward the war can be discerned in both the public sentiment and the movies during 2004 and 2005; however, movies after 2005 show a clear shift from the right to the left, reflecting society's growing disaffection with America's course.

Reflection theory also accounts for the postmodern spirit in contemporary films. Modernism is rooted to cultural changes taking place in the late nineteenth and early twentieth centuries. Modernism is shaped by an enhanced scientific leaning toward gaining knowledge: technology and industrialization are emphasized as a means for transforming society for the better. In cinema, modernism celebrates strict linear progression and technological mastery. The storyline is straightforward and the spectacle becomes supreme: *Trip to the Moon, The Great Train*

Robbery, Birth of a Nation, and *Gone with the Wind* are just a few representative modern films that span the first half of the twentieth century. Somewhere along the line during the second half of the twentieth
century a shift toward postmodernism begins to take place and becomes
increasingly pronounced as the twentieth century rolls into the twenty-
first century.[14] There is, however, no clear break that separates the modern era from the postmodern one.[15] This results in considerable overlap
between these two points, which is the reason why Boggs and Pollard
hold that modernism-postmodernism inhabits a cinematic continuum.[16]
Still, postmodernism tends to depict considerable disenchantment with
social arrangements and takes a more critical, alienated worldview that
borders on the nihilistic. Postmodern films are more fragmented, reflecting this social alienation (see *Stranger than Paradise,* 1984; *Brazil,*
1985; *Smoke,* 1995; *Il Divo,* 2009); postmodern cinema also interprets
events from multiple viewpoints, rejecting the dominant metanarrative
of modern filmmakers (see *Rashomon,* 1950; *The Thin Blue Line,* 1988;
Crash, 2004; *Waltz with Bashir,* 2008).

The plot-driven metanarrative is readily discerned in films made
about World War II that were made during the war years. Films in
the immediate aftermath of World War II begin to show a postmodern
bent. The "darker" social perspective is especially discernable in film
noir movies that gained ascendancy toward the end of the war with
the release of Billy Wilder's *Double Indemnity* (1944) and Edward
Dmytryk's *Murder, My Sweet* (1944). Film noir cinema was marked
by its moral ambiguity, which is a sharp departure from the moralistic
and clearly defined good versus evil duality of the majority of movies
that preceded them. Post–World War II films reflected the angst of
the returning veterans, who inhabit a world dramatically different from
the one they left, and where they question their place in the new, alien
social order. *The Blue Dahlia* is an excellent representative of this new
breed of film since it melds the alienation of the returning veterans with
the moral ambiguity of noir: Johnny (Alan Ladd) returns home to a un-
repentant cheating wife, and his friend Buzz (William Bendix) exhibits
violent and erratic behavior because of a steel plate in his head from a
wartime injury; the overall feel of the movie is one that depicts, in the
words of Wheeler Dixon, "a world of hopeless, terminal despair."[17] The
rise of the Cold War pushed these morally equivocal films out of the

limelight as America once again faced a clearly defined foe whose values were antithetical to those of red-blooded Americans.

The postmodern era in film was flirted with in the immediate aftermath of World War II when social and financial uncertainties loomed over the immediate postwar years, but the postmodern image became a marked cinematic convention following Vietnam, due largely to the moral ambiguity of the Vietnam conflict, which became clearer in the aftermath of the war than during the war itself. McCrisken and Pepper argue in a chapter subheading entitled, "The Bad War," the reason behind this shift:

[t]he moral certitude of the World War II era, and indeed, the early Cold War was thrown into disarray by America's first defeat in war. The network of corruption, lies and abuse of power in Washington coupled with revelations of massacres and other heinous acts committed by U.S. forces in Indochina, served to undermine the way Americans thought of war as a unifying force that, when undertaken by the U.S., served some higher purpose. . . . Vietnam brought about a period of disillusionment with combat. . . ."[18]

The first major feature film about Vietnam that incorporated distinct postmodern elements was *The Deer Hunter*. *The Deer Hunter* is illustrative because it remains quintessentially a modern film with a straightforward storyline with a clearly defined foe (Viet Cong), and yet is dusted with noir elements: the grainy, black-and-white cast of the Pennsylvania coal mining town that the decent but going-nowhere main characters inhabit before going off to war; the Russian roulette scene which captures for Ronald Davis "the risk, insanity, and despair experienced by the Vietnam soldiers in raw, existential terms."[19] Considerably more postmodern in its tone is *Apocalypse Now* (1979), which distains to camouflage American involvement wrapped in some higher purpose and depicts instead the sheer surreal madness of war. The film leaves the viewer to ponder just who is mad, Kurtz (Marlon Brando) or the American imperialists, particularly in the guise of Colonel Kilgore (Robert Duval), who Auster and Quart view as the embodiment of "American arrogance and ethnocentrism in his incapacity to believe that some small Asiatic people could hurt or even defeat his country or that there are other countries and people who have complex political and social interests and needs of their own."[20]

This postmodern vision is reflected in many of the films that depict American involvement in the Middle East after 9/11. The moral certitude that led to America's early involvement is intensely debated in movies made between 2004 and 2005, but increasingly questioned in films after this period. The metanarrative voice-over view that America is saving the world is also challenged in films after 2005. This is seen in the fragmented style of many post-9/11 war films. Fragmentation serves to disrupt the film's coherence, so prevalent in modern films. It also allows for multiple, often disjointed viewpoints. Some of the postmodern 9/11 films give voice to how those on the "other side" see things, while other films express the existential views of some of "our own" on the front lines who question their reason for being there and their doubt regarding the difference they make by their presence.

Another legacy of postmodern films is the tendency to promote a social vision that will lead to change. This aspect of postmodernism goes beyond the passive societal-culture connection of reflection theory and is more appropriately addressed under the other cultural-societal prong, where the cultural artifact is seen as shaping societal values.

Films may reflect society and provide a glimpse of what people believe, but people also recognize that the message may be distorted to reflect the values of those individuals or vested interest groups that make or produce the film. This aspect of reflection theory may be better described using the metaphor of refraction since the point of view that is propagated tends to refract the values and beliefs of the proselytizing individual or group. The refracted message can be taken as reality by the viewer. Refraction theory suggests that recurring exposure to a film's message may not just reinforce existing attitudes and beliefs but shape them.

Though the metaphor of refraction is new, the analysis of the vested interest of groups whose views are refracted is quite common. Films have long been criticized because they promote the views of the producer or director.

Marxism is one of the more prevalent schools that examine the refracted message. The Marxist analysis relies heavily on the base-superstructure relationship, which is rooted to the society-to-culture perspective: Cultural products (superstructure elements) are shaped by the economic base. Cultural items that arise from this base serve to perpetuate the ideology of the capitalist social class—the owners of the means of production. Marxists acknowledge the society-to-culture connection, but their analysis focuses on how the cultural object shapes values.[21] This is especially the case with neo-Marxists in the Critical School, which Grossberg argues is one of the most influential interpretations relied upon in communication studies.[22] The Critical School has its roots in the 1930s and 1940s, and even though Strinati feels that their approach is both narrow and outmoded today, he nevertheless is compelled to acknowledge that their analysis of popular culture continues to be extensively utilized, so much so that any "contemporary analysis of popular music [and elsewhere] still commences . . . [with] Adorno's [1941] theory."[23]

Proponents of the Critical School focus extensively on the superstructure; they explicate how cultural objects such as music, movies, and television maintain the ideology of social elites by pacifying and stupefying the consumer.[24] Their perspective has been applied to movies with some validity, particularly those made during World War II and the Cold War.[25] The disruption of the old Hollywood system, however, would suggest that the ability to control a singular, monolithic ideological motif is more difficult in contemporary cinema, which helps explain a strong counter-hegemonic theme in many post-9/11 Iraq-Afghanistan war films.

In the best Marxist tradition, the Critical School felt that art forms such as movies should raise the consciousness of the masses to their exploitation.[26] This is exactly what postmodernism accomplishes. It rejects the monolithic metanarrative voice and promotes a plurality of views and interpretations of events. A heterogeneous perspective is celebrated over a homogenous elitist one. This is accomplished in postmodernism without a Marxist referent. Postmodernism also embraces popular culture, while post-Marxists following the Critical School tradition tend to dismiss mass culture forms such as films for their banality. There are certainly many films that fall into what Jameson calls nostalgic films and perpetuate an idealized and naïve view of the past, such as *Peggy Sue Got Married* and *Back to the Future*, or relate simplistic myths and stereotypes about the past, such as the *Raiders of the Lost Ark* and

National Treasure series, the *Lord of the Rings* trilogy, and just about any "classic" western.[27] These types of films lend credence to Jameson's charge that postmodernism is a hopelessly commercial culture. The present crop of films, however, would challenge this post-Marxian view of popular culture because it is anything but "commercial" and tackles sensitive contemporary topics while also painting a complex picture of current events that defy an easy solution.

The problem with a Marxist analysis is that it limits the interpretation of cultural events by placing all such activities within the Marxian social class framework. The metaphor of refraction avoids this a priori orientation, which sometimes forces square pegs into round holes. The refracted view *may* represent the view of social elites who are attempting to promote the dominate ideology—both *FarhenHYPE 9/11* and *Michael Moore Hates America* (2004) ideologically and unabashedly promote the Bush war agenda; but the refracted view may represent an alternative, though likewise biased, perspective that is not rooted to perpetuating ruling class interests. Michael Moore's *Fahrenheit 9/11* fits more neatly into this alternative viewpoint. So do a host of other post-9/11 films that deal with the Iraq-Afghanistan conflict. A substantial portion of the post–2005 war-related films, rather than serve the interest of elites, attempts to expose the viewer to how elites have distorted certain realities.

Seeing culture only as a shaping instrument has been legitimately criticized by Ann Swidler as fundamentally misleading because it assumes that culture shapes action by supplying ultimate ends or values.[28] At the same time, Swidler recognizes that culture can affect social values. This is the reason she proposes that when looking at the culture-society connection the focus should be less grandiose and should examine the cultural artifact as a kind of "tool kit" of symbols, stories, and worldviews that people may rely on to help them construct strategies of action. Refraction theory does just that by recognizing that *all* films refract a political message that may influence the viewer to interpret their world in certain ways.[29] Some of these messages are starker than others, and not all the messages, in the Marxian tradition, attempt to cloud the issue. The Critical School's criticism of film was that cultural artifacts are always used by elites to dull social awareness. It was their contention that cultural objects should reveal the face behind the mask—the false ideology of the ruling class—and stimulate praxis by depicting "shimmers of resistance." This term might have been used by a Marxist critic but was in fact coined by Patricia Zimmerman to describe early films made by American filmmakers about the Iraq-Afghanistan conflict.[30] Indeed, the films made between 2004 and 2005 reflected but also helped to shape the public debate about American involvement in the Middle East, which after 2005 moved increasingly to expressing an antiwar sentiment.

The reflection-refraction metaphor is a sound heuristic device for studying cultural objects because it provides a framework for approaching the cultural form. It is misleading, however, because it overanalyzes one aspect of the cultural object and neglects, or at least minimizes its counterpart. Studies by Markert on music lyrics and television shows, as well as the present analysis of films, would suggest that the culture-society connection is recursive.[31] In other words, social attitudes, social context, and movie themes are interconnected and each interacts with and influences the other. Movie themes are often rooted in a specific time frame and social group and tend to reflect the values of that group. People select a movie because the theme relates to them and their social world. In turn, the movie's theme acts as a socializing agent by suggesting how the viewer should interpret their social world: those who "buy into" the film's thesis have their views authenticated by the movie experience, while those who do not have clearly formed attitudes toward the depicted theme are likely to be influenced to some degree by what they see on the screen. This is clearly discerned in the present analysis and is the reason for the chronological division of the book. In the immediate aftermath of the attack on the World Trade Center (WTC), there was considerable social support for American intervention in Iraq and Afghanistan. But a few years later some issues about how Americans might have been mislead about the weapons of mass destruction (WMD) by members of the Bush administration, and which prompted America's incursion into Iraq, began to percolate in society and in film. The public debate was intense between 2004 and 2005; it began to turn in 2006 and has since escalated. The wars—particularly Iraq—are now seen with a more jaundiced (camera) eye. Films certainly reflected this social shift, but they also helped promote the change in social attitudes while avoiding any attack on those who sacrificed for their country and put their lives on the line in a hostile terrain. How films managed this tenuous balance is a key aspect of this analysis.

One last perspective needs to be taken into account because it helps to assess the shaping of film content. The production-of-culture (POC) perspective is less a theoretical orientation than a self-conscious attempt to take into account extraneous factors that influence the content of a cultural object. The POC perspective raises slightly different questions than the other two theoretical orientations. Production seeks to examine the cultural objects more from an organizational (rather than societal) perspective by examining the process by which cultural artifacts are actually produced. The POC approach borrows from organizational and industrial sociology and refers to the process of selecting, manufacturing, marketing, distributing, exhibiting, and evaluating the cultural artifact. This view holds that cultural products such as film are subject to certain production constraints. Peterson pioneered the POC perspective and initially identified five constraints that affect the content of a cultural product, later expanding this to six.[32] The six external constraints that shape a picture include (1) law, which may prohibit certain content from being aired; (2) the structure of the industry, which would take into account whether the industry is monopolistic, or oligopolistic, or highly competitive and loosely coupled; (3) organizational structure, which takes into account the size (large versus small) of the firm making the film and the division of labor within the organization; (4) occupational careers; (5) technology; and (6) market, which refers not so much to who actually consumes the product as it does to those who make the product feel is the intended audience, the premise being that it is their perception of the audience that will influence how they make and market the product. Not all these constraints work in tandem all the time, but certain aspects do influence what is filmed, how it is filmed, and how it reaches the public.

In this analysis, production constraints will always remain in the foreground as possible explanations for the film's content. One constraint, the structure of the industry, notably the more competitive nature of the film industry today in contrast to its earlier oligopolistic structure, has already been mentioned a number of times as it affects content. A second constraint, organizational structure, is immediately addressed because the majority of films between 2001 and 2007 that covered 9/11 war-related events were documentaries made by small independent companies that could take more risks than the studios who market their films toward a larger, more homogenous audience and are often fearful that controversial subject matter might offend their audience and possibly reduce revenue. Organizational structure is intertwined with a third constraint, occupational careers. Film careers today are not tied as tightly to the old Hollywood system and this allows more freedom to develop movies without the "credentials" normally required by financial backers. A fourth constraint is technology because break-throughs in filming and film processing helped independent producers develop their work more expeditiously than the larger studios. A fifth is market, or more specifically, the access to alternative delivery methods to reach an audience: The role of small "art houses," the multiplexes, many of which because of their size can premiere pictures for a smaller audience, and the rise of DVD sales and rental outlets that make these films available to a wider audience beyond the movie house. The only constraint that has not been touched on is law. There is, of course, no explicit law that forbids films about the war from being made. However, the government has used its muscle to channel reporting of the war within the mainstream media. The often sanitized public face of the war has prompted the appearance of independent, documentary filmmakers to fill a critical fourth estate role to make the public aware of a darker side of the war than they had been exposed to on television.

DOCUMENTARY FILMS

Documentary films have a distinctive aesthetic which differentiates them from feature films and those with which most moviegoers are fa-miliar. An appreciation of documentaries is important because this was the predominant cinematic means that was used to "appraise" post-9/11 events and the war in Iraq and Afghanistan. Documentaries were relied on initially to "interpret" the terrorist attack on the WTC because they can be quickly produced, often by threading together existing footage with a narrative ribbon. They were relied on to present a picture of the war in Iraq and Afghanistan for at least three reasons. First, they were a way to get information to the public about the war on the ground that people were not being exposed to through the mainstream media. This led to the second reason for the surge in documentaries: those who wanted to reveal another side of the war could do so because the technology to make a documentary is economically within the reach of small, independent filmmakers, a situation that is particularly so with portable cameras and computer technology today; this makes documentaries relatively inexpensive, compared to production costs for even a B-list movie. And third, documentaries are typically not made with a profit motive in mind so they can tackle sensitive issues more readily than Hollywood producers who might fear alienating potential audiences.

Documentaries are also a primary form relied on in wartime. The "Why We Fight" series that was made during World War II (1942–1945) is an excellent example of wartime documentaries (see also the two short cinematic compilations, *World War I: Films of the Silent Era* [1916] and *History of World War I: America Goes Over* [1918], as well as the Army Signal Corps film, *The Korean War: The Big Picture* [1953]). The "Why We Fight" series was overseen by Lieutenant Colonel Frank Capra and the battle sequences in particular—*The Battle of Britain* (1943), *The Battle of Russia* (1943), and *The Battle of China* (1944)—were largely composed of government footage taken on the scene and made available to Capra, whose job was to weave it into a coherent native.[33] The series also illustrates another historical aspect of documentaries—their support, if not outright financial backing, by the government to promote an "orientation," to use the preferred, less value-laden term the U.S. government employed when referring to the strongly propagandistic slant of the "Why We Fight" series.[34]

The government did not promote any films to justify its incursion into Iraq and Afghanistan. From World War I through the Korean Conflict, the primary visual interpretation of events was through photojournalist magazines, such as *Life* and *Saturday Evening Post*, and movies, both of which relied extensively on government support by receiving approved footage or access to military instillations. Today, television (and increasingly YouTube)[35] replaces film as a way to visually inform the public of events occurring in the world, and how to interpret those events: the ground wars since Vietnam—Granada, Panama, and Gulf Wars I *and* II—were largely government-orchestrated television spectacles.[36]

Post–9/11 war documentaries, then, are atypical because they become a way for countervailing (nongovernmental) voices to be heard.

The government's monopoly on post–9/11 war-related media images was strong. The orchestrated landing of President Bush on the carrier *Abraham Lincoln* with the large banner unfurled in the background proclaiming the war to be over is one illustration of the government's manipulation of television exposure. Likewise, the toppling of Saddam Hussein's statue appeared on the major news networks to reflect the glee that Iraqis felt toward the American "liberators" as they surged toward the fallen statue of the former dictator, stomped and spitted on the rubble, and "whooping [as] they dragged its head through the street," even though a long-shot photo by Reuters and a BBC photo sequence of Firdos Square showed that it was nearly empty.[37] The silences—what was not covered—were also very "loud." During President Bush's two terms, over 3,876 military personnel were returned home in body bags,[38] but the President made sure no media would photograph the bodies. By flying them to Dover Air Force Base in Delaware where reporters and photographers were not given access, this reflects the governments out-of-sight, out-of-mind mentality[39]; similarly, by interring reputed terrorists within the confines of Guantánamo Naval Base in Cuba only military personnel (or those approved by the military) would have access to them and be able to appraise their treatment or the conditions under which they were held. This is not to suggest the media was totally silent. Voices were occasionally raised in the print media, but these palled with the coverage by the major television networks, which are the primary means by which the majority of Americans learn about world events: 58 percent of the public rely on television news for their primary source of information on national and international events.[40] This left the responsibility to visually report on the war in Afghanistan and Iraq to documentary filmmakers.

One of the unique attributes of the documentary form is its representation of fact. Indeed, Rosco and Hight hold this to be a privileged position among documentaries: their *claim* to truth.[41] Documentaries are viewed by audiences as "objective" since the camera ostensibly never lies. This assumption is largely based on the popular notion that a picture is worth a thousand words and that if it is a picture of something that putatively happened, then it must have happened. Many people believe that seeing something is visual proof that what is depicted actually took place. This is why documentaries carry so much weight with the public: documentaries ostensibly show real people in real-life events, unlike fiction, which by its very definition is artifact. This is why fictional violence is not terrifying. Fictional violence today relies on special effects to portray violence, but the graphics are so "carried away" that it leads to sensory overload. As Joel Black put it, such over-the-top gothic horror films as Wes Craven's *Scream* (see also *Lara Croft: Tomb Raider*, 2001; *The Mummy: Tomb of the Dragon Emperor*, 2008) or the meticulously choreographed violence of John Woo's or Ang Lee's action films "could be mistaken for the real thing only by viewers who are either mentally incompetent or culturally illiterate."[42] This makes the violence depicted in documentaries seem so much more real. It also appears to capture reality more truthfully because the characters telling the story are not actors but real people who were on the scene and who share their experiences with the audience. The intimate gaze of the camera as it captures the reaction of real people facing real events only serves to heighten the audience's identification with the events depicted.

The camera's intense scrutiny of events and the reaction of those on the scene are further heightened by certain cinematic techniques widely employed in documentary films. One is the shaky, handheld camcorder

The intense gaze of a believer listening to a political speech outside a mosque in Iraq in Fragments.

The gaze of vigilance: On patrol in _Gunner Palace_.

with its not-quite-perfect jumpy camera angles and grainy texture that
manages to give the film an authentic feel precisely because it is not
associated with the quality, airbrushed camerawork audiences expect
from feature-length fictional movies. This cinematic technique marks
the documentary from its origin with _Nanook of the North_ (1922), and
was a driving force for the audience confusion with the highly successful
fictional movie that didn't seem like a fiction film, largely because of the
poor quality photography in _The Blair Witch Project_ (1999). It is a tradition that frames the majority of post-9/11 documentaries and, as we will
see, is often interjected into fictional films that deal with the post-9/11
events to add credence to the storyline.[43]

The narrator's voice is another well-established documentary technique that is widely employed in post-9/11 films. Contrary to the popular adage, a picture is _not_ worth a thousand words. Indeed, the picture
itself is worthless unless it is framed and can be understood—turn
the sound off and watch the cascade of pictures on the evening news:
The pictures are meaningless without a context. The narrator's voice
in documentaries tells us what is going on by interpreting the event
depicted. This is also accomplished by the framing of interview questions and by reference to experts who are interviewed to shed light on
the event. These techniques characterize Michael Moore's work, from
his first work, _Roger and Me_ (1989) through his recent films, _Bowling_

for Columbine (2002), *Fahrenheit 9/11* (2004), and *Sicko* (2007). The narrator's voice—the voice-over explanations or the interview voice—is a stock technique in all the post-9/11 films. The penetrating questions are particularly provocative because they attempt to ferret out the interviewees' existential reaction to events that affect and shape their lives, and by inference, all our lives, since the events depicted are mired in the major social issues of our day. Experts add a layer of depth to the events and sanctify the refracted narrator's point of view by suggesting the opinion expressed is widely shared.

The reflective component of post-9/11 documentaries is obvious. They reflect concern about major social issues that are taking place at the time the film is made and often reflect the popular mind-set of at least a segment of the population in the film's country of origin. The refractive aspect is noticeable in the interpretation of events documented. Some films refract the views of those filmmakers who feel America's military incursions are necessary and justifiable to deal with international terrorists, while others refract the views from the other side. With the narrator's obtrusive presence, the refractive is more obvious in documentaries than fictional films. But a major component of refraction theory is not just that they "refract" the views of those involved in making the film, but the film acts didactically by teaching us something about our world.

Documentaries directly teach us about some slice of our world; fiction is more likely to do it indirectly. Indeed, the more direct didacticism of documentaries suggests that their meaning cannot be escaped; for example, there is no equivocation in Al Gore's 2006 Oscar-winning film, *An Inconvenient Truth*. Nor can documentaries be dismissed because they are not profitable—an indictment that implies they are not popular—or because they reach a limited art house segment of the population at theaters. This criticism does not take into account their extended life through DVD rentals or sales. Those who view these films, even if they watch them at home with half an eye, cannot fail to notice the overall tone and thrust of the storyline, which is more likely to be lost when watching fictional films at home, especially if one is engaged in other activities while viewing the film.

In an excellent analysis of documentaries over time, Jack Ellis and Betsy McLane critique documentary films at various historical periods:

Flaherty's work (1922–1929), early Soviet films (1922–1929), European avant-gardists (1922–1929), and so forth.[44] They point out that the term itself—document—comes from the Latin *docere*, to teach, and that is precisely what they find documentaries to do, whether it be *The Plow That Broke the Plains* (1936), which served as an indictment of the lack of planning that caused the Dust Bowl, to *Super Size Me* (2004), which showed just how much harm ingesting fast food does to one's physical *and* mental health, and how quickly. These documentary films, and a host of others that scholars and film critics have examined, certainly attempt to teach the viewer something about the world we live in (see *Food, Inc.*, 2009). And that is their purpose. Whether one actually learns anything from what is viewed is harder to ascertain, but awareness that something is happening is a precondition to changing one's opinion. For those with an open or inquisitive mind who wish to learn about events that they might not otherwise be exposed to, documentaries are a step in the process of (at the very least) expanding—and possibly challenging and changing—one's worldview.

Documentaries historically have raised consciousness. This is the purpose of documentaries and is cited in interviews as the reason the overwhelming majority of post-9/11 filmmakers made their film.[45] And post–9/11 war-related documentaries, perhaps more than any documentary form in the history of cinema, have this ability because (1) they are free from governmental oversight that may require certain aspects of the film not be addressed,[46] preventing filmmakers from exposing slices of the world they might have liked to reveal, and (2) contemporary documentaries have the potential of reaching a wider audience than any documentary in the past because of their availability to potential viewers outside their theatrical release.

A METHODOLOGY NOTE

More than 200 films (N=210)* were identified that dealt with 9/11-related events between 2001 and 2009. These films can be broken into three categories. The first category consists of films that deal with the

---

*The capital letter "N" is used to designate the total number of films in the group; the small "n" is used to indicate a subset within the larger group. These designations are used throughout the book.

enemy (n=20): Saddam Hussein or Osama bin Laden. A second category of films depict 9/11 events (n=32) and analyze either what happened on the ground in New York City or in the air with United Flight 93. Both these categories are addressed in chapter 1. The third and largest category deals with the war on the ground in Iraq and Afghanistan (n=153); this category also includes a number of films depicting, in some detail, the terrorist threat today (n=5). This third category is chronologically examined: America's initial foray into these regions is critiqued in chapter 1; subsequent chapters examine transition films that "argued" the merits of American involvement (2004 and 2005), and finale films (2006 through 2008), a term used not because the war was concluded during this period but because the public and cinematic debate had moved decidedly toward an exit strategy, and these films assert the reason this is desirable, generally—but not always—without denouncing those who serve in the military.

The majority of films dissected are movies intended for movie house release. The fact that they are available on DVD greatly expands the initial movie house audience. Also included in this analysis are those feature-length films and documentaries that were released on television as long as they were available on DVD, which expands their "movie-viability"—DVD releases available on movie sites geared toward a movie audience.[47] For example, the DVD release of HBO's miniseries about the war, *Generation Kill*, greatly expands the audience beyond those who subscribe to this pay-per-view movie channel. Similarly, many documentaries might have initially enjoyed limited release at local art houses but their availability on DVD allows those in small towns without art houses and those who were unable to attend the event during its typically limited run the ability to rent and view the movie.

All the identified movies were purchased or rented and subjected to a detailed content analysis. A critical evaluation of the plotline is not difficult even if one is not trained in film criticism, since films are fairly easy to understand, Nowell-Smith argues, "if only because in the great majority of cases they have been designed to be instantly accessible to audience with no special esoteric competence."[48] Potential authorial misinterpretation is tempered, however, by relying on input from other sources. One source often available on DVD releases is the director's comments, which are generally taken into account since they shed light on how the viewer is expected to interpret events depicted on the screen or how the director and actors hoped the scene would be interpreted; commentary by those involved with the film generally includes remarks regarding their motivation for making or appearing in the film. Also taken into account is commentary by film critics that assesses the film's merits. This analysis also sometimes uses insights by lay reviewers at online movie sites, especially when their assessment of the film radically departs from those of film critics. Lay reviewer remarks are often quite insightful, and should not be discounted because they are not from "legitimate" critics.[49] For example, movie critic Roger Ebert gives the film *Southland Tales* one-and-a-half stars, and says "[a] Schwarzeneggerian actor, related to a political dynasty, has been kidnapped, replaced with a double, and—I give up. A plot synopsis would require that the movie have a plot. . . ."[50] A Netflix reviewer, prominently displayed on the site, gives it one star and basically agrees with Ebert, saying "I'm glad I didn't walk out of this film if only because I earned the right to one-star it. In a world where people work hard to secure funding for their projects, to follow a complex and meditative indie darling with this 8-figure bathtub fart suggests a level of self-importance that I didn't expect of [director] Kelly." Seventy percent of the 410 people who read this lay review's remarks indicated that it was helpful in determining their desire to rent it. These lay reviewers, then, can influence perspective viewers as much as film critics. Films where lay reviewers merely reflect the views of critics, however, are given less weight than those movies where the lay reviewers sometimes dramatically differ from the critics.

This analysis also takes into account other cinematic techniques beyond the storyline. Stories are convincing not only because they "tell a story" but because the success of the story goes beyond plot and includes music and cinematic techniques, such as camera angle, to hook the viewer. These aspects are taken into account when discussing the story, otherwise the cinematic critique amounts to little more than plot summary. Any analysis, to be truly a film analysis, must go beyond the overt messages conveyed in the film. This includes an appraisal not only of how the messages were delivered, but also includes an appreciation of silences in the film. This tripartite formation—the overt messages, the techniques used to convey the messages, and what is *not* addressed in the film—leads to a new knowledge of the text. It also recognizes that a film may have more than one message to convey, and thus follows Macherey's lead by rejecting the interpretative fallacy: the assumption that films have a single meaning and it is the task of the critic to uncover.[51]

Finally, it is important to point out that not every film is discussed in the body of the text. Films that are dissected are considered representative of those in the category being examined. Films that were produced in the years critiqued are delineated at the beginning of every section, even if they are not subjected to detailed analysis.

CONCLUSION

People have always lived in a visual society. The visual aspect has become increasingly pronounced during the last hundred years, owing largely to the widespread diffusion of cinema, television, and more recently, the Internet and YouTube. The problem is that the sheer pervasiveness of images prevents people from pondering what they have just seen. And precisely because they are images, people often unreflectively interpret them to be the truth. Like Thomas, who would not believe that Christ had been resurrected until he had seen the wounds, people are convinced that an event has unfolded in a particular way because they have seen it.

The truth of images may be debatable, but since the images often do reflect part of the everyday world, they are less likely to be questioned. Reflection theory holds that because photographic images do reflect things people are familiar with, they are likely to accept them. This means that people might not recognize the refractive point of view when they see it. Refraction theory suggests that all images are shaped. They may be shaped by the time period such as postmodernism, or by production constraints such as laws prohibiting the image from being displayed; just as likely, they are shaped to refract the perspective of those who are responsible for manufacturing the image. The same image of the president on FOX will be interpreted differently by network executives than the same image on "The Daily Show." Because it is the image of, say, the president stepping off Air Force One, people accept that the president is deplaning—or is he getting on Air Force One? People have to be told, and they are also told why he is aboard Air Force One, and what his actions will mean to them.

Fiction can be mistaken as a representative of reality by the viewer. This is more likely to occur if the fictional event reflects a slice of the world with which the viewer is already familiar—showing Cleopatra stab Julius Caesar on the steps of the Senate would not be accepted as fact because every schoolchild knows it was Brutus, among others, who assassinated him, whereas Comte de Salvo's actions during the French Revolution may not be familiar to people and, thus, the viewer is more likely to accept the movie of de Salvo's life as at least partially truthful. Viewer familiarity with the event depicted is not a precondition in documentary film, however. This is because the tradition of the documentary is that it purports to *document* an event. Consequently seeing is often taken at face value by the viewer. But even the best documentary needs to be framed, which is to say, it must tell a story, and the storyteller tells his or her interpretation of events. In some cases, the interpretation is overly didactic and the narrator says this action or event means this or that. More often than not the viewer fails to recognize the storyteller's interpretation because it subtly purports to simply record events, even as the storyteller nudges the viewer to see the events in a certain way by the way the images are assembled. This believability is enhanced in the documentary format by the on-the-scenes shaky, handheld camera effect that makes even staged events seem real.

Documentaries are of particular concern in this analysis of films revolving around post-9/11 events because they were the predominant means by which people became familiar with distant events that affected their everyday lives. Most Americans witnessed the collapse of the WTC on television, but they got to know those affected through films that depicted the lives of those on the ground and in the air. Similarly, the war in Iraq and Afghanistan has been only summarily seen in the news. It was left initially to documentaries to tell people "the truth" about what was taking place "over there." Later fiction took up the story and continued to inform Americans about the war and what it meant, both to them and to those in the field. Fiction often followed the interpretation of events already established in the documentaries, adding validity to the documentary point of view, which, in turn, gave credence to the fictional portrayal.

To some degree, the cinematographic depiction of WTC-related events reflects social attitudes, but in other ways it refracts the mind-set of those who made the films. This book is about the reflective-refracted dimension of films that deal with the WTC and America's war on terrorism in Afghanistan and Iraq. It will be seen that while at times the reflective prevails, at other times the refractive view does. This suggests the effects of films about these events are recursive: social attitudes, social context, and movie themes are interconnected and each interacts with and influences the other. The next chapter begins the analysis by dissecting those films that set the stage for the subsequent incursion into Afghanistan and Iraq: the collapse of the WTC and the depiction of Saddam Hussein and Osama bin Laden as America's most-wanted terrorists.

NOTES

1. Leo Lowenthal, *Literature, Popular Culture, and Society* (New York: Prentice-Hall, 1961), 79; Ian Watt, *The Rise of the Novel* (London: Chatto and Windus, 1957).

2. Gerald Mast and B. F. Kawin, *A Short History of the Movies* (New York: Macmillan, 1992).

3. Luigino Bruni and Luca Stanca, "Income Aspirations, Television and Happiness: Evidence from the World Values Survey," *KYKLOS* 59 (2006): 209–25; *Nielsen Media Research 2000 Report on Television: The First 50 Years* (Kingsport, Tenn.: A. C. Nielsen Company, 2000): 1–27.

4. There is a scarcity of current research in this area, largely because the findings are so well established. Sociologists focused on this issue during the early years of television, largely abandoning the field in the mid-1960s to communication scholars who, after replicating the earlier research, in turn abandoned the field in the mid-1980s. Melvin L. DeFleur and Mary M. Cronin, "Completeness and Accuracy of Recall in the Diffusion of the News from a Newspaper vs. a Television Source," *Sociological Inquiry* 61, no. 2 (1991): 148–66. See also Neil Postman, *Amusing Ourselves to Death* (New York: Penguin, 1985); Neil Postman and Steve Powers, *How to Watch TV News* (New York: Penguin, 1992); W. Russel Neuman, "Patterns of Recall Among Television News Viewers," *Public Opinion Quarterly* 40, no. 1 (1976): 115–23.

5. Neuman found the remaining viewers watch it either "to relax" or are labeled "casual viewers" because they "fall into the undifferentiated middle mass" who either just happen to catch the news that night or who watch it regularly but "express no special interest in keeping informed." Abelman et al. have

added another reason besides the habitual nature that drives so much television viewing among that group that seeks information (news)—the desire for companionship, which appears to drive local station loyalty among those who watch the news more than network loyalty and may, the authors speculate, reflect "the success of some stations in building an image as a community 'friend.'" Neuman, "Patterns of Recall Among Television News Viewers," 115–23; Robert Abelman, David Atkin, and Michael Rand, "What Viewers Watch as They Watch TV: Affiliation Change as a Case Study," *Journal of Broadcasting & Electronic Media* 41, no. 3 (1997): 360–82.

6. Mediamark Research and Intelligence, "Media Multitasking Usually Exception, Not Rule," www.marketingcharts.com/television/media-multitasking (accessed 23 February 2009). See also Donald F. Roberts and Ulla G. Foehr, "Trends in Media Use," *The Future of Children* 18, no. 1 (2008): 11–37.

7. The MRI study indicated the most common nonmedia activity to engage in while simultaneously using media is chores, but never defined chores or provided a statistical breakdown. Mediamark Research and Intelligence, "Media Multitasking Usually Exception, Not Rule."

8. Aviva W. Rosenstein and August E. Grant, "Reconceptualizing the Role of Habit: A New Model of Television Audience Activity," *Journal of Broadcasting & Electronic Media* 41, no. 3 (1997): 324–44; George Comstock, *Television in America*, 2nd ed. (Newbury Park, Calif.: Sage, 1991).

9. In door-to-door interviews, Heeter was surprised to learn that 23 percent of all respondents answered, "I don't know, I just watch TV" when asked to identify what channels they commonly viewed. C. Heeter, "Program Selection with Abundance of Choice: A Process Model," *Human Communication Research* 12, no. 9 (1985): 126–52.

10. Realistic here means believable; that is, the character's actions are "realistic," even if the events are not (see *Wizard of Oz, Alice in Wonderland, Star Wars*). Joel Black, *The Reality Effect: Film Culture and the Graphic Imperative* (New York: Routledge, 2002); Paul G. Cressey, "The Motion Picture Experience as Modified by Social Background and Personality," *American Sociological Review* 3, no. 2 (1934): 230–44.

11. See David J. Hogan, *Science Fiction America: Essays on SF Cinema* (Jefferson, N.C.: McFarland, 2006); Trevor B. McCrisken and Andrew Pepper, *American History and Contemporary Hollywood Film* (New Brunswick, N.J.: Rutgers University Press, 2005); Mark C. Carnes, ed., *Past Imperfect: History According to the Movies* (New York: Henry Holt, 1995).

12. Herbert J. Gans, "Popular Culture in America: Social Problems in a Mass Society or Social Asset in a Pluralist Society?" in *Social Problems: A Modern Approach*, ed. H. Becker (New York: Wiley, 1966): 562.

13. See E. McLaughlin, "Television Coverage of the Vietnam War and the Vietnam Veteran," www.wabirdforum.com/media (accessed 12 November 2009); D. F. Schmitz, *The Tet Offensive: Politics, War, and Public Opinion* (Lanham, Md.: Rowman & Littlefield, 2005); Don Oberdorfer, *Tet! The Turning Point in the Vietnam War* (New York: Da Capo Press, 1984).

14. E. Deidra Pribram, *Cinema and Culture: Independent Film in the United States, 1980–2001* (New York: Peter Lang, 2002).

15. Steven Alan Carr, "Mass Murder, Modernity, and the Alienated Gaze," in *Cinema and Modernity*, ed. Murray Pomerance (New Brunswick, N.J.: Rutgers University Press, 2006), 57–73; Pribram, *Cinema and Culture*.

16. Carl Boggs and Tony Pollard, *A World in Chaos: Social Crisis and the Rise of Postmodern Cinema* (Boulder, Colo.: Rowman & Littlefield, 2003).

17. Wheeler Winston Dixon, "The Endless Embrace of Hell: Hopelessness and Betrayal in Film Noir," in *Cinema and Modernity*, ed. Murray Pomerance (New Brunswick, N.J.: Rutgers University Press, 2006), 38–56.

18. Trevor B. McCrisken and Andrew Pepper, *American History and Contemporary Hollywood Film* (New Brunswick, N.J.: Rutgers University Press, 2005, 93.

19. Ronald L. Davis, *Celluloid Mirrors: Hollywood and American Society since 1945* (Fort Worth, Tex.: Harcourt Brace, 1997), 115.

20. Albert Auster and Leonard Quart, *How the War Was Remembered: Hollywood and Vietnam* (Westport, Conn.: Praeger, 1988), 66.

21. Terry Eagleton would rightfully call this a simplified, "vulgar" Marxism because it does not account for the complexities of a Marxist approach; nevertheless, it captures the essence of the Marxist critical approach. Terry Eagleton, *Marxism and Literary Criticism* (Berkeley: University of California Press, 1976), 17; see also John Storey, *Cultural Theory and Popular Culture: An Introduction*, 4th ed. (Athens: University of Georgia Press, 2006), 48.

22. Lawrence Grossberg, *Bring It All Back Home: Essays on Cultural Studies* (Durham, N.C.: Duke University Press, 1997).

23. Dominic Strinati, *An Introduction to Theories of Popular Culture* (New York: Routledge, 1995), 52. See also J. Marcus, ed., *Surviving in the Twentieth Century: Social Philosophy from the Frankford School to the Columbia Faculty Seminars* (New Brunswick, N.J.: Transaction Publishers, 1999); A. van den Berg, "Critical Theory: Is There Still Hope?" *American Journal of Sociology* 86, no. 3 (1980): 449–78.

24. See George Ritzer and Douglas J. Goodman, *Sociological Theory*, 6th ed. (New York: McGraw Hill, 2004), 273; Deborah Cook, *The Culture Industry Revisited: Theodor W. Adorno on Mass Culture* (Lanham, Md.: Rowman & Littlefield, 1996).

25. See Thomas Doherty, *Projections of War: Hollywood, American Culture, and World War II* (New York: Columbia University Press, 1993); Bernard F. Dick, *The Star-Spangled Screen: The American World War II Film* (Lexington: University Press of Kentucky, 1985); Tony Shaw, *Hollywood's Cold War* (Amherst: University of Massachusetts Press, 2007).

26. Theodor Adorno, "On Popular Music," *Studies in Philosophy and Social Science* IX (1941): 17–48.

27. Frederick Jameson, *Postmodernism, or, The Cultural Logic of Late Capitalism* (Durham, N.C.: Duke University Press, 1991). See also Storey, *Cultural Theory and Popular Culture*; Jean Baudrillard, *Simulacra and Simulation*, trans. S. F. Glaser (Detroit: University of Michigan Press, 1995).

28. Ann Swidler, "Culture in Action: Symbols and Strategies," *American Sociological Review* 51, no. 2 (1986): 273–86.

29. Bilge Ebiri, "The Ravages of War and Occupation: An Interview with James Longley," *Cineaste* 32, no. 1 (2006): 38–41; Margo Kasdan, Christine Saxton, and Susan Tavernetti, *The Critical Eye: An Introduction to Looking at Movies* (Dubuque, Iowa: Kendall Hunt, 1998).

30. Patricia R. Zimmerman, *States of Emergency: Documentaries, Wars, Democracies* (Minneapolis: University of Minnesota Press, 2000).

31. John Markert, "Sing a Song of Drug Use-Abuse: Drug Lyrics in Popular Music—From the Sixties through the Nineties." *Sociological Inquiry* 71, no. 2 (2001): 194–220. See also W. Weber, "Beyond Zeitgeist: Recent Work in Music History," *Journal of Modern History* 66, no. 2 (1994): 321–45; Jay R. Howard, "Contemporary Christian Music: Where Rock Meets Religion," *Journal of Popular Culture* 26, no. 1 (1992): 123–30; John Markert, "Superstitious Peasants: Religious Images on Spanish-Language Television in the United States," *Sociological Imagination* 43, no. 2 (2007): 21–35; John Markert, "The George Lopez Show: The Same Old Hispano?" *Bilingual Review* 28 (2007): 148–65; John Markert, "Divergent Gender Messages on Spanish-Language Television in the United States: Cracks in the Edifice, Unlatching the Window of Change," *Sociological Imagination* 45, no. 1 (2009): 41–61. See also James W. Chesebro, "Communication, Values, and Popular Television Series—A Twenty-Five Year Assessment and Final Conclusions," *Communication Quarterly* 51, no. 4 (2003): 367–418; Demetrus W. Pearson et al., "Sport Films: Social Dimensions Over Time, 1930–1995," *Journal of Sport & Social Issues* 27, no. 2 (2003): 145–61; I. C. Jarvie, "Film and the Communication of Values," *European Journal of Sociology* 10, no. 2 (1969): 205–19.

32. Richard A. Peterson, "The Production of Culture: A Prolegomenon," in *The Production of Culture*, ed. R. A. Peterson (Beverly Hills: Sage, 1976), 7–22; Richard A. Peterson, "Five Constraints on the Production of Culture: Law,

Technology, Market, Organizational Structure, and Occupational Careers," *Journal of Popular Culture* 16, no. 1 (1982): 143–53; Richard A. Peterson, "Six Constraints on the Production of Literary Works," *Poetics: International Review for the Theory of Literature* 14, nos. 1/2 (1985): 45–68; See also John Markert, "Romance Publishing and the Production of Culture," *Poetics: International Review for the Theory of Literature* 14, nos. 1/2 (1985): 69–94.

33. The first three films were an attempt to break the spirit of isolationism that was still strong in the country, even after Pearl Harbor. These films cover the period from 1918 to 1941 by documenting the increase in Japanese aggression in Asia and the growing menace of Hitler in Europe: *Prelude to War* (1941), *The Nazis Strike* (1943), and *Divide and Conquer* (1943). All seven films, including *War Comes to America* (1945) were compulsory for military personnel before leaving for overseas duty. Some of the films were made available for civilian audiences through theatrical exhibition. See Jack C. Ellis and Betsy A. McLane, *A New History of Documentary Film* (New York: Continuum, 2005), 133.

34. Ellis and McLane, *A New History of Documentary Film*, 131.

35. YouTube started in February 2005 and relied extensively on independent, user-generated video content. By the close of the decade, it was getting more files from the major networks. This trend is likely to increase in the years to come.

36. Boggs and Pollard, *A World in Chaos*; Zimmerman, *States of Emergency*.

37. Sheldon Rampton and John Stauber, *Weapons of Mass Destruction: The Uses of Propaganda in Bush's War on Iraq* (New York: Tarcher/Penguin, 2003); see also Anthony Arnove, "Cautionary Tales: Documentaries on the UN Sanctions and War with Iraq," *Cineaste* 2, no. 2 (Spring 2003): 21–23.

38. Another 28,530 military personnel had been wounded in Iraq (as of October 1, 2008); these causalities also receive limited media attention.

39. The ban on news coverage of the return of war dead was instituted during Gulf War I by President George Walker Bush. It was lifted within months of President Obama taking the oath of office.

40. The "big four" (CBS, NBC, ABC, and FOX) are heavily relied upon and are used by 34 percent of the public as their primary source of national news; CNN adds another 12 percent with another 9 percent relying on local news, which largely is a take on the affiliate's national slant. The other primary media sources include newspapers (17 percent), radio (10 percent), magazines (2 percent), and the Internet (12 percent). See Jonathan S. Morris, "Slanted Objectivity? Perceived Media Bias, Cable News Exposure, and Political Attitudes," *Social Science Quarterly* 88, no. 3 (2007): 707–28.

41. Jane Roscoe and Craig Hight, *Faking It: Mock-documentary and the Subversion of Factuality* (Manchester: Manchester University Press, 2001).

42. Black, *The Reality Effect*, 112.

43. The technique of introducing real "grainy" black and white clips from historical periods is increasingly frequent in mainstream fictional film; however, because it is a fictional film it is more likely to be appreciated by the audience as technique and not real (see *Forrest Gump*).

44. Ellis and McLane, *A New History of Documentary Film*.

45. David A. Goldsmith, *The Documentary Makers: Interviews with 15 of the Best in the Business* (Switzerland: RotoVision, 2003).

46. David Robb critiques at some length how the government required changes in a host of military-themed films and includes in his analysis of films that are self-censored to gain official approval of the film, typically to access military personnel or equipment. David L. Robb, *Operation Hollywood: How the Pentagon Shapes and Censors the Movies* (Amherst, N.Y.: Prometheus Books, 2004). See also *The Tuskegee Airmen* (1995) and *Afterburn* (1992).

47. Most made-for-television documentaries tend to be shorter, cheaper, and tackle safer issues, and because they are on television they are not watched as closely as movies made for the big screen. They may initially reach larger audiences but are more likely screened as on-offs with little expectation of a repeat [DVD] screening. See Roscoe and Hight, *Faking It*, 27.

48. Geoffrey Nowell-Smith, "How Films Mean, or, from Aesthetics to Semiotics and Half-way Back Again," in *Reinventing Film Studies*, eds. C. Gledhill and Linda Williams (London: Arnold, 2000), 9.

49. Saying simply "This movie is crap" or "I loved this movie" does not qualify as critical analysis.

50. Roger Ebert, "*Southland Tales*." *Chicago Sun-Times*, 16 November 2007, www.rogerebert.suntimes.com (accessed 12 August 2009).

51. Pierre Macherey, *Theory of Literary Production*, translated by Geoffrey Wall (New York: Routledge, 2006). See also Storey, *Cultural Theory and Popular Culture*, 59.

CINEMA SIMPLICITY

Heroes and Villains

THE VILLAINS

The collapse of the World Trade Center in 2001 witnessed a potpourri of early films about the tragedy. The specific cinematic face of the enemy did not occur until 2002 to 2003. It would be a good twelve-plus months after 9/11 before a film about bin Laden would appear, but Saddam Hussein garnered attention even before Iraq was invaded on March 20, 2003. Saddam's cinematic progression mirrors the postinvasion search and subsequent trial. No doubt, Saddam's historical chronology provided filmmakers with a narrative flow, in contrast to the endless, fruitless search for bin Laden that, after a while, added little to the cinematic storehouse of existing knowledge. The first group of films critiqued appraise Saddam Hussein; the second group, Osama bin Laden:

Uncle Saddam (2002)
Marooned in Iraq (2002)
Saddam's Bombmaker (2003)
We Got Him: Capturing Saddam (2004)
Buried in the Sand (2004)
WMD: Weapons of Mass Destruction (2004)
Ace in the Hole (2005)

Saddam's Secret Tunnels (2007)
America at a Crossroads: The Trial of Saddam Hussein (2008)
House of Saddam (2008)

Osama (2003)
Osama bin Laden: In the Name of Allah (2004)
Meeting Osama bin Laden (2004)
The Hunt for Osama bin Laden (2004)
Our Own Private bin Laden (2006)
Triple Cross: bin Laden's Spy in America (2006)
The al-Qaeda File (2006)
Targeted: Osama bin Laden (2007)
The Search for Osama bin Laden (2007)
Where in the World Is Osama bin Laden? (2008)

Saddam Hussein

Saddam Hussein garnered public attention before the invasion and well before 9/11. There was the Iran-Iraq War (1980–1988), and then Gulf War I (August 1990–February 1991). He remained in the news throughout the 1990s because of the difficulties and obstacles that faced the United Nations inspection teams that were trying to ascertain the existence and extent of any weapons program. The American perception of the Iraqi leader was firmly set in the public's mind prior to the invasion because of the political rhetoric surrounding Saddam Hussein's weapons of mass destruction (WMD).[1] Indeed, the public's perception was considered to be so entrenched that there was little doubt who the John Goodman character was railing about in the 1998 film, *The Big Lebowski*, when he offhandedly cursed "that camel fucker in Iraq." The attitude toward Saddam as a "nutcase" is certainly reflected in the first feature film about him, *Uncle Saddam*, and considering the poor quality of the film is most likely to have received the attention in did in the United States, Anthony Arnove argues, because it "fit the current mood in Washington."[2] The film reflects a rather simplistic and stereotypical perception of the Iraqi leader. This is no doubt the reason the film, shot in 2000, was finally shown in post-9/11 America, just a few months before the invasion of Iraq.

Uncle Saddam was made, according to CNN.com (22 Nov. 2002), by the French filmmaker, Joel Soler. The French filmmaker's attribution suggests that the television journalist has a history of filmmaking; however, his website reveals he has made only two other feature films, both after *Uncle Saddam*, and neither of any repute and in limited release: *Osama bin Laden* and *Uncle Hitler*. His film *Uncle Saddam* did, as the cover of the DVD release indicates, win a number of film awards, though the awards themselves are local awards and may reflect more the public attitude toward Saddam at the time of its release than any cinematic merits: *Uncle Saddam* won in the best documentary category at both the Northampton Festival and New Orleans Film Festival. The reception of the film by the media tends to reinforce this perspective since the qualities of the film are given scant attention, compared to the "appreciation" of Soler's portrait of Saddam that was the focus of attention in interviews with those involved with making the film.

> The cult of personality around Mr. Hussein is mocked by the soundtrack music—including "No Regrets" and "La Vie en Rose" and the tongue-in-cheek narration written by the comedian Scott Thompson of the "Kids in the Hall" troupe.
> "I wanted to bring a deadpan tone," said Mr. Thompson.
> "You're dealing with such a monster, there's no need to oversell it through words."[3]

> *Interviewer:* What did you learn about what makes Saddam tick?
> *Soler:* In everything that he does, his primary focus is to remain in history. He restored Babylon using bricks with his name on them. He's building the biggest mosque in history—so that he can be closer than anyone to God. It even has an island in the shape of his thumb that is covered with an enormous mosaic of his thumbprint.[4]

> The film opens with a running list of Saddam [crazy] fun facts [a history of his rise to power: at 6, at 42, at 43, in his 50s]. . . . [Then] things take a bizarre turn. Saddam is a fanatic about cleanliness, which he regards as no laughing matter, even if we do, since, we are told [by the film's narrator], "Saddam likes to be greeted with a kiss near the arm" (footage is shown depicting a steady stream of black-bereted minions with copycat mustaches puckering up to plant one between Saddam's armpit and areola). The butcher of Baghdad, it turns out, has all sorts of ideas about personal

hygiene. Sitting behind a desk in a wide-brimmed hat and flashy suit that make him look like a Newark pimp."[5]

The film, which aired on Cinemax in late November, is given documentary status because of how the film was made. Soler ostensibly gained entry into Iraq by indicating he wanted to make a film about Iraq's culture and architecture. He states in interviews that he was initially well received but eventually had to flee the country when his true purpose became known. It seems almost humorous today that such a self-proclaimed "pussy" would have the audacity to pull off a covert film on Iraq, given his fleeting familiarity with Arab culture and inability to speak the language,[6] or be able to pass for an Arab when making the film:

> I wanted to film Saddam's newest palace—his biggest one yet. The officials wouldn't let me, so I played sick one day and went to the palace dressed as an Arab. Anyone filming anything related to Saddam can be shot to death on the spot. I spent an hour filming in the trees. You can tell that footage in the movie because it's so damn shaky.[7]

At the time the movie was made in 2000, and given the pre-invasion climate toward the Iraqi dictator in the United States,[8] Soler's bravado was taken at face value, and the shaky filmmaking tradition of the documentary form lends credence to his assertion of his surreptitious filmmaking technique.[9] The film as first-person documentary is dubious, however. Arnove even suggests "Not Actual Footage would be a more accurate title for the film."[10]

It might perhaps be more accurate to say, "hardly any actual footage." There are a number of short interviews with "talking heads" interspersed throughout the film, which Soler obviously filmed, of former Iraqi officials commenting on Saddam's habits, and on a few occasions, of unidentified males remarking on Saddam's life. This comprises less than 10 percent of the film, but is enough to suggest to the viewer that the other pictures of the Iraqi leader were made by the filmmaker, when in fact they are taken from file footage. Indeed, in the credits only one cameraman is identified as being involved in the film but archival material is attributed to a variety of sources: Iraq TV, Cinema Archive Baghdad, Prime Time Jordan, U.S. Department of Defense, IBC, Egyptian

Tourism Office, which provided a picture of the pyramids when Soler mentions that Saddam spent some early years in Egypt, British Tourism Office, Danish TV, UN TV Switzerland, IIN Reuters, and AFP. Since few viewers bother to watch the end credits, this formal recognition would largely go unnoticed. Nor did the filmmaker make any attempt to suggest in the body of the film that what the viewer saw was not shot by him.[11] He did not say it was, but he certainly never said it was not.

There is certainly nothing wrong with using file footage to depict events of an otherwise inaccessible person. The depiction of Saddam rests less on this than the *interpretation* of the pictures by the filmmaker, especially considering that if taken in context many of the actual activities and remarks of Saddam are quite innocuous. The following representative comments could be said by or about *any* leader:

"The first thing he likes to do when he wakes up is to have a cup of coffee." This is accompanied by a picture of Saddam sitting at his desk drinking from a cup and saucer while sifting through paperwork.

Saddam, we are told, is "obsessed" with personal hygiene because, the Iraqi leader says, one "should not appear at public gatherings with his body odor trailing behind him."

The viewer learns that Saddam takes great pains to project the proper image. Pictures are shown of him in various public guises, where we learn from the narrator that he "regularly dyes his mustache a *rich and regal black.*" [narrator's falsetto emphasis]

"Several rules [are] established by doctors [picture of two physicians walking a hospital corridor is shown]. They tell you [basic rules of protocol] how to shake his hand, how many centimeters there should be between you and him."

In an interview in *The Sunday Times* (1 Oct. 2000), Soler says that the reason there is such a wealth of available material on Saddam in Iraq is "[b]ecause of Saddam's considerable ego" and has nothing to do, apparently, with his stature as the Iraqi head of state.

How basic statements such as these are slanted to pander to the American audience can be gleaned in the following two illustrations from other segments of the film.

The narrator is talking about how Saddam likes to shoot off weapons at public demonstrations. The viewer sees two images, one of Saddam shooting a rifle off over his head in the country, the other of him firing a handgun into the air before a large assembly of cheering Iraqi's. With the sound of the cheering crowd still ringing on the audio, a murky black and white clip of a man with a pistol shooting a man in the head appears with the caption in the lower left, "Government sponsored execution."

Later, we see Saddam sitting on a stoop in a street with a sack handing out apples to a bevy of children. The viewer is told, "He likes to tell jokes and is supposedly good with children, even if the apple he is offering them here is a bit rotten" [there is a small, quarter size blemish on one side of one apple]. The clip concludes in a mocking tone by stating, "It's the thought that counts."

Such misattributions are likely to go unnoticed by the viewing audience, largely because this was the public image of Saddam fostered in the public sphere in the United States (see also *Weapons of Mass Deception*). The film no doubt debuted on Cinemax precisely because it captured the public sentiment toward Saddam, but in so doing, even when the viewing audience might have recognized that it does not give a comprehensive picture of the Iraqi leader, it reinforced and possibly strengthened the public view of him as more of a nutcase than as a dangerous despot. The film is rated three stars by viewers of Netflix. Member reviews (from www.netflix.com), much like the stories in the press about the debut of the film on Cinemax, indicate that the "bizarre" is vividly recalled even when the film might be taken with a grain of salt.

Rather cheesy and somewhat bizarre documentary but as far as I know, it is perhaps the most comprehensive collection of footage of modern Iraq (presumably Baghdad), and of several Iraqi citizens (or subjects?). The portrayal of Saddam and his eccentricities is extremely bizarre. Unfortunately, the somewhat satirical and derogatory nature of the documentary forces me to be very skeptical of much of the anecdotal information presented in the video. If you can exercise your own judgment and some skepticism, this is a pretty interesting film.

Wow. This is an alarming and funny [sic] look inside the bizarre world that, until recently, was Iraq. The filmmaker should be commended for risking this life to get a lot of unflattering footage of Hussein and for giving Saddam's lackeys plenty of rope and getting out of the way as they expose how crazy their cult-like society is in their own words. The only flaw is that, like a lot of recent media coverage of Iraq, this film overlooks how U.S. policy during the Cold War and the Iranian revolution helped make Hussein a monster that we would finally have to hunt down and remove from power decades later.

Saddam Hussein was, unquestionably, a sinister despot who committed numerous atrocities—notably against the Kurds. He was also a complex man who ruled in a society few Westerners fully appreciate. People, however, like the face of evil to be clear and unequivocal. This is the portrait that emerges on film, but it is also the portrait painted by the Bush administration and popularized in the media. The implication: if the other is bad, we are good. This type of simplified Manichaean duality is common practice in times of conflict. It is only in the aftermath of conflict and with the mist of time that a more nuisance picture of the enemy emerges (see *All Quiet on the Western Front*, 1930; *The Bridge on the River Kwai*, 1957; *Das Boot*, 1981). It is not surprising, then, that subsequent, postinvasion films that deal with Saddam Hussein (or bin Laden) are stark in their depiction of the madman.

Most of the films that follow *Uncle Saddam* rely on the same format: talking heads, file footage, judgmental narrative. In part, the simplified picture that is found on many of these films is related to their status as television documentaries that are ground out for the Military Channel, History Channel, and Discovery Channel, whose logo, "*Entertain* your brain" [author's italics], is itself indicative of their approach to current events. Their inclusion here is due to their availability on movie sites. They are dealt with summarily, largely because they add little to the documentary format or to the portrait of Saddam or Iraq that has not already been critiqued in *Uncle Saddam*. They do, however, reflect a popular mind-set toward Saddam in the United States, and their initial showing and subsequent viewing only served to reinforce the popular belief about him.

The first in this group is *Saddam's Bombmaker* (2003). It obviously garnered early attention because it tells the story of Dr. Khidhir Hamza, who was, as the title indicates, the physicist Saddam relied on to build his putative nuclear arsenal. Hamza's story was widely circulated by the Bush administration to validate the existence of Saddam's weapons capabilities. A clip is shown of Hamza testifying before Congress of his firsthand knowledge of Saddam's weapons program, after his "harrowing" escape from Iraq, which is reenacted for the viewing audience. The docudrama format, where the viewer is shown the scene being reenacted as the event is described, is the key difference between this film and *Uncle Saddam*. It is important to point out that when this is done, no disclaimer appears on the screen, since this is an entertainment channel and not a news channel, which could lead the viewer to assume the event, like the other file footage clips that are interspersed throughout, is one that was actually filmed at the time of the occurrence.

Hamza decides to flee Iran near the end of eight years of war with Iraq, after Saddam uses chemical weapons against his neighbor to the East. The eight-year war is glossed over. The number of causalities is remarked on in this section of the film: "350,000 Iraqi dead, Iran has close to a million." The Iran-Iraq conflict is boiled down to two key points for the American audience. One mismanaged "fact" is that "Iraq [is the] first to use nerve gas on a battlefield," when in fact it was first used by the German army on April 22, 1915, at Ypres, Belgium.[12] This point takes on an ominous cast since the use of chemical weapons was because "time [was] running out." The implication is that Saddam has WMD—his own weapons expert asserts this point throughout—and if he is pushed into a corner by the United States, he will use them. Though no WMD had been found since American troops entered the country, the film reasserts that they are there *somewhere*. It would not be until near the close of the first decade of the twenty-first century that Americans began to appreciate how they were sold the WMD premise. When this film was aired in 2003, 72 percent of the American public still believed Iraq had WMD: 33 percent felt they had been smuggled out of the country, while another 28 percent said they were stashed somewhere.[13] *Saddam's Bombmaker* catered to this popular belief. Any self-serving basis for Hamza's testimony—he agreed to provide information to the CIA if they got his wife and children out of Iraq—is lost sight of in the patriotic rhetoric that could only tug at the heartstrings of the American viewer:

> "I loved the U.S. from day one," he says as we learn that he obtained his doctorate from MIT, after which he obtained a teaching post at Florida State University, where he remained until he was forced to return to

Baghdad because of threats to his father (who is never again mentioned in the film) if he didn't. Ultimately, he was able to return to the country he loved and escape a ruthless dictator, thanks to the CIA, where, we learn at the end, "Today, the Hamzas [are] living the American Dream."

We Got Him: Capturing Saddam . . . and What Comes Next (2004) aired on the Discovery Channel, *Ace in the Hole* (2005) on the Military Channel. The movies are cut from the same cloth; the Military Channel is a subsidiary of Discovery. They are similar to one another, though the one on the Military Channel has more military talking heads and focuses on the military operation in greater detail than the one on Discovery.

There are a few interesting aspects to these films that are worth a brief comment. *Ace* is perhaps the first time that the American public gets to see the grim casualties of the war: Three rows of flag-draped caskets are seen being transported home on a cargo plane, a pair of

Saddam Hussein: *We Got Him.*

parade-rest honor guards standing in front of the coffins, while a single-column of military personnel stands respectfully along one side of the coffins. This is a jarring picture, largely because of the absence of such pictures in the media. The initial reason given by President George W. Bush for the continued ban on returning coffins is that they might be taken out of context and used by antiwar propagandists. This picture is permitted because the dead *are* contextualized. This is a story about the military and the threats they face on the front line, and their tenac-ity and grit in finding the fled Iraqi leader. These flag-draped coffins represent the fallen heroes in a war against a tyrant and the sacrifices of American troops—"[a bullet] could come from anywhere," we're told—that viewers of the Military Channel are likely to appreciate.

The political and military situation is given considerable context. The context is missing, if not bastardized, when the situation in Iraq is dis-cussed in these films. In *We Got Him,* for example, a well-dressed Asad Gozh is interviewed. The viewer learns that Gozh is a Kurdish survivor, but nothing is ever really contextualized about the Kurkish situation in the Middle East, nor the longstanding internecine hostility between the Kurds and the Iraqi people. Gozh's comment has more to do with a justified Kurdish animosity toward Saddam because of the persecu-tion of the Kurdish people, but his comment is lost as it is rolled into the whole. "Too many [Kurds] have died," says Gozh. This is why, the narrator says, "like so many Iraqis, he's looking forward to Saddam's day in court." The whole—the overall satisfaction of Iraqis regarding Sad-dam's fall, not just the Kurds—is decontextualized earlier in the film when the we see a tight shot of a half dozen cheering demonstrators in a park while some people mull around watching, and the narrator tells us, "Across Iran and around the world, celebrations erupt at the news [of his capture]." Such a worldview is one of the reasons for American puzzlement, if not outright anger, when it is learned that not everyone shares the American perspective toward the war in Iraq. The large, bold-type headlines in the *Washington Post* aptly portray the animosity toward those who share a different perspective: "Axis of Weasel: Ger-man and France wimp out on Iraq."

Both films end by acknowledging the war is dragging on, but imply an end is in sight. *Ace* concludes by saying that the "U.S. pinned end of Iraqi resistance on capture of Saddam Hussein, but the violence would continue. *However*, the capture of Saddam means that Iraqis are guaranteed a future free of their former dictator [narrator's emphasis]." *We Got Him* goes even further by suggesting that soon, very soon, those in the field will find what has eluded them to this point [2004]:

> The CIA will use its best [sic] techniques [on Saddam] to try to learn the answer to many enduring questions. Where are Saddam's remaining lieutenants hiding? Where are the caches of weapons and bomb making material used by the insurgents? And where *are* the weapons of mass destruction that have eluded investigators and haunted the Bush administration for months? [narrator's emphasis]

Three years later, the History Channel explains the failure to find the weapons is because of *Saddam's Secret Tunnels* (2007). The existence of this subterranean empire is not successfully established in this documentary. The casual television viewer may be impressed, however, with the diagrams of tunnels, which the Secretary of Defense proclaims, run "for miles and miles and miles" underneath Baghdad in a file footage speech given before the invasion four years earlier. The viewer is then shown a diagram of tunnels that, we're told, many believe connect the various government buildings. Viewers learn, as they watch the extensive connect-the-dot tunnels diagrammatically depicted on the screen, that "one of [these] *could* be an escape route leading all the way to the airport" [author's italics]. If the viewer is riveted to the diagram, then the viewer might not digest the verbal disclaimer at the end of this sequence when the narrator accedes that "the Pentagon now says such an extensive route does not exist."

The Trial of Saddam Hussein naturally follows his capture. It aired on PBS in 2008. The film opens with the now de rigor picture of Saddam's statue being tumbled in the square. The increased insurgency taking place in Iraq in 2006 is glossed over by suggesting that once justice has been served and Saddam has been brought to trial, and the Iraqi people see how democracy works, any countervailing opposition to the new government will fade away.[14] It is not easy, however, since the Iraqi people do not grasp how the American system of justice works—the viewer learns of numerous assassinations of lawyers involved with the case. The failure to appreciate how the democratic system of justice works is an often stated explanation for why things did not proceed smoothly.

Nevertheless, this flawed system is still better because it is "not court like Saddam had where you're whisked off in the middle of the night."

There are fourteen charges against Saddam and his seven codefendants. Their case is heard by a five-judge panel. The presiding judge is criticized midway through the first of two trials for being too lenient on Hussein, because he tolerates Saddam's outbursts in the courtroom; this is mentioned over file footage of Saddam standing, shaking his fist and railing. He is replaced by a more hard-line judge who, intolerant of Saddam's disruptive behavior in court, ultimately banishes all but one of the eight defendants from his courtroom for their ill-behavior during proceedings. The implication is that the court needed a hard-line judge to take charge for the court to run smoothly, like they do in the United States, sidestepping parallels to Judge Hoffman's hard-line and biased behavior toward the Chicago Eight in September–October 1969 and which was applauded by then-President Nixon.[15]

A second trial commences after the first ends, and the new judge, the narrator says, "shocked everyone when he made a sympathetic remark to the former dictator [that] 'you are not a dictator.'" Such a statement outraged officials [in the Iraqi government] and the judge resigned. The outcome of the trial, we are told, is breathlessly awaited: "All Iraq has waited three and one-half months for [the] verdict.'" This statement is accompanied by visuals of the "common man" in the streets glued to their television set, ostensibly awaiting the foregone conclusion of the trial. The verdict is unanimous. This is the point the viewer learns something that few realize—one of the judges who was soft on Saddam was secretively removed, apparently to ensure a unanimous verdict. This happened because of the increased assertiveness by the new government. This assertiveness was earlier mentioned as the reason America was "losing control" of the trial process, and was an implied explanation for any "flaws" in the Iraqi judicial process. This impression becomes an important assertion when the viewer witnesses Saddam's execution. The official version of Saddam stoically being led to the gallows and then hanged is first shown, as it initially aired, without the audio portion. Then we see the unofficial version that was secretly taped and released after the execution. In this tape the audio version is heard and the full execution (dangling of corpse) is shown. A near hysterical mob taunts, insults, and lashes out at the former Iraqi leader, chanting the name of Saddam's nemesis, the Shiite firebrand cleric whose father Saddam was reputed to have killed: "Muqtada! Muqtada! Muqtada!" An American official remarks that, "The spirit of vengeance and savagery that was on display in the execution chamber [was] exceedingly distasteful." This is followed by a quip from a well-dressed Iraqi official: "Saddam's execution went wrong. But it's over. To hell with him." Given the tone of this and other documentaries, and the prevailing view of Saddam in the United States, few American viewers would disagree and any miscarriage of justice is lost because he received his comeuppance.

The documentaries ultimately come together in a four-hour minise-ries that was a joint venture of HBO and the BBC, *The House of Saddam* (2008). It is the only fictional movie of Saddam Hussein. The late arrival of a feature film about Saddam is because people know every-thing about Saddam, or at least what Americans (the HBO audience) or Britains (the BBC audience) need, or want, to know. The film, however, gives viewers insights into others in his entourage that the documenta-ries only briefly touch on, if they mention them at all: Saddam's wife, his child-bride and cousin, Sajida; his sons, Uday and Qusay; Saddam's "married off" daughters and their husbands, Raghdad and General Hus-sein Kamel al-Majid and Rama and Saddam Kamiel al-Majid; Saddam's strikingly attractive blonde mistress, who eventually becomes his second wife, Samira Shanbandar; along with other key members of his inner circle, such as cousins, General Adnan Khariallah, his Defense Minister, and Tariq Aziz, his Deputy. The family connections are strongly mined in the movie, which smacks of familial nepotism to Westerners,[16] and does not clarify the importance of family bonds to Arabs, aptly captured, accordingly to Raphael Patai, in one of the most frequently quoted Arabic proverbs: "I and my brothers against my cousin; I and my cousin against the stranger (or 'against the world')."[17]

The movie nicely fictionalizes the life of Saddam that is captured in the three documentaries about his life. The first thirty minutes of part I delve further than the documentaries into his rise to power, but that is because there is little early documentary footage of Saddam as a deputy president and a fictionalized version can depict these events by filling in the pictorial gaps. It is a well-done film that undoubtedly reached more viewers than any of the televised documentaries. It adds little, however, to the storehouse of knowledge about the man himself and perpetuates most of the fanaticism viewers associate with the former dictator.

Film critics and lay reviewers alike are in general agreement that this is a well-acted but otherwise thin movie: limited, episodic plotline that is short on historical details—the British journalist Thomas Sutcliffe, writing for *The Independent*, captures the absences nicely when he asks, "who the hell airbrushed the Americans out of the picture?"[18] It is an unnecessary question. The Americans have clean hands. They have seldom been mentioned in *any* of the documentaries aired in the United States, and if they are mentioned in any dubious way, their complicity in Saddam's rise to power and their tact support of his more dubious acts are passed over as if it were a minor point.

The complaint by many critics is that the film focuses too much on the family, but this is precisely what makes *House* watchable . . . for four hours! These are the people behind the man and their stories do hold the audience because they are key unknowns. It is true that the "bloody bits are passed over" but this is standard in an *entertainment* program that is aimed to captivate and titillate, as most made-for-television movies are—as, in fact, most movies are.[19] The complaint that the film could have been longer and given more historical detail misses the point that movies typically run ninety minutes and are not about historical accuracy, especially when the history is recent and well known.

The strongest segment is the first thirty minutes of part I, which delves into Saddam's life as deputy president—in itself, a historical fact that is not widely known—and his elevation to president. This is also why part IV is the least successful: the hunt for Saddam Hussein was widely reported by the news media and part IV simply rehashes the familiar—the soldiers searching for Saddam in a green-tinted night scene is straight out of *We Got Him*.[20] Parts II and III gloss over the Iran-Iraq conflict and Gulf War I for the same reason.[21] These two parts manage to hold the viewer by portraying others in his house. Both parts are particularly successful at putting a face to Uday's craziness: Part II opens with Uday firing a handgun into the air from the band shell of a packed disco and laughing manically; in part III, Uday arrives late for a dinner gathering at the palace and tosses food at one of Saddam's generals after Hussein leaves the room; later in part III he singles out the lone female among the passing wait staff—"You!"—and we hear him copulating with her in the restroom, afterward curtly dismissing her with a wave of his hand as he leans over the sink to do a line of cocaine.

Saddam's father, who he never knew, his mother tells him on her deathbed in part I, was "bad blood." The movie suggests the bad seed was transmitted to his son, Saddam, who in turn passed it on to his son, Uday. Had Saddam not been deposed and the reins passed to his son, things would be worse, for a least Saddam knew what his son didn't: "You think violence is a pastime?" he screams at his son, "It is a tool! What are we? Barbarians?" The answer in the minds of many is, yes!

Osama bin Laden

There is the same number of films about Osama bin Laden as there are about Saddam Hussein. The tact is largely the same, as well. The majority sketch his personal, somewhat eccentric history and how he ultimately became the world's most wanted man. The first, however, is distinct. It is the only fictive feature film about Osama, released by United Artists and produced by the Japanese Broadcast Company in 2003. It is misleadingly but aptly titled *Osama*.

The film is not about Osama bin Laden but a young, twelve-year-old girl in Afghanistan under the Taliban who, in order to survive, cuts her hair short to pass as a boy and adopts the common name Osama. While not about bin Laden, it nevertheless depicts the havoc wrecked by the Taliban in Afghanistan. It promotes itself as "the first [film] to be made in a post-Taliban Afghanistan" and utilizes a cast of nonactors that "adds integrity to the heartbreaking story." Critics generally praise the insights the film provides into what life was like under the Taliban. The only criticism, made primarily by lay commentators, is with the slow, often plodding pace of the film. This pacing is critical to the films ability to allow the viewer to step back into time and get a true taste of a simpler, albeit harsher way of life (see also *The Story of Qiu Ju*, 1993; *Into Great Silence*, 2005). The story is in the tradition of a select few of other Islamic films that attempt to place the subjugated role of women into context in Muslim society (see *Daughters of Afghanistan*, 2004;[22] see also *Two Women*, 1999; *The Circle*, 2000; *Baran*, 2001). It is all the more stark in this film because of the strict, fundamentalist interpretation of the Qur'an under the Taliban.

The film opens with a large group of burka-adorned women marching, chanting in Arabic, "We want the right to work. We are not political. We are hungry." Moments later a young boy runs by shouting, "Run! The Taliban are coming! Run!" as machine-gun mounted trucks roll up disgorging Taliban males who begin to round up the women, locking those they catch into primitive cages in the back of the trucks. The scene ends with a nice cinematic touch: A Taliban raises a club high and begins to march toward the camera that is ostensibly covering the march. The point of view is from behind the camera, which suddenly goes dark. The fate of the "infidel journalist" is revealed later in the film.

The next scene is of one of the women in the protest march who has escaped. She has returned to the hospital where she works, along with her daughter. No one has been paid in months and the hospital, the administrator tells her, is being closed for some inexplicable reason simply because it is the wish of the Taliban. The Taliban arrive, then depart. They are not seen in this shot, only heard; this is a common practice throughout, suggesting their menacing, ubiquitous presence. This scene too fades out to some nice camerawork: long shot from the rear of a decaying hospital corridor with patients slowly filing out, one hobbling, being steadied by a friend; another marching ploddingly, rolling his IV tube along with him; a young boy on crutches that no one is helping who slowly gets left behind as the others disappear around the corner to the outside world. The camera lingers on the boy, helpless, and now alone in the corridor. His plight is clear. He will never survive in this harsh, cruel Afghan world ruled by the Taliban.

It is only now that the story of Osama begins, but the viewer already has an inkling of her fate—as a female.[23] The mother is talking to her. The viewer learns that her husband was killed in the Kabul wars; her son in the Russian war. With no men in the family, and the Taliban prohibition against women working, they will not survive, unless she cuts her hair short and passes for a boy. This accomplished, she gets a job with the local merchant, who knows the child is really a girl, but accepts the façade and tells her, "Come to work early, boy!" Soon after, the Taliban recruit Osama into their school of young boys, where they learn the Qur'an and how to fight. It is only a matter of time before Osama is unmasked.

Shortly after the revelation, "She is a girl!" the viewer witnesses Taliban justice, knowing that Osama's fate will also be decided. The infidel journalist, who doesn't appear to understand what is going on, is given the death sentence by a reclining judge, and taken away. The sound of machine-gun fire is heard shortly thereafter. A white, blond-headed Western woman, who was seen briefly with the marchers in the opening, is brought out, accused of promoting profanity. The judge rules, "She shall be stoned to death." She is then placed in a pit up to her neck and the sentence is carried out. Surprisingly, Osama is given a reprieve. Of sorts. The viewer expects her to receive a similar death sentence since "In Holy Islam, this has never happened before," and perhaps her fate is worse than death: she is married off to an old, toothless man, who grinningly thanks the judge, "God will reward you." That night, they arrive in an oxcart before his house, where numerous other young wives are locked in separate rooms. Tears streaming down her face she climbs the ancient wooden ladder to her fate, the old man behind her. The film ends with him performing the ritual of postcoital cleansing that he earlier had taught the boys. The tear-stained face of Osama is then seen. The movie fades out with her dreaming of skipping rope, a recurring motif that runs through the film to signify lost innocence. This film, though not specifically about bin Laden, does give insight into the form of Islamic fundamentalism that shapes bin Laden's worldview.

If the documentaries fail to convey the horrific situation of life under the Taliban, they do touch on the plurality of wives that bin Laden had and the excess of his brand of Islamic fundamentalism. Those documentaries that trace his early years (*Osama bin Laden: In the Name of Allah* and *Meeting Osama bin Laden*) dwell on the fact that he was the son of his father's tenth wife and that he took his four wives to Afghanistan with him. The number of wives is meant to cast aspersions on his way of life to monogamous Westerns. It is reminiscent of documentaries about Saddam Hussein that reveled in exposing his eccentricities. In both Saddam and bin Laden's cases these peculiar tendencies are, ostensibly, preconditions that later explain their more bizarre behavior. Also at the heart of these and most documentaries about bin Laden is the excessiveness of his Islamic beliefs. For example, in *Meeting Osama bin Laden*, we are told that as a young man he attended "university to

study economics, but once there spent most of his time studying Islam
in its most austere and strict form," and while there he met the "radical
fundamentalist teacher, Abdullah Azzam." The movie *Osama* is much
more successful in conveying the full nature of this form of radical fundamentalism.

The various documentaries are a matter of emphasis. The two histories, *Osama bin Laden: In the Name of Allah* and *Meeting Osama bin
Laden*, ultimately stray into bin Laden's activities in Afghanistan against
the Russians, and his subsequent evolution as a terrorist, but focus on
his path to terrorism: his time in Saudi Arabia and in Afghanistan. The
other two documentaries mention his early years but focus on the period after American troops entered Afghanistan: *The Hunt for Osama
bin Laden* and *Targeted: Osama bin Laden*. These two later films explain how he slipped away in the mountainous regions of Afghanistan
and boldly state that now that Saddam Hussein has been captured and
the situation in Iraq is no longer as critical, forces are being shifted to
Afghanistan and bin Laden will soon be found. The two-disc Frontline
series, *The al-Qaeda File*, marries the early years with the hunt. The bin
Laden documentaries, much like those depicting Saddam, tend to be
familiarly Procrustean.

In the Name of Allah is illustrative of this Procrustean tendency: manipulating data to make it fit some preconceived point of view. The call to
Afghanistan to expel the infidel Russians was embraced by many Muslim
young men. The time spent in the forbidden terrain of Afghanistan is
glossed over. It was just one big party. According to a CIA talking head,
the whole thing was "Like Woodstock. Like Club Med." And as for bin
Laden's self-proclaimed military bravado: "Not everyone remembers
Osama bin Laden as a war hero," says another CIA field agent, who dismisses bin Laden's time in the mountains and the ten-year Afghanistan-
Russian conflict with a metaphorical wave of his hand by stating that
none of the Arabs were ever involved in a major combat battle. This is
because bin Laden's role was primarily financial: he was the "Ford Foundation for terrorists." Bin Laden, we learn from a psychological profiler
in *The Hunt*, is just a nutcase: "[He] suffers from malignant narcissism
. . . underneath [the] grand façade [is a] person consumed by self doubt
. . . [who must] compensate with dreams of glory." So much for the background and expertise of America's most wanted man.

America's Most Wanted from *The Hunt for Osama bin Laden*.

The bin Laden films all bear a striking resemblance to the search for Saddam, with two exceptions: the satiric feature film by Morgan Spurlock, *Where in the World Is Osama bin Laden?* and the French-made documentary, *The Search for Osama bin Laden.*

Morgan Spurlock follows the success of his critique of fast food in *Super Size Me* (2004) with his second feature film, *Where in the World Is Osama bin Laden?* (2008). He takes a humorous approach, a radical departure for a movie that touches on such tragic events. Alas, he is nowhere near as successful in combining these two as Roberto Benigni in *Life Is Beautiful* (1997), though his style is less condescending, and thus more engaging, than Michael Moore's.

The film opens with a view of feathery white cirrostratus clouds seen angelically from above. The voice-over says, "Man, life is good . . . then one day everything changes." The viewer sees the city below and hears a bomb going off. It is not 9/11: A young woman holds up her pregnancy test and announces, "I'm pregnant." He is doubtful: "From just one test?" She holds up five other tests. The world has changed!

The connection to bin Laden? "What kind of world am I [sic] bringing a kid into?" He has to do something, and taking his cue from the many action films he has seen, where "complicated world problems ultimately [are] solved by one lone guy," he sets off to find Osama bin Laden, failing to understand how a country with "the strongest military, the sneakiest spies, [and] the coolest technology in the entire world" cannot find him. All this is accompanied by visual cartoon characterizations of bin Laden. Spurlock then sets out in the format he successfully employed in *Super Size Me* to prepare himself for the undertaking. He goes to the doctor to learn about *all* the shots to travel abroad, then embarks on a series of self-defense courses, where he learns how to duck a grenade, how to tell from blood spatters on the wall the direction the sniper is firing from and how to say to a terrorist, "Don't take me, take the cameraman." The remainder of the ninety-minute film is a trip to hot spots in the Middle East where he conducts people-in-the-street interviews: Egypt, Jordan, Israel, and so forth. The interview style fails: He asks his questions in English and then listens knowingly, sagely nodding his head to the often lengthy native-speaking answer. Spurlock's translator is briefly seen in two or three shots standing beside him, but the interpreter is never seen translating for the audience—Spurlock simply summarizes what his translator must have told him.

Film critics found the movie trite, giving it two stars (of five) or less. Jim Emerson at the *Chicago Sun-Times*, Wesley Morris of the *Boston Globe*, and A. O. Scott of the *New York Times* were all critical of the film's merits. Scott here summarizes the views of many when he says, "It's impossible to disagree with much of what he [Spurlock] says . . . but it's also impossible to learn anything about war, terrorism, religion, oil, democracy or any of the other topics a less glib, less self-absorbed filmmaker might want to tackle."[24]

One thing the film critics do not mention, but that is particularly noteworthy, is that Spurlock does tackle one aspect of terrorism not addressed in any of the other documentaries: America's role in fostering terrorism. Spurlock asks a young man in Egypt if he voted in the last presidential election, only to learn that he hadn't because the country "isn't a democracy." Spurlock then explains to the viewing audience that President Mubarak has been in power for twenty-six years, thanks to the Americans, even despite some questionable and decidedly undemocratic behavior. The viewer then sees a cartoonish FDR-like character, resembling Uncle Sam, sitting at a bar with a child puppet on his knee, a white shoulder-to-waist sash identifies the puppet as "Dictator Trujillo." Uncle Sam explains: "He may be a son-of-a-bitch, but he's *our* son-of-a-bitch." Spurlock explains that during the Cold War the United States made some unsavory allies, including the Shah of Iran and Saddam Hussein, who "was a SOB, too, but while he was fighting the Iranians, he was *our* SOB." A picture of our sons-a-bitches is then seen lined up at the bar, glasses of beer upraised in a toast at the money that's been poured into their country (regime) by the Americans.

Despite addressing an aspect of terrorism that explains why many parts of the world (e.g., Iran) are anti-American, the segment fails. One reason for the failure is the cartoonlike depiction of the topic, which itself detracts from its seriousness. The other is that, despite mentioning America's role in supporting state terrorism in some countries, it was not directly done by the Americans (the regimes did it, not the United States) and the viewer never really knows who these people are or how they ruled their country with an iron fist.[25]

The critical failure of the movie does not mean the movie was unsuccessful. Though none of the lay critics signaled out the sequence about America's role in sponsoring terrorism that Spurlock took some pains to insert, the movie achieved a successful rating of 3.5 stars from 21,357 people who took the time to rate the film on Netflix,[26] which is substantially higher than the film critics accorded it. In this sense, the director achieved his aim, which was to sensitize the viewer as to what other, everyday young people think about terrorism and Americans.

> *Netflix reviewer 1:* "The most shocking part of this film shows how warmly Spurlock was treated by the people of such collectively distrustful nations."
> *Netflix reviewer 2:* ". . . this is a pretty interesting journey. For me it opened a window into the daily life of people in 'those other' countries—particularly Muslim families."
> *Netflix reviewer 3:* "I was laughing through the whole thing . . . [but nevertheless found it] intriguing and arousing."

Spurlock was certainly more successful in getting his point across than the other outcast documentary, *The Search for Osama bin Laden* (2007), which was made by two French journalists, Emmanuel Razari and Eric de Lavarence. It is obviously made for the U.S. market as the two journalists speak English throughout. Nevertheless, the film is made from the French point of view and develops a distinctly different perspective toward bin Laden—that the Americans let him escape and don't want to find him. They make their point by interviewing, among others, (1) a group of Taliban fighters in the mountains who say, "We're fighting Americans because they took our country away"; (2) warlords in the Tora Bora region where bin Laden fled after the invasion; and (3) French troops stationed in Kabul and in the remote area of Jalalabad, an area that has "long [been] a gathering place for Taliban fighters, [and] now seems cut off from the rest of the world. Our cameras aren't welcome." The regions are thematically linked: "From Kabul to Jalalabad, accusations against the Americans [for letting bin Laden slip away] are growing." The proof is in the pudding. In one instance, a "highly respected warlord" in the Tora Bora region, "one of three Afghan commanders that helped Americans during the Tora Bora attack," tells the investigative journalist that the decision to surround the cave where bin Laden was supposedly hiding before the 8 a.m. bombing commenced didn't happen because of "Pakistani pressure [on the Americans]."[27] This confirms an earlier report made by a French soldier in Jalalabad when, the narrator tell us, "*twice* the special French forces had Osama bin Laden in their gun sight [narrator's italics]," but word never came down to pull the trigger: "It's true," the voice of the French soldier says, "I can testify [that] in 2003 and 2004 . . . [I] had [him] in [my] gun sight."

American complicity for bin Laden's escape, a perspective not reflected in any of the other documentaries about bin Laden, may explain the film's failure to gain a foothold in the United States. It did not air on any of the traditional television outlets that regularly featured related documentaries about bin Laden. It has gained only modest attention on DVD sites. Its perspective on the war is not a point of view that Americans want to appreciate, not after bin Laden and the al-Qaeda claimed responsibility for 9/11.

SACROSANCT MEMORIES: THE HEROES OF 9/11

Certain events are seared into the collective memory of those who lived at the time the event occurred. Those most affected are those who ex-

perienced the event during their critical ages of adolescence and early
adulthood; those least affected are those who are born after the event
occurred because of their psychological distance from the event.[28] The
attack on Pearl Harbor and the assassination of John F. Kennedy may be
historical footnotes for those born after the event, but few that heard of
the tragedy at the time fail to remember where they were or what they
were doing when they first learned of its occurrence. The collapse of the
WTC may be even sharper on the mind than earlier historical events for
those who lived through it. In part, this is due to the extensive television
coverage that took place as the twin towers collapsed and to the ensuing
search for survivors and cleanup efforts that followed. In part, it is also
owing to the video-recording equipment widely available to the man on
the street. This visual coverage of the collapse of the twin towers, the narrator of *In Memoriam: New York City 9/11/2001* points out, is the reason
it is "the most documented event in history." The amount of film footage
also explains the outpouring of documentaries examining the collapse.

The first part of this section examines the proliferation of documentary films revolving around the terrorist attack that took place on
September 11, 2001. The terrorist attack itself is the reason for the
increased support of the military and the desire to get even with those
responsible, which was at its highest immediately after the attacks.[29]
The visual carnage that American viewers were continuously exposed
to through films well after 2001 helped maintain support for the war on
terrorism, even as the body count of American soldiers in Afghanistan
and Iraq climbed in 2005 and 2006 and the tide against the wars began
to turn.[30] These films inevitably cast those on the site of the disasters in
a positive light—altruistic, self-sacrificing, patriotic—even if the print
media, as we will see, sometimes took issue with this portrayal. This is
not to say that some of the films about 9/11 did not criticize aspects of
9/11. Film criticism, however, focused on only one aspect of the problem: the government's failure to prevent the disaster (see *On Native
Soil*, 2005; *9/11: Press for Truth*, 2006). In so doing, the films continued
to portray the event and the actions of those on the ground in an unequivocal positive light. Films in this group include:

America: A Tribute to Heroes (2001)
WTC: The First 24 Hours (2001)

9/11 (2002)

Why the Towers Fell (2002)

WTC: Anatomy of the Collapse (2002)

World Trade Center: In Memoriam (2002)

In Memoriam: New York City 9/11/2001 (2002)

New York Firefighters: The Brotherhood of 9/11 (2002)

Twin Towers (2002)

Engineering the Future WTC: Rebuilding Ground Zero (2004)

Thomas L. Friedman Reporting: Searching for the Roots of 9/11 (2004)

On Native Soil (2005)

Answering the Call: Ground Zero (2005)

Aftermath: Unanswered Questions from 9/11 (2005)

The Road to 9/11 (2005)

Inside 9/11 (2005)

9/11: Press for Truth (2006)

Portrait of Courage: The Untold Story of Flight 93 (2006)

Saint of 9/11 (2006)

9/11: The Myth and the Reality (2007)

9/11: Inside the Twin Towers (2007)

911: In Plane Site (2007)

Blocking the Path to 9/11: The Anatomy of Smear (2008)

The second part of this section delves into the fictional treatment of 9/11 events. The WTC is certainly at the heart of these movies, but the focus broadens in 2005 and 2006 to address not just those on the ground that day but the psychological trauma of those who lived through the event, something the documentaries seldom assessed. Indeed, only one fictional film, Oliver Stone's *World Trade Center*, deals with events at Ground Zero, and may be considered a modest critical and box office success. Stone's movie deals with the rescue efforts to find survivors after the collapse of the WTC. Many critics rated it two stars, finding it, like Kenneth Turan of the *Los Angeles Times*, "pious [and] conventional," while those that did rate the film higher (3 or more stars) did so less for the cinematic effort than, Owen Gleiberman writes for *Entertainment Weekly*, for its merits as "a tribute to those who died, and survived, on Sept. 11."[31] The film adds nothing to the abundance

of documentary footage that addressed the heroic efforts on those dealing with events in the wake of the twin towers' collapse and which was
already firmly established in the public's mind by the time Stone's film
appeared in 2006. This is the reason the movie is given little attention in
this section on feature films. The other feature films that address WTC
events, though hardly blockbusters, are given more attention because
they approach the subject from an angle not appraised in the documentaries. Similarly, other films attempt to give a face to those events that
are not detailed in the documentaries. *DC 9/11* attempts to give insights
into what happened at the Pentagon and in Washington on that fateful
day—the only real visual of the event being the picture of the plane that
demolished one side of the building. A number of other films give faces
to the voices aboard United Flight 93. Films in this group include the
following:

DC 9/11: Time of Crisis (2003)
Homeland Security (2004)
Flight 93 (2005)
WTC View (2005)
The Path to 9/11 (2006)
World Trade Center (2006)
United 93 (2006)
The 9/11 Commission Report (2006)
Reign Over Me (2007)

Documentaries

The first show to deal with 9/11 beyond the extensive news coverage
that focused on events at Ground Zero was a two-hour star-studded
television special to raise funds for the victims, *America: A Tribute to
Heroes*. The show opened with an original number by Bruce Springsteen, "My City of Ruins." Interspersed between songs that fit the occasion—Stevie Wonder, "Let Us Pray to See the Light"; Tom Petty, "No,
I Won't Back Down"—during the commercial-free program were other
stars, such as Tom Hanks, who recalled some act of heroism by those
caught up in the events. The show closed with Clint Eastwood reading

the words from "America, America." The show is worth a brief mention here because (1) it was the first show to address the events of 9/11 beyond the news coverage, (2) it mentioned two brothers who lost their lives in the rescue efforts the day the WTC collapse and who would be the subject of a subsequent documentary, and (3) it reminds us a decade later of the somberness of the tragedy that has lost some of its intensity with the passing of time.

The television special was much more trenchant in its depiction of 9/11 events and more effective in stirring a passion for those who were lost than the first documentary, *WTC: The First 24 Hours*. The failure of this film was that it was too hastily assembled, appearing within weeks of the event. There was no time for the editing process to frame the events. The idea was sound: The film was promoted as devoid of music and commentary as a means to capture the essence of the tragedy. The absence of music and commentary, however, was more likely owing to the quick montage of disjointed images, all of which had been seen repeatedly on the news. The show also failed because of its brevity: It was promoted as a feature depicting a horrendous twenty-four-hour period but only ran twenty "hard" minutes. Viewers on Netflix gave it a mean rating of less than 2 stars. The rationale for the abysmal rating is captured by one lay Netflix reviewer:

[T]his film, although somewhat interesting, just showed the buildings still left standing, ground zero and dust and debris. There was no depth or real sense of why we were seeing the same shots over and over. . . . [All] we see is the same empty blown out windows and dust. For the years of crying I have done for losing a family member on the flight, this film did not even evoke one tear.

More successful was a retooled, already shot A&E one-hour special on the WTC. The film was initially to be a part of the architectural marvels series. It had been filmed in February–March 2001 and featured many individuals who worked in the WTC. The architectural features depicted in the documentary were updated by a somber host who reminded the viewer of what took place a few months later and often mentioned that some of those who were just seen on the taped interview lost their lives in the terrorist attack of 9/11.[32] The film was originally titled, *WTC: A Modern Marvel, 1973–2001*, but was released as a tribute to those who lost their lives on 9/11, *World Trade Center: In Memoriam.* Though audience information is proprietary, I suspect the film did exceptionally well on the cable network and in the subsequent video release because it is one of the few to appraise the building itself, and because it focused on the structure's architectural and engineering features, it made its destruction all the more salient for the viewer who gleaned a deeper appreciation of the uniqueness of what has been lost. Of particular interest to this analysis is the optimism of those who were interviewed, who detailed the uniqueness of the building, and who talked of the ability of the structure to withstand even a commercial jet crashing into it, a point reinforced in the closing that discussed the failure of the 1990 terrorist attack to cause any significant structural damage, despite the fact that the bombs were designed to collapse the WTC. These points will be returned to later in this section and have a direct bearing on those documentaries that suggest the government should have been able to avoid the 2001 disaster.

The overwhelming majority of WTC films depict events on the ground on that fateful day, and the rescue efforts in the aftermath of the towers' destruction. Despite the span of time that separates them (2002–2007), the films are remarkably consistent in their appraisal of events. They are much more successful in depicting the tragedy than the hastily assembled *24 Hours* film. The earlier ones (2002–2004) are more successful than the later films, largely because the images are still fresh and the release date makes the films less of a historical analysis than a story about unfolding events. Two of the better representative ones are critiqued. Both focus on the rescue efforts of those on the ground. They are unique because unlike the typical collage of images from diverse sources (e.g., *In Memoriam: New York City 9/11/2001; Answering the Call: Ground Zero*) these two films are works in progress about New York City firemen (*9/11*; see also *New York Firefighters: The Brotherhood of 9/11*, 2002; *Saint of 9/11*, 2006) and police officers (*Twin Towers*) that because of events developing on the morning of September 11 turned into a close-up look of rescue efforts of those on the scene when the towers collapsed.

9/11 runs two hours, with an hour of bonus material on the DVD that is comprised primarily of testimonials by New York Fire Department (NYFD) personnel. It was made by two French filmmakers, Jules and

Geodeon Naudet, and is narrated by a friend of theirs who is one of the firemen from Engine 7, Ladder 1, and who receives directorial credit. The film was initially to be a documentary about a rookie New York firefighter. After following the cadets through graduation, Tony Benetatos is selected to be the focus of the film. He is assigned probie status and starts his career at Engine 7, Ladder 1, which is the fire station proximate to the WTC. The film is not going anywhere because Tony is marked by a "white cloud" since no fires occur during his shift—there is nothing exciting to film. The irony of this is not lost on the viewer, who knows the American nightmare is about to begin.

Ladder 1 is located six blocks from the WTC. On the morning of 9/11, Ladder 1 is called to the scene of the WTC for a routine gas leak. It is just one of many calls they have made to the WTC over the years. One of the brothers, Jules, follows the firefighters for some camera practice. They are on the scene when the first jet hits, which allows Jules to record the first crash. Geodeon has remained at the station house. This provides the viewer with back-and-forth shots of events taking place both on site and the response of those at the fire hall. Because Ladder 1 was already on site, Jules captures some of the only film that was taken inside the WTC after the first plane hit Tower 1. The film flits to the lone fireman who is forced to stay behind to man the station house. The frantic efforts on the ground, which the lone fireman on duty is watching on television, are strikingly juxtaposed with the quiet and isolation of the placid firehouse. The clock over the mounted television gives the time: 9:30, 9:40. The first tower is about to collapse; it starts to go down at 9:59. Geodeon goes in search of his brother. In the process of making his way to the WTC, he films some of the expressions of on-the-street New Yorkers and captures some of the chaos that was occurring on the ground.

The framing of the story departs from traditional films about the disaster, which typically show the first plane hitting Tower 1, the "Oh, my God" response of those on the ground, then the second plane hitting Tower 2, followed by the collapse of the two towers and the screams and frantic attempts of those on the ground to avoid the debris. 9/11 opens in the traditional manner, but then adds depth by flashing back to the history of Ladder 1 and the selection of Tony Benetatos upon his graduation to be the featured rookie as he finally becomes the fireman that he has always wanted to be. He lost his life on 9/11. The film ends with a pictorial montage scroll of the firemen who lost their lives that day to the fade-out song, "Danny Boy."

Unlike *The First 24 Hours*, the thickness of the dust, the extent of the debris, and the pure panic of the civilians who were in harm's way is given sharper focus, largely because of the cross-cuts to the sereneness of the station house, the interior images of firemen in the building trying to figure out what is going on after the first plane crashes into Tower 1, and the pride of Tony Benetatos at his graduation from the academy at finally fulfilling his lifelong dream. The camera angles also work to give depth to the film as a documentary. The shots of the graduation ceremony and the initial scenes at the firehouse are sharp and crisp and professionally edited, while those that take place on site are rough cuts: jittery, often blurred, fuzzy images that convincingly convey the franticness of on-site filmmaking during a chaotic period.

9/11 initially aired on CBS, which excluded it from Oscar nomination. The film that did win the Oscar for best documentary in 2002 was the thirty-minute short, *Twin Towers*, which was released by Universal. Like *9/11*, it too was a film in progress, in this case a planned television program about the members of the elite Emergency Services Unit (ESU) of the New York Police Department. The setup is the same as *9/11*. The film opens with the picture of Tower 1, then the plane hitting Tower 2, and the collapse of the twin towers. This is followed immediately by a crawl that twenty-three New York City police officers died on 9/11, fourteen of whom were members of the ESU. The focus on the ESU team is justified because of the 37,000 police officers in New York only 350 are members of the special forces of New York City's police department. The film then moves away from the events of 9/11 and for the next seventeen minutes follows members of the ESU team as they go about their daily business: serving high-profile warrants—kicking in doors and wrestling dangerous suspects to the ground—or rescuing five children trapped in icy waters. The narrator tells us, "If there's a problem, these are the guys to go."

Like *9/11*, the story focuses on one member of the team, Joe Veigiano—he and his brother, who both lost their lives that day, were specifically named in the tribute special. Like the firemen from Ladder 1, the ESU team was among the first cadre of police on the scene shortly after Tower 1 was hit. The story of events at the WTC now begins: "Suddenly," one of the officers says, "there was a massive explosion in South Tower [just as they were getting ready to go into Tower 1]. When the second plane hit, we knew what was happening at that point." Joe was one of those who was in Tower 1. The officers "were told to pull out, but he [Joe] stopped . . . there were hundreds of people coming down [that needed help]." We are told by another ESU officer, "I knew Joe'd stay in that building . . . till he could do everything he could possibly do." The scene of the WTC ends with a video of the fireman at the site pausing to carry out a flag-draped coffin. A police officer remarks, "Can't believe three thousand Americans in there . . . fourteen of my best friends [are] in there." The video ends with a speech by Mayor Giuliani: "Couldn't have better heroes than Joseph and his brother and his fellow members of Emergency Services. They are entitled to a special place in our history as true patriots." A rolling "In tribute" scroll of the officers killed on 9/11 ends the film.

Those who watched the terrorist attack on the WTC unfold on film have the sense that shortly after the second plane hit Tower 2 (North), the buildings collapsed. These films tend to reinforce that perspective, even though nearly an hour separated the events. The North Tower was hit at 8:46 and shortly thereafter, striking the other tower at nine times the speed it would have been flying during a typical accident, United Flight 175 hit the second tower at 9:02. It was the second hit tower, the North Tower, which fell first at 9:59; the South Tower stood for a full thirty minutes more. Watching the films, one has the sense that the two planes hit close in time to one another, which they did, but the sense is that almost immediately thereafter both towers collapsed simultaneously. This clouds the strengths of the two towers. One can understand the optimism of those who were interviewed in *World Trade Center: In Memoriam* concerning the tower's invulnerability. Indeed, William Langewiesche writes, "One of the many astonishments of that day is that the building was able to swallow a whole 767, and to slow it from 586 mph to a stop in merely 209 feet . . . if not exactly shrugging off the hit, the South Tower had absorbed it well."[33] Recognizing the time lapse between the second plane hitting and the collapse of the first tower helps explain who so many emergency service workers were on the ground still trying to evaluate the two buildings and were caught by surprise when the North Tower disintegrated.

The majority of films detailing events of 9/11 revolve around the destruction of the WTC and the heroic efforts of those who lost their lives or who sacrificed to help others caught in the buildings. Susan Faludi in her book, *The Terror Dream*, points out something provocative about these images that only becomes apparent when viewed as a whole and not in isolation from one another: the male hero has been reborn, the female relegated to her traditional subordinate place.[34]

> On the fifth anniversary of the attacks, Bush again offered a lone antidote to exemplify post-9/11 virtue: the story of Rose Ellen Dowdell, who lost her husband, a New York firefighter, but was a "proud mom" because her two sons, recent graduates of the New York Fire Academy and West Point, had stepped into the protective gap. When Bush ran for reelection in 2004, the most ubiquitous photo op featured the president wrapping his arms around a girl whose mother had died in the twin towers. The new designation of roles was nicely spelled out in the first two scenes of a Daryl Cagle cartoon that ran in *Slate* called "How We Remember September 11th": in the first frame, titled, "The Heroes," a square-jawed fireman in a helmet clutches an ax; in the second, titled "Silent Victims," a little girl in pigtails weeps.[35]

Faludi's book is about the disappearance of women as proactive portraits in post–9/11 United Sates. There is some justification for this. Police and firefighters are disproportionately male enclaves. And those that were on the scene of the WTC did indeed act heroically. But this glosses over the everyday members of the various emergency service units that worked tirelessly to do what they could to help: men *and* women. Or, more accurately, if it does not "gloss over" them, it enshrouds them in a heroic halo by default. But by focusing exclusively on the men on the ground—policemen and firefighters, in particular—it ignores the role of women as active social agents and pushes them into the background where they are passively relegated to remembering their men.[36] This, as will be shown later in this section, is the only time women move to the foreground in these films (see *On Native Soil*; *9/11: Press for Truth*).

Further mythologizing the heroic ideal in these films is the silence—the idealized image of those on the ground is never assailed. This is understandable in the aftermath of the terrorist attack. The early movies glorified the "heroes versus villains" mind-set typical of early conflict situations, and rightfully so given the patriotic fervor that swept the United States at the time. However, the passing of time often gives rise to a more critical (re)appraisal.[37] This did happen in 2005 and 2006 with those WTC-related films that questioned the government's failure to foresee the disaster. But no films question the behavior of those on the ground, though some of the behavior was less than heroic.

One of the few articles to cast a shadow on the behavior of those on the ground was a three-part feature story by William Langewiesche in the *Atlantic Monthly* entitled, "American Ground: Unbuilding the World Trade Center."[38] Part I and II are generally positive, with a few brief critical asides, but part III goes into some detail about the dubious behavior by some on the ground. One of the more problematic, especially given the otherwise dominate heroic portrait of police and firefighters in the popular press and in film, was how some in these groups actually impeded progress. The longstanding police-fireman rivalry commenced almost from the start but turned overtly hostile on November 2, 2001, in what has been called "the fireman's riot," alternately, "the battle of the badges," that resulted in five policemen injured and the arrest of twelve bystanders, most of whom were firemen. At the root of the riot was Mayor Giuliani's order that the fireman, who would often stop the clearing of the construction site to honor *their* dead comrades, were hindering the cleanup efforts. The firemen certainly had a vested interest in honoring their dead, but the animosity was with the police who felt their own were being slighted with a "tag-them-and-bag-them" mentality. Mayor Giuliani's order that cleanup efforts be coordinated among the vested interest group was an attempt to move forward and stop the tribalism that was occurring on-site. In the end, the greatest loss of life was civilian and the firemen's obstinacy in promoting their own often hindered the cleanup effort and at times actually risked lives.[39] The press touched on these events at the time but has largely ignored them since, and film has totally glossed over the tainted behavior of some emergency services workers at Ground Zero, including some of the flagrant looting by firefighters, police, and construction crews that followed the collapse of the twin towers.[40] The silence toward these less-than-heroic actions is shrill.

In a similar vein, the silence percolates to a barely audible murmur in those films that attempt to explain the root cause of 9/11. The films about Saddam Hussein and Osama bin Laden skirt this issue; they simply suggest these are crazed, nefarious men. But that does not explain the animosity toward the United States that is raised in *Where in the World Is Osama bin Laden?* It is important to realize why the United States is considered by many in the Middle East to be the Great Satan. A historical appreciation of the longstanding, strongly fundamentalist stance of many Middle Eastern Muslims suggests a ready solution— finding bin Laden, executing Saddam Hussein—is not going to resolve the tension between Middle Eastern Muslims and the Christian West. The appraisal of the historical factors that shapes Middle Eastern attitudes is only halfheartedly attempted in those documentaries that delve into the roots that lead to 9/11.

Thomas L. Friedman Reporting: Searching for the Roots of 9/11 (2004) and *The Road to 9/11* (2006) are two documentaries that attempt to appraise the root causes that give rise to the Middle East's hostility toward the United States. Both purport to answer the question, "What motivates Muslim men to kill?" They are only marginally successful. Their failure is twofold. First, they only briefly sketch the historical aspects that shape existing attitudes so the depths of these entrenched views are not fully appreciated. The first part of *Road to 9/11* discusses how the Middle East was shaped by colonial powers after World War I, but spends most of its time focusing on Turkey's success in adapting Western ways, rather than how colonialism shaped Arabic anger toward the West. An hour on this would be very unsettling to most viewers, who tend to hold a rather naïve attitude toward Western participation in other countries' affairs. Likewise, we learn most Middle Eastern countries gained their freedom from colonial tyranny after World War II, that the Arabic League rejected the United Nations' creation of the state of Israel, embarrassingly lost the Six Day War to Israel, and that soon thereafter they fell under the orbit of the Soviet Union, which is why so many countries, like Iraq and Iran, have deteriorated into tyranny. This is a quick summary of the program, *Road to 9/11*, which does as much justice to it as it did to the emergence of anti-Western attitudes among many in the Middle East.

These shows failed for another, more problematic reason: They fail to engage the viewer. In *Road to 9/11* file documentary still photos wash over the viewer with little time to pause and consider what was just flashed on the screen. Thomas Friedman is even more problematic. The show revolves more around him than the Middle East—he is watched talking for almost an hour (see *South of the Border*, 2009).[41] This film might make a good audiobook, but film, by its very nature, requires visuals to hold the viewer.[42] His visuals are largely, like Spurlock's film, of him interviewing Middle Easterners, who often tell him of their animosity toward the United States, but he fails to follow through with an appreciation of the rationale for this anger. For example, one young female student in Qatar tells him that though she personally disapproves of violence, sometimes it is the "last way [for some] to get their point across." Friedman asks, "Which is?" And she responds, "That Americans should not try to boss around the whole world." Shortly thereafter another student says, "We know people [in the United States] are good . . . but it's the foreign policy, the double, hypocritical standard." Friedman does not follow up on either of these critical points: how, exactly, does the United States boss people around? What is the hypocritical standard the United States employs? Later, when he learns that a young Egyptian believes that the WTC was a Jewish conspiracy—there was a story circulated shortly after 9/11 that four thousand Jews who worked at the WTC were told of the attack so they would not perish in it—he mocks the fact that she gained this (mis)information from the Internet and Arabic magazines: "Obviously," he says, "[she] had misinformation about what is going on in the United States." He fails to mention that the Internet and other press sources often foster unreliable information for many (young) Americans regarding Arab culture and beliefs, as well.

In the end, Friedman is a columnist, not a journalist; he is playing to his audience more than informing them. He goes to Belgium to investigate Western attitudes toward the Middle East, and thus deflects the issue away from the United States—it happens over there, not in the United States. He also repetitively uses the keyword, "democracy": The viewer sees a picture of the Arab League and is told ominously that "almost none of [them] were democratically elected." Toward the end of the program, we learn things are changing for the better as the democratic system of government begins to be embraced. The viewer sees burka-clad women in Bahrain are "finding their ways to the polling booths," Friedman quips, "even when [she] can barely see through the slits [in her burka]."

In the case of these explanatory documentaries, a little knowledge may not be harmful, but neither is it particularly helpful. Two separate student focus groups were assembled to ascertain what they learned about Arabic culture. One group watched *Road to 9/11*, the other *Thomas L. Friedman Reporting*. Before watching the films, we spent a half hour discussing their knowledge of Arabic culture. There was no discernable deeper appreciation of Arabic culture after the programs were viewed. If anything, the students, gained no substantive knowledge from *Road*, but felt the Arabs to be more "backward" after viewing *Thomas L. Friedman*, largely owing to their "lack of knowledge about the United States" and their failure to embrace the democratic way of life.

The historical issue is more often socially and cinematically addressed by the question, "What went wrong?" than "What motivates terrorists?" More precisely, the question raised might be, "Why didn't the government prevent the disaster?" Two fictional films of exceptionally poor quality focus on this problem: *Homeland Security* (2004) and *The 9/11 Commission Report* (2006).[43] The five-hour docudrama, *The Path to 9/11* (2006), which aired on ABC over two consecutive nights (Sunday–Monday) without commercial interruptions likewise appraises this issue, turning the 9/11 Commission Report, Executive Producer Mark Platt tell us, into something that is "accessible" to most people.[44] One of the story's heroes, John O'Neill (Harvey Keitel), was the FBI agent who repeatedly warned of the al-Qaeda threat, succulently summarizing the thrust of the film when he says, "Despite all the red flags, no one's taking terrorism seriously."[45] The other two films that address this issue are more germane to this section on documentaries: *On Native Soil* (2005) and *9/11: Press for Truth* (2006).

On Native Soil mimics the fictional treatments by focusing on the 9/11 Commission and its investigation into the cause of 9/11. Testimony is heard from a variety of witnesses, the first being one of New York City's most decorated firefighters, who speaks before the commission as an "Ambassador of the dead." While the lack of airport security is raised and the breakdown of communications to alert fighter pilots of the hijackings is assessed, the thrust of this film revolves around the testimony of those women who lost loved ones and who are pressing for answers.[46] These women, who came to be known as the Jersey Girls, and their search for the truth is at the heart of the other documentary, *9/11: Press for Truth*. They want to know why the president just sat there in the school he was visiting for seven minutes after Tower 2 was hit and did nothing. The government had forewarnings: "The country was at risk from terrorists—and incompetence." It was as a direct result of their efforts that the 9/11 Commission was formed. Thomas Kean was appointed to head the commission after the women marshaled a successful effort to prevent Henry Kissinger from being appointed; quips Kean, "I wouldn't want to be in the way of some of these [women]." The final report, however, the narrator tells us, "failed to meet many of the families' expectations." These women wanted someone to be held accountable, but the film ends with the failure of anyone to take accountability. The film suggests they just wanted some in the government to acknowledge they might have done a better job and that this never happened. In actuality, blame was accepted in the conclusion of *On Native Soil*, which had been made the previous year, when Richard Clark, former National Security Council Counterterrorism Coordinator testified and said, "Government failed you; we failed you," and asked for understanding and forgiveness. Clark's apology was well received by the families: "finally someone just admitted they made a mistake and said sorry." This ending was expunged from the Jersey Girl's story in *Press for Truth*. Their defiance was applauded—they stood up to the government and continued to press for answers. The 2006 film ends with a chastisement of the fourth estate, the press, for failing to adequately uncover the truth,[47] and with a tribute to the fifth estate[48]—watchdog groups such as the Jersey Girls, whose right to dissent, we are told in the conclusion, is integral to democracy. This latter, stand-tall-against-the-government ending is more in keeping with the groundswell of dissent that was beginning to take place circa 2006 among the American public, which was starting to acknowledge that the Bush administration might have distorted the WMD issue leading to the quagmire in Iraq, and fictional films were increasingly raising (see also *9/11: The Myth and the Reality*, 2007).

Both these documentaries, and fictional treatment of the 9/11 Commission Report, have perfect 20/20 hindsight. It is always easy to blame

Looking for survivors in 9/11: *Press for Truth.*

the government, and these films cater to the building distrust of the Bush administration (see also *911: In Plane Site*, 2003; *9/11: The Myths and the Reality*, 2007; *Blocking the Path to 9/11: The Anatomy of Smear*, 2008). Indeed, the films are constructed in a very Procrustean manner to reflect and, in turn, shape the public's cynicism of big government. The Jersey Girls mock President Bush for just "sitting there" after the attack on the second tower for seven minutes and doing nothing. They

Testifying in 9/11: *Press for Truth.*

do not address the question: "Just what was the president to do in those precious seven minutes that would have changed events?" Indeed, since he was being covered by the press in the classroom with the elementary school children, a preemptive action on his part might have been misconstrued and broadcast to the public, causing more panic. The president himself is acknowledged to have said in *On Native Soil* (see also *DC 9/11: Time of Crisis*[49]) that the reason he didn't want to react too precipitously was so that he wouldn't cause panic.

The chain of causation is also much too clear in these films. Conflicting data is expunged. The viewer only hears from those who have connected the bin Laden dots to the WTC, so viewers end up shaking their heads in disbelief because the evidence is so clear. The viewer is told, in *On Native Soil*, that Secretary of State Condoleezza Rice is "either lying [to the families] or didn't know [about the attack], which is just as scary." There is no middle ground of uncertainty at the mass of information that the various agencies had gathered. The complexities of the secretary of state's job in sifting through the mountain of contradictory data are also glossed over. Similarly, the problems of communication that are intrinsic to complex organizations is glossed over: "Tape after tape," the commission learns from one witness, "showed communication between FAA, its air traffic control center, and the military—was a mess." The fact that all this was going on within a frantic and very narrow time frame, and that air traffic on any given day is fraught with errors and problems of tracking, tends to be forgotten as the list of the failures to prevent the attack are detailed.[50] In fact, in *In Memoriam: New York City*, we learn at Mayor Giuliani's press conference that "all we know [at the moment] is that two planes have hit the World Trade Center" and that within this hour, the Mayor has been on the phone with the White House [and apparently the Pentagon], and "We ask air space around New York be sealed"—and it was.[51] As anyone who has worked in even a modestly sized organization knows, information does not pass quickly and reliably through the system. The following figure is a revision to a Simple City Health Network, outlined by organizational theorist Charles Perrow[52]; it is here used to designate those organizations along the eastern seaboard that were involved in passing communication between them on the morning of 9/11. It should also be remembered that the WTC withstood an earlier terrorist attack and that few saw the tow-

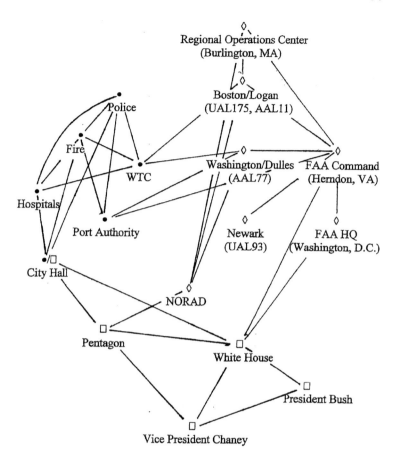

• NYC agencies
◊ Air traffic control
□ Political agencies

Critical Agency Network: Morning of September 11, 2001.

ers collapsing as something that would even remotely occur—it was felt that the buildings would be able to withstand one commercial airliner hitting it, not two planes simultaneously hitting both towers shortly after takeoff with a full load of jet fuel. The optimism of those who worked in the WTC in the A&E show, *World Trade Center: In Memoriam*, is a reminder that the skepticism that followed the event did not precede it.

Fiction

Fictional films in 2004 and 2005 were beginning to challenge the monolithic mind-set that followed in the wake of the terrorist attack, but not fictional films that dealt directly with the terrorist attack. One set of two films continues to eulogize the heroic spirit of those who died on 9/11: *Flight 93* and *United 93*. Another set of two films deals with the survivors: *WTC View* and *Reign Over Me*.

Flight 93 is an A&E made-for-television movie. The opening shows United Airline pilots going off to work in the early morning of 9/11, one kissing his sleeping wife and baby good-bye. The next ten minutes is filled with buildup: passengers, including the hijackers, going through airport security; people boarding their flights; airplanes in queue for takeoff. The next twenty minutes is spent at the American, United, and FAA Command Centers as air traffic controllers frantically track the flights, then the visual of three of the four missing planes hitting their designated targets. The viewer then joins the passengers and crew aboard the missing airline. The rest of the film shows the passengers aboard United 93 talking on cell phones to their loved ones, the hijackers taking control of the plane, the passengers being huddled to the rear of the plane, and, finally, after they learn that the WTC and Pentagon had been attacked, stoically charging the cockpit and spoiling the hijackers' goal of hitting yet another target, most likely, the viewer is explicitly told in the concluding crawl, the White House. The film ends with sirens wailing toward the wreckage. The viewing audience knows there were no survivors.

Flight 93 comes in as a poor second cousin to the "big budget" feature, *United 93*, which is sharper in tone and more tightly woven. This is partly because the versatile director, Paul Greengrass (*Bloody Sunday*, 2002; *The Bourne Supremacy*, 2004) was at the helm.[53] *United 93* also received a substantial amount of prepublicity attention, largely over whether it was too soon or appropriate to graphically depict what happened on this flight, a concern that preceded Stone's *World Trade Center* as well. *Flight 93*, which appeared a year earlier on television, did not provoke the same attention.[54] This appears to be largely owing to some astute marketing. When the trailers ran in Manhattan prior to the opening of the movie, the audience responded with cries of "Too soon!"[55]

This was capitalized on by Greengrass in a flurry of interviews shortly before the file was released, giving the film a lot of free prerelease publicity. In one interview, Greengrass says, "Why are people saying it's too soon? Like the people on that flight, we need to agree about what to do about terrorism. And I think we need to have that conversation now." In another interview, he says, "I've tried so hard to stick to my principles and guidelines—that you honor and dignify the memories of innocent people who are the victims to political violence. You do it because it's the right thing to do."

Both films depicted the same event in pretty much the same manner. The financial constraints of made-for-television movies that often result in low-budget films, such as *Flight 93*, may have deflected some of the attention. And there is little doubt that *United 93* is a better film cinematically, even though both movies were generally well received.[56]

Both movies spent considerable time, first with the setup—following the terrorists through airport security, airplanes taxiing down runways, passengers waiting for their flight to be called—and then in the various flight control centers as air traffic controllers were frantically sorting out what was going on before ultimately focusing in on the passengers aboard Flight 93. The movies are, therefore, thematically similar, but there are two major differences in the treatment of events.

Until *United 93*, it was typical to scapegoat those in the various flight control centers for their ineptitude at failing to know (and therefore to minimize if not prevent) what was occurring in the air (*9/11: Press for Truth*; *On Native Soil*; see also *Portrait of Courage: The Untold Story of Flight 93*). This does not occur in *United 93*. Air traffic controllers are feverously working to ascertain what is taking place and attempting to forestall further problems. In one scene the flight control supervisor screams, "Get Langley on the phone. We need [interceptor] planes in the air, NOW!" In another scene, the supervisor is trying to figure out from the National Security Council what the rules of engagement are: "We have no shoot-down order at this time," he tells those in flight control. "[It] has to come from the president, and only the president," and later, "Get the Pentagon on the phone, I need action!" The confusion was undoubtedly widespread in the various control towers because so many things were going wrong in the air at the same time—a point made explicit in one of the tower control scenes—but the viewer gets a more realistic picture of the problem facing those who were attempting to do their job (see figure on page 39). Cinematically, the time devoted to this aspect of the movie, a good thirty minutes, was successful because the frantic information that was coming into the towers is tightly juxtaposed with a series of placid scenes taking place aboard United 93: copilot chitchat, bored passengers, food being served, and other mundane activity.

The other major contextual difference is that those on the plane are acting more realistically. In *Flight 93*, the hijackers take over, kill the pilots and one of the flight attendants (off-screen), and force the passengers to the back of the plane. The passengers appear dazed and confused over what is taking place, make some calls to loved ones on the ground to say good-bye, and then decide to take action and stop the hijackers. This also occurs in *United 93*, albeit more graphically—the stewardess is shown having her throat cut by a hijacker with box cutters—but the viewers see not just confusion among the passengers, but fear! The passengers are scared! They are terrified! And they initially decide to attempt to stop the hijackers, not in some altruistic effort to save the world, but to save themselves, even if they might in the end feel, after learning of the other terrorist attacks, that they have to attempt to take the cockpit, despite that it could well mean their own deaths.

United 93 is a much more realistic portrait of how people react to a life-threatening situation, and Greengrass, who had previously successfully portrayed Irish terrorism in *Bloody Sunday*, was familiar with human reaction to terrorism. Others had shied away from this, not wishing to tarnish the heroic image of the passengers on Flight 93. This is most likely due to the well-entrenched heroic tradition that was firmly established in the press and among other WTC-related movies.[57] Greengrass was concerned about this too. He says that he remembers "sitting down with one of the widows and saying, 'I'm going to have to be pretty explicit about the violence and not sanitize it,'" and was told, "She said, 'You don't have to worry . . . I know what happened, and there isn't a night that I don't think about it. You need to show it in every detail.' This was [a] pretty common sentiment in the families."[58]

The subtle changes in the treatment of some aspects of 9/11 that takes place in *United 93* is also seen in two other films that begin to focus on a dimension of the disaster often overlooked, and cinematically neglected:

the effect of the WTC collapse on the survivors. These are the unsung heroes of 9/11.

WTC View was written by Brian Sloan, based on his own post-9/11 experiences attempting to sublet an apartment that the day before, when he placed the ad, had a view of the WTC. It opened as an off-Broadway play in 2003 and debuted as a feature film in 2005. It was directed by the author and the lead characters in the play performed in the feature: Michael Urie played the role of Eric, and Elizabeth Kapllow appeared as Josie.[59]

Eric places an ad in the Village Voice for a roommate to share the expense of his modest walkup in lower Manhattan, twelve blocks from the WTC. The plot revolves around the interviews as a series of potential roommates visit the apartment and share their views on the tragedy. The view, Eric's window, is the focal point that leads to the topic: "Nice view. Could you see them from here?" Another inquires, looking out the window, "Been down there yet?" One doesn't vocalize, but his actions speak the same thought as he peers through the window and his eyes slowly roll up to where the towers once stood. Eric mentions to his sister, Josie, how difficult it has become to rent in New York where he could once find a roommate in a day or two. The potential roommates all call and leave messages on his machine, giving halfhearted explanations on their change of mind and their decision to leave New York. In the end, Eric too leaves the apartment with all its memories, but not New York. The film manages to capture the author's intention:

> The phrase "I love New York" is not just a slogan for people who live here. . . . It's been a struggle to live here ever since but it has made the last few years the richest and most challenging years of my life in New York. I still love the city but it's now a different love, tempered by age and sorrow and events beyond anyone's control. Not unlike a real relationship.

The film received modest critical attention but lay reviewers rate it well: it often garners four stars, and quite often five.[60] The film does capture the struggle of those who lived there to deal with the aftermath of the tragedy. It deals with somber events without wallowing in self-pity. One of the more trenchant aspects of the film that is hard to get across in a visual medium is the olfactory dimension. Images of rubble always arise when the WTC is shown or thought about, but View figuratively introduces the smell of carnage. Eric sometimes opens the windows, coughs, and slams it shut; he is often wandering around the apartment with an aerosol air freshener. On one visit by Josie, Eric lights a cigarette and, offended by the smell, she asks him to open the window, which he reluctantly does—they both choke on the stench and ram the window closed. On another visit, Josie says upon entering the apartment, "I cannot believe it's still smoking," and later, in yet another entrance scene, she practically screams, "It's *still* smoking! Can't they stop it?"

View manages also to convey the psychological impact of the disaster on those that live there. In a near concluding scene while Eric is interviewing a prospective roommate, a siren is heard wailing from the street below. Eric panics, "Oh, my God. . . . Something is going on. . . . We're under attack." The prospective roommate dismisses the event, "It's just a siren." The psychological damage to those who lost someone on 9/11 is better captured by the survivor feature film, *Reign Over Me.*

Reign Over Me was released by Columbia Pictures in 2007. It was directed by Mike Binder (*Indian Summer*, 1993; *The Contender*, 2000) with a strong cast that included, Adam Sandler, Don Cheadle, Liv Tyler, Robert Klein, Melina Dillon, and Donald Sutherland. The studio and cast ensured that it would get broader distribution and critical attention than the small-budget production, *WTC View*. It did not fare well critically (less than three stars), owing largely to meandering subplots, but it was, again, well received by the Netflix viewers, who rated it four to five stars.

The movie focuses on Charlie (Adam Sandler) who seems lost in a daze, the result, we learn as the movie progresses, of post-traumatic stress: Charlie hasn't been the same since losing his wife and three daughters in the WTC disaster. The former dentist, looking like a youthful, bedraggled Bob Dylan, is now puttering aimlessly around the city on a motorized scooter. An old school chum, Alan Johnson (Don Cheadle) recognizes him, and attempts to rekindle their old dental school friendship. The plot revolves around Alan's attempts to "restore" the old Charlie and with the help of his friend, a therapist—who too coincidentally is also the therapist for the sexually obsessed young woman who is stalking happily married Dr. Johnson—some progress begins to be made toward the film's end. The story is at its best when it attempts to explore the sense of loss Charlie cannot bring himself to face all these years later, and his friends attempt to understand and help him. The movie puts a face to the deep sense of loss survivors like the Jersey Girls struggle to express.

The main problem the critics had with the movie was the multiple subplots, which unnecessarily pulled the film from its focus. The main subplot revolved around a sexually obsessive female with Charlie's friend, the successful dentist, Alan, which vengefully led to sexual harassment charges when the overtures were repulsed. The director probably thought this subplot was necessary to give the film momentum and suspense because it broke up the drudgery of Charlie's aimless wandering. Unfortunately, the subplots undercut the mood that is needed to convey the depth of Charlie's grief. There are also the Dickensonian coincidences that come together too neatly: Alan's friend, who is the therapist and eventually helps Charlie, just happens to be the therapist of the sexually obsessed female stalking Alan. But if the movie is directed at the everyday movie viewer, these same flaws may keep the pace of the movie moving forward. Lay viewers certainly seem to connect with the central plot in their comments about the movie and don't get sidetracked by the subplots. Indeed, many who critiqued the film on film sites find the subplots tie back into and reinforce the movie, such as Alan's general disaffection with his pretty-good life, as well as the overly didactic closing by the judge (Donald Sutherland) who is hearing the case that weighs whether Charlie should be committed. Many are quick to pick up on the music, too, including Charlie singing to himself The Who song, "Reign Over Me," at the beginning of the movie, and the use of '80s rock [Charlie collects vinyl records] to push the main character into an earlier, more quiescent time in his life . . . before 9/11.

CONCLUSION

It might be wistful to imagine life in a world untouched by the effects of 9/11, but the reality is that this is no longer possible. The terrorist attack of 9/11 made the United States, and her citizens, vulnerable like never before. A decade later, people are still going about their business under the shadow of 9/11. Still, the malaise that swept the country in the immediate aftermath of 9/11 is less intense today. In part, this is due to the passing of time. In part, it is because the media has helped people explore and understand what happened.

Woody Allen asserts that film, including tragedy, should be "calming and reassuring."[61] Not everyone would agree that this is the purpose of film. Indeed, many of the films that will be examined in subsequent chapters that specifically address the conflict in Iraq are very disquieting and are meant to disturb the viewer. Nevertheless, those films that address 9/11 events are specifically made to calm and reassure people. This is often stated in interviews with many of those involved with making these films, and it is clear in their intent—the film's content.

Saddam Hussein and Osama bin Laden are clearly villains, and the world is a much better place without them. Iran, if not a perfect world without Saddam, is moving in the right direction now that he has been deposed, discovered, justly tried, found guilty, and executed for his crimes. Osama bin Laden would not be located until mid-2011, but films during this period (2002–2008) indicated that his capture was imminent, and though he had not been located to this point, films reported that other members of the al-Qaeda terrorist network had been tracked down and the Taliban presence in Afghanistan had been dramatically curtailed, thanks largely to the intervention of the United States. It is calming and reassuring to know the world is a better place now that these dictators no longer wield power (Saddam Hussein) or, at least, not the power they were once able to muster (Osama bin Laden). It is also calming and reassuring to know that though a great tragedy has occurred with the destruction of the WTC, not only have those responsible paid, but it brought out the best in the behavior of those confronting the tragedy, and that they died honorably and in self-sacrifice, and will always, to quote Mayor Giuliani, "have a place in America's heart."

The heroic actions of some that occurred when the WTC collapsed needs to be remembered, and that is why the silences that might taint these memories are so pronounced. It is calming and reassuring to know that tragedy brings out the best in people. That this does not occur among all those involved is a point that can be left to rest. It may be, like the concern about the timing of some of the other movies, such as *World Trade Center* and *United 93*, too soon to bring up the miscreant behavior of some because it could tarnish the images of those who did act bravely and sacrificed their lives trying to help others, like Tony Benetatos (*9/11*) and Joe Veigiano (*Twin Towers*). The pain is also too recent and deep for those who lost love ones in the wake of 9/11 (see *9/11: Press for Truth*; *Reign Over Me*).[62]

The memory of those who lost their lives on 9/11 is not likely to change in the foreseeable future: it is reassuring to know that those responsible have paid,[63] or that those who died lost their lives for a reason, altruistically sacrificing their lives to help others. Nor are films likely to take a closer look at the reasons behind 9/11. Those films that do (*Where in the World Is Osama bin Laden?*; *Thomas L. Friedman Reporting*) are a bit simplistic. Rather than root out the real cause of Arabic anger, their premise is really that all Muslims do not hate the United States, just some of the more extremist, radical ones, like bin Laden and those involved with al-Qaeda. Ultimately, taking the other's perspective and trying to understand why they consider the United States to be the Great Satan, might suggest "they" are right and "we" are wrong, and that is not a human characteristic. It may even be unhealthy at the nationalist level to seriously entertain such a potentially destabilizing idea. It certainly is neither calming nor reassuring. The problem, however, is very complicated, perhaps too complicated for films to grapple with given the time constraint of movies, or even television documentaries that can be stretched over a few days. It is much easier to "satisfice": search a limited number of straightforward alternatives along familiar and well-worn paths, selecting the first satisfactory solution that comes along.[64]

The approach toward Saddam Hussein and Osama bin Laden has not really changed. To some degree, this is because an understanding of Middle Eastern ideology and actions is extraordinarily complicated. But it is also because it is a fait accompli: the deed is done and cannot be undone. In other words, people want to think it was a correct course to invade Afghanistan and Iraq to depose Saddam Hussein and Osama bin Laden. The fait accompli notion also holds for those who lost loved ones in the WTC collapse: They cannot be brought back and it is common for survivors to sanctify the memory of those who have died.

Though it is unlikely that Americans will see (or want to see) films that taint the memory of those who died on 9/11, or suggest Saddam Hussein or bin Laden were less than evil despots, films about WTC-related events are beginning to change. To some degree, this reflects a growing skepticism toward the Bush administration that followed his reelection in 2004 and what those in the administration might have known. The changing social attitude is reflected in those films that attack the Bush administration for failing to protect Americans from the attack.

Films are also beginning to move beyond the day of the attack. The face of the pain experienced by survivors, such the Jersey Girls in *9/11: Search for Truth*, is pungently depicted years later in *Reign Over Me*. This movie is important not only because it bespeaks of the suffering of those who lost love ones on that tragic day, but it also shows the long-term effects of such a loss, and the need for survivors to grapple with that loss and move, however tenuously, on with their lives. *WTC View* addresses another aspect of the WTC "day of infamy"; it shows how even those who did not lose someone in the attack were affected by it, and also, how they too need to grapple with the loss of a comfortable, familiar world and move on with their lives. This adumbrates a potential new direction in WTC-related cinema: Films may begin to explore other nuances of the multifaceted tragedy on those who were further removed from the disaster but no less affected by it.[65] These films, however, are shuffled to the rear of the cinema queue at the moment as the wars in Iraq and Afghanistan, and America's involvement in them, clamors for attention. The cinematic debate about the two-front war begins in 2004, and soon rises to a clamor.

NOTES

1. *Marooned in Iraq* was released in 2002 and made by the Kurdish director, Bahman Ghodadi (see also *A Time for Drunken Horses*, 2000). It is the only foreign fictive feature film made in this group. Saddam's atrocities are recognized in the film but its main purpose, apparent in the cinematography but made explicit by the director in an interview, is to acquaint the viewer with the beauty of northern Iraq (see also *Himalaya*, 1999). "The story," Ghodadi tells us, "is just an excuse to take the audience around and show them the different corners of Kurdistan." The film is not critiqued in any detail because the body of the film is more of a travelogue than a critique of Saddam's treatment of the Kurds, even though this is raised quite explicitly near the end of the film.

2. Anthony Arnove, "Cautionary Tales: Documentaries on the UN Sanctions and War with Iraq," *Cineaste* 28, no. 2 (2003): 22.

3. Ted Loos, "An Avuncular Uncle He Is Definitely Not," *New York Times*, 24 November 2002: 36(2).

4. Genevieve S. Roth, "A New Documentary Reveals the Tyrant at His Most Bizarre," *Esquire* 138, no. 6 (December 2002): 152

5. Refus Jones, "Iraq's Crazy Uncle," *The Weekly Standard*, 18 November 2002, www.weeklystandard.com (accessed 15 September 2009).

6. The *New York Times* interview indicates Soler "knew little about the Arab world until he started traveling in Dubai and other Middle Eastern cities when he was in his twenties" and only recently took up studying Arabic. Traveling the Middle East in one's twenties might add insight into Arabic culture, but later in the interview Mr. Thompson, who worked with Soler on the film, is quoted as saying that "Joel was very young and more cavalier when he started [the project]." Loos, "An Avuncular Uncle He Is Definitely Not," 36(2).

7. Roth, "A New Documentary Reveals the Tyrant at His Most Bizarre," 152.

8. The initial launch of the film did not include the filmmaker's native country. "I got so much backlash for this film in France," Mr. Soler said. "I got one letter from a network saying that they didn't want to buy an American propaganda movie." Loos, "An Avuncular Uncle He Is Definitely Not."

9. There were numerous grainy, black-and-white home video clips inserted into the film that were likely taken by family members or social intimates and may be interpreted by the viewer to have been filmed by Soler, since the source of the video is not identified and no disclaimer as to its origin is made by the filmmaker.

10. Arnove, "Cautionary Tales," 22.

11. Toward the end of the documentary there were a few obvious television clips of an event related to the story—such as a picture of a helicopter when one of Saddam's "turned" family members died in a "mysterious [helicopter] accident." At the bottom right of this clip was the traditional television disclaimer: "Not actual footage."

12. World War I is often referred to by historians as the chemist's war because of the production and deployment of war gasses such as chorine, phosgene, and mustard that endangered not only those on the battlefield, but proximate civilians, as well as chemical workers on the home front who were involved in the large-scale manufacturing process. See Paul Fussell, *The Great War and Modern Memory* (London: Oxford University Press, 1975); G. J. Fitzgerald, "Chemical Warfare and Medical Response during World War I," *American Journal of Public Health* 98, no. 4 (2008): 611–24.

13. Debora L. Acomb, "Foreign Affairs," *National Journal* 35, no. 222 (2003): 1801–6; Alexis Simendinger, "In Credible Standing," *National Journal* 35, no. 23 (2003): 1782.

14. In *We Got Him* (2004), the capture of Saddam Hussein was to end this violence by Iraqis. Four years later, this will supposedly happen with his just punishment.

15. The opening of Graham Nash's song "Chicago" mentions Hoffman's behavior: "So your brother's bound and gagged, and they've chained him to a chair." On November 21, 1972, all of the convictions were reversed by the U.S. Court of Appeals for the Seventh District on the basis that the judge was biased.

16. This is seen in the movie when, after the attempt on his life, Saddam dismisses his half-brother, Banzan Ibrahim, as his bodyguard and replaces him with a member of the family that shares direct blood ties; Saddam explains, "Son in [the] future will be responsible for [my] personal safety. I trust him . . . [he's] my blood." To Western eyes, the dismissal appears unjustified because Ibrahim is loyal to Saddam; however, from the Arabic familial perspective it is more unusual that such a distant (nonblood) relative would have been given such a sensitive, insider post in the first place.

17. Raphael Patai, *The Arab Mind, Revised edition* (New York: Hatherleigh Press, 2002).

18. Thomas Sutcliffe, "Last Night's TV: *House of Saddam*, BBC2," *The Independent*, 31 July 2008, www.independent.co.uk/arts-entertainment/tv/reviews/last-nights-tv-house-of-saddam-bbc2 (accessed 20 September 2009).

19. Jen Phillips, "Film Review: *House of Saddam*," *Mother Jones*, 5 Dec. 2008, www.motherjones.com/media/2008/12/film-review-house-of-saddam (accessed 20 September 2009).

20. Part IV was necessary, however, to conclude the story of *The House of Saddam*. As soon as he was pulled from the hole and uttered his now famous statement that he is "ready to negotiate" the film ends with him being led out of the courtroom, with the voice-over that he has been found "guilty of five separate crimes against humanity" and the crawl that he was executed on December 30, 2006.

21. The two brief scenes leading up to the invasion of Kuwait that are developed are those that are not popularly known: Saddam's meeting with the Kuwaiti emir in Switzerland *asking* him to stop the financial squeeze on Iraq by Kuwait undercutting oil prices, and his meeting with the American ambassador at the palace and her equivocal response that prompted his understanding that the United States had "no opinion" on what they considered an internal (Arab to Arab) issue.

22. *Daughters* is a Canadian documentary that uses interviews with Afghan women to depict their plight under the Taliban.

23. The reason why the burka is required in Muslim society is explained in an earlier scene. The mother is given a ride from the young man whose father she tended in the hospital because she is not supposed to be unaccompanied in public. She dons the burka and is sitting sidesaddle on the bicycle seat. The

camera lingers on the touch of flesh on her foot that protrudes. The Western viewer wouldn't think about any problem with this scene until the bicyclist is stopped by an unseen Taliban male, whose husky voice admonishes her for her tasteless behavior: "men will be aroused." Her hand hastily reaches down and the garment is pulled over the naked flesh.

24. A. O. Scott, "Looking for a Terrorist, but Not Too Hard," *New York Times*, 18 April 2008, 16(E).

25. Dictator is spelled out on the sash over Trujillo's chest, but only the first few letters of his name are discernable. The viewer would have to know who he was from those few letters and what country he was from to have any appreciation of the consequences of his rule to those in the Dominican Republic.

26. Most of the documentaries critiqued to this point are rated by only a handful of viewers: mean equals 800. *Osama* is an exception, but *Osama* is a feature film and not a documentary; it was rated by just short of 100,000 people who accorded it 3.6 stars, on a rating par with Spurlock's film.

27. This is "Operation Anaconda." *Hunt* glosses over the failure to capture Osama as "coalition forces encircled the area" by mentioning that later that same month (March) they captured the third ranking member of al-Qaeda in Pakistan, "just one of many [arrests] to come in the months ahead."

28. Howard Schuman and Willard L. Rodgers, "Cohorts, Chronology, and Collective Memory," *Public Opinion Quarterly* 68, no. 2 (2004): 217–54.

29. Andrew Kohut, "Trends in Political Values and Core Attitudes: 1987–2007," *The Pew Research Center*, 22 March 2007, www.pewresearch.org/trends-in-political-values-and-core-attitudes-1987-2007 (accessed 13 March 2009). See also "Post September 11 Attitudes," 6 December 2001, www.people-press.org/report/144 (accessed 13 March 2009); "A Year after Iraq War," 16 March 2004, www.people-press.org/report/206 (accessed 3 March 2009); "Foreign Policy Attitudes Now Driven by 9/11 and Iraq," 18 August 2004, www.people-press.org/report222 (accessed 12 March 2009).

30. See Jody T. Allen, Nilanthi Samaranyske, and James Albrittain Jr., "Iraq and Vietnam: A Crucial Difference in Opinion," 22 March 2007, www.pewresearch.org/pubs/432 (accessed 13 March 2009); "Public Attitudes toward the War in Iraq: 2003–2008," 19 March 2008, www.pewresearch.org/pubs/770 (accessed 13 March 2009).

31. Kenneth Turan, "The Easy Way Out: Ghastly Events Forced into a Feel-Good Formula—It's Not the Memorial Sept. 11 Needs," *Los Angeles Times*, 9 August 2006, www.latimes.com/2006/august/09/entertainment/et-wtc9 (accessed 23 October 2009); Owen Gleiberman, "World Trade Center," *Entertainment Weekly*, 11 August 2006, www.ew.com/ew/article/0,,1222149,000 (accessed 23 October 2009).

32. The host appeared after every commercial break to "frame" the story in contemporary terms before returning to the taped interviews. On the video, the commercial interruptions are not there and the sudden appearance of the host appears more contrived than it would have on television.

33. William Langewiesche, "American Ground: Unbuilding the World Trade Center, Part I: The Inner World," *Atlantic Monthly*, July–August 2002, 73.

34. Susan Faludi, *The Terror Dream: Fear and Fantasy in Post 9/11 America* (New York: Metropolitan Books, 2007).

35. Faludi, *The Terror Dream*, 6.

36. *Heroes*, Faludi writes, "is a sixty-four page all-color poster book—featuring such images as a fireman carrying a limp woman away from the smoldering ruins. . . . . On the book's cover, [an ineffective Superman] stands gazing up at a sea of men in fire helmets, hard hats, and police caps (and two female medical workers, who stand, literally, at the margins) and says, 'Wow.'" Faludi, *The Terror Dream*.

37. This is admirably done in *From Here to Eternity*. The men at Pearl are all flawed. The two leading male characters are involved in questionable relationships: 1st Sergeant Milton Warden (Burt Lancaster) is having an affair with his Captain's wife (Deborah Kerr) while the self-righteous Private Robert E. Lee Prewitt (Montgomery Clift) is involved with a woman of ill repute (Donna Reed) and has gone AWOL. However, when Pearl is attacked they both put their personal desires aside and, despite pleas by their women to remain with them, heroically attempt to rejoin their unit and serve their country.

38. William Langewiesche, "American Ground: Unbuilding the World Trade Center, Part I: The Inner World"; William Langewiesche, "American Ground: Unbuilding the World Trade Center, Part II: The Rush to Recover," *Atlantic Monthly*, 2 September 2002, 47–79; William Langewiesche, "American Ground: Unbuilding the World Trade Center, Part III: The Dance of the Dinosaurs," *Atlantic Monthly*, 3 October 2002, 94–126.

39. Langewiesche, "American Ground: Unbuilding the World Trade Center, Part III," 103.

40. A fire truck was discovered under the rubble filled with dozens of new pairs of jeans from the Gap, a WTC store. It appears, writes Langewiesche, "that the looting had begun even before the first tower fell, and that while hundreds of doomed firemen had climbed through the wounded buildings, this particular crew had been engaged in something else entirely, without the slightest suspicion that the South Tower was about to hammer down." Langewiesche, "American Ground: Unbuilding the World Trade Center, Part III," 102.

41. Friedman is often wearing a black pullover, which causes his features to be the focal point of the interview. This is a classic Hollywood technique that many stars use when on the television talk show circuit to promote their film because it serves to frame the speaker's face, so the viewer remembers the person (and hence the film) being interviewed more than the substance of the interview.

42. *9/11: The Myth and the Reality* finds favor with a limited number of Netflix viewers (n=30) who appear to be predisposed to conspiracy theories. But even the individuals who find the information "cold, hard and INDISPUTABLE," or "eye opening," feel the production value of questionable merit and the method of delivery "boring." This is because the viewer simply watches the narrator at a podium talking for four hours, and when dissolves do occur, they tend be "very confusing and detract from the message. . . ."

43. *Homeland Security* was a two-hour pilot for a television series of sixty-seven-year-old Scott Glen chasing bad Muslims around the world. The fact that the series never materialized indicates the lack of interest in this show. *The 9/11 Commission Report* may have won the dubious distinction of the poorest-reviewed movie about 9/11 by Netflix reviewers, who are generally in agreement with the following composite review: "[T]his film played like a bad History Channel reenactment by a film school student. [It] was really bad! I mean awful acting . . . and the camerawork looked as if it were done by a freshmen year film major."

44. Gail Pennington, "ABC Turns 9/11 Commission's Report into 5-Hour Drama," *St. Louis Post-Dispatch*, 10 September 2006, 1(F).

45. O'Neill left the FBI and became head of security at the WTC. He died in the terrorist attack on 9/11.

46. This reinforces the depiction of gender that Faludi raises. Those that come before the commission (at least on film) who are women, are there because they lost a loved one (husband or child) in the WTC collapse. Men give testimony, but it is never for a loved one (wife or child) lost. Faludi, *The Terror Dream*.

47. One woman castigates the press, "Facts dribbled out over such a long period of time, the effects [were] lost on the American people," while another says bluntly, "The press should have been doing a better job." There is a brief rebuttal by the executive editor of the *Washington Post*, who defends the press by saying they did get "the stuff out," and that what the women wanted "is not the job of reporting . . . [but] the job of editorial pages."

48. The term fifth estate is used by me and is not used in the film. The film does suggest a fifth estate mentality for those watchdog groups that have to do the job the press (the fourth estate) once did.

49. *DC 9/11: Time of Crisis* is another poor quality, hastily produced made-for-television movie. But it does fit more snugly into the early view of WTC events. In this film, the president (and his cabinet) is presented as a strong, take-charge leader. Throughout the film his repetitive mantra is, "We're gonna kick the hell out of whoever did this. . . . We're gonna get the bastards."

50. There was considerable confusion over which flight had hit the tower and which was missing en route to Washington. This point was directly addressed at some length in the film. Ignored, however, was the fact that while there was some confusion over which plane was where, those at flight control center were following the flight that was making its way to Washington on radar and were attempting to make responsible individuals in D.C. aware of the imminent threat.

51. Jane Garvey, head of the FAA, according to *Time Magazine*, "almost certainly after getting an okay from the White House, initiate[ed] a national ground stop [at 9:26 a.m. on 9/11], which forbids takeoffs and requires planes in the air to get down as soon as is reasonable. The order, which has never been implemented since flying was invented in 1903, applied to virtually every single kind of machine that can take off—civilian, military, or law enforcement." Military and law enforcement flights were allowed to resume at 10:31 a.m. "U.S. Congress, House Committee on Transportation and Infrastructure, 9/21/2001," www.historycommons.org/context (accessed 15 April 2009).

52. Charles Perrow, *Complex Organizations: A Critical Essay*, 3rd ed. (New York: McGraw-Hill, 1986), 196.

53. Greengrass was nominated for an Academy Award for his direction of *United 93*. The film was certainly good, but I suspect the nomination was more a bow to the topic (that had not previously been touched by feature films) than any cinematic strengths of the film.

54. Mick LaSalle, "Agony, Heroism of 'United 93' Shown with Nearly Unbearable Realism," *San Francisco Chronicle*, 28 April 2006, 1(E).

55. Lou Lumenick, "He Rolls with the Punches—Too Soon for a 9/11 Movie? *United 93* Director Says No," *New York Post*, 20 April 2006, 50.

56. Netflix viewers gave *Flight 93* a mean rating of three stars; *United 93* received four-plus stars.

57. Faludi traces the sanctified image of those who lost their lives in 9/11 in an array of publications, from *Time*, *Newsweek*, and *Vanity Fair* to Marvel Comics. Faludi, *The Terror Dream*.

58. Lumenick, "He Rolls with the Punches," 50.

59. A handicap of the film is the newness of both the director and cast to presenting theoretical material in cinematic form. It reads too much like

a play—transition scenes between prospective tenants are filled by a weak montage of WTC-related events and the movie viewer never gets to look out the window and see what Eric sees. This works in theater but could have been more visually filled in the movie. The cast is also used to the more pronounced, histrionic gestures that are often necessary on stage for those in the audience to appreciate the actions and moods that are being conveyed. The close-up camerawork of cinema makes this unnecessary, so when the theoretical gestures are captured on film it makes the actor's action appear contrived.

60. The review section on the *WTC View* homepage is thin. Only two major papers are mentioned giving positive comments about the film: *LA Times* and *Variety*. The others are from *LA Weekly*, *Philadelphia Gay News*, *Next Magazine*, and *Philadelphia City Paper*.

61. Richard Schickel, *Woody Allen: A Life in Film* (Chicago: Ivan R. Dee, 2004).

62. It was initially proposed by Congress that four men on Flight 93 receive gold medals for their heroism under the new True American Heroes Act. Lori Guadagno, whose brother died on Flight 93, felt he should receive a medal too because he was trained in law enforcement and thus wouldn't have stood idly by and not acted. Hamilton Peterson, whose son died on the Flight 93, told the *Pittsburgh Tribune* that everyone on board was a hero and they all deserved recognition. In the end, everyone received medals, including every officer, firefighter, emergency worker, and government employee who responded to the terrorist attacks on 9/11, as well as Mayor Giuliani, Governor Pataki (NY), and the port authority commissioners. Faludi, *The Terror Dream*.

63. The doctrine of *lex talionis* (an eye for an eye) is an ancient one, and while the argument rages over whether it is still appropriate to apply in contemporary society, the survivors of victims whose murderers are on trial are seldom satisfied unless those found guilty forfeit their lives for the ones they took.

64. Herbert A. Simon, *Administrative Behavior*, 3rd edition (New York: Free Press, 1973); James G. March and Herbert A. Simon, *Organizations* (New York: John Wiley & Sons, 1958).

65. Tens of thousands of people across the country were stranded for extended periods of time with strangers when airspace was frozen and their planes had to remain on the ground: Canada alone received 226 of some 500 diverted flights and launched Operation Yellow Ribbon to deal with the large numbers of grounded planes and stranded passengers. The uncertainty of the period caused many of those stranded to forge strong bonds that remain years later. This is one aspect of 9/11 that, though not as apparent as those who lost their lives or suffered from their loss, could be the subject of a future WTC-

related movie, as too would a film about "people on the street" whose lives were forever changed by 9/11, even though they were not on the scene and did not know someone whose life was taken that day. Once films begin to move beyond the event itself, a mine of potential films emerges.

②

THE CINEMATIC DIALECTIC

Movies Begin to Debate the Wars

The terrorist attack on the WTC on September 11, 2001, set the mood for, and justified, the subsequent invasions of Afghanistan (January 17, 2001) and Iraq (March 20, 2003) to most Americans: 85 percent of the American public supported military action against terrorism following the attack on the WTC, and just shy of 80 percent felt sending troops into Iraq was justified.[1] The American public continued to rally round the flag, even as the number of people who felt that the United States overreacted to the threat of terrorism was increasing among America's allies.

Films in the United States tended to reflect the popular sentiment, decrying the attack on the WTC and painting the faces of Osama bin Laden and Saddam Hussein as terrorists directly responsible for the attack and who deserved their subsequent fate. These films, as we saw in the last chapter, reflected, and thus served to reinforce, the public sentiment toward the wars.

Bush's sweeping reelection victory in November 2004 suggests that the public remained steadfastly behind the administration's prowar policies. Still, all was not placid in America. Voices of dissent started to occur shortly after Iraq fell in 2003 and no WMD were found. Public criticism increased somewhat during 2004 and 2005 but it would not

Table 2.1.   U.S. Overreacting to Terrorism

	April 2002	March 2004
France	30%	57%
Germany	33%	49%
Britain	20%	33%
United States	—	13%

Source: www.people-press.org/report/206/a-year-after-iraq-war

become pronounced until 2006. The growing dissent is reflected in the movies during this two-year period. These two years are cinematically significant because film went a long way in giving a voice to the debate that had generally been muted in the public sphere.

Dissenting voices were heard before the war started, but once it started, they became rare. The public reaction to comments by Natalie Maines of the Dixie Chicks is illustrative of the mood of the country. Her aspersions of President Bush just before the invasion of Iraq would cast a long shadow over the group's subsequent career that would not

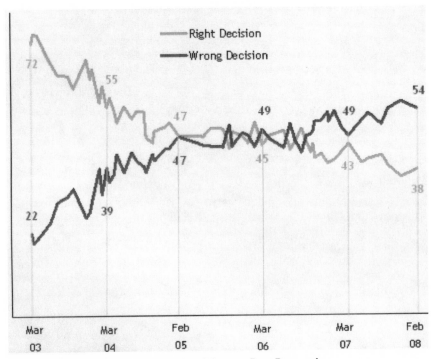

Decision to Use Military Force in Iraq? *Source:* **Pew Research.**

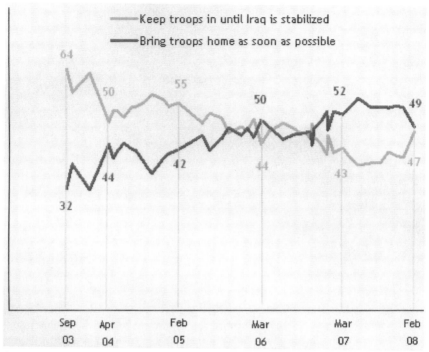

Should U.S. Keep Troops in Iraq? *Source:* **Pew Research.**

reblossom until 2007.[2] Before her infamous remark to fans that she was ashamed to be from the same state as President Bush, the group was featured on two television specials in 2002 and sang the "Star Spangled Banner" at Super Bowl XXXVII in 2003. In fact, Clear Channel Communications, which owns more than 1,200 radio stations was heavily promoting the Dixie Chicks' 2003 Top of the World Tour but pulled them from their playlists after Maines's remark during the London concert. After the incident on March 10, 2003, they were largely banished from the airwaves. Even their March 2006 comeback single, "Not Ready to Make Nice," was ignored by country radio and failed to penetrate the top 35 on the Hot Country Songs Chart, even as the subsequent album, *Taking the Long Way*, released in May 2006, went gold in its first week despite the lack of airplay.

A similar fate befell antiwar activist Cindy Sheehan and the other female protestors outside the Bush ranch in Crawford, Texas, in 2004 and 2005. The women demonstrators were not given wide credence by the mass media. Only a few demonstrators were seen on the news when the press covered Bush's forays to the Western White House. Even when seen, the public only caught glimpses of protestors. This gave the impression that the sentiment to bring the troops home was limited to a small, marginalized segment of the population, which allowed the public to easily dismiss them, a tactic reminiscent of the coverage of the student protestors in the early days of the Vietnam conflict.[3] It would not be until September 2005 that the first large-scale antiwar protest took place when over 100,000 protestors marched on Washington to demand the president end the Iraq war.[4]

There was certainly negative media coverage as early as 2003. The *Boston Globe* was the first to make the Vietnam quagmire analogy in June 2003, not long after the war was declared officially over on May 1 of that year.[5] Other issues garnered attention throughout 2004. On April 28, 2004, *60 Minutes II* aired a program on the Abu Ghraib abuses by members of the 320 Military Police, just before Seymour Hersh, who broke the My Lai massacre story three decades earlier, ran an exposé on the prisoner abuses in the *New Yorker* on May 10. Adding to the negative publicity on the war in Iraq was the release in June of the 9/11 Commission Report that concluded that there was no collaborative relationship between Iraq and al-Qaeda and that there was no evidence Iraq was in any way involved in the 9/11 attack on the WTC. Despite all this, the administration's battle-cry clamor that followed in the wake of 9/11 remained consistently shrill throughout 2004 and 2005. Both the president and vice president relied on their symbolic capital to claim privileged insight. Symbolic capital, like economic capital, accumulates over time with privileged access to resources.[6] The administration dismissed the 9/11 Commission Report by bluntly stating commission members were not privy to the same inside information that they had access to and that the Abu Ghraib abuses were isolated incidents committed by errant individuals and were not sanctioned by either the administration or by upper-echelon military personnel.[7]

The public appears to have accepted the administration's explanation, given Bush's sweeping 2004 reelection. Even though a good three-quarters of Americans in October 2003 felt the Bush administration had mislead the public as to how long U.S. military forces would have to remain in Iraq, they remained convinced the president had told them the truth for the most part: an attitudinal poll by University of Maryland in April 2004 showed a majority of Americans (57 percent) believed Iraq was providing substantial support to al-Qaeda and even after the 9/11 Commission Report, a Gallup poll conducted in October 2004 found that 62 percent of Republicans still believed Saddam was personally involved in the 9/11 attacks *and* 33 percent of the Democrats were of the same mind.[8] One reason for the continued support of the war by the public is the relentless, though slightly modified administration rhetoric. After the failure to find any WMD—the most cited reason for sending troops into Iraq by the administration—justification for the continued presence in Iraq shifted to the threat of terrorism in general. The terrorist connection was made by the president as early as 2002 but it now became a stable of the administration's rhetoric: 82 percent of the post-invasion public addresses by Bush, Cheney, and Rice made a link to the war on terrorism.[9]

The support for the war in the United States remained high because of the general perception that the wars were successful: both Afghanistan and Iraq had been liberated; Saddam Hussein had been deposed and captured (2003), tried (2004–2005), and executed (2006); and even though bin Laden would not be found until 2011, other members of the al-Qaeda terrorist network have been tracked down, and the Taliban had been ousted from power in 2001 when U.S. forces entered the country. These images, reinforced by the news media and by strong, forceful, recurring statements from members of the Bush administration, helped establish a false memory among many Americans: original misperceptions, once established by repetitive news stories, remained intact even in the face of subsequent counter information. The process of establishing the symbolic high ground began by strategically controlling press information about the war.

Attempts by the government to control media access to ensure the party line is promoted have long existed.[10] In Gulf War I, reporters were corralled at a central command post to receive combat news.[11] In Gulf War II, a similar staging took place: the Pentagon built a $1.5 million press conference room in Doha, Qatar, where the seven hundred journalists from around the world were regularly debriefed on how the war was going.[12] Victoria Clarke, the Pentagon's assistant secretary of defense of public affairs, is credited with developing a new strategy for covering the war in Iraq: embedding reporters with the troops. Embedding allows carefully screened reporters to travel with military units. This had been done in the past but never to the scale that took place in Iraq, nor with these results. It was, says Lt. Col. Rick Long, the former head of media relations for the U.S. Marines, a gamble, but "we were very happy with the outcome."[13] Riding shotgun with military personnel gave reporters a bird's-eye view of the fighting, but always from the vantage point of the men they were following. The journalist shares the risk and is dependent on the soldiers he is traveling with. The result of this distinct perspective, according to media critic Todd Gitlin, is that "the reporter approximates the view of the government's own camera. War reporting becomes a travelogue."[14]

The "bombs bursting in air" spectacle has become central to modern war reporting.[15] Television requires images. The reliance on these images has credited a television mind-set: Unless one is visually held by the images on the screen, people are quick to graze for another televised image that grabs them.[16] This mind-set is compounded by 24/7 news networks like CNN and MSNBC because they rely on a barrage of constantly new images to feed their viewers. This helps explain the success of these 24-hour news networks during the Iraq war which is where some 70 percent of the public was getting their input about the war.[17] Because there is no substantive analysis relating to the images, the end result of all this viewing is that "the more TV [news] people watch, the less they know."[18] Indeed, one study found that twenty-four-hour cable news channels were particularly insidious since viewers tended to lose 0.08 percent on their civil literacy test scores for each hour they spend each week watching TV news.[19]

The administration's control of the rhetorical high ground and the reliance of news organizations on the stunning visual effects of the war on the ground—supplied by the military when not taken in the field by embedded journalists—meant the American people were not being exposed to alternative perspectives of the war. Those who did manage to raise their voices were often shouted down by the Patriotic Police, the loudest of whom were found on FOX. The Patriotic Police were quick to denounce any media pundit for their lack of patriotism if they did not unflinchingly and completely support America's war effort. But Michael Moore was used to attacks, and is always on the lookout for a good skirmish, so his movie, *Fahrenheit 9/11*, was, if not the first to raise issues about the war, the one to garner attention and spark the public debate about it.

THE DIALECTICAL PROCESS

It is one of the few axioms in sociology: a social problem does not exist until it is identified. There is no issue if everyone accepts the status quo of doing business. Someone has to object. Just identifying an issue, Julia Wood argues in a provocatively titled article, "Saying It Makes It So," gives rise to conflict because it reorders and redefines the experience.[20] The process of "naming it"—tobacco causes lung cancer, drunk drivers should be punished for their irresponsible behavior, sexual harassment is inappropriate conduct in the workplace, American citizens were misled about the threat Saddam Hussein posed—raises alternatives to the status quo acceptance of the topic. This results in conflict between disputed approaches: the "old" way and the "new" way. Ultimately, one approach is adopted over the other; the old way is reasserted or the new way becomes the prevailing thought, or some compromise between to the two approaches is arrived at and agreed upon. This is the dialectic process.

The dialectic method has a long and distinguished history. It is rooted to the Socratic Method and was popularized by Plato's Socratic dialogues. Two or more people with different perspectives argue the merits of their respective ideas with the goal of ultimately arriving at some new insight. The dialectic method was significantly advanced by the eighteenth-century German philosopher, Friedrich Hegel, in his now-famous dialectical model: thesis, antithesis, synthesis. The thesis gives rise to a reaction, an antithesis, which contradicts the thesis, and the tension between the two ultimately results in a synthesis. Marx did not find fault with the Hegelian dialectic so much as that he found it too abstract,[21] so he rooted it to the more concrete realm of class conflict.[22] Marx saw the capitalist bourgeoisie holding sway (thesis) but felt they would increasingly be challenged by the growth of the proletarian workers (antithesis). The conflict between these rival class ideologies would eventually result in a synthesis: a new communal, classless social order

Marx called communism. These dialectical thinkers, as well as those who followed, including dialectical filmmakers, are intent on unmasking the taken-for-granted prevailing reality with the ultimate goal of changing it.

The administration's thesis following the attack on the WTC was that those responsible for the tragedy had to be stopped. This thesis was widely supported by the American people who steadfastly supported the invasion of Afghanistan. The administration's charge against Saddam Hussein was that he had WMD—and because he was "crazy" he would likely use them—was also largely supported by the American people and justified the subsequent incursion into Iraq. There were some antiwar demonstrations before the invasion of Iraq, but much of the antagonism toward the Iraqi war dissipated once the war began, largely because it was viewed as unpatriotic to not support American troops in the field when at war. The administration's thesis began to be challenged in the public realm some months after the war ended and no WMD had been found. The administration managed to maintain its status quo position by shifting the argument away from the missing WMD and by focusing on Saddam's terrorist connection. The few antithetical voices that were raised about events taking place in Iraq—the 9/11 Commission Report and Abu Ghraib stories— did not appear to spark a dialectic about the war.[23] The dialectic would not be "lit" until the movies started to weigh in against the war.

INITIAL VOLLEYS

There were two films in 2003 that examined facets of the war not directly connected to the hunts for Osama bin Laden and Saddam Hussein. One is the hour-long *National Geographic* special, *21 Days to Baghdad*; the other is *Uncovered: The Whole Truth*, which revisits the WMD issue but from a distinctly vituperative perspective. These films can be considered forerunners of the cinematic debate because one weighs in on the war's side while the other questions the premise of sending troops into Iraq.[24]

The first film, *21 Days to Baghdad*, details the military incursion into Iraq and documents the first twenty-one days of war. The film is not much different from what people in their living rooms were exposed to on the nightly news as the war unfolded on television. In mimicking televised events of the war, it underscores the visual aspect of the war. It goes further, however, because it inadvertently provides insight into how embedded journalists covered the war because, says Joe Galloway from Knight-Ridder, "This is what war is. The difference is we got to look over their shoulder this time and see some of it."

The first third of the movie is interspersed with images of the president. It shows him addressing Congress after 9/11, and then, somewhat later, his declaration that Saddam "get out" of Iraq within forty-eight hours. Between these two bookend speeches, the film is filled with stock footage that inventories America's military arsenal: the Apache and Blackhawk helicopters, the FA-18 Hornet, F-14 Tomcat, and the B-2 and B-52 long-range bombers, as well as the Stealth Bomber are just some of the sophisticated arsenal the United States has ready for combat. This inventory of military technology is justified by the narrator because the United States is about to "deploy the world's most advanced weapons . . . to stop a dictator and end his brutal twenty-four year rule." It is toward the end of this prelude that the viewer learns what is unique about this film: a *National Geographic* reporter will be embedded with the 3rd Infantry, 1st Marine Division as they go into Iraq.

Much of the rest of the film shows the images the world is familiar with from television as troops moved into Iraq. Most of these images are very visual. The night bombings and the resulting flames dotting the Baghdad skyline are shown. A *National Geographic* reporter, who remained at the hotel where many of the journalists in Baghdad stayed to report on events in the city, comments of the missiles exploding over the city, "Incredible. . . . It's a spectacular display." One would think he was talking about a July Fourth fireworks display. It's almost as if he were watching the bombing and saying, "Wow! Cool!"

Relatively little is actually reported by the embedded journalist. Only a handful of scenes show the cameras following the 3rd Infantry, 1st Marine Division. The scenes are obvious from the camera angle: the back of Marines running with raised rifles across a road, Marines checking their gas masks in a moving truck, the back of a military convoy taken by the journalist from atop another vehicle. No real fighting is ever shown. Fighting may result in deaths and mangled corpses. This might unsettle the viewer, especially if the bodies are our soldiers. The face of death is banished.

The viewer is told of the tragedy of war, however. The viewer just doesn't see the tragedy of war. We learn that Jessica Lynch was rescued in the "first rescue of a missing soldier behind enemy lines since World War II," and see her being carried on a stretcher to a waiting helicopter. To get her out, we are told simply that there was "a firefight in and a firefight out." The viewer does learn that elsewhere in Iraq that day six soldiers were killed in a helicopter crash on their way back from a mission. The clause, "on the way back from a mission," seems to make their deaths more heroic than tragic since they accomplished their task before sacrificing their lives. The grieving but proud mother and wife of one of those who died are shown back home. The death of these and others are acknowledged, but quickly passed over: There were "several friendly fire incidents [sic]," and to date eighteen American and British combatants had lost their lives because of "human error and software glitches [sic]." Quick fade to action sequence: "Today, grunts of the 3rd Infantry, 1st Marine" drawl up to a heavily defended bridge. "Suddenly," the embedded reporter reminisces, "I heard gunfire, I heard explosions, and I saw black puffs of smoke over our column." Puffs of smoke are shown. No "action" takes place, however.

The fighting at the airport is recalled by Joseph Galloway with Knight-Ridder, who reminisces, "We [sic] took it [the airport], boy, just like that. . . . It was a shooting gallery. . . . The enemy had no chance defending the airport (or the country) because they simply were no match for the sophisticated weaponry of allied forces." The narrative focus on the technology throughout *21 Days* (see also *Wings over Afghanistan*, 2004) tends to cloud the horror of death: "If you see death," Galloway says, "you're never the same. It will always be with you. You'll carry it with you to the grave." Galloway is undoubtedly correct, and that is perhaps why the viewer is left with the spectacle of technology and doesn't see the face of death. In one of the few scenes where death is shown, it isn't seen. The embedded *National Geographic* journalist says of the death of a little boy that he is "missing his face." His face is not shown; he is seen being cradled in the arms of a helpless medic, the boy's body pressed to the chest of the medic. The close-up of the boy's body never shows his missing face. His death is a tribute to the ugly side of war. At the same time, his death is quickly dismissed; he was simply in the wrong place at the wrong time. How he died and who was responsible is a moot point.

The ugly side of war, like the ugly underside of society on the nightly news, is wiped away by the ending of the film. The nightly news typically ends with a cute, upbeat story, which helps the viewer forget the downbeat news of the last thirty minutes. This film ends in a similar fashion, with a similar effect. Whatever price that might have been paid—and the film suggests throughout that it was not very high, thanks to technology—the end result is that Saddam had been ousted. The closing visual is of Saddam's statue being pulled down. For the Iraqi people to see this, Joe Galloway of Knight-Ridder intones, as the viewer sees the statue topple and watches the images of cheering Iraqis, "set off the real jubilation" that, it is intimated, swept the country. It is a very visual depiction of an event and response that was a very effective, but staged, event.

The twenty-one-day war is whittled down to a riveting hour. It is sufficient because the images that were depicted in *21 Days to Baghdad* were the images that were widely entrenched in the public mind by the time Iraq fell. So *21 Days* recycles, and consequently reinforces, the view of the war that the Bush administration wished to propagate, and one that had widespread appeal among the American populace in 2003. But an antithetical view of the war was beginning to emerge. The new view did not directly challenge the war, but it did cast doubts on the motives for the war, and, like those sporadic voices that were starting to be raised in other media outlets, it challenged the prevailing Bush party line.

Uncovered departs radically from the early prowar cinematic stance of films. It is the first to fire a cinematic volley directly assailing the justification for declaring war; by doing so, it "popularized" a topic that was just beginning to gain media attention in 2003.[25] The film opens with a rolling montage of key military and intelligence personnel by establishing their credentials to speak about the war. The experience of these individuals—twenty-two years as a CIA analysis, a retired army colonel who was the former Chief of Middle East Intelligence at the Defense Intelligence Agency—intimates this is going to be another film of talking heads mouthing the administration's party line. This misperception is quickly put to rest as one spokesperson after another assails how the administration mined data to fit their prior beliefs that Saddam Hussein was a terrorist who had WMD. Their insider status gives them symbolic capital and makes their testimony believable. Mel Goodman, who was a senior analysis with the CIA for twenty years says that the "Bush administration made up its mind to go to war on 9/11/2001. From that time on you were dealing with rationalizations and justifications [for going to war]; there was no clear and present danger." Ray McGovern, who was with the CIA for twenty-seven years, concurs: "Weapons of mass destruction was a convenient way of tricking the Congress into giving the president authority to wage the war."

Parades of other insiders testify before the camera to the same effect. Their testimony is interspersed with clips of Bush and members of the administration making overreaching statements: Bush is at the podium addressing the nation that "We cannot wait for the final proof"; a jump shot shows the vice president stating, "There are al-Qaeda in Iraq"; this is followed by a clip of Secretary of State Rice proclaiming with her trademark scowl, "Saddam Hussein consorts with terrorists." A number of analysts convincingly debunk these statements by stating categorically that they know Saddam had "no connection to terrorists."

The film received some good critical press upon its release that tended to sidestep the film's liberal bias—it was produced by the Center for American Progress. Nevertheless, the film appears to have had limited release, and hence effects, in the public forum. The film holds up better today because the charges of data mining made in the film in 2003 are more widely recognized. It would be much harder to avoid the second volley, which landed with all the impact of a mortar shell the following year: Michael Moore's *Fahrenheit 9/11*.

POINT/COUNTERPOINT: *FAHRENHEIT* OR *FAHRENHYPE?*

It might be best to begin with the title of Moore's film since it has received so little attention. Neither noted film critics Roger Ebert with the *Chicago Tribune* nor A. O. Scott with the *New York Times* mention the title in their generally positive reviews; Terry Lawson with the *Detroit Free Press* does, but only in passing: "the title was appropriated without approval from Ray Bradbury's *Fahrenheit 451* [1951], a novel about a government that burns books to keep its citizenry in the dark."[26] Perhaps it was assumed that the public made the connection, especially since a central tenet of the book—and Moore's film—is that the [Bush] government uses television to channel information to the people to keep them complacent. The connection to the book may not be one readily made, however, given the state of cultural illiteracy Hess and others find among many in contemporary society.[27] For example, Hess found that only 45 percent of seventeen-year-olds could identify Oedipus, 45 percent knew that the biblical Job was known for his patience in suffering, 44 percent think that *The Scarlet Letter* was either about a witch trial or a piece of correspondence, and 38 percent knew Geoffrey Chaucer wrote the *Canterbury Tales*.[28] In a related study, Ravitch found that few high school seniors (12 percent) knew the content of John Bunyan's *Pilgrim's Progress*.[29] A solid majority in Ravitch's study, 60 percent, knew that Dickens's *Tale of Two Cities* described events occurring during the French Revolution, though one cannot get overly excited about this increase in literary knowledge since 60 percent is still tantamount to a D–. Dickens's story may be more widely recognized because of the popularity of *Les Misérables* and the innumerable movies and television series that have been made of Dickens's novel.[30] This suggests that Moore's reference to Bradbury's book may be more widely recognized in the near future since Frank Darabont has plans to remake the now-dated 1966 version of the film, originally made by Francois Truffaut with Oskar Werner starring as the fireman Guy Montag.

Michael Moore's attack on Bush in *Fahrenheit 9/11* generated a substantial amount of critical and popular attention for a number of reasons. First, Moore has widespread name recognition. The extent of this recognition is unprecedented for a documentary filmmaker; he is on a directorial par with such feature filmmakers as Spike Lee, Quentin Tarantino, Ron Howard, and Penny Marshall. Moore's name recognition as a documentary filmmaker is intertwined with the second point: *five* of his films are in the top ten grossing (1982–2010) political documentaries, with *Fahrenheit 9/11* capturing the number one slot by a significant margin. The third reason helps explains why *Fahrenheit 9/11* achieved the top grossing slot: He won the Oscar for best documentary, *Bowling for Columbine*, the previous year, so is able to build on his cinematic momentum, and *Fahrenheit 9/11* received a fifteen-minute standing ovation when it premiered at the Cannes Film Festival in May 2004 where it was awarded the coveted *Palme d'Or*, the first documentary to receive this award since Jacques Cousteau and Louis Malle won the award in 1956 for *The Silent World*. And lastly, there was a substantial amount of prerelease publicity, not just to promote the film but because of the subject matter: Moore's antipathy toward Bush was heard by millions in his diatribe against the president at the time he received the Oscar the previous year; notoriety regarding the film's release was exacerbated by media coverage that revolved around the pressure on subsidiary Miramax by Michael Eisner at Disney corporate to withdraw backing for the film.

The popularity of *Fahrenheit 9/11* captures the growing antipathy toward the war in Iraq. It is the first strong sign that the policies of the Bush administration, despite being swept into office in the 2004 elections, are not embraced by a significant proportion of the American people. People who saw this film were most likely to agree with the filmmaker since people do not generally go to a movie to have their worldview challenged, though certainly some conservatives watched the movie to learn the face of the enemy. It is unlikely, therefore, that the movie changed opinions toward the war. As one member of the audience who was lined up to hear Michael Moore speak, said, when asked what they found so endearing about him in the counterpoint movie, *Michael Moore Hates America*, "He keeps it real," a euphuism for "He tells it like I think." Later in the film, this is stated more explicitly by

Table 2.2. Total Grosses for Political Documentary Films: 1982–2009

Rank Title	Gross Box-Office Revenue	(Rounded Millions)
1	*Fahrenheit 9/11*	$119.2
2	*Sicko*	$24.6
3	*An Inconvenient Truth*	$24.2
4	*Bowling for Columbine*	$21.6
5	*Capitalism: A Love Story*	$11.6
6	*Expelled: No Intelligence Allowed*	$7.7
7	*Roger and Me*	$6.7
8	*The Fog of War*	$4.2
9	*The Corporation*	$3.5
10	*Control Room*	$2.6

Source: www.boxofficemojo.com

another audience member: "I don't think anyone not predisposed to Michael Moore is going to come out [from film or talk] saying, 'I've never looked at it that way.' You go in with the same notion you go out with." Nevertheless, the stringency of Moore's message, even among those of similar minds, could only serve to reinforce, and possibly inflame, the public's growing antagonism toward President Bush and the war in Iraq. It certainly made them think more about the reason for the war, which was Moore's point in making the movie.

This movie is the most vituperative attack on the status quo of any of Michael Moore's movies. Only the scene raking Charlton Heston over the coals in *Bowling for Columbine* comes close to the level of sarcasm that is the recurring motif of *Fahrenheit 9/11*.

The movie opens with Florida Secretary of State Katherine Harris conceding the state's electrical votes, and hence the election, to Bush. The implication is that no such theft of a presidential race ever took place in American politics before this; Moore conveniently forgets that a federal panel in 1876 awarded twenty disputed electoral votes to Rutherford B. Hayes, effectively making him the nineteenth president of the United States by one electoral vote. Moore states that Bush's victory only happened because his brother was governor of Florida and that the Supreme Court didn't hear the case because they were all "daddy's people," when, in fact, George H. W. Bush only appointed two of the nine justices. The theft of the election by Bush is reinforced with close-cropped depictions of signs held by demonstrators in Washington on Inauguration Day that read it's a "Sad Day," and that this is only happening because "Bush Cheated." Moore then inaccurately proclaims that "No president has ever witnessed such a thing on inauguration day," this time forgetting about the 60,000 Vietnam protestors (versus 20,000) that marched in Washington protesting Nixon's 1972 inauguration.

Despite his election, however, Moore says that things were not going well for the president during his next eight months in office because he "couldn't get his judges appointed, couldn't get his legislation passed." His approval rating at the polls began to sink; this is proclaimed over a chart showing his slipping popularity—53 percent in May to 45 percent in September—so, the viewer is told, he did what anyone might do under such circumstances, "he went on vacation." In fact, he was on vacation, Moore tells us reading from the *Washington Post*, "42 percent of the time." This is mentioned over a series of vacation videos: in one, the president is swinging a golf club; in another, he is riding in a golf cart with his feet propped up; in yet another, he is proudly holding up a fish he caught. It is only now, ten minutes into the film, that the opening credits roll, by which time the viewer already has clearly learned two key things: Bush is a lazy president who stole the election.

Immediately after the credits, the film very effectively goes dark for a full minute while the audience hears the awestruck, bewildered screams of those at Ground Zero on 9/11. The dark screen to the "Oh, my God," horrified voices of pedestrians on the streets of Manhattan is a particularly effective cinematic technique precisely because the images are so firmly entrenched in the public eye that to *not* see them rehashed is more pungent than seeing them yet again. The camera fades from the dark screen to pan the upraised, horror-stricken faces of those looking up at unfolding events at Ground Zero, then to the president at the Emma E. Booker Elementary School in Florida where he is vacationing at this moment in time. The viewer sees the president sitting immobile and staring mindlessly into space. Moore tells us that "When informed of the first plane hitting the World Trade Center . . . Mr. Bush decided to go ahead with his photo opportunity. . . . When the second plane hit and he was told the nation was under attack, [he] just sat there and continued to read *My Pet Goat*." The camera scans to the clock on the wall, then back to the blank face of the president, then back to the clock: "Seven minutes passed with nobody doing anything," Moore intones.

Two movies provide a counter perspective. One is *Michael Moore Hates America: A Documentary That Tells the Truth about a Great Nation*, written, directed, and produced by Michael Wilson, intently parodying the opening of a Michael Moore film. The other is *FahrenHYPE 9/11*. Curiously, this film has no opening credits and the vested interest personnel responsible for the film are revealed only at the end, where the viewers learn, if they are paying close attention, that the conservatives who produced and wrote the movie are the same ones who voiced their opinions throughout the film: Lee Troxler, Dick Morris, Eileen McGann, and Alan Peterson, among others. These films directly assail Moore's manipulation of information.

Michael Moore Hates America is more of a critique about *Bowling for Columbine* than *Fahrenheit 9/11*; there are only two or three very brief remarks in *Michael More Hates* that bear on the Iraq war in the first part of the movie—one relating to Disney's stopping Miramax from distributing *Fahrenheit*—and one lengthy segment in the latter part of the movie that criticizes the segment in *Fahrenheit 9/11* when Michael Moore ostensibly walks through Walter Reed Hospital and comments on the neglected state of health care for those who have served in Iraq. The movie still works as a challenge to *Fahrenheit*, however, because it effectively critiques Moore's movie-making techniques and shows how many scenes are manipulated to distort what really took place. It is flawed, to be sure. It is Michael Wilson's first film and the director inexplicitly relies too much on running criticism by Penn Jillette of Penn and Teller comedic fame, and on comments from attorney David Hardy, who provides questionable psychological insight: "Michael Moore has all the symptoms of narcissist personality disorder," which, Hardy says, is characterized by inner self-hate and an enormous ego—flit to scene of Michael Moore at podium proclaiming, "I'm the biggest selling author in America. I've the biggest watched documentary of all time. . . ." At the same time, Wilson does not capitalize on commentary by Albert Maysles who he interviewed and who has a long and distinguished career of documentary filmmaking dating back to 1955—best known for making *Gimme Shelter* (1970) and the original *Grey Gardens* (1976). Maysles is eminently qualified to judge Moore's documentary style of filmmaking, but his credentials are not firmly established until the end of the film.

Michael Moore Hates America is clearly the better of the two films because the director seems to sincerely want to learn why Michael Moore hates America. And there is enough footage that pertains to Iraq, however modest it might be, to allow the viewer to recognize how Michael Moore's distortions in his other movies can carry over to *Fahrenheit 9/11*.

FahrenHYPE pales in comparison because the talking heads that are the glue to this film simply parrot the familiar FOX clichés lambasting Michael Moore. Nevertheless, *FahrenHYPE* does more convincingly address the infamous seven minutes at the elementary school by allowing Gwen Tose-Rigell, the African American principal of the school, to speak on behalf of Bush's action during those critical seven minutes. The appearance of Tose-Rigell at the outset of the film is particularly

convincing because she clearly has a different ideology than the president or the film's commentators: "I didn't vote for him, but on that day,
at that moment, I could have . . . [it was] the first time since in office
that he looked presidential."

Her question, "What should he have done?" has been asked by conservative commentators, but seldom as effectively—there is a scene in
FahrenHYPE where the female political commentator and author, Ann
Coulter, flails her arms about and rails, "What was he suppose to do?
Run out of the room [like Superman] and tear open his shirt." In a more
level-headed and convincing manner, Principal Tose-Rigell says, "I was
very pleased at the way [the president] handled [himself]. That he took
a few moments to gather himself." She also addresses the book he was
reading, *My Pet Goat*. The title of the book garnered a certain amount
of attention in the media, and Michael Moore made sure to mention it
in his critique of how Bush spent his time in the classroom. The focus
on the book suggests it was preferred reading material of the presidents,
when it was a standard text for second graders that he was given to follow their recitation. The principal also adamantly addresses another
point that was widely commented on by the media and states emphatically that "the president was reading the book right side up." A freeze
frame of the president reading makes it difficult to determine from the
back of the book cover any script, but the ISBN bar scan is clearly visible in the lower part of the book where it should be if he was reading
the book right side up and confirms the principal's observations, which
she should know because, she says, "I was standing right behind him."

Immediately following the lapsed seven-minute episode, Michael
Moore says that after the 9/11 attacks 142 Saudi nationals were permitted by the president to leave the country, 24 of whom were connected
to the bin Laden family. This took place despite the freeze on airspace,
which affected, we learn, everybody else, even "daddy." But not all
planes were grounded. Moore inserts a file footage picture of a plane
talking off, ostensibly with the 142 Saudi nationals aboard, accompanied
to the lyrics of "We Gotta Get Out of Here." Then an old black-and-
white Jack Webb *Dragnet* segment is shown—to the dramatic beat
of dum, de dum, dum—where hard-nosed Detective Webb fingers
a suspect from a photo lineup and then interrogates a fidgeting family member on her front stoop. As the *Dragnet* segment is watched,

Moore comments that you "usually want to talk to family members to find out where they think you might be. . . ." He then makes an insipid, but provocative, analogy: "Could you imagine after the Oklahoma City bombing, President Clinton arranging a trip out of the country for the McVeigh family?"

All this seems particularly ominous. A moment's informed reflection, however, would suggest that members of the Saudi royal family, who, if associated with the embassy would enjoy diplomatic immunity, are not subject to interrogation. Besides that, they would likely, and rightfully, want to get out of town in anticipation of the subsequent hostility by Americans to anyone identified with the Muslim community. This point is passed over by Michael Moore but is raised in *FahrenHYPE* when the narrator, quoting from a highlighted paragraph in the 9/11 Commission Report, says, "We find no evidence that any flights of Saudi nationals . . . took place before the reopening of national airspace" and that they were only allowed to leave after being cleared of involvement by the FBI.

All three filmmakers assail the others for manipulating data and all three go beyond the neutral lens advocated by legendary documentary filmmaker Albert Maysles. The propagandist charge that is rightfully leveled at Moore's film by the other two can be turned on its head and equally leveled at them. They might *all* be an excellent source of dissection for a propaganda documentary that, to slightly modify (from singular to plural) the comment of the narrator in *FahrenHYPE* about *Fahrenheit 9/11*: "Eighty years from now film schools will still be studying *these* films as *among* the most effective propaganda movies ever made."

Propaganda relies on a number of time-tested techniques, other than taking a scene or comment out of context and making it appear as other than it initially was. Another technique that all three filmmakers rely on is a rapid-fire delivery that might be called information overload: facts bombard the viewer. This information overload is artfully constructed so that the viewer hears or sees a wealth of "facts" but does not have the time to digest them to ascertain any flaws. Just as Moore relies on this technique when he talks about the time Bush spent on vacation, *FahrenHYPE* counters using the same technique by stating that some of the time that Moore took into account as vacation time is unfair because it included weekends, and then a voice-over runs showing how active the president was on just one week of his so-called vacations, then running a number of weeks together to make the list all the more impressive. The running verbiage rolls active events together with passive ones. Active events are those where real work was done; passive events are ones that did not require an investment of time. Illustrations of the latter are meant to imply that his "vacation" was really another workweek because he did all the following, and then some: visited an elementary school, held a brief press conference, announced the appointment of the new chairman of the Joint Chiefs of Staff, and took the time to issue a proclamation honoring women's equality. This is a variation of another aspect of propaganda that Michael Moore is captured acknowledging in a speech that is, in its turn, spun by Michael Wilson: "The best [scenes], the ones that work, have a strong kernel of truth to them." This is why one cannot say that it is an outright fabrication, even though the "fact" is stretched beyond its initial application.

Another propaganda technique is to wave the flag. All three filmmakers make extensive use of this technique. Each sees himself as the only true American, which implicitly, and quite often explicitly, cast aspersions on their opponents' right to speak for the American people.

Both *Michael Moore Hates* and *FahrenHYPE* parade their American roots. Michael Wilson starts his film by saying, "Michael Moore pissed me off. . . . Always talking about how great Canada is . . . [Well], I was born February 18, 1976. My mother worked at Wal-Mart, my dad worked the line [making] pre-fabricated homes. . . . [We] didn't have much, but parents did best they could." His father told him when he got laid off, that "We've been here before, we'll be here again. . . . In America, if you work hard and never quit, you can make it." And that is what Michael Wilson did, going off to college, getting married, and had a daughter who was told by Michael Moore that she wouldn't be able to get ahead because "she was enslaved by corporate interest." This is refuted by a successful immigrant who has achieved the American dream during his interview: "Here in America," he says, "the individual is in the driver's seat of his own life. [That's the] reason why American is so appealing to young people around the world." The individuals in *FahrenHYPE* do not go to this length, but their Americanism is obvious in their approach to the war on terror and what took place on 9/11. David Drum, for example, is identified as a fellow of the American Enterprise Institute and a former member of the George W. Bush administration; in another segment, the viewers see

American flags waving in the breeze over the graves of those who lost their lives while a flutist plays "The Star-Spangled Banner."

Michael Moore's "Americanism" is more in keeping with Guy Montag, the gadfly in Bradbury's novel who rebels against the Fascist system to enlighten others. In a scene reminiscent of Bradbury's novel, Moore holds up a highly censored document that is largely blacked out because "It is important to not let others know how we collect information" about what happened on 9/11; Moore then goes on to say that James Baker, a longtime friend of the Bush family, was hired to fight the families that had lost loved ones on 9/11. Moore proclaims his Americanism by holding those in power up as corrupting the meaning of America. He shows a Marine captain speaking on camera saying, "We have to bring the idea of democracy and freedom to the city"; Moore then flashes to a house door being kicked in by soldiers and two women cowering and crying in the corner. In another scene a soldier states, "We're here to do a job," and then the viewer sees a bunch of soldiers standing over the body of a dead Iraqi male on a stretcher and laughing, while one kicks the dead man's feet and says, "Ali Baba [here] still has a hard-on." Moore is implying he is more of an American than some Americans who are acting very un-American.

This flag waving is used by all three in how they depict Sergeant Peter Dawson of the Army National Guard who lost both arms during his tour of duty in Iraq. We first meet Sgt. Dawson in Michael Moore's film. It is a very brief section. Moore is talking about how George W. Bush is supporting the troops with verbal platitudes and not in any meaningful way because he's (1) cutting combat soldiers' pay by 33 percent and assistance to their family by 60 percent, (2) opposed giving veterans a billion more in health-care benefits and wants to close [some] veterans hospitals, and (3) tried to double the prescription drug cost for veterans and opposed full benefits for part-time reservists. To drive home the horrors of war and the plight of veterans, Moore then takes us to Walter Reed where we see a number of amputee soldiers. One (not identified) soldier is Sgt. Dawson who appears heavily drugged and needing the drugs because of his pain. This is a very brief scene that comprises about one minute in a two-hour movie.

Sgt. Dawson plays a central role in the other two films. He is interviewed sometime after his release from Walter Reed and is at home with his wife and child. The sergeant tells the interviewer that he was surprised to learn that he was in Moore's film and that Moore was never in Walter Reed. In these films we learn that the interview was, in fact, from an NBC Nightly News segment, though because it was not identified, and Moore's voice-over commentary was heard while the scene was shown, Moore certainly left the impression that he was there in person. The same, however, holds true for the other two films. Both use identical footage of Sgt. Dawson, which indicates that someone else did the actual interview. The viewer, however, is left with the impression the interview was conducted by the respective filmmakers.

The sergeant is very critical of Moore for bashing those who serve: "I'd like an apology from Michael Moore to the military for the way he portrayed them in his film." This is stated over a picture of a company of fatigued soldiers standing smartly at parade rest. We see the dual amputee sergeant wearing a prosthesis device on one arm. His agility is captured when he drops a jigsaw piece and reaches over to pick it up with this hooked hand and tells us, "I was just doing my job and an unfortunate accident happened." At least he lived; a fellow soldier didn't. He is angry about how he was portrayed in the movie since he is adapting and functioning: "I don't feel like I'm being left behind at all. I'm fine, as you can see." But does the viewer see? Does the viewer identify with the functioning Dawson? The answer is a matter of perspective.

Interpretation is in the eyes of the beholder. In the Oscar-winning movie *Annie Hall* (1977), there is scene where Woody Allen and Diane Keaton are seeing their separate counselors. The split screen shows each with their respective therapists discussing the same thing but with distinctly different interpretations: How often do you have sex, the therapist asks Alan, who replies "hardly ever," and to which Keaton says "constantly" (see also, *Divorce His, Divorce Hers*, 1973). The same holds for Sgt. Dawson. In the scene where we see him reach down and pick up the jigsaw piece, he does it with some difficulty. Liberals viewing this movie would be sure to see the problem he was having, which belie his statement that he is functioning well; on the other hand, conservatives would be struck by his dexterity and admire him for how well he is managing. In another parallel scene, Sgt. Dawson says that by joining the National Guard his life has been changed for the better because the problems he was having in his marriage have now been resolved.

As he makes this statement, he is leaning on the kitchen table with his hooked arm prominently displayed in front of his face. Liberals would be dubious of his statement about how much his life has been improved and feel, no doubt, that he is besotted—Marx would hold he is laboring under a false consciousness; on the other hand, the primary audience for this film is conservatives and the lingering camera shot and Dawson's pride at having served despite his loss would be viewed as admirable.

Sgt. Dawson's story is illustrative of another aspect of these blatantly propagandistic documentaries: they do not promote a point of view so much as push it. When Dawson was shown in the hospital in *Fahrenheit*, he appeared embittered and relying heavily on drugs to numb his pain. When Dawson was shown in the rebuttal films, he states that he was simply describing phantom pain.

In the end, Michael Moore's film is quite slick. This is to be expected. First, Michael Moore is a seasoned documentarian. Second, it is a big budget picture: Miramax put up $6 million to make the picture. This is a lot for a documentary, but certainly justifiable given Michael Moore's box office track record. And the movie continues to garner attention, at least in part because it reflects a wider perspective about the war that is held by the American public today compared to when it was first released.

At the same time, Michael Wilson's film holds up quite well. It does so for similar reasons. In this case, Wilson's novice status may not have worked to enhance the film but it is offset by his sincerity in making the film and trying to figure out just why Michael Moore hates America. Its low-budget status even works in the film's favor because it makes the film more "gritty" in depicting everyday people doing everyday things much as Michael Moore accomplished in his first film, *Roger and Me* (1989). And lastly, it does make the viewer question Michael Moore, which makes this a successful movie because that is what Wilson set out to do. He does this because Michael Moore fails to respond to his repeated and persistent requests to grant him an interview, a technique that Moore often employs in his films and which is now turned against him. In one scene, for example, Wilson is finally able to approach Moore. After his presentation at the university, those in the audience have the opportunity to ask Moore questions. Wilson patiently waits his turn. Moore was not ready for him, and seemed to be anticipating the standard recitation regarding his provocative and insightful filmmaking style. Wilson introduces himself as one of the wackos Moore is always talking about and then asks why he won't give him his requested forty-five-minute interview. Moore avoids the request by denouncing Wilson: "Everything I do is because I love America. It's people like you that hate America." Wilson walks out, defeated because the "Master [was] cheered by 7,000 fans." Outside, however, he approaches some of those same fans as they leave the auditorium, and they all agree on the one thing that comes off clearly in Wilson's film: says one person, "It took a lot of courage to do [what you do] and I believe in your right [of free speech] to do it"; another quips, "I thought it was kind of sad [Moore's ridiculing Wilson's point of view]," while another commented, "I like Michael Moore; I like what he stands for. But I will give you this, he should have answered your questions. And in all honesty, he should give you the interview." Wilson quite successfully turns Moore's own cinematic technique against him. The fact that Moore didn't answer Wilson's question and ducked Wilson a number of other times during the film, *Michael Moore Hates America*, presents an unflattering portrait of Michael Moore that is particularly effective because Moore uses these same avoidance techniques in *all* his films to besmirch others.

BEYOND MICHAEL MOORE: THE DIALECTIC CONTINUES TO RAGE

Michael Moore's film sparked the cinematic debate, though this debate was already beginning to intensify in the public arena in 2004. This occurred because Americans continued to die in a war that was declared over May 1, 2003. Films in this section extend the dialectic into areas only tangentially raised by Michael Moore. On the one side are those films that more stridently question why American troops were deployed in the first place. The argument here hones in on how the Bush administration misled Americans about Saddam Hussein and his notorious WMD. This issue was raised in *Fahrenheit* but the threat he posed to the United States was not specifically addressed. Films on the other side skirt the WMD issue. They tend to follow the lines promoted by the Bush administration after failing to find WMD: America's involvement was necessary to depose a ruthless tyrant who posed a threat to world peace, and a continued presence was necessary to ensure stability to a very unstable part of the world. The point–counterpoint cinematic argument follows the classic thesis-antithesis dialectic delineated by Hegel, and, in the best Hegelian tradition, results in a kind of synthesis. The last film analyzed in this section, *The War Within*, is not clearly linked to one side or the other and is the only domestic fictive feature film to be released during this two-year period.

Thesis Films
Buried in the Sand: The Deception of America (2004)
Weapons of Mass Destruction (2004)
Wings over Afghanistan (2004)
The Blood of My Brother (2005)
Confronting Iraq: Conflict and Hope (2005)

Antithesis Films
Aftermath: Unanswered Questions of 9/11 (2004)
Battleground: 21 Days on the Empire's Edge (2004)
Life and Death in the War Zone (2004; critiqued in chapter 3)
Rush to War (2004)
Uncovered: The War in Iraq (2004)
WMD: Weapons of Mass Deception (2004)
The Oil Factor (2005)
Poison Dust (2005)
Why We Fight (2005)

Synthesis Films
Last Letters Home (2004)
The War Within (2005)

Thesis: A Just War

These films pound home the point made by President Bush and "argue" that the United States did the right thing by going into Iraq. They somewhat halfheartedly acknowledge that maybe Saddam Hussein did not have WMD, but focus on the "fact" that he was still evil and was a threat to the United States, even if he was not directly responsible for 9/11. In short, they adapt the rhetoric the administration took after entering Iraq and finding no WMD. This is hardly surprising since these films have a strong conservative slant. Their purpose is to make sure the American people know that we are fighting a just war.

Generally, the films in this section are much like the films examined under America's villains in the last chapter. *Wings over Afghanistan*, for instance, is mentioned in the section about Saddam Hussein, even if it is about the war in Afghanistan, because its raison d'être is simply to catalog the technological sophistication of America's arsenal. The same applies to *Weapons of Mass Destruction* (2004), which could just as easily have been fitted into those films that examine *Saddam Hussein*. It is placed in this chapter only because the topic is WMD rather than Saddam Hussein, though the two are so closely woven together no real cinematic distinction separates them, hence the subtitle, *The Murderous Reign of Saddam Hussein*. This body of film, much like those under the section on Saddam in America's Villains, is a lengthy depiction of Saddam's brutal tyranny of the Iraqi people that is enough, they assert, to justify America's intervention.

Buried in the Sand: The Deception of America (2004) is produced by CYHL (Can You Handle Life) Pictures. It is noteworthy because the deception is placed at Saddam Hussein's feet, not President Bush's. The film does not live up to its stated purpose, however, which narrator Mark Taylor indicates will be "disturbing" because it "presents a perspective never before seen in the national media. . . . A true look into the hearts and minds of our enemies." Alas, not so. Basically, it repeats the litany of horrors performed during Saddam's reign. The focus is on the brutality of the regime and passes over any abuses by Americans by making them look incidental. The American "abuses" at Abu Ghraib prison are viewed as inconsequential, committed "by [a] small number of rogue American military personnel," in comparison to the "30,000 people Saddam Hussein executed here." This point is well taken. It is hammered home by the time devoted to the prison: still photos are quickly shown of the American abuses in a segment lasting a little over 60 seconds while the abuses committed by Saddam are more graphically depicted and nearly thrice as long. In this same vein, other issues are rolled together to make it all appear to be Saddam's doing. We are told or shown the following at the end of the Abu Ghraib segment:

- "Saddam Hussein's oldest son, Uday, used to beat offenders on the bare feet with a cane." This is apparently regularly done for a host of trivial things, like simple grammar mistakes. It is important that this list starts here so the viewer will connect all the other abuses to the regime.
- Three men are shown sitting on the ground being hit with canes. The lashes are relatively mild and all three men get up and run away without being chased.
- A tight shot of someone hooded being shot in the head, public execution style. There is no context, so the punishment is not related to the seriousness of the offense; the viewer is led to conclude that it is likely for some trivial thing, like a grammar mistake.
- A public beheading is shown. It is from Saudi Arabia, not Iraq.
- A stoning is depicted which is described as "extremely barbaric." Such a method of punishment may be barbaric to Western eyes but it is a common method of punishment in Arabic culture, much as hangings (Utah) and the electric chair are in the United States for people who have been convicted of a capital offense, which some have held to be likewise barbaric.

To this end, the photo gallery extras on the DVD are impressive because the viewer gets to linger over the still photographs of abuses that took place under Saddam's twenty-four years in power. This leads to a key question that is seldom addressed: Why after twenty-four years of tyranny did the United States *now* decide to intervene? This film answers that question at the end when a young Palestinian is talking about martyrdom and the narrator talks about how "[America's] defenseless civilians are their target." But now that 9/11 has occurred the extremist will find, as Saddam has, that they "have awoken a sleeping giant," just as the Japanese did after their attack on Pearl Harbor—with similar consequences. "God bless our troops. And God bless the United States of America." The end!

Confronting Iraq: Conflict and Hope (2005) starts with the traditional unfolding of world events that ends with the tragedies on 9/11: Tehran in 1979; Beirut, Lebanon, 1983; the downed airliner in Lockerbie, Scotland, 1988; Kuwait, 1990; Mogadishu, Somalia, 1993 (see *Black Hawk Down*, 2001); Khobar Towers, Saudi Arabia, 1996; Tanzania and Kenya, 1998; Aden, Yemen, 2000.[31] The point of this roll call of catastrophic terrorist attacks on the United States and its allies is that America—notably Carter but especially Clinton—stood by and apparently did nothing. Says James Woosey, first director of the CIA under Clinton, "[The United States] never moved against them . . . [we] just sent in the attorneys." The difference is that finally, today "George W. Bush is willing to fight for a new Middle East."

This film is of interest as it is one of the last loud cries from the conservative right. Increasingly after 2005, there was an onslaught of films that staunchly attacked America's involvement in Iraq. The mood of the country, and the cinematic debate, had clearly shifted in 2006 toward an antiwar sentiment—though as we'll see, not an antimilitary sentiment, à la Vietnam. But in 2005 the Bush administration still held tenuous sway, and *Confronting Iraq* clearly promoted the new party line. In doing so, *Confronting Iraq* stood in opposition to those films that were critical of American involvement.

Confronting Iraq did not sidestep the WMD issue either. It did, however, deal with it summarily and quite accurately, if somewhat misleadingly, by reframing the issue. The talking heads, who are largely published authors of right-wing books on the war, do not say anything about *not* finding WMD. To the rhetorical question, "Did he have weapons of mass destruction?" the answer is an unequivocal, "Yes!" The proof: "He used them against the Kurds, used [them] against Iran." There is not time to digest this misinformation as another person immediately points out "Saddam Hussein was a brutal dictator." Pausing to reflect, however, would indicate that we are now dealing with a postinvasions interpretation of WMD, not a preinvasion one. Preinvasion WMD were construed to be at least short-range and possibly long-range nuclear missiles; WMD are now being constructed as chemical weapons, which Saddam certainly had and did use during the Iran-Iraq conflict, and against the Kurds. The framing of this is very neat. If WMD are defined as chemical weapons then Saddam had them and used them, which is why he is a brutal dictator, and this leads to the inevitable conclusion: If he could have, he would have used them against the United States,

so he had, using Bushesque rhetoric, to "be taken out." Bush's speech
to the United Nations is interspersed throughout this segment. None of
the featured clips contained reference to WMDs, even though WMD
were a prominent part of Bush's rationale before the United Nations to
justify military intervention in Iraq.

Does this mean then that the United States has to become embroiled
with Iran, which is obviously an enemy of the United States and if it
doesn't have nuclear weapons its leaders are certainly making strides
to obtain them? Be assuaged, the narrator tells us, because while that
may be true, "there is no need to attack" since there is "strong internal
opposition to [the] extremist ruling party" that is comprised of students,
women, and "most of [the] clergy." The implication of this segment is
that the United States is in Iraq for a good, solid reason, but this does
not mean it will be embroiled elsewhere, and once things in Iraq settle
down, American troops will be pulled out, the Middle East is now
stable. Syria may pose another problem, so the viewer is simply told it is
a Baathist state to the north of Iraq.

Confronting is illustrative of the new, postinvasion approach to Iraq
from conservatives. It is otherwise a thrice-told story. *The Blood of
My Brother*, on the other hand, is a more nuanced view of the Iraqi
situation. The story revolves around nineteen-year-old Ibrahim whose
brother was ostensibly killed by American soldiers for no apparent reason. It becomes clear as the film progresses that the shooting, though a
tragic accident, was justified. Ibrahim learns from a friend that while it
is true that his brother, Ra'ad, didn't himself have a rifle, his companion
did. His friend uses his fingers to show how the two were walking side
by side and that Ra'ad's companion had a rifle slung over his shoulder
with the muzzle protruding in the air, so it was not possible to tell who
had the weapon, and because they didn't stop when challenged, American soldiers opened fire. Ibrahim refuses to accept this explanation and
steadfastly continues to blame the Americans: "God didn't kill him. The
Americans did."

Though there are scenes in *Blood* that would soften the justification
for American involvement in the region, other, more powerful ones, put
it decidedly in the thesis camp. One shows the Americans busting into a
house in the middle of the night and wrestling the apparently innocent
family to the ground: "Go, go, go! Get down! Get down!" The family is

not innocent, however. A rug covering a trapdoor in the floor is found to contain a cache of weapons. The men are hooded and loaded into a military vehicle. The viewer is forced to interpret the raid and the detention of the men as a justifiable action—had Berends ended the scene excising the trapdoor and showing the men detained after the house intrusion, a different interpretation would be warranted and might have moved the film from the thesis to the antithesis category. The ending likewise reinforces the thesis stance of the film by showing the instability of the region, and hence the necessity for a continued military presence. Masked terrorists are shown thrusting their rifles into the air in Sadir City. They are incited by the infamous cleric, Sayid Moqtada al-Sadar, and as they march down the street to confront Iraqi police, chant in unison, "Mohammad, grant victory to Moqtada. Moqtada! Moqtada!" The concluding scene shows Ibrahim, who has toyed with the idea of joining Sadir's army, at his brother's grave denouncing the infidels: "When I see an American or a Jew, I want to kill him." Any sympathy for the grief of the family at Ra'ad's death is tested by these scenes.

Antithesis: An Unjust War

Two films in this group can be quickly appraised as neither is of particular cinematic significance. *Aftermath* (2004) is a thirty-five-minute montage of talking heads that is produced by the Guerilla News Network whose extreme leftist perspective is readily discerned; they hold the radical Weatherman of the Sixties to be a "unique treasure."[32] Their "guerrilla" format in *Aftermath*, less blatant than in *Battleground: 21 Days on the Empire's Edge* (2004) but still obvious, is best exemplified by their choice of narrator, hip-hop artist Paris. Otherwise, the film simply delineates eleven questions surrounding 9/11 and each is ticked off by an "expert" who raises a specific point. The first question asks, to what extent should the airlines have been prepared for 9/11? The second question ponders just what the Bush administration knew and when did they know it. These two questions are answered by references to historical precedents. In the first case, a similar hijacking took place in Jordan on September 1970, and therefore the airlines are culpable since they should have known this kind of thing could occur; in the second case, the viewer learns that the Pentagon had detailed drills to deal with an airplane striking it, so they therefore knew it was going to happen. The left-wing selectivity of talking heads is as blatant and unconvincing as any of those produced by the right.

Uncovered: The War on Iraq was released near the end of 2004. It is certainly slanted, but its distinction as a film owes more to its crass attempt to cash in on the popularity of Michael Moore's film. It is simply a recycled and slightly extended version of *Uncovered: The Whole Truth about the Iraq War* that was released in 2003 and which was discussed in the "Initial Volleys" section of this chapter: it even has the same cover of a hand drawing back the American flag to uncover the White House (and its secrets) in the background (see also *Rush to War*, 2004). The 2003 version ran fifty-eight minutes and was earmarked for the DVD market; the 2004 version was extended into a ninety-minute film that was theatrically released. The spark that Michael Moore ignited with his film and the theatrical appearance of the re-edited *Uncovered*, plus Robert Greenwald's earlier success in 2004 with *Outfoxed: Rupert Murdoch's War on Journalism*,[33] justify the film commentary of the 2004 release that escaped the 2003 version. Generally, however, most film commentators sided with Ward Harkavy at the *Village Voice* who found there "are some fascinating *nuggets* to be fished out of the flash flood of quotes" (author's italics) but that the film generally lacked any substantive narrative thread.[34]

Why We Fight is accorded a higher order by film commentators largely because it is done with a deft hand by director Eugene Jarecki, who did *The Trials of Henry Kissinger* (2002), and because of its skillful editing. It won the Sundance Grand Prize in the documentary category in 2005. It is also very popular; it is rated just out of the top ten tiers of grossing documentaries at the number eleven spot.

Why We Fight (2005) takes its name from Frank Capra's series of World War II films. For those conversant with Capra's films, the title suggests a strong prowar approach: the allies (coalition forces) are fighting to rid the world of tyranny. The choice of titles is provocative precisely because it goes against type. Most film critics found the treatment insightful.

> I can't think of a better way to kick off the new movie year than with Eugene Jarecki's potent provocation to see what's right in front of us. . . .

Table 2.3. Other Iraq-Related Top 100 Political Documentary Films

Rank	Title	Gross Box-Office Revenue (Rounded Millions)
11	Why We Fight*	$1.4
12	No End in Sight	$1.4
14	Where in the World Is Osama Bin Laden?	$.4
28	Taxi to the Dark Side	$.3
30	The War Tapes	$.3
32	Uncovered: The War on Iraq*	$.2
34	Iraq in Fragments	$.2
51	Body of War	$.07
54	Voices of Iraq*	$.06
56	Weapons of Mass Deception*	$.04
85	The Prisoner, or: How I Planned to Kill Tony Blair	$.02
92	Return to the Land of Wonders*	$.04

*Films critiqued in this chapter

Source: www.boxofficemojo.com

Jarecki's film—fluidly edited by Nancy Kennedy—mounts a strong case against those who would exploit patriotism and human lives as a business proposition.[35]

A parade of [incisive] sound bites lays out American foreign policy from President Kennedy to the second President Bush, and Jarecki masterfully maps the simultaneously expanding militarism, first as a reaction to the growth of communism and later propelled by the war on terror.[36]

Jarecki's passion enlivens the stream of historical images and statistics, and he knows the persuasive value of an image (cue the video footage of Rumsfeld shaking hands with Saddam Hussein in 1983).[37]

Their points are well taken, but so too is Roger Ebert's, who acknowledges the film's "skillful assembly of its materials" but feels it falls flat as a documentary because it adds little after it makes its initial point regarding the military-industrial complex.[38] The truth, as it often does, lies somewhere in-between.

The film starts with the televised farewell address to the nation by President Eisenhower in 1961. It was the first time the military-industrial complex had been publicly linked in such a nefarious way. Eisenhower issued a stern warning about the dangers of such an alliance. His

concerns carried particular weight because of his long and distinguished
military career. Ebert argues that the rest of the movie is anticlimactic
since it adds little to what we already know, the military-industrial complex becoming such a staple since Eisenhower left office. Nevertheless,
many younger viewers (less than fifty) have a feeble grasp of history.[39]
A report card issued by the Intercollegiate Studies Institute after conducting a random sample of 2,508 Americans on their basic knowledge
of America's "founding principles and texts, core history, and enduring
intuitions," ISI's basic definition of civic literacy, gave a D to 17.8 percent of the respondents and an F to 71.4 percent.[40] This suggests it *is*
necessary to drive the historical point home, and to do so utilizing the
contemporary visual medium of film. However, the historical connection that many critics applaud is the film's greatest weakness. It is close
to nonexistent. The only depth of the historical development of the military-industrial progression occurs two-thirds of the way through the film
when we are told that putting land forces into a country "is a ritual we've
been seeing for decades." This is stated over a map montage stamped
with dates and places that the United States has been embroiled in. The
implication is that all such involvement has been financially motivated,
starting with Guatemala in 1954 and then in rapid-fire chronological
order: Lebanon, Cuba, the Congo, Dominican Republic, Indonesia,
Cambodia, Chile, Angola, Afghanistan Libya, Nigeria, Angola (again),
El Salvador, Grenada, Chile (again), Bolivia, Panama, Sudan, Yemen,
Philippines, and ending with Haiti in 2004. There is no time for reflection as to American involvement in any of these countries. It is all laid
at the feet of the military-industrial complex. The connection is made
emphatic at the end of this roll call of empire building by airing a Halliburton promotional film from 1951 that shows the United States is in
the Middle East because of the money to be made from oil (see also *The
Oil Factor*, 2005).

The driving point behind *Why We Fight* is clearly made, if sometimes
overplayed. In one early scene, for example, some children are asked
what we are fighting for and they proudly and smilingly both proclaim
"freedom." Later, the astute viewer will notice that when this setting is
reframed a third of the way through the film, the children are now "situ-
ated": They were attending an aerial display by the Blue Angels on the
military base at Pensacola, Florida, where the word "freedom" had no

doubt been widely bantered about in the festivities entitled, a "Celebration for Freedom." But the viewer is led to believe—and we are later explicitly told—that "freedom [today] is simply a platitude . . . [relied upon solely] to expand the American empire. We are the new Rome!"

Why We Fight is no more distorted than any other documentary film that has been examined in this series. It is lifted above some of the other films because it does manage, David Ansen at *Newsweek* argues, "to look beyond individual villains," where so many of the other films wallow, and examines "the bigger idea: that we've become an empire in the thrall of a system whose economic survival depends on preparing for, and waging constant war."[41]

Despite the big picture approach *Why We Fight* takes, the most successful aspect of this film is accomplished at the individual level. The viewer meets Witon Sekzer on a subway ride into New York City; as the subway rounds a corner, he gazes out the window to where the Twin Towers once stood. Sekzer is a retired New York City police officer who lost his son on 9/11. Sekzer wants vengeance. The early introduction of Sekzer suggests that this "why we fight" analysis is going to follow the Capra tradition: "I want to see their [those responsible] bodies stacked up for taking my son." A clip of Bush standing amid the debris of the WTC appears immediately after Sekzer's statement. "The people," Bush says, "who knocked these buildings down will hear [from] us soon." His proclamation is greeted with wild cheers from those working the site, followed by their chants, "USA . . . USA. . . ." One suspects that if Sekzer were among the throngs, he'd be chanting too. Later we learn he feels a sense of justice because his letters to those in power at the Pentagon have been answered and his son's name was put on a bomb. Pictures are sent to him that show his son's name scrawled on a precision bomb—"In loving memory of Jason Sekzer"—with a note that read it was dropped on April 1 with "100 percent success."

Sekzer's anger turns well into the film as he becomes enlightened. The fault does not lie without; it is the fault of the military-industrial complex. Near the conclusion of the film, over an inserted clip of the president speaking on television, he hears the president belatedly acknowledging that there is now "no evidence Iraq [was] involved in 9/11." Sekzer says his first thought was, "You're [Bush] a goddamn liar. . . . I'm from the old school [Vietnam vet]. Certain people walk on water. The president of the United States is one of them. If I cannot trust the president of the United States . . ." he pauses, and then continues, shaking his head, "I don't know. Terrible! The government exploited my feelings of patriotism, of a deep desire for revenge . . . and I was [so] insane in wanting to get even, I'd believe anything."

Sekzer's dismay is mimicked by a parade of experts that have been seen throughout the film, each re-lamenting America's involvement. Ike is again heard giving his dire warning about the military-industrial complex. Retired Lieutenant Colonel Karen Kwiatkowski gives the final summation as the screen goes dark: "So, why do we fight? I think we fight because too many people are not standing up saying, I'm not doing this anymore" (see *Network*, 1976).

Why We Fight focuses on the overreaching military-industrial complex. This is the reason it stands out. It is the only film that directly, and at some length, addresses this issue and this is, at least in part, the reason for its success (see Table 2.3). The misleading of Americans that is raised at the end of *Why*, is addressed in *WMD: Weapons of Mass Deception* (2004).

Deception has strong parallels to *Outfoxed*. Both analyze the media and how it distorts the news. The reason *Deception* is critiqued in this section and not the more successful *Outfoxed* (no. 20) is that *Deception* (no. 56) focuses on the media's misinformation as it revolves around 9/11-related events while *Outfoxed*, though it touches on this issue, is more of an analysis of how Fox News distorts information in general.

The director, Danny Schechter, bears an unsettling resemblance to Michael Moore, both in his disheveled appearance and in his brusque manner. The subject matter had been touched upon earlier: it was raised by the 9/11 Commission Report in June 2003 and was a central motif of the first *Uncovered* film in 2003. By 2004, when this film was released, it was becoming more of a public issue.

Deception does not add significantly to what was known at the time. Nor does it succeed in painting a solid picture of how news is mangled. Indeed, the critique of how the news mismanages information has a long and tarnished history.[42] The director himself edited a book with William Browning on the subject, *The More You Watch, The Less You Know* (1997). The problem with the film is that there is no coherence, or, as Ned Martel at the *New York Times* put it, the film is an "uneven, unpolished documentary . . . [that] takes on far too many antagonists."[43] One of these antagonists, Fox News, is also an easy target that is more successful and cogently assessed in *Outfoxed*. Schechter does raise some valid points about the issue of embedding that will be taken up later in this chapter, but these issues had wide circulation among journalists even before the invasion and had wide social currency by the time this film was produced. There are some nuggets among the barrage of outtakes, such as an early name bantered about for *Operation Iraq Freedom—Operation Iraq Liberation*—which was discarded because of the questionable acronym (OIL), or how Michael Wolf of *Vanity Fair* raised the issue of journalists being corralled for debriefings during the Iraq war and was shown being told by the military debriefed to "shut the fuck up." Such nuggets, however, are not enough to make *Deception* of particular cinematic interest; however, the film does have a certain amount of popular appeal, judged simply by its slot in the top 100 grossing political documentaries.

In the final analysis, *Deception*'s unevenness may be owing to Schechter's rush to cash in on a hot topic; the end result, a hastily edited and somewhat choppy film (see also *Fire over Afghanistan*, 2003),[44] further encumbered by the time and attention devoted to Schechter as the focal point of the story. At the same time, the topicality of the film also helps make the film mildly successful. His film credits indicate he is finely attuned to topical issues: as the economy became *the* issue that would eventually sweep Obama into office, Schechter made *In Debt We Trust* (2006; see also Michael Moore's *Capitalism, A Love Story*, 2009), and as Obama's popularity soared after capturing the presidency in 2008, Schechter hastily assembled *Barack Obama: The People's President* (2009). His hot topic savvy is undoubtedly linked to his days as a producer for some of ABC's topical "20/20" programs. This fast-track television connection is a double-edged sword: It helps account for the success of his films in the public domain, but it also accounts for his lackluster achievement as a craftsman of documentary films.[45]

Synthesis: *The War Within*

The Day After was a 1983 television movie about the effects of a nuclear attack on the United States. It garnered considerable attention before it was released. The conservatives didn't want it to be televised because they feared that it would turn people against the arms race then in progress. The liberals wanted it aired for just that reason: They felt it would show the consequences of a nuclear arms race and rally people against the continued arms buildup. The day after it aired, both camps were satisfied. The conservatives felt it clearly showed what would happen if the United States did not have a viable nuclear capacity to deter such an attack. The liberals felt it clearly showed the logical consequences to the existing arms race. In short, what is depicted on screen tends to be interpreted through the prism of one's existing beliefs. Such is the case with *The War Within* where conservatives can see it as a validation of their concerns that America continues to be threatened by extremist groups; the liberals will see this as affirmation that the problem of terrorism is created by American foreign policy, and to defeat terrorism requires a dramatic change in Bush-era politics (see also *Last Letters Home*, 2004).[46] Neither perspective is addressed in such a trenchant manner in any of the other films to date. In this sense, it offers a kind of synthesis because it gives relatively equal weight to both points of view.

The War Within is about the threat posed within the borders of the United States by a suicide bomber. The bomber was created by America, however. A Pakistani is suddenly mugged and thrown into the back of a van as he walks leisurely down the streets of the Latin Quarter in Paris. Hassan (Ayad Akhtar) is taken to an unknown destination in Pakistan where he awakens in a dark cell. An unseen inmate quips, "Welcome to Karachi, brother," to which Hassan replies, in an often repeated lament made during his torture and imprisonment, "I didn't do anything." "Makes no difference," the voice says in French, and tells him not to despair, "The Brotherhood is here for you." Hassan snaps, "I don't want to have a fucking thing to do with your Brotherhood." But after being abused for information he does not have—and in flashbacks we get an idea of the extent of some of the torture inflicted when his captors ignite a blowtorch—he makes an ardent member.

Hassan is then seen, three years later, arriving secretly in a shipboard container at Port Authority in New York Harbor. His target is Grand Central Station. He reunites with an old boyhood friend, Sayeed (Firdous Bamji) and stays with him and his family until he has a chance to fulfill his destiny. Sayeed is thoroughly Americanized and cannot under-stand his anger, or the reason for his extremism. In one scene, Sayeed asks, "How did you become so pious?" to which Hassan retorts, "When did you forget your heritage?"

The director, Joseph Castelo, could have made Hassan's pilgrimage to Grand Central Station the focus of his film. Such a focal point could easily carry the film—it was accomplished, as will be seen later in this chapter, by Hany Abu-Assad in *Paradise Now* (2005). There are enough obstacles and interruptions in Hassan's hajji (pilgrimage) to Grand Central that would allow for this single-focus depiction to be dramatically successful. The stopover with the family is, however, important to the message. It vividly shows the assimilation of Muslims in America. In fact, Sayeed is so fully assimilated that when he ultimately learns that Hassan is making a bomb in the basement, he calls the FBI and turns him in as a terrorist. The irony, purposely framed, is that because Say-eed is a Muslim foreigner the FBI takes him into custody.

The film ends with Hassan fulfilling his destiny. He is seen walking down 42nd Street on his way to Grand Central. He passes a cluster of American flags attached to a pole, waving in the breeze. An illuminated marquee in the background reads, "Democracy is best taught by ex-ample, not by war." Standing in the midst of Grand Central Station, he silently mouths prayers, while his trembling hand alights on the button to detonate the explosives strapped to his chest. The film goes dark, but it is not over. A television announcer appears and says that a suicide bomber has struck; it is the first of its kind to occur in the United States. The number of causalities is not yet known. Sayeed's face is shown, and we are told that he's been arrested because he was "harboring the bomber."

Robert Koehler, writing for *Variety*, found it difficult to believe that a "Pakistani cell is able to work in security-conscious Gotham to craft a plan to detonate several bridges and Grand Central Station."[47] But that is the point: The United States remains vulnerable, and despite increased security, terrorism is still a threat. This is precisely why a conservative watching the movie would proclaim that the United States must remain eternally vigilant. And while one lone bomber, Hassan, did get through, the terrorist cell itself was disrupted and many of the extremists caught before they could do the damage they had in mind. Flipping this over and looking at it from the liberal perspective, the ending is chilling, and finishes where it started: an innocent man is suddenly seized and imprisoned. The ending suggests that the United States propagates terrorism by rounding up people like Hassan, and possibly Sayeed, and turning them against principles they once applauded. It is, to be sure, a low-budget movie and tends to overaccentuate its points, which is why Owen Gleiberman at *Entertainment Weekly* assigned it a B–.[48] Nevertheless, it "is quite a movie," writes Teresa Wiltz with the *Washington Post*, which is precisely why the dark, somber tones of the movie are so successful; they serve to both "foster a chilling sense of growing menace and to reflect Hassan's turmoil, his war within, as he struggles with his conscience and his faith."[49]

VIEWS FROM THE FRONT

The front has been seen only peripherally in cinema to this point in those villain films where soldiers searched for Saddam Hussein and Osama bin Laden. The films in this section examine in greater detail what is taking place on the front lines in Iraq. The initial footage of coalition forces crossing the border into Iraq and marching toward Baghdad is already familiar to most viewers who watched the stories unfold on the nightly television news. The films in this section likewise depict the "March to Baghdad" progression. But if that were all they did, they would have little documentary worth. They go beyond the initial move into Iraq, however, by doing three things that are crucial to the documentary tale: (1) the films give the viewer insight into the lives of the men and women fighting by tracing their military career before they went into combat; (2) they show the effects on the lives of family members left behind; and (3) they provide insight into how the combat experience and extended stay in Iraq has affected the worldview of those who served overseas during this early period. The following movies are the viewer's first in-depth look at those fighting in Iraq: *Soldier's Pay* (2004); *Battlefield Diaries: Kiowa Down* (2004); *Gunner Palace* (2005); *Off to War: From Rural Arkansas to Iraq* (2005); *Occupation: Dreamland* (2005).

When one thinks of the war in Iraq, one thinks of those in the military who are stationed in Iraq. The viewer is reminded in this second grouping of films that there are others on the front lines. This group of films focuses less on the solider than on the journalists who covered the war. The issue of embedding arises in these films and the answers that are verbally given by journalists at the front do not "line up" with the visual context that the viewer sees. These films are meant to show how journalists also sacrificed to cover the war to bring it to viewers back home. The following films are the journalists' stories, and they are not pretty: *War Feels Like War* (2004); *Inside Iraq: The Untold Stories* (2004); *War with Iraq: Stories from the Front* (2004).

The Grunt's View

Soldier's Pay is the first to address the plight of the grunt. It is produced by David O. Russell (with Tricia Regan and Juan Carlos Zaldivar) who made the successful *Three Kings* (1999) movie about Gulf War I that starred George Clooney and Ice Cube. It is a scant thirty-five minutes which keeps it from being theatrically released. The film was intended as bonus material to the *Three Kings* DVD re-release, but, sensitive to the political climate, Warner Brothers decided against including it. It was subsequently released by Cinema Libre, who was also responsible for *Outfoxed* and *Uncovered: The War in Iraq*, both by Robert Greenwald, and whose logo clearly indicates it has a mission to accomplish: "Opening Eyes and Minds One Film at a Time." The film did ultimately debut on the Independent Film Channel. Russell was certainly correct when he proclaimed his short to be cinematically "nothing fancy."

Though a documentary, *Soldier's Pay* is strongly linked to *Three Kings*. The three primary Arabic spokespeople who voice their opinion in *Soldier's Pay* were all extras in *Three Kings*. The resemblance goes beyond a cast reunion, however. The storyline of *Soldier's Pay* is reminiscent of the cynical plot of *Three Kings* and, like *Three Kings*, deals with common soldiers trying to cope and who end up having to make a moral decision.

Both film plots revolve around looting: gold bullion in *Three Kings*, dollars in *Soldier's Pay*. This is not a *Three Kings* movie, however. This film opens with one of the central themes that all the other films in this section underscore: no one wants to be there, no one really cares, and all are in the military because they have no other life options. Perhaps the most cinematic noteworthy depiction in the film is a speech by President Bush about the need to "demonstrate civilized behavior"—appar-

Cultural insensitivity from *Soldier's Pay*.

ently to these backward Bedouins, whose history stretches back five thousand years—over a picture of a grunt standing before the scribbling on a wall, which reads, "Ha! Ha! Our God is better than your God." The picture of the scrawl is followed by Major General J. Michael Myatt (USMC, retired) lamenting the very *un*civilized behavior of American MPs that took place at Abu Ghraib: "the darkest cloud to descend on the military in my lifetime."

Another dark hour in this ostensibly balanced portrait of a soldier's life revolves around the looting of the Iranian national museum while Secretary of Defense Donald Rumsfeld ruminates, and in so doing devalues the historical significance of the objects destroyed: "My goodness, were there that many vases? Is it possible there were that many vases in the whole city?" His cavalier comment dismisses the historical significant of the objects destroyed. But the darkest hour of all is spent over the moral crisis of two ordinary soldiers, Specialist Jamal Mann and Sergeant Matt Novak who found the pot of gold: 320 million American dollars under the floorboards in a raid. They stuffed as much as they could in their uniforms: "it was coming out everywhere," says Mann.

Their surprise was not at their behavior but that so many others "didn't take a dime."

Eventually, someone figures it out and they were read their rights. CID investigator James Mead, in a statement seen in the *L.A. Times*, said in an interview that Sergeant Novak came forth with the complete truth after being offered amnesty, and "the information that he gave us did identify additional subjects." The end result, however, was that his Commanding General did not feel the amnesty was appropriate and Novak was dishonorably discharged. So, the narrator asks Novak, "Are you the fall guy?" to which Novak nods adamantly, "I *am* the fall guy!" A crawl indicates he was unjustly vilified by citing his record: twelve years of service in both Gulf Wars I and II, eighteen medals, combat and service ribbons, "and just the month before [his discharge] he was awarded the army achievement medal for 'exceptional performance' during the war." The film then nears its conclusion by suggesting Novak was the fall guy (despite his guilt) because other money has disappeared. This leads to a rather tenuous connection: the $1.7 billion in contracts that Halliburton has been awarded—stolen is the implication; this, the viewer is told, amounts to one-third of the $3.9 billion allocated to fight the war in Iraq.

The film does not fail to mention Vice President Cheney's association with Halliburton. It concludes by mentioning the inflated incomes of Halliburton employees, who make twenty times the amount the combat solider makes, and yet it is the soldiers who are the ones who put their lives on the line and, ironically, are the ones who have to protect the Halliburton employees.

A connection not made—the silence—in all these films is that for the "grunt on the front," the E-2s, 3s, and 4s (privates, specialists, corporals), low pay is quite common, even when those who hold these ranks are the most common on the front lines, and the ones who are most likely to pay the final price (see also *Last Letters Home*, 2004). This is as true of any of the wars since World War II (if not before) and is not unique to contemporary military action in Iraq or Afghanistan. Unlike previous wars, inclusive of Vietnam, the "quality" of the soldier is, at least insofar as their occupational versatility is concerned, more limited. The draft equalized the ranks: one was as likely to be in a foxhole with a store manager as a mechanic. The all-volunteer army recruits are largely going-no-wheres. All the films in this section make this clear, though the point is not dwelt on. When asked in *Occupation: Dreamland* why they joined, one after another says, "Didn't have any money"; "Didn't know what [I was] gonna do with [my] life," to which another immediately agrees; another says, that he was in college studying liberal arts, "Yeah," another chimes in, "a bull shit degree." One admits, "Well, [I was] not a model citizen before [joining]." In *Off to War*, one member of the group from home joined because his buddies were. He was accepted but before deploying was [undesirably] discharged. It is clear that he slipped through the crack in the military's need to find recruits—an issue scathingly addressed in *Fahrenheit 9/11*—and that not only was he in difficultly with the law, but he has some severe psychological problems. The "quality" of the recruits is more of a central theme in *Occupation: Dreamland* than the other two movies that depict life on the front line. It is important to point out that while many might have joined because of limited life options, none of the films purposely or directly demean them. The military is viewed as a way out, a means to occupationally move forward. Many see it as a means, with their limited income, to, once discharged, get an education; others are promoted or get special training and remain in the military.

Regardless of their educational attainment or occupational future, these men and women have one key thing in common with military personnel in combat situations across time. They may not wish to be there, but they are there and they will do the job they have to do; nevertheless, the overriding goal at the moment is to just stay alive (see also *Kiowa Down*, 2004).

Gunner Palace is the first to really give a detailed look at the combat soldier's life—not just news journalists clips of an isolated military action. The title takes its name from the gunner's new place of residence in Baghdad, a former palace of Uday, now occupied by the 2/3 Field Artillery: 2nd battalion, 3rd field artillery regiment, 1st armored division. The reality of war is contrasted throughout with the out-of-touch world back in Washington. The tone is established in the opening voice-over crawl, repeated here in full:

9/5/2003 Baghdad, Iraq

Greetings to the Iraqi People

Hello, I'm Donald Rumsfeld, the United States Secretary of Defense. It is a pleasure to be back in your country.

When I visited four months ago, the regime of Saddam Hussein had just fallen—and I was pleased to be able to celebrate your liberation with you.

The changes that have taken place since then are extraordinary.

Baghdad is bustling with commerce.

[See cameraman taping generally empty main commercial street; then see two men with firearms, followed by intermittent shooting.]

[Crawl continues with Rumsfeld speaking.]

Major combat operations ended four months ago.

[The voice-over ends. The crawl concludes.]

THIS IS MINOR COMBAT

At first, combat doesn't look all that bad. The now militarized palace seems like a grand place to be stationed. We're given a tour by the "mayor" of Gunner Palace, Specialist Jessie Potts, where, we hear from a voice-over from back home, morale is high and troops [are] dedicated to getting the job done." Uday's luxurious swimming pool is shown where some of the four hundred men and women stationed at Gunner Palace are enjoying a swim, while others are putting on a makeshift golf green. Later, as some of the palace's contingent rides though the city, waving to some of the people on the street from atop their trucks behind the mounted weapons, we're told, "Here they have to be policemen, social workers, politicians." The fun, however, is short-lived as much of the rest of the film shows.

Contrasting worlds are constantly depicted. In one scene an explosion occurs. "What the hell was that?" the civilian narrator asks. "Just an RPG" (rocket propelled grenade), we learn, to a voice-over from home by Rumsfeld, "Coalition forces are making steady and remarkable progress toward stability in Iraq." In a related scene, Rumsfeld is heard saying, "Iraqis [are] coming forward with useful information and that's led to scores of raids," while we watch soldiers taping "most wanted" reward posters of Saddam Hussein to poles down a main thoroughfare. The point, should anyone miss it, is driven home by the closing question of various soldiers in close-up shots. In response to the question, "Do people understand [back home]?" we learn that there is not a remote possibility: "At home [they're sitting] on [the] couch watching TV complaining because [the] pizza's five minutes late. No way [are they] gonna be sympathetic to this. . . . After watching this film, they'll go get their popcorn out of the microwave and talk about what I say, and then forget."

The film closes where it began, finding it necessary to accentuate the point, which is driven home throughout, just in case anyone missed it. It closes with a crawl from Specialist (SPC) Stuart Wilf, who not only was featured in the film but coincidentally was one of the three soldiers to appear on *Time Magazine's* cover for "person of the year" (along with a female soldier who is one of the few females to appear in any of the films).[50] The date of Wilf's closing comment in *Gunner Palace* is April 10, 2004, almost a year after Rumsfeld's opening remark that major combat operations had ended: "Tell the politicians back home that are sitting around their dinner table talking about how hard the war is on them that we're under attack twenty-four hours a day, not fighting for Iraq, but simply to stay alive."

Unlike *Gunner Palace*, which received considerable critical commentary, *Off to War: From Rural Arkansas to Iraq*, a ten-part series that runs close to eight hours (four discs), received scant critical attention. The lack of critical attention is related to its debut on the Discovery Channel, one of the smaller cable networks. It is also a rather choppy film to watch in installments on television; ironically, it is a bit of a marathon to watch on DVD, especially because it does not significantly add to the viewer's knowledge about life on the front.

Off to War follows the exploits of a handful of members from the Arkansas National Guard as they deploy to Iraq. The choice of Arkansas guardsmen was simply because the directors, Brent and Craig Renaud, are themselves from the Mockingbird State, grew up in Little Rock, and know someone who was a retired ranking officer in the Guard; they also had many childhood friends in the Guard who were about to be deployed in the largest (3,000) call up in Arkansas since the Korean War. Appropriately, each episode opens with Springsteen singing "Small Town Boy."

Philosophical discussion in *Occupation: Dreamland*.

The life of the soldier is more cogently depicted in *Gunner Palace* and *Operation: Dreamland* (see also *This Is War: Memories of Iraq*, 2007). *Off to War* adds little to the other films in its depiction of a soldier's life at the front: "Even roughest neighborhoods back home," one guardsmen says, cannot hold a candle to what they're seeing in Iraq; another, commenting on the Arabic spoken in the streets, "You know they're talking

Grunts in *Occupation: Dreamland*.

shit, you just don't know what they're saying"; another quips in the best, wanna-get-out-of-here tradition, "I will kill anyone here who will keep me from going home without even thinking about it." *Off to War* goes beyond the other films, however, because it is one of the few that captures the input and impact of deployment on the families. The viewer gets to know their families. In fact, the first episode is more about the families than the men. The families are also interspersed throughout the film, so while we are watching someone in the two-by-four-foot space in the barracks writing home, we get to see their loved ones reading the letter and interpreting its effect on *their* lives back home. For example, in one back-and-forth scene, we see the strains on a young couple's marriage: He makes a call home, the conversation is terse, then the viewer listens to his comments about their relationship, then we get to hear her comments about the relationship. In another husband-wife exchange, the viewer learns that Sergeant Betts, who is shown in one scene reading from a Bible, is told by his wife that he is having the church he built taken from him, despite having been promised that he would not be permanently replaced while stationed overseas.

The Guardsmen angle is also unique to this film, though it is far from a focal point. Many military personnel serving in Iraq are from the National Guard. This one is one of the few films to specifically address the consequences of the guardsmen status, on the men serving and on those who remain at home. The viewer is reminded, if only incidentally, that many guardsmen are vastly unsuited for military duty, having joined the Guard, as many have historically done, for financial reasons, to pick up a few dollars, with no realization that they would actually be activated. Standing in formation after being called up, the drill sergeant welcomes them to Ft. Hood and explains military life to them: "[It's quite] simple. [Just] be there when you are supposed to be there . . . and turn [those] stupid cell phones off!" An officer explains small arms weapons training to them: "Sorta like a laser game . . . you're 'dead' when [the] laser hits," then, turning toward the narrator, "They never had to do this stuff [in the Guard]."

The troops never come off badly in these movies. Sometimes they are insensitive to the Iraqi people, and often they are calloused because of the work they have to do: "These people don't appreciate anything we're doing [for them]," says a soldier in *Off to War*," they couldn't care less

. . . they just want to watch us die. Makes me sick." A soldier at Gate 2 in *Gunner Palace* who has to decide whether the information locals are bringing is reliable and he should admit them to the palace or turn them away, laughs when he recalls how he pulled his weapon on one big, 6'2" man who was giving him a hard time, and, then mimicking the Iraqi's behavior, showed how the civilian started to cry and whimper. These scenes are often counterbalanced with attempts to understand and help the locals: a grunt in *Operation: Dreamland* remarks that he "Cannot blame them for not really wanting us here . . . gotta admit, we're pretty fuckin' intimidating when we roll in, weapons pointed . . . [guess] they have to fight back." Another in *Dreamland* says that rounding up and taking women and children into custody is "indecent."[51] The ultimate depiction is that they are simply doing their job and trying to make the best of a bad situation. The reporters who were embedded with the troops say pretty much the same thing: covering the war is a job that's got to be done. Their view of the war, however, is distinctly different from the soldier's views.

The Reporter's View

The movie *21 Days to Baghdad* (2003) was one of the initial volleys that showed the effect of embedding on the journalists. The films in this section do not significantly differ in the way the journalists see the troops with whom they are embedded. *War with Iraq: Stories from the Front* (2004) is similar to *21 Days* because it too is little more than threaded together segments that had initially appeared on the ABC Nightly News. *War with Iraq* is slightly different only because it dissects the contribution of each branch of the military: the Air Force, then the Army and Marines in some detail, concluding with the Navy. The impact of embedding is clearly seen, despite Peter Jennings's cutely turned phrase that this does not mean journalists are in bed with the military; embedding, he states, simply allows a better view of the battlefield than one would normally get, and this allows the viewers to watch the war in real time. Still, it seems that the journalists, "cannot say enough good things" about their [Air Force] helpfulness, and proceed to glowingly describe military personnel; for example, the viewer is told that Major General Blount [USAF] is the "quintessential [leader]: a tall Mississippian with a soft voice . . . [there's] also Lt. Col. 'Rock' Marcone, who graduated from West Point where he played football, but [nevertheless] is a 'no-nonsense guy.' And tough!" And even though he's in charge of Charlie Company, he's still "a real good guy." Death occurs, but it is depicted hygienically. The viewer is told that one young Marine steps on a mine: too bad, he was really a nice kid, the "most well-liked in [the] company." He died in the helicopter on the way to the hospital—out of sight! Somberly, the viewer is told, "This is serious, serious business."

It was interesting to see in this four-hour, three-disc set how the Navy was depicted since Iraq is a land war. They are given precious little space, but have to be included since it is about the various military branches. Their very short fifteen minutes of fame boils down to watching "red shirts" on the flight deck flagging jets down on a carrier; later, the journalist aboard is shown being taken by the XO (Executive Officer) into the sonar room so he could see "the real shock and awe" that was taking place over Iraq on television. There is a touch of irony in this section: The journalist is in the war zone but has to watch the war he is reporting about on television.

To give grit to all the segments in *War with Iraq*, each embedded journalist finds it necessary to establish the significance of the unit they are following: Bob Woodruff says the members in his unit are "getting ready [in Kuwait] . . . they'll be the tip of the spear, at front edge of attack. Likely to be first if there is a war." John Berman, following the 3/2 (3rd battalion, 2nd regiment), says of his unit, "these guys might be the first to cross into Iraq"; Ronald Claiborne aboard the *Abraham Lincoln* says the fleet was on its way home when it received new orders to steam toward the Gulf: "It's coming," Vice Admiral Keating is shown saying to the crew, "Get ready!" This is classic television on DVD; if it is not first, it is not newsworthy.

At the start of the war, the issue of whether journalists would be affected by being embedded with troops was widely debated. In the aftermath of the war, the effect of embedding is now clear—it altered how journalists reported the stories. Lindner did a random content analysis of 742 articles written by 156 journalists (March 2003–May 2003) to determine if the coverage by embedded journalists was any different than that covered by independent journalists.[52] Embedded journalists tended to focus on the perspective of the soldiers they were with while

Baghdad-based reporters best captured the Iraqi experience; independent reporters, he argues, "were able to report on both . . . [and also] produced, on the whole, the most balanced reporting [and used more varied sources] of the war [even though] embedded reporting with its more limited view was the dominant journalistic vantage point in this war."[53] These videos support the research by *showing* just how journalists were influenced. These particular videos do more, however. They show what might be called the "Roland Hedley factor," named after the less-than-intrepid journalist who covers the Iraq war in *Doonesbury*.

It is really tough out there in the field, one reporter after another proclaims. After all, it's "not fun" when "you have to learn how to not shower for two to four weeks at a time"—curiously shown over a picture of a solider bathing in a makeshift field shower. One has to "learn to live with a lot less . . . and learn [a] whole new set of interpersonal skills," which means, aboard ship in this film, "you had to share [a] room [sic] with sixty other guys. . . . We were all in the same boat, literally and figuratively."

They are really not literally in the same boat, however. They are not being shot at and often protected by the soldiers they cover. They are not at the same risk of being killed. It is true that a number of journalists lost their lives in Iraq, but that is a rare event. One reason for this is that they are *not* out there in the field. This is very clear in *War Feels Like War*, a sixty-minute documentary produced by InFocus Produc-

Table 2.4. Journalists Killed in Iraq (Motive Confirmed)

Year	Deaths
2003	14
2004	24
2005	23
2006	32
2007	32
2008	11
2009	4
2010	5
Total	145

Note: (1) The majority of journalists killed were Iraqi (83.6%); (2) Five percent (n = 7) of all those who were killed were embedded; (3) Two journalists (1.5%) were American; 13 (9%) were European.

Source: Committee to Protect Journalists, www.cpj.org/reports/2008/07/journalists-killed-in-iraq

Table 2.5.   Coalition Military Fatalities in Iraq

Year	US	UK	Other	Total
2003	486	53	41	580
2004	849	22	35	906
2005	846	23	28	897
2006	822	29	21	872
2007	904	47	10	961
2008	314	4	4	322
2009	150	1	0	151
2010	60	0	0	211
Total	4,431	179	139	4,749

Source: Iraq Coalition Casualty Count, www.icasualties.org

tions for the BBC. Despite its name, the film never manages to capture the feeling of war. This may be because the journalists spend most of their time at the Baghdad Hilton, and despite occasional blackouts, they are well comforted, having rooms with clean sheets, a well-stocked bar in the lobby where they fraternize with each other over drinks and hot food while someone plays the grand piano that sits in the corner (see *Liberace of Baghdad*, 2005). So far removed are they from the war that they cannot wait to see a dead body: "The whole time we've been here [we] hadn't really seen dead people," one journalist says, who is excited, and quite pleased, that they finally get pictures of some wounded civilians in a hospital.

"That was fun," says another about her exploits on the front line: shots are heard in the distance; she ducks behind a pile of sandbags with a silly grin on her face; sticks her head over the top of the pile, tentatively steps from behind the sandbags, more shots [not at her], she jumps back behind the sandbags; a long moment passes, then she darts toward a car with a "press" sticker affixed to the front windshield; the car roars off while she idiotically laughs (see *Oh, What a Lovely War*, 1969). In another scene, on the road to Baghdad, the journalist's car is waived over by a military policeman (MP), a rifle in his other hand. The photojournalist gets out of the car while he directs traffic and stands in the middle of the road taking snapshots. The MP from the 101st Airborne frantically waves her back to her vehicle. As she ambles toward her car he shouts at her, "You're going to get us killed. Stop it!"

In the end, these journalists are much too pampered to want to really be on the front line, a point some, but all too few, have made.[54] This is nicely summarized toward the end of *War Feels Like War* as the journalist's car pulls up to the Tikrit checkpoint, one of the more dangerous areas in Iraq at the time. The MP suggests they go back. He's asked, "So, do you think it is just way too dangerous? I mean, I just don't really want to get shot. We want to cover [the] story, but not if it's dangerous." She asks if the road is protected if they decide to proceed and is told that the "road is not constantly covered by military personnel. It's war. . . . If it was me, I wouldn't go up there without a gun." The journalist turns around and returns to the Baghdad Hilton.

The journalist in *War Feels Like War* may not be particularly intrepid, but they are in Iraq. *The War Tapes* (2006; see also *Bad Voodoo's War*, 2007)[55] may be the ultimate journalist prophylactic and is the reason these later films are critiqued here. In *The War Tapes* three National Guardsmen attached minicams to their helmets, gun turrets, and dashboards to record their experiences as they moved about in Iraq. One thousand hours of footage was edited down to a ninety-minute documentary by the self-styled virtual filmmaker, Deborah Scranton, from the comforts of her mountain home in New Hampshire. The film itself does give a firsthand view of the war which may be why it was voted best documentary feature when it debuted at the 2006 Tribeca Film Festival. Nevertheless, *War Tapes* is no more (or less) successful in depicting life on the front line than others that give the soldier's view of war. *War Tapes* does have the refreshing advantage, unlike *War Feels Like War* and *Inside Iraq*, of not having the journalist as the focal point of the film—but then the journalist wasn't there, so she cannot be the focus of the story.

Inside Iraq: The Untold Story is about a reporter who ostensibly is not embedded and has to sneak into Iraq to bring the world the story not covered by the mainstream news media. Sneak is the reporter's word; it is not quite accurate. Mike Shiley enters Iraq with an ABC convoy of white bulletproof Suburban vans from Jordan; only two passengers per car in case of an attack, each car bookended by Suburbans with armed paramilitary personnel (see also *Iraq for Sale: The War Profiteers*, 2006). Reaching Baghdad after his less than harrowing journey, he hires a young Shiite male to serve as his guide and proceeds to go places other journalists have not ventured: a special "market" where he needs to "watch his back" because it is underground—a thriving porn market previously banned under Saddam's rule; a technical college that teaches computer skills on a whiteboard because all the computers have been stolen; a bombed out shelter where 242 Iraqi civilians were incinerated by a smart bomb; a stretch of barren land marked with red warning skull-and-crossbones signs where Saddam Hussein laid over 30 million landmines "*in his own country*" [narrator's emphasis] and where workers today are paid $10 a day to remove them.

The film does venture into places typically not depicted in other films. But it is still a travelogue, and Mike Shiley wants to do more than this. He wants to be in the action. When he found out that "no one from ABC" wanted to be embedded with the 3rd Army Calvary because they were stationed in the vast "wild wild west . . . wasteland" near the Syrian border because it is one of the "most dangerous . . . places in the country . . . I immediately signed up." Shiley should be commended for going where no other journalists dared. He is right when he says earlier that it is "one thing to see a car bomb on TV and see a car bomb when it really happens." The problem with this is, of course, that we *are* seeing it on TV, or in this case a filmed documentary, so the viewer really cannot connect. The same holds with Mr. Shiley's bravado: it does not come off well, it's all a game, and he's having a grand ol' time—or so it appears on film.

Shiley "wants to spend some time on the front line actually [sic] being a soldier." He is assigned to ride in one of the Abrams tanks that patrols the region. The sergeant, however, is protective of the untrained journalist and requires him to ride in the belly of the Abrams tank and so ensconced, he couldn't see anything. He wants to be a gunner on the tank turret. To ride there, however, he has to be weapons certified. "Great, let's get started," says Shiley, and in the blink of the camera's eye we see him learning how to fire a weapon in the desert. Now he's a gunner: "Can you believe it . . . on a $2 million Abrams?" The tone changes with his promotion from the third person (the soldiers did this, did that) to the first person plural, "We did this. . . . We did that."

At the end of *Inside Iraq*, Shiley returns to his central framing device: himself. The events that have been portrayed in the film are updated, but they are all seen through the first person singular prism, which tends to minimize, even if it does not completely negate, the horrors of war, simply because the tragedies are so quickly summarized and not seen: "On March 8, 2004, just after Mike visited the Chaldean Church in Baghdad . . . a car ran into a parking lot after Sunday services and exploded . . . "; On September 4, 2003, just after Mike filmed the land mine removal, two land mine experts were shot by unknown assailants"; "after Mike went on patrol" troops [he was embedded with] were ambushed."

QUASI-FOREIGN DOCUMENTARIES

Not surprisingly, films about the Iraq invasion that are made outside the United States, especially those made by Arabs in the Middle East, are likely to have a different interpretation of the war. This often occurs. There is, however, a group of films that are here labeled "quasi foreign" because they *seem* to be made from the Arabic point of view but are interpreted through a distinctly Westernized frame. The first is *Voices of Iraq* (2004) that, while it purports to document the everyday events of Iraqis going about their business, is edited with an American hand. Two others, *About Baghdad* (2004) and *Return to the Land of Wonders* (2004), are made by expatriate Iraqis whose films reflect their contemporary Western ties while simultaneously capturing their Iraqi roots. The last in this category is the highly successful film *Control Room* (2004) made by the Egyptian-American director, Jehane Noujaim.

The viewer is emphatically told in the opening of *Voices of Iraq* that it is "filmed and directed" by the Iraqi people. It is certainly filmed by Iraqis. One hundred and fifty lightweight video cameras were dispensed to Iraqi civilians who passed them along to more than 2,000 Iraqis; this resulted in 450 hours of videotapes that were edited down to an eighty-five-minute film. The preponderance of happy, smiling faces, however, jar with the devastation and anger that most other films, American and foreign, depict. The disgruntlement is there, just not the anger. One says, "The Americans did good things for us. They kicked Saddam out . . . but I didn't know it was going to be like this. It's a miserable situation"; another complains that there is "No stability, no safety [now]. Wish [we] had Saddam back." Despite these sporadic outbursts that dot the film, the overall feel is appreciative of the U.S. presence, which recognizes that if the United States pulls out now, the future is bleak. Besides, one Iraqi says, "Americans have helped Iraqi children by rebuilding schools." This is stated over the smiling countenance of school children; no reference is made to the fact that Americans are rebuilding schools they destroyed. The "they love us" depictions far outweigh the sporadic discontentment of a few isolated Iraqis. There are also a disproportionate number of Kurds in this movie, which gives it a positive turn since the Kurds were persecuted under Saddam's regime and directly benefited from the American invasion.

The film, more than most in the foreign category, dwells on the nefarious rule of Saddam Hussein. This reinforces the reason for the invasion. Its success is clear. The viewer sees a television clip of Saddam being pulled from his hole, then an Iraqi male is asked how he reacted when he saw this on television; "I danced like this," he says and then shows how wildly he danced at the news. Another is asked about the Abu Ghraib scandal. We're told it is inconsequential: "I was personally tortured much worse," one says; another comments that America's torture, compared to what took place under the former regime, is a "nice kind of torture."

There were charges when this film was released that it was covertly funded by the conservative right.[56] Turvey alludes to this but goes on to point out that these charges were never substantiated, because, he writes, there is no evidence "that the footage is in any way inauthentic."[57] Turvey is no doubt correct—the footage *is* authentic; however, this does not mean it was not skillfully edited to present a flattering face of a happy, free people.[58] Turvey is also right that the film depicts a less triumphal celebratory mood (see Rumsfeld's comments throughout *Gunner Palace*) and is more one of cautious optimism, but that is in keeping with the postinvasion depiction of Iraq fostered by the Bush administration. It also reflects the mind-set of an occupied people, for if one cannot hope that the future is going to be better, one can become terribly despondent. Cautious optimism is a classic response of the occupied to the occupier.

In the final analysis, *Voices*, is of two worlds. It is the honest view of some Iraqis. It purports to be balanced by giving the negative along with the positive. But it is also the view that Americans want to see. In this sense, it is an American film, painstakingly edited to promote a point of view. Its ultimate goal is to show a variation of "mission accomplished."

The war is not over, but things are improving. American troops are still there, but it is necessary for them to be there, and most Iraqis, even though they might wish the Americans gone, are appreciative of that fact. This point is made clear by the multitude of smiling faces studded throughout this film. The mood is slightly darker in the other two films made by Iraqi expatriates returning home, but the sense of cautious optimism pervades them both.

Maysoon Pachachi follows her diplomatic Iraqi father, Adnan Muzahim Amin al-Pachachi, home in *Return to the Land of Wanders*. Adnan al-Pachachi spent most of his years under Baathist rule in exile. He returned home as part of the Iraqi Governing Council in July 2003 to help write the new Iraqi constitution. His daughter attempts to capture his journey on film. It is not particularly successful, despite Maysoon Pachachi's cinematic credentials: she graduated from the London Film School and has numerous television credits.

The problem is not so much with the filmmaking as the subject matter. Filming a diplomat—unless he happens to be particularly colorful (see *Fidel*, 2002, 2009; *Che*, 2005, 2008; *Michael Collins*, 1996)—is a tad boring: We see him sitting at his desk staring off into space, thinking, sifting through papers, amiably chatting with other committee members. This is disappointing because her eighty-year-old father is a vociferous critic of U.S. policy and a key Iraqi insider in the emerging Iraqi government. None of this is truly captured on film. The director appears to realize that her subject is not particularly cinematic and intersperses the "home video" segments with tours of Baghdad that often deteriorate into Better Business Bureau outtakes and childhood remembrance sequences: The blue-doomed Iraqi monument to soldiers killed in the eight-year war with Iran is seen from a long-lens shot; the ancient Persian palace outside Baghdad that was built in the third century and where she fondly remembers family picnics; the market where she once shopped as a little girl. She laments the changes that have taken place. However, the changes owe as much to the thirty-five years she has been away than the consequences of the American occupation. Her tour of Baghdad does show some of the more problematic aspects of the city: a man's story of his false imprisonment at Abu Ghraib by American troops; a woman's anguish over her husband who has been missing for fourteen years; a car backfire that resulted in a friend's death because American military personnel mistook the sound for a bomb and opened fire on the driver. These stories are intercut with the tedium of her father's diplomatic pondering and a Better Business Bureau tour of the city; in the end, the "man on the street" stories do not come off as successful as they do in *About Baghdad*.

About Baghdad is a collage of interviews that took place three months after the fall of Saddam Hussein. It is produced and directed by InCounterProductions, which, it is learned at the film's conclusion, is comprised of Arabic expatriates, who are all affiliated with American universities. The issue is not with the filmmakers' academic credentials but the fact that they are the talking heads that appear throughout the film. Since their identification is not made evident until the end of the film, the viewer watches the film under the impression that, when they appear on camera in the film, they are Iraqi nationals living and working in Iraq.

Unlike *Land*, this film focuses on how "the man on the street" in Iraq views current conditions. Its singular focus makes it more successful than *Land* in accomplishing its stated goal: "The structure of this film reflects the disquieting chaos and violent disorder that has engulfed the lives of Iraqis and fractured their space and psychic." The people who are interviewed generally perceive the removal of Saddam Hussein by the Americans in a positive light; they also largely agree that nothing has really changed. The American armed forces have simply replaced Saddam: it is they who are responsible for the bombing of the city, the looting of the Academy of Fine Arts (seen) and the Iraqi national museum (mentioned), as well as equipment shortages at the hospital and the high unemployment rate. These issues are all related to the central motif of the film—the widespread animosity toward the continued occupation and the everyday person's desire for Iraq to achieve self-rule: "Americans liberated us, and we thank them . . . but Saddam Hussein is gone. Now we want to rule ourselves." In this, the film deftly succeeds.

Iraqis want freedom in more than name only and their bitterness at their disempowerment ekes through: "This is occupation, not freedom," says one; another complains that George W. Bush "didn't bring security [as promised]"; while still another complains, "Where is the democracy?" It's just been one endless series of events, says another: "sanctions, war, [now] occupation." Some of the fault is shared, however, with other Muslim countries: "Who's at fault?" ponders one old man, in a verbal sidebar, "Saddam [first and foremost] but also other Arab and Muslim countries that could at least have severed diplomatic ties with Saddam Hussein." Still, the shock and awe that destroyed sections of Iraq is exacerbated by America's postinvasion cordon-and-sweep policies: The indiscriminate arrests of Iraqi civilians without the due process Adnan al-Pachachi insisted be a vital part of the new Iraqi constitution in *Land*—he was talking as much about the tyrannical rule of Saddam as he was the Americans, a point made much more cogent in *About Baghdad*. The Iraqi's view of the prevalent cordon-and-sweep policies is distinctly different from those films that depict the soldiers' views of the night raids of private homes. Videos taken by military personnel inevitably show cordon-and-sweep tactics as a key means to stopping the insurrection and saving American lives. The Iraqi view of cordon and sweep goes a long way in explaining the strong sense of outrage many Iraqis feel toward the continued presence of coalition forces: kicking in doors, wresting unarmed men to the ground, hooding and removing people in the middle of the night for no apparent (or explained) reason. It is not just that Iraq is an occupied country, it is how the occupying coalition forces behave that raises the ire of Iraqis and stimulates their desire for self-rule. In the end, however, this anger is tempered because the film is framed in such a way that the destruction of Iraq that is frequently mentioned is offset by the camera tour of the city at the end of the film, which shows as many prosperous, thriving sections as there are destroyed ones. Indeed, the number of thriving sections is curious so soon after the war, and considering the lament of Iraqi citizens, tends to undercut their complaint of just how bad things are in Iraq under the American occupation. The way this is accomplished suggests the producers are aiming to please two markets. Iraqis watching this film would have their views of self-rule vindicated, while Americans watching the film would take their complaint with a grain of salt, sagely nodding in agreement with the American soldier who says, "[I've] never met anyone who complained [about our presence]. They always say thank you for being here. When you're not [patrolling], they're afraid."

Control Room provides a unique journalistic perspective on the war in Iraq. It focuses on how Al Jazeera covered the war in Iraq from its onset until the fall of Baghdad. The Doha, Qatar, headquarters of the

Arabic media outlet did not provide it any advantage. Like the legions of other media, the Arabic network was confined to the media compound at Central Command (CentCom) in Doha. In fact, the title does not refer as much to the room from which Al Jazeera reported on the war but to the control room at CentCom. In this, it is as much about the problem the media had gaining access to information as the problem Al Jazeera faced in reporting the war. This is shown clearly in the house of cards scene in the film, where the journalists at CentCom are shown the infamous deck of cards at a briefing but were not allowed to have access to and inspect the cards. Al Jazeera reports on the widespread media disgust at how journalists are being denied critical information and not allowed to do their job.

Control Room is not about the media, however; it is about how Al Jazeera, speaking from the Arabic perspective, reports events. This perspective is like nothing seen on American television. It still was not an acknowledged perspective a year after the war was declared over when the film was released in the United States, a few weeks prior to the debut of Fahrenheit 9/11. This is why numerous reviewers applauded the film. Ty Burr at the Boson Globe, for example, finds the film refreshing, and likens it to "an open window that sucks the smog out of the room."[59] This distinct perspective, and the generally positive reviews, helped nudge Control Room into the coveted top ten spot of political grossing documentaries, and is one of only of a small handful of films in the top ten to be inhabited by someone other than Michael Moore (see Table 2.2). Al Jazeera's perspective, however, is anything but impersonal, as A. O. Scott reports in the New York Times.[60] There is a definite agenda in the presentation of information at Al Jazeera. It may not be as overbearing or blatant as the news reported by some of the other networks; nevertheless, a strong undercurrent flows through the verbal reporting and pictorial depiction of events.

Al Jazeera's view of events was widely criticized by the president and members of his administration. Donald Rumsfeld is seen stating in Control Room that "Al Jazeera [is] pounding the people in the [Middle East] day after day with things that are not true, which is what they do." The clip then flits to a montage of American soldiers shoving innocent people to the ground. It might have been more provocative to insert, after Rumsfeld's self-serving statement, a clip of Fox News "pounding the people in the [United States] day after day with things that are not true, which is what they do."

Just as American news sees events through an American lens, Al Jazeera views events from an Arabic one. Like any news program, it must keep its audience in mind when reporting the news. This is clearly seen on Fox, which caters to a right-wing conservative audience, and thus casts the news in a similar format (see *Outfoxed*); this is also seen on CNN and BBC, which has a more liberal-leaning audience and so interprets events to cater to them.[61] This does not mean that the news outlet overtly manipulates the news to kowtow to its audience. It is done much more subtly than this, as Herbert Gans showed some time ago in his landmark media study, *Deciding What's News*.[62] Media organizations lean toward a liberal or conservative orientation. Journalists hired by the organizations are hired because they fit, which means they have a conservative or liberal slant on how things unfold, so when they do a story, they tend to see things from their preexisting perspective. The same holds for Al Jazeera: they cater to an Arabic audience but their journalists are also fellow Arabs who see things from the Arabic perspective and thus interpret events through an Arabic lens. Reporting on the Palestinian-Israeli conflict is one instance of how this is done. Kaplan finds that whenever Al Jazeera covers the Israeli-Palestinian dispute, its reports clearly side with the Palestinians, as is obvious from the "tear-jerking features about the suffering of the Palestinians [which is] not matched with equal coverage of the Israeli human terrain."[63]

The Arabic slant should not be surprising. The network was born in 1996 after the Saudi government forced the closing of the BBC's World Service Arabic language television station because of censorship demands. This is the reason Al Jazeera, which means, appropriately, "the island," is located in Qatar's capital. Its independent status is a driving force behind its phenomenal success: many Arabs see it as more trustworthy than other government-controlled Middle East media outlets.[64] As an independent source of news for the "person on the street," Al Jazeera sees its mission to present the plight of the masses: the weak and oppressed people throughout the Middle East.[65]

Despite its Arabic bias, Al Jazeera presents a view of the world that Westerners are seldom exposed to and goes to some length to report stories with some depth.[66] It also attempts to provide a balanced portrait.

This is accomplished in *Control Room* in a scene where Samir Khader, a senior producer for Al Jazeera, berates a journalist for arranging an interview with an American academic critical of the war. "This is [a] news [program]," he snaps, "[we] want balance. [It's] not an opinion show."

Many reviewers cite this segment of the film to underscore its impartiality. Roger Ebert says that *Control Room* is a film that for the most part is "just watching and listening" in the best cinéma vérité style of filmmaking.[67] The truth, however, is distinctly Arabic, which is one reason the film *is* refreshing—it's a point of view that Westerners are seldom exposed to and *not* heard in the public domain in the United States until this film was released. It does not seem as pronounced or unique a decade later, but it was a stunning and refreshing perspective for liberals in 2004.

Control Room unfolds around three independent but interrelated stories. One, already noted, focuses on the media in general. Al Jazeera is in the same boat as American journalists. The American connection is strong but subtle. The key players are mostly Western educated and speak fluent English. Samir Khader, a senior producer at Al Jazeera, grabs the [American] audience's attention when he admits that despite everything else, if he were offered a job in the United States, even if it were at Fox News, he'd take it without a moment's hesitation. This jarring admission is one Americans would appreciate, but so too would many in less-developed countries: America is, despite everything, the land of opportunity and the place many dream of living (see *Sin Nombre*, 2009; *Goodbye Solo*, 2008; *Brick Lane*, 2007; *Amreeka*, 2009). Khader is being hyperbolic, however. Fox is not going to hire him because he is so ideologically disparate and he knows that the ideological gulf is precisely why he will never be offered a job at Fox. This is very disingenuously done.

Another key player in the film is the journalist Hassan Ibrahaim. One of his roles is to dot the film with witticism. At the start of the war Ibrahaim is in front of the television watching the war at Al Jazeera. The staff is stunned as they watch what is taking place and Ibrahaim nicely, and quite succulently, sums up the perspective of those watching the start of the war: "Wow! Democracy!" he says, shaking his head in stunned near silence as bombs burst in the air over Baghdad. In another segment, while watching American troops patrolling the city and stopping to shake hands with the locals, he adapts the song "Yankee Doodle Dandy" to contemporary Iraqi exigencies: "Yankee Doodle went to town / Riding there on Sunday / Found some people living there / Killed them all by Monday." Later he laughs at a report shown on the BBC. "It was the funniest report ever," he says, referring to a reporter who was surrounded by a group of kids chanting against Bush, "but he didn't know Arabic. He hears the name Bush [and reports], 'I'm surrounded by a bunch of children cheering President Bush.' . . . They were [really] a bunch of kids cursing Bush."

The film is not really about what is taking place seven hundred miles away in Baghdad. It is how what was happening was debated in the offices of Al Jazeera in Doha. Ibrahaim's sarcastic witticisms serve to underscore the film's second storyline—how Al Jazeera provides insights into events not covered by the mainstream media. In this, it was quite successful. We watch the fall of Saddam Hussein's statue on television in reel time[68] with Al Jazeera staffers, who are quick to notice that "It was a media show . . . [the people in the square] "weren't Iraqi; I can recognize an Iraqi accent." They were also quick to see that the camera angle was a tight shot and that there were not many people gathered to topple Saddam's statue. Later, staffers point out as they watch people looting the banks and burning money that they were not Iraqi but Kurds and that they were doing this because the "Kurds are using a completely different monetary system . . . so what we're seeing [Kurds burning Iraqi money] is meaningless."

Ibrahaim is also central to the third storyline in *Control Room*, the conversion of Lt. Josh Rushing. Rushing was the Marine press officer for CentCom at the time of the invasion of Iraq. As might be expected, Rushing is the idealist young Marine who believes 110 percent in the party line. He has all the passionate naïveté of Harrison Carter MacWhite (Marlon Brando) in *The Ugly American* (1963).[69] In one early exchange, Ibrahaim asks him, "When? When did Saddam Hussein threaten to use weapons of mass destruction?" "He had the will," answers Rushing. In a subsequent exchange, Ibrahaim accuses the Americans of "bombing the hell out of Baghdad." Rushing rejoins that "We have the most precision munitions in the world." Ibrahaim persists: "You're killing civilians." "Nothing," rejoins Rushing with a metaphorical wave of the hand, "compared to the carpet bombing of Germany; the carpet bombing of Tokyo." Ibrahaim trumps him: "[The] bombing of Dresden was before the days of television. Since Vietnam, the picture has changed. And now in [the] Arab world . . . see massacres in Palestine and how people are butchered [sic] . . . the idea of another Arab capitol occupied is really fueling [a lot] of anger." By the end of the film, Rushing is often found siding with the Arabic perspective. He's come around. His cinematic conversion was not appreciated by his superiors who reassigned him and prohibited him from talking to the press when the film was released in 2004, which is why, when his tour of duty was up, he resigned his commission. His conversion is now complete: He is presently working for Al Jazeera English.

Rushing's conversion is a parable for the film's intent: the conversion of the viewer. It is not, as many have reported, a neutral story where the camera simply records events. Jehane Noujaim, the film's skillful director (see *Startup.com*, 2001), uses her lens quite incisively. Her camera shows certain events and not others. In doing this, she tells a story about the war that reflects the view toward the United States that is widespread, though by no mean ubiquitous, in the Middle East. This would make the film appealing to the Arabic market. She does this in such a way, however, so the film does not alienate American viewers. Marketing a film to tap two widely disparate audiences is no mean feat. The critical assessment of the attack by the United States is there—still thin in the public sphere in 2004—but the fault lies not with the "warmongering" American people, so much as it does the contrivances of the Bush administration, a point that was starting to play in the United States around this time (see *Uncovered*, 2003, 2004; *Why We Fight*, 2003; *Fahrenheit 9/11*, 2004). Noujaim further manages to promote Al Jazeera's view as even handed in two other ways. First, one storyline revolves around the media and how they (not just Al Jazeera) are being kept from accurately reporting on the war. The second way this is done is by showing Lt. Rushing slowly being won over as the "facts" are laid out for him in the best dialectical tradition. Rushing could have been excised from the film. He is there because he plays a pivotal role. Had the film only examined Al Jazeera's perspective, it could have been too easily dismissed as one-sided, which would open it up to Rumsfeld's charges that it is overly propagandistic. Had it come off as less evenhanded, it would have not endeared itself to critics and mostly likely would not have achieved its top ten grossing status.

FOREIGN FILMS

The purpose of a documentary is to inform the viewer about a slice of the world with which they might otherwise be unfamiliar. But if one is immersed in that world, documentaries are not likely to garner particular interest. There are only two documentaries in his section that are made by Iraqi nationals. One is *Dream of Sparrows*; the other is *Boy of Baghdad*. They are refreshing simply because they depict the war from the Arabic perspective, though *Dream of Sparrows* is much more effective than *Boy of Baghdad* in capturing the trauma of war-torn Iraq.

While documentaries are meant to inform, feature fictional films are made to entertain. This does not preclude their heuristic value. It is simply a matter of emphasis: documentaries (D) inform while they entertain; fictional films (F) entertain while they inform:

Boy of Baghdad (2004, D)
Daughters of Afghanistan (2004, F; see chapter 1)
Liberace of Baghdad (2005, D; see under heading Reporter's View in this chapter)
The Dream of Sparrows (2005, D)
The Tiger and the Snow (2005, F)
Turtles Can Fly (2005, F)
Paradise Now (2005, F)
Brothers (2005, F; see chapter 4 in its original and 2009 American remake)

The other films in this section are fictional films. Other than the fictive features that depict WTC-related events, there have only been a handful of fictive feature films: the Japanese production *Osama* (2003), the HBO special *House of Saddam* (2008), the low-budget adventure yarn *Wings over Afghanistan* (2004), and *The War Within* (2005), the first film to address the consequences of rendition. Here fictive features move to the foreground. They are particularly informative for Western eyes because, while the story entertains, it provides insights into the Arabic mind that the other, domestic films have failed to achieve. They certainly refract a point of view. Still, their fictional framework makes them less overtly didactic than the documentary format, and this tends to make them more palatable to an American audience.

There are three fictive features in this section. One is the Italian film *The Tiger and the Snow*. The other two are Arabic features. One of these is the disturbing film *Turtles Can Fly*. The other, *Paradise Now*, is about a suicide bomber and does not fit snuggly into the post-9/11 criteria because it is really about the Palestine-Israel situation. Nevertheless, it is one (1) whose theme is quintessential to the Muslim experience; (2) that revolves around a point raised, even if it is not dwelt upon, in American films that assesses the death among American military personnel that is caused by improvised explosive devices (IEDs); and (3) that is the subject of *The War Within* but here is examined from a Muslim perspective without being filtered, as *War* was, through an American lens. Because of the topic, the later Arabic fictive feature, *Making of* (2006), which is also about suicide bombers, is included in this last section.

The foreign films examined in this section are not all encompassing. They are limited to those released in the United States. Their purpose is not only to entertain their native audience but to give others, notably Americans, insight into how Muslims view the American presence in the Middle East. Most are Arabic films and deal with the impact of the war on the lives of people living in occupied territory.[70]

Baghdad from the Iraqi Perspective

One documentary, *Boy of Baghdad* (2004), was never theatrically released in the United States but it is available on DVD and accessible at most film rental outlets. The film lingers over the innocent, doe-eyed expression of a twelve-year-old boy, Kheer Allah, as he goes about his daily business. The film purports to show "the chaos of Najaf and Falluja"; it is not particularly successful for a number of reasons, but mainly because the markets and places that are seen are in no way chaotic, and the young man's poverty is no worse than many in this part of the world who lack education and skills. In this, it is no more or less successful than any of the quasi films critiqued in the last section of this chapter. The other documentary is more successful because it presents a distinctly different perspective of the unfolding war in Iraq.

The Dream of Sparrows is a first-time documentary by Iraqi film-maker Hyder Mousa Daffar, who subsequently went on to make *Sadar City Soccer* (2007). Daffar prefaces the film by saying he is one man with one camera who is just looking for the truth (see *Man with a Movie Camera*, 1929). He tells us an opening story about a man whose wife is giving birth, and who, unable to find anyone to assist, delivers the baby himself. The child is held up crying; the mother dies in childbirth. Daffar explicates the connection: "This movie is what happened to the child . . . to the new Iraq." The title suggests this with the use of sparrows. Birds are often revered in Islamic literature, and in Sufi tradition represent the soul's journey to a better world (the heavenly kingdom). At least that's the dream.

The main accomplishment of *Dream*'s otherwise hodgepodge of unrelated events is to present a fairly balanced portrait of the mixed emotions the Iraqi people have toward Saddam Hussein and America's intervention. The first scene sets the tone. A number of people are seen gathered in a public area watching Saddam's capture on television. Happiness is expressed by many; at the same time, others express their disbelief and laud Saddam as their savior. Shortly thereafter, a girl's school is visited where one girl says, "I drew this [pleasant scene] because I feel safe now"; others, however, are drawing pictures of planes and bombs. In a later extended scene, the views of two former military men who served under Saddam are juxtaposed. One says Saddam was never a threat and deplores the number of innocent people killed by the Americans, "who invaded against all international laws," while the other talks about how bad Saddam was and thanks the United Sates "for saving us from Saddam." The tenuous balance the director has maintained throughout this film slips away toward the end. After bemoaning the stupidity of the IEDs taking place throughout the city, which kills fourteen Iraqi civilians for every American soldier who loses his life, the viewer is treated to a concluding scene that depicts the death of an Iraqi by Americans. Sa'ad Fakher, an associate producer for the film, was driving into Area 55 when the Iraqi police (for some reason) opened fire on his vehicle; Sa'ad sped away in the opposite direction into the American sector where American troops, thinking the careening car might be a suicide bomber, opened fire. We are told he was hit *only* 15 to 20 times before he was taken to a hospital where he died, but his car, shown in a still shot, was riddled with 122 bullet holes. The director, looking slightly crazed in a sleeveless, ribbed undershirt, then launches into a long diatribe: "Baghdad! Baghdad is hell, really hell, and you in New York . . . a paradise, no Osama bin Laden, no Saddam Hussein . . . [everyone here] all happy Saddam Hussein gone [but] nothing new . . . more explosions. U.S. troops very hard hearted. Cowboys, like Clint Eastwood." Fade to black over the concluding crawl, "In loving memory of Sa'ad Fakher," who is shown in a still photograph, smiling at the camera, strumming the guitar that he loved to play.

Turtles Can Fly is a fictional film made by the Kurdish director, Bahman Gholbadi, who also did *Marooned in Iraq* (2002)[71] and *A Time for Drunken Horses* (2000). The film is much more effective in depicting events in Iraq than *Dream of Sparrows*, in part because Gholbadi is a more seasoned filmmaker, and in part because he is not foregrounded and lets the film speak for itself.

The main character is a thirteen-year-old boy whose given name is Soran, though everyone knows him as Satellite because he installs satellites for the villagers in northern Kurdistan. It is a few weeks before the American invasion of Iraq. Satellite is the go-to guy. The elders, on those occasions when they creep into the film, depend on him to set up their televisions and to organize his adoring band of boys to clear mines from their land. He is always charmingly boastful. Soon, Satellite tells an old man, the Americans will be coming. "Who are Americans?" asks the old man. "Have you seen the movie *Titanic*, Washington, San Francisco, Bruce Lee, Zinedine Zidane?" The old man retorts that Zinedine Zidane is not American. No, Satellite says, "he's French and a Muslim and I know him well."[72] In another scene, an elder asks him what George W. Bush, who appears on television, is saying. "Rain tomorrow," he says, flaunting his linguist (in)abilities, though, in a way, he is figuratively accurate.

The central motif of *Turtles Can Fly* is the landmines that litter the Kurdish countryside. These were obviously put there by Saddam Hussein but America is complicit, since they provided them. This point is subtly made when Satellite tells his rag-tag team to collect only the American mines, not the Italian ones, because American mines are better, which is why they bring a bigger bounty. The landmines certainly are effective. Most of the boys are missing limbs from their efforts to

Surviving amid the rubble in *Turtles Can Fly.*

collect them. Nevertheless, it is their only source of income so they eagerly volunteer for the dangerous tasks Satellite dispenses, even if, as one elder says of the boys Satellite assigns him, "half of them don't have hands."

To keep the endless tromping through the minefields from growing tedious, the director introduces three key characters that play off of Satellite. One is the young girl Turtle, whose given name Agrin is only mentioned in passing. She is shown in the opening of the film standing suicidally atop a cliff looking down into the mists below. Her face is not seen, so we don't immediately recognize her when she wanders into Satellite's sphere of influence. Satellite is immediately attracted to her youthful beauty: "I've been looking for a girl like you for years." She does not return his affection and remains distant throughout the film. Later, in a flashback, we understand her aloofness: she was gang-raped by Saddam's soldiers who plundered and massacred those in her village. She is accompanied by her armless brother, Hangao. Despite his apparent handicap, Hangao is quite competent; he is shown disarming mines with his teeth. He and Satellite are often at odds and in one scene after an argument, Hangao lowers his head and rams into Satellite, bloodying his nose. As Hangao wanders off, Satellite yells at him from the ground, "I'll cut off your legs [next time]." The third character is a rather large blind baby, Riega, who Turtle often carries on her back; he appears to be about two years of age and besides his physical handicap, appears to be mentally challenged. He is a bastard. Turtle is responsible for him because his parents have been killed in the massacre that took place in her village, though Roger Ebert, reviewing the movie for the *Chicago Tribune*, suggests the baby might be her own, the product of her sexual molestation.[73] In either case, Riega is a burden to Turtle, who ultimately abandons him. She ties him to a tree before going off to kill herself, wiping a tear from her eye as she leaves him behind. His fate too is sealed: he breaks free of the rope and stomps around in a minefield. Satellite futilely tries to rescue him. A bomb goes off and the screen goes dark, then we see Satellite being carried to an elders' tent for care, his foot wrapped in a bloody bandage. In a closing shot, Hangao goes to the top of the cliff and, using his teeth, picks up the shoes his sister left behind when she jumped to her death. He gives the shoes to Pashow, Satellite's crippled friend, and we watch as Satellite and Pashow gimp into the sunset.

Turtle is a very effective movie of the hardships, and resilience, children face in wartime, and the devastation Saddam's reign had on the Kurds. It remains a moot point whether the war that is commencing as the film comes to a close will bring any changes. It is certainly a disturbing movie, and the director would be pleased it rocked the world of a number of viewers. One lay Netflix reviewer wrote that it "is one of the most upsetting films I've seen"; another commented that the "movie is heartbreaking, especially if you are a parent with young children . . . [And] although the film was very well done, it is a gut-wrenching tale that leaves you with a very ugly feeling." It is too bad that in order to get the movie's taste out of one reviewer's mouth the couple had to cleanse their palate by watching "the movie *Ratatouille* in order to get to sleep due to the disturbing images [in *Turtle*]."

Baghdad from the Italian Perspective

The Tiger and the Snow is not a particularly good movie. At least it received more than its share of negative critical reviews: Young, at *Variety*, charitably said the movie was "lame," whereas Kevin Thomas, writing for the *Los Angeles Times*, was more caustic, referring to its plot as "an endless series of cockamamie adventures."[74] Nevertheless, it deserves special, albeit limited, attention as a movie in its own right for two reasons: (1) it is one of the few films to this point that addresses the war in Iraq from the perspective of another Western country; and (2) despite its failure to garner critical attention, the director and star of the film, Roberto Benigni, is well known to American audiences after winning the Oscar for his film, *Life Is Beautiful* (1997), which was sure to generate public attention. The popular appeal of Benigni means that more people will get an alternative insight into the war in Iraq than many foreign films achieve in the United States. *Tiger* was also released in English in the United States, unlike the other foreign features, which makes it more palpable to Americans who struggle with subtitles.

Benigni's character, the poet Attilio De Giovanni, is in love with Vittoria (Nicoletta Braschi). She ends up in Iraq because she is writing a book on Attilio's Iraqi friend, Fuad (Jean Reno) who has decided to return to his homeland. Fuad calls Attilio from Iraq, where the war has just broken out, to inform him that Vittoria is in the hospital. Attilio overcomes a variety of obstacles to get to Baghdad. Much of the plot in Baghdad revolves around his attempt to find medicines that are in short supply but which are necessary if Vittoria is to survive. These are the endless series of cockamamie adventures that Thomas lamented. And Thomas is right, they are cockamamie. Nevertheless, there are a number of scenes that are of interest for presenting a face of the war seldom seen in the United States, even in 2006—the film was released by Warner Brothers in Rome in 2005 but did not open in the United States until late 2006.

Attilio calls Fuad when, after a series of misadventures, he finally gets to Baghdad. Fuad fetches him under the outstretched arms holding two scimitars that mark the main entrance into the city. It is a scene of desolation: empty streets, destroyed vehicles. Later, the two talk while watching the bombs burst over the city as they sit under a headless statue of Saddam Hussein, arms outstretched, the surroundings all rubble. Fuad acknowledges in his conversation with Attilio that he finds no refuge in religion. Attilio is surprised the next morning when he sees Fuad entering a mosque, oblivious to Attilio's futile shouts of greeting. Later in the day, Attilio goes to Fuad's home and we see the scholar's papers being blown about. Attilio steps into the courtyard and finds Fuad has hanged himself: interestingly, he is hanging from a tree in full flower, which is typically, symbolically, a sign of rebirth. The scene works if only because it gives a personal face to the impersonal deaths of Iraqis that are occurring across the country as coalition bombs fall.

The face of America is shown in Attilio's encounter with American soldiers. In one early scene, he is stopped by MPs at a checkpoint. He's strapped some medical supplies to his chest so he appears to the soldiers to be a suicide bomber. He's rousted—or at least that is the way it is made to appear—then finally allowed to proceed after he makes his profession known, which they snigger at. Attilio encounters MPs again after finding his friend hanged. Dazed, he's wandering the streets when he is caught in a roundup that appears to be taking place for no apparent reason. He is imprisoned in an outdoor barbed-wire encampment with other Iraqis, mumbling over and over as the night closes in (and somewhat more weakly as the dawn breaks), "I'm Italian, I'm Italian." One of the MPs finally recognizes the voice, "[It's] the poet," and Attilio is freed. The film ends with him (and Vittoria) back in Italy.

Half the film is devoted to the Iraqi sojourn. The two scenes discussed tend to put a face to the tragedy that is taking place—Benigni's point, since he had declared himself against the war from the start. The medical search, which occupies the majority of Attilio's time in Baghdad, serves primarily as a vehicle for Benigni to indulge his somewhat slapstick comedic routine. It is successful in depicting the Iraq war only insofar as it shows the effect of the bombing on those living in the city.

A View from the Other Side: The Suicide Bomber

It is fitting to conclude this section, and this chapter, with two films that assess the suicide bomber. One is *Paradise Now* (2005), written and directed by Hany Abu-Assad. This film is about two Palestinian young men who are recruited in the war against Israel. Typically, this movie would not be included since it does not specifically address the wars in Iraq or Afghanistan. But the topic does. It arises in most of the films that address combat forces in Iraq. Just about every documentary that follows soldiers patrolling the streets of Iraq touches on the issue, as do most films that delineate the plight of journalists covering the war. It is raised by Benigni in *The Tiger and the Snow* and is a subject that reoccurs in subsequent films (see *The Kingdom*, 2007). It was the central motif of *The War Within*. In *The War Within*, however, the motivation driving Hassan, the suicide bomber, is his anger at having been unjustly imprisoned and brutally tortured. This is an understandable motivation, but it is too simplistic. Many suicide bombers are never tortured. *Paradise Now* provides a closer, more nuanced look at the motivation for those recruited to be suicide bombers (see also *Gaza Strip*, 2002). The other film, *Making of* (2007), is made by the Tunisian filmmaker, Nouri Bouzid, and is critiqued here out of sequence because it too assesses the suicide bomber from an Arabic perspective. This film, more than *Paradise Now*, relates to the central theme of this book because it is tied to the Iraq war.

The theme ties these two movies together. They also depict the suicide bomber in a similar vein. In *Paradise Now*, two young men, Said and Khaled, are just hanging around. They are young twenty-something car mechanics who don't really care about their job and go off and lounge about on a grassy knoll overlooking the city where they while away their time listlessly sharing a hokum and listening to music. As young men are inclined to do, one teases the other about Suha, an attractive Palestine female who has recently returned to her homeland from France: "[I] think she likes you!" Bahta (Lofti Edbelli), the twenty-something central character in *Making of*, is a break-dancer by profession; at least that is how he looks at what he does when he is hanging out with his peers, which is most of the time (see *La Haine*, 1995). He too has limited goals and life chances. This is implicit in *Paradise Now*, but explicitly made in *Making of*. Bahta has dropped out of school and his only real goal is to get smuggled into France, where he seems to think the good life will somehow magically occur. The result is a lot of posturing, tough-guy stances, which underlies the central motif of his life: his struggle with his identity. In one scene, reminiscent of René Descartes's famous philosophical dictum, *Cogito ergo sum* ("I think, therefore I am"), Bahta screams into the night, "Bahta exists, Bahta dances, [therefore] I'm a man."

Poverty and the futility of existence for young men[75] with limited life opportunity is a popular belief to be the driving force behind their conversion to terrorist suicide networks and has been perpetuated in public addresses by such luminaries as the Dalai Lama, Bishop Desmond Tutu, Secretary of State Colin Powell, and Elie Wiesel when he accepted the

Killing time from *Paradise Now*.

Nobel Peace Prize in 2001.[76] Both filmmakers perpetuate this spurious belief, which is challenged by a growing body of contemporary research.

The suicide bomber is much more likely to be an educated individual with some university training and twice as likely as the indigenous population to be established in a job that has some life potential.[77] In short, they are anything but the crazed religious fanatics that have nothing going for them. Indeed, their educational achievement vis-à-vis the wider populace explains their success. Berrebi offers a number of reasons why education is positively correlated with suicide bombers: (1) educated individuals are better equipped to understand moral and religious justifications invoked by terrorist groups; (2) educated individuals may be more aware of social barriers and restrictions that block their advancement in a closed society that poor individuals don't even know exist; and (3) poorer individuals are more likely to be preoccupied with daily matters and devote less attention to militant struggles.[78] To Berrebi's list, we might add that they are more likely than less-educated individuals to be capable of accomplishing their mission.

People with limited education are not as likely to be versed in weaponry or have the skills necessary to carry through with their intentions. The failure rate of successful bombings in Afghanistan underscores the need for competent (i.e., educated) suicide bombers. In Afghanistan, at least through 2005 when Taliban insurgents relied on local recruits, the number of individuals killed by the suicide bomber was practically nonexistent. This is because most were rural farmers with limited education who, in fact, were often severely mentally impaired or physically handicapped, and more often than not ended their lives by setting off their vest before they reached their target.[79] This is not the case in many other areas of the Middle East and where suicide bombers are much more successful in accomplishing their nihilistic goals precisely because they are educated: Hassan's study of 250 terrorists found *none* were uneducated, desperately poor, or simpleminded, while Russell and Miller's profile of the modern urban terrorist found two-thirds to have had some university training, or be university graduated or postgraduate students.[80] Education seems to be necessary because suicide bombings are based on rational, cost-benefit decisions. Hafez calculates that conventional military tactics in the Palestinian-occupied territories resulted in an average of one Israeli casualty for every twelve Palestinians killed, while suicide bombings within Israel's 1948 borders yielded nine Israeli deaths per martyr.[81] Outsiders may look at the act as irrational, but it is clearly a rational decision for those committed to the cause.

These flaws aside, the films generally paint a fairly accurate picture of the suicide bomber. They do tend to be younger, unmarried males who live in urban areas. Both films also accurately rectify two popular misperceptions linked to the suicide bomber. All three protagonists are normal individuals and none are particularly religious. The antiheroes in both films may be misguided and misunderstood youth, but they are clearly everyday people (see *Rebel without a Cause*, 1955; *Easy Rider*, 1969; *Clerks*, 1994). Nor is religion a key motivating factor for joining the terrorist organization, just as it is *not* a major factor for most terrorists.[82] Fundamentalist zealots may use religion as a motivating tool, but their hook is often the offer of an embracing sense of community for socially alienated individuals as a restorative for the humiliation they and their countrymen have suffered at the hands of the occupier. This is the selling point for the young recruits in both these films. In *Paradise Now* Said and Khaled are told that they need to stand up to Israel because it is "an answer to injustice . . . there is no other way to fight it. Israel continues to confiscate [our] land, Judizing Jerusalem, and carrying out ethnic cleansing." America is complicit with Israel: "They use their war machine and their political and economic might to force us to accept their solution." This same pitch is made to Bahta in *Making of*. He is given a tape to watch that depicts the massacres that "began in Sabra and Chatila." He then sees bombs bursting over Baghdad, followed by the planes hitting the WTC, as if, in the order it is presented, the WTC attack was in response to the attack on Baghdad. A picture of Osama bin Laden follows, saying, "The only way to rid ourselves is by Jihad . . . and suicide bombs. A free man refuses to be dominated." The recruiter reinforces the taped message the next day when he sees Bahta: "[The West] imposes its point of view on us. They sacked our land and humiliate us."

This focus on how these young men and their countrymen have been humiliated by the occupier is a quintessential feature of Arabic society that has been characterized as a shame society.[83] Honor and shame are two sides of the same coin. Honor is connected to one's public face (*wajh*) which, Patai argues, a man will attempt to preserve even if he has committed a dishonorable act.[84] This is because appearances are everything. Shame, not guilt—which is an internal state of consciousness—motivates Arabs to preserve one's honor. The shame of being conquered pressures Arabs to act honorably, which in this case means that they must do something to preserve the shame of being subjugated.

One course of face-saving publicly is to attack the person (government) that has shamed them, even if it means taking their own life. This is as important, if not more important, than obtaining some coveted benefit in the hereafter. Religion then might be used as a pretext to recruit individuals to "the cause," be it Hamas or al-Qaeda, but the specific goal is secular: to coerce occupying forces to make significant political and territorial concessions.[85] Westerners may dismiss this as an idealistic goal, but it does sometimes work. In 4 of 7 cases that culminated in 186 suicide attacks that took 5,587 lives that Pape studied, 4 (Lebanon, West Bank, Sri Lanka, and Turkey) resulted in partial or complete withdrawal of occupying forces with the remaining 3 (Chechnya, Kashmir, and Saudi Arabia) goals to force withdrawal still ongoing.[86] Atran argues that converts to the cause will continue to take place not only because Iraq is occupied by a foreign power but because of the people's moral outrage at what took place at Abu Ghraib prison, as well as the often apparent random search-and-seizure activities that regularly occur (see the section in this book "The Grunt's View").[87] At least one of the three protagonists in these two films accepts this honorific pretext and accomplishes what he sets out to do.

Both films are well made and equally deserving of viewing. They are solid dramatic stories that attempt to show how young men are recruited and why they might be duped into sacrificing their life in such a way. The directors of both films are Muslim Arabs. As such, they attempt to portray something that is too often fobbed off by Westerners as the antics of crazy people.

Despite their common theme, the directors tell different stories, in different ways, and with different endings. Bouzi's film *Making of* is enhanced by a traditional narrative device that is seldom used in dramatic cinema, and this, in itself, makes it particularly effective—the narrative aside. Bahta, the central character in *Making of*, is being seduced by a fundamentalist who preys on the young man's search for identity, his need to belong. During a conversion sequence well into the film, the lead character, Lofti Edbelli, suddenly stops in the middle of the scene and walks off the set. Cameras continue to roll and the viewer sees cameramen and crew standing around. Lofti demands to see the director. He will not tolerate the fundamentalist character demeaning his dancing. He admonishes the director: "He attacked dancing. I am a dancer [in real life] . . . Who are you [director] to forbid dancing?" "Calm down," the director tells him. . . . It's [the character's] opinion, not mine." Others involved with the film encourage him to resume filming. "I'm going home," Lofti says. In the end, the director is able to convince him to return to the set, though not without resignedly murmuring, "I think this will be my last film." The film suddenly resumes where it was interrupted. A similar incident reoccurs slightly later in the film. Lofti storms off the set demanding to see the director: "I'm Muslim. You're using me in this film to attack the Muslims." This time we have a lengthy statement to Lofti made by the director that is important to quote at length because what he is doing is explaining his Muslim point of view to the audience in case they don't pick it up from the film itself.

"I read the Qur'an before doing this film," the director tells Lofti, "in Arabic and French. Sufi [another character] can find what he needs in it, peace and love. If someone wants war, he'll find the verses that suit him. In my opinion, Islam was useful in its time. Nowadays, we should be secular. Love the Qur'an as a belief, not a tool to resolve our daily problems. . . . I want to show how a young person can be brainwashed. That's why I'm doing this film. . . . I am not anti-Islam, I am anti-terrorism. . . . I accept the struggle against occupation. . . . Trust me!"

Part of the bonus material is an interview with the director, Nouri Bouzid. The interviewer asks him "what everyone wants to know" and that is whether this was done purposely. It is an unnecessary question since there was no cut when these scenes occurred and the cameraman followed the asides in a continuous take. Bouzid curiously prefaces his answers by first remarking that we need to appreciate that all Tunisian films receive 30 percent of their funding from the government. He then goes on to answer the question in the affirmative. This link to the Tunisian government would suggest that the government felt the film needed to somehow make the point clear that the film was not attacking the Muslim religion. It was no doubt left to the director as to how to do this and he was quick to accept this solution, which was offered by Lofti. The director himself later says in the interview that the film deals with this hair-trigger issue rather subtly. The asides, then, are a way to deflect any potential misreading of the film as an attack on the Qur'an or Tunisians' religious beliefs.

In *Making of*, Bahta dies at the end. His conflict is obvious—to do or not to do. He has the vest and visits his mother one last time, telling her that "God has chosen me." The mother refutes the fundamentalist's earlier pitch that all mothers want their sons to die martyrs; she tries to stop him, saying, "You're crazy. . . . You want to kill people." Bahta is then seen roaming the street with the armed vest strapped to his chest. He sees one of his recruiters walking by and attacks him, throwing him to the ground and repeatedly striking him, screaming, "Don't you want to be a martyr with me?" The police arrive and Bahta flees. He is seen eluding the police at the docks, jumping from cargo container to cargo container. In a long shot, we see him fall into one of the containers, or between the containers, and the bomb explodes. Fin!

In *Paradise Now*, many of the same recruiting techniques take place. The ending is different, however, as is the camaraderie between the two protagonists. In *Making of*, the protagonist is clearly a conflicted, socially isolated individual. Such a person is obviously at risk of being induced to join an organization that promises a sense of belonging and identity: in an early scene, the fundamentalist recruiter gives Bahta some money, to which Bahta says, "No one has ever done that to me before."[88] *Paradise Now* portrays a more common social characteristic: 68 to 75 percent of those who join a terrorist organization are prompted to do so because of friendship bonds with someone in the group or because of a family tie.[89]

Said and Khaled are longtime friends who join the group together because they do things together and this seemed a good idea at the time. The strength of friendship bonds are made clear in a scene where they are separated after being fitted with their vests. The recruiters think Said might have been captured and betrayed them. Khaled emphatically denies this would happen and has to find him because he might accidentally discharge his vest. They remain together to the very end. At least until the final scene where Khaled, who's had a change of mind— "Suha is right. [We] won't win this way"—and tries to talk Said out of finalizing his intentions. Knowing Khaled won't take no for an answer, Said agrees not to go forward, but after Khaled gets into the car that is going to return home after dropping them off to proceed to their target, Said tells the driver to "Go." As the car speeds away, Khaled looks back tearfully at his friend through the rearview window, knowing he'll never see him again. The movie concludes soon after with Said standing on a crowded bus, his hand on the trigger in his pocket. A close-up shot of his face, then the crowded bus, then back to his face, and darkness!

Roger Ebert made some positive comments about the movie but was wistful because he would like to finally see a movie about a suicide bomber who is not religiously motivated, factiously closing his column on the movie by saying, "When higher powers are evoked to justify death on both sides of a dispute, does heaven [really] send four [sic] angels?"[90] The point is that the two young men are not particularly religious and even the scene that Ebert cites where one asks "What happens?" after you die, and is told "Two angels pick you up," misses the distinctly unreligious way this is conveyed as the dialogue continues: "Are you sure?" "Absolutely!" Matter resolved! Not really. It is not taken as a serious answer by the character in the film, nor was it meant to be a serious answer. Indeed, it is not religion that motivates Said to ultimately take his life and the lives of those around him; it was his humiliation. He completed his task, unlike Khaled who abandoned it, because, unlike Khaled, his father was unjustly killed as an Israeli collaborator when Said was ten, and Said has had to endure the shame and humiliation of this, he tells us repeatedly, his whole life.

Both films leave one big hole—the silence! The end result of their intended acts. By focusing on the bomber, the victims are forgotten. Even when Said touches the trigger in his pocket on the packed bus, we forget the innocent men and women who are about to lose their lives, and feel pity not for them but for Said. The focus in *Paradise Now* is on the tragedy of Said's lost life. It is important that the viewer appreciate that the suicide bombers are just ordinary people and not the stereotypically crazed fanatic. But the humanism of the bomber denies the horrors that are committed, a point cogently made in the documentaries that are discussed in the next chapter that assess the plight of returning, combat-injured veterans, many of whom were maimed by IEDs.

CONCLUSION

The Bush administration dominated the public discourse at the outset of the war years. Most of the public and cinematic attention focused on Iraq. This is because Iraq, more so than Afghanistan, unfolded in a major city with a clear focus: the entrance of American forces into the city of Baghdad and the removal of Saddam Hussein from power. The attention toward Iraq was also facilitated by the extraordinary number of journalists who covered the war. Some issues arose during the early stages of conflict with Iraq, but most concerns about the war were brushed aside before 2005. The Bush administration charged that members of the 9/11 Commission (2004) were not privy to the same insider information members of the administration had, and therefore could not state that Saddam Hussein did not have WMD—in any event, he was still a tyrant who had committed numerous atrocities, which itself was (ostensibly) reason to remove him from power. And while the behavior at Abu Ghraib that came to light in 2004 was clearly inappropriate, it was laid at the feet of a few errant individuals and was not something that was promoted by either ranking government or military personnel. The public, however, was not as convinced as they were at the outset of the war. Public opinion, while it had not turned, was beginning in 2005 to debate involvement in Iraq to a greater degree (see figures on pages 58 and 59).

The public was nudged to debate American involvement in 2004 by cinema since most other media sources either promoted the party line or did not challenge it—the Abu Ghraib scandal being the exception, but that came to light after Michael Moore's film debuted, which explains Moore's failure to reap this low-hanging fruit in his diatribe against the administration. One of the first films to directly assail the status quo was *Uncovered* in 2003, which countered Bush's heretofore unassailable symbolic capital by relying on key insiders who could claim their own privileged positions allowed them to state that no WMD existed, and that the president knew that no WMD existed but that he cherry-picked the evidence to find "facts" that supported his a priori contention. Nevertheless, *Uncovered*, in its limited release, truncated 2003 version, did not garner much attention. This cannot be said about Michael Moore's runaway hit, *Fahrenheit 9/11*, which appeared in early 2004.

The attention Moore's film achieved served as a major catalyst to stimulating the antithetical debate because it raised such a shrill voice against the status quo. Public voices had been raised before Moore's film, but to little account. The Dixie Chicks paid dearly for their offhand remark about the president, and Cindy Sheehan was often dismissed by the press as a lone, dissenting voice in the wilderness. The war was talked about more after Michael Moore's film debuted, even by those who had not seen his film. Though it had a decidedly liberal slant, Moore's film accomplished what he set out to do, which was to get people to at least see the other side of things. Seeing here means discussing the war, appreciating a different perspective, and giving it weight. It does not mean that he convinced people to change their minds. But a necessary antecedent to changing people's opinion is for them to appreciate an alternative to the one accepted. Moore's film did this, though many of the points he made were successfully refuted by two much smaller films, *Michael Moore Hates America* and *FahrenHYPE 9/11*.

The public's opinion on many topical social issues often mimics normal distribution, with roughly half the population leaning toward the liberal side and the other half leaning toward the conservative side. At the tail end of the distribution are some 20 percent of the population who are strongly locked to that side and little is going to change their perspective. In between resides the body of the populace who are roughly equally divided. Those closest to the middle ground are the ones most likely to appreciate the other perspective since they are not as entrenched as those further along the continuum. These are the ones who might see a film that proposes an antithetical view and be struck by its points, and change sides. Moving from a 50/50 split to even a 52/48 one can makes a big difference in the course of history: John F. Kennedy, who was largely responsible for escalating American involvement in Vietnam, won the 1960 presidential election against Richard Nixon by a fraction of the popular vote (49.72 percent to 49.55 percent), and George W. Bush beat Albert Gore by taking Florida, which gave him 50.37 percent of the electoral votes to Gore's 49.44 percent.

The dialectic years (2004–2005) began to challenge the administration's preeminent position. People were discussing the war more. If nothing else, the films helped to keep the issue alive. This made people think about the wars more than they otherwise might. This debate would change the world—at least for Bush and the Republican Party. Prior to 2004, the Bush administration held the high ground. In 2006, there was a decided change of opinion against involvement in Iraq and the president's handling of the war. Films preceded the public change

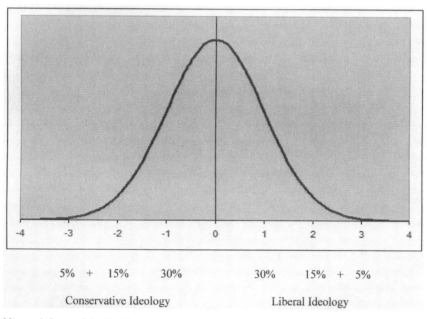

Normal Curve Distribution.

in attitude. In 2003, coverage of the war was solidly in Bush's camp; in 2004, the year the cinematic debate was launched, films were roughly evenly divided; one year later, domestic films against the war outnumbered films promoting involvement by a margin of 2:1. It would not be until 2006 that the public opinion toward the war started to shift and turned against keeping troops in Iraq. In subsequent years, as will be seen in the next two chapters, antithetical films basically took over the debate, and the shift against involvement in the war that began to coalesce in 2006 would significantly rise.

Despite the growing cinematic antagonism toward the war, numerous films promoted a positive view of those who fought. The movies that fall into what we've labeled the "grunt at the front" show the troops going about their everyday business. The grunts do not always come off in the most positive light and their attitudes toward the locals sometimes appear quite benighted. Ranking military personnel had not foreseen this. They were so focused on selling the picture to embedded journalists—who they often (at least tacitly) required to submit their material to them before disseminating it—that they did not realize that the ground troops were taking videos of their day-to-day activities and sending the footage home without any seal of approval. And because the men were talking among themselves, their comments are often quite stark. These comments come through loud and clear in many of the videos, and they sometimes represent "America's finest" in a tarnished light. Despite some of the more questionable insights these rank-and-file military members share with their audience, they are generally portrayed as simple, honest men and women who are doing a difficult job and just want to come home alive.

The everyday activity of the soldiers helps to differentiate this war from Vietnam. There was no humanization of the men on the ground in Vietnam. The result was that the negative attitude toward the war carried over to the troops. The humanization that took place during Gulf War II was helped by embedded journalists who so strongly identified with the men and women they lived with that it was nearly impossible for the journalists to be impartial. The journalists' biases in reporting events would subsequently be substantiated by research on the stories they filled and how they depicted events. The military, however, favorably regarded the results of embedding, which minimized the need to censor stories from the front. Ironically, and quite inadvertently, the journalists do not come off anywhere near as positively as the military personnel they depict. In fact, most of the documentaries that feature reporters' perspectives reveal that the reporters often put the men in the field at risk because of their lack of knowledge of military protocol in a combat zone.

A potpourri of other films increased the antithetical margin during this pivotal period from 2:1 to 3:1. This is a significant increase when one recalls that at the time the public was evenly splintered on the war. The margin is raised by quasi-foreign and foreign films. These films are generally critical of the war efforts, the sole exception being *Iraq in Fragments*, but *Fragments* is the only film in the group that is not really made by those with a Middle Eastern background, even if it was shot, not edited, by Iraqis. These films garnered attention precisely because the films examine the conflict in Iraq and Afghanistan from an insider's perspective. They present a face on the war that was generally not covered in the popular press.

The most successful of those in this category is *Control Room*, the only foreign film to inhabit the rarefied top ten slot for a political documentary released in the United States. It managed to capture the public's attention because it does not overly accentuate the Arabic perspective. This is nicely accomplished in *Control Room* because it is as much about the problem the media had in finding out what was taking place on the front lines as it is about Al Jazeera. *Control Room* portrays Al Jazeera as just another media source, simply wanting to report the truth. This focus keeps the film from strongly challenging the viewer's perspective while succeeding, at the same time, by giving the viewer insights into an organization that few in the West know much about. In the best dialectical tradition, *Control Room* hoped to convert the audience in much the same manner the rational discourse that unfolded in the film brought around by Lt. Rushing.

The other films in this category are much more value-laden in promoting the Arabic perspective, some more blatantly than others. One of the stronger antithetical films in this group is the quasi-foreign film *About Baghdad*. The film depicts a face of everyday Iraqis that has been seen in numerous other films: "We're glad America removed Saddam." The "other" side of the war that is depicted is one not often captured in the domestic product—the growing disgruntlement toward the continued American presence in Iraq: "Saddam is gone. Now we want to rule ourselves." The hostility toward the continued American presence is made even starker because it is one of the few films during this period that challenges the grunt's view that their cordon-and-sweep endeavors are not appreciated—grunt documentaries justify the raids as necessary to promote stability by rounding up insurgents. It is surprising that so few films have raised the point that these activities are problematic, but then American forces don't seem to feel their tactics are flawed. It was not until 2009 when a directive came down from General Stanley McChrystal in Afghanistan that bursting into homes in the middle of the night might not be appreciated: "We didn't understand what a culture line it was," McChrystal said of the regular night raids.[91] *About Baghdad* is the earliest voice to cast doubt on activities by American forces that had not heretofore been examined.

The other films in this latter group are unique to this period because they are among the rare set of fictive features to assess the war and its consequences. *Turtles Can Fly* examines the consequences of Saddam's war with Iran by looking at the minefields which litter northern Iraq. It is not a direct attack on occupying forces but it still falls into the anti-thetical camp for two reasons: (1) the mines that have injured so many are American-made, which underscores the complicity of the United States with Saddam's regime; and (2) the arrival of coalition forces does not adumbrate any significant improvement in the lives of the Iraqi people or in the fate of the nation. The same holds for both *Paradise Now* and *Making of* that depict the recruitment of suicide bombers. They, too, lean toward an antithetical assessment of the situation in the Middle East. Neither promotes the use of IEDs as a solution to the problem, but they do suggest that the seeds for sowing terrorism are at least partially the result of conditions in the Middle East fostered by American foreign policy. These issues are addressed more forthrightly in subsequent documentaries and in the surge in domestic fictive features that begin to appear.

NOTES

1. Job ratings are tied to war: FDR's popularity rose to the highest level of his four-term presidency and hit 84 percent after the Japanese attacked Pearl

Harbor; Truman's hit 87 percent after FDR's death and the war marched toward its conclusion; JFK's reached 83 percent after the Bay of Pigs invasion; and George H. W. Bush's climbed to an all-time high of 89 percent during Gulf I. Sheldon Rampton and John Stauber, *Weapons of Mass Deception: The Uses of Propaganda in Bush's War on Iraq* (New York: Jeremy P. Tarcher/ Penguin, 2003), 144; "Post September 11 Attitudes," 6 December, 2001, www .people-press.org/report/144 (accessed 13 March 2009); Jody T. Allen, Nilanthi Samaranyske, and James Albrittain Jr., "Iraq and Vietnam: A Crucial Difference in Opinion," 22 March 2007, www.pewresearch.org/pubs/432 (accessed 20 September 2009).

2. At a sold-out concert in London, Maines said, "Just so you know, we're on the good side with y'all. We do not want this war, this violence, and we're ashamed that the president of the United States is from Texas [like us]."

3. See Frank E. Dardis, "Marginalization Devices in U.S. Press Coverage of Iraq War Protest: A Content Analysis," *Mass Communication & Society* 9, no. 2 (2006): 117–35; Howard Tumber and Jerry Palmer, *Media at War: The Iraq Crisis* (Thousand Oaks, Calif.: Sage, 2004); Todd Gitlin, *The Whole World Is Watching: Mass Media in the Making and Unmaking of the New Left* (1980; repr. Berkeley: University of California Press, 2003).

4. There were numerous large-scale demonstrations before the war commenced, but after the invasion of Iraq these demonstrations became rarer and when they did take place seldom exceeded a few thousand protestors.

5. Brian A. Patrick and A. Trevor Thrall, "Beyond Hegemony: Classic Propaganda Theory and Presidential Communication Strategy after the Invasion of Iraq," *Mass Communication & Society* 10, no. 1 (2007): 95–118.

6. Adam Hodges, "The Political Economy of Truth in the 'War on Terror' Discourse: Competing Visions of an Iraq/al-Qaeda Connection," *Social Semiotics* 17, no. 1 (2007): 5–20; see also Pierre Bourdieu, *Distinction: A Social Critique on the Judgment of Taste* (Cambridge, Mass.: Harvard University Press, 1984).

7. See Hodges, "The Political Economy of Truth in the 'War on Terror' Discourse."

8. Patrick and Thrall, "Beyond Hegemony," 106, 114; Hodges, "The Political Economy of Truth in the 'War on Terror' Discourse," 8.

9. Patrick and Thrall, "Beyond Hegemony," 113.

10. Robert S. Prichard, "The Pentagon Is Fighting—and Winning—the Public Relations War," *USA Today*, July 2003, 11–14(A); G. Ridge, "Embedded: The Media at War in Iraq," *Military Review* 84, no. 1 (2004): 74–75.

11. Ridge, "Embedded: The Media at War in Iraq."

12. Ridge, "Embedded: The Media at War in Iraq"; Tumber and Palmer, *Media at War*.

13. Jeffery Kahn, "Postmortem: Iraq War Media Coverage Dazzled but It Also Obscured," 18 March 2004, www.Berkeley.edu/news/media/releases/2004/03/18_iraqmedia (accessed 8 August 2009).

14. Kahn, "Postmortem"; see also Lori Herber and Vincent F. Filak, "Iraq War Coverage Differs In U.S., German Papers," *Newspaper Research Journal* 28, no. 3 (2007): 37–51; Patricia R. Zimmerman, *States of Emergency: Documentaries, Wars, Democracies* (Minneapolis: University of Minnesota Press, 2000); Carl Rising-Moore and Becky Oberg, *Freedom Underground: Protesting the War in America* (New York: Chamberlain Brothers/Penguin, 2004).

15. Zimmerman, *States of Emergency*, 57–60.

16. James R. Walker and Robert Bellamy, eds., *The Remote Control in the New Age of Television* (Westport, Conn.: Praeger, 1993); Robert Bellamy and James R. Walker, *Television and the Remote Control: Grazing on a Vast Wasteland* (New York: Guilford, 1996).

17. Rampton and Stauber, *Weapons of Mass Destruction*, 174; Gitlin, *The Whole World Is Watching*.

18. Rampton and Stauber, *Weapons of Mass Destruction*, 175; Justin Lewis, Sut Jhally, and Michael Morgan, "The Gulf War: A Study of the Media, Public Opinion and Public Knowledge," Center for the Study of Communication, University of Massachusetts at Amherst, February 1991, www-unix.oit.umass.edu/~commdept/resources/gulfwar (accessed 4 August 2009); see also Neil Postman and Steve Powers, *How to Watch TV News* (New York: Penguin, 1992).

19. "Our Fading Heritage: Americans Fail a Basic Test on Their History and Institutions," *Intercollegiate Studies Institute 2008*, www.americancivicliterarcy.org (accessed 5 August 2009).

20. J. T. Wood, "Saying It Makes It So: The Discursive Construction of Sexual Harassment," in *Conceptualizing Sexual Harassment as Discursive Practice*, ed. S. G. Bingham (Westport, Conn.: Praeger, 1994), 17; see also John Markert, *Sexual Harassment: A Resource Manual for Organizations and Scholars* (Spokane, Wash.: Marquette Books, 2010).

21. This is what is generally meant when it is said that Marx "turned Hegel's dialectics upside down" or that Marx believed Hegel was "standing on his head."

22. Karl Marx, *A Contribution to the Critique of Political Economy* (1859; repr., New York: International Publishers, 1970); Karl Marx and Fredrick Engles, *The German Ideology* (1924; repr., New York: Prometheus Books, 1998).

23. See Tumber and Palmer, *Media at War*; Piyush Mathur, "More Whitewash: The WMD Mirage," *Third World Quarterly* 27, no. 8 (2006): 1495–1507.

24. *Baghdad in No Particular Order* was shot prior to the invasion (December 2002–January 2003) and released in the United States in 2003. The movie is not critiqued here because it does not deal with the invasion. It is a refreshing film, however, because it is a montage of everyday Iraqis going about their everyday businesses which, at the time it was released, jarred with the bombs-bursting-in-air depiction of Iraq that most viewers were exposed to on the nightly news. The film had a distinct agenda, however. It was made by Paul Chan for the antiwar group Voices in the Wilderness, which had been working since 1996 to end economic sanctions and warfare against the people of Iraq.

25. Some sources suggest that the intelligence reports were clearly misinterpreted but an examination of various Congressional documents from 1990 to 2003 shows that a substantial number of reports released under the Freedom of Information Act still, as late as 2002 and 2003, maintained that Iraq, if it did not actually have WMD, had the capability to make them. Craig R. Whitney, ed., *The WMD Mirage: Iraq's Decade of Deception and America's False Premise for War* (New York: Public Affairs, 2005); see also Jeffrey Richelson, ed., "Iraq and Weapons of Mass Destruction," *National Security Archive Electronic Briefing Book No. 80*, 2004, www.gwu.edu/nsarchiv/NSAEBB/NSAEBB80 (accessed 9 September 2009); Mathur, "More Whitewash."

26. Terry Lawson, "Moore, Please: Snide, Bush-Bashing 'Fahrenheit 9/11' Stoops Low and Reveals Little." *Detroit Free Press*, June 24, 2004, www.debateforamerica.com/forum/printhead.php?t=1066.

27. Frederick M. Hess, "Still at Risk: What Students Don't Know, Even Now," *Common Core* 110, no. 2 (2009): 5–20; Diane Ravitch, *What Do Our 17-Year-Olds Know?* (New York: Harper and Row, 1987); Mark Bauerlein, *The Dumbest Generation: How the Digital Age Stupefies Young Americans and Jeopardizes Our Future* (New York: Tracher/Penguin, 2008); "Our Fading Heritage," 2008; E. D. Hirsch, *Cultural Literacy: What Every American Needs to Know* (Boston: Houghton Mifflin, 1987).

28. Hess, "Still at Risk."

29. Ravitch, *What Do Our 17-Year-Olds Know?*

30. In 1978, it was made as a high-quality television miniseries that is still available on DVD—Anthony Perkins plays the role of Chief Inspector Valjean. The movie was remade, first as a musical (*Les Misérables in Concert*, 1996) and then as a dramatic movie by Bille August in 1998. The French six-hour miniseries starring Gerard Depardieu as Valjean and John Malkovich as Javert was shortened to a three-hour television version for the American audience that was televised in both France and the United States in 2000.

31. See Peter Travers, "Why We Fight," *Rolling Stone*, 20 January 2006.

32. Guerilla News Network went dark in November 2009 and is now only accessible to registered members; A. Lappé, "The Weather Underground," *Guerrilla News Network*, May 3, 2003, www.upstatefilms.org/weather/guerrilla (accessed 16 August 2009).

33. *Outfoxed* is not listed in Table 2.3 of top-grossing political films because it does not directly pertain to post-9/11 events. It should be noted that *Outfoxed* is ranked no. 20 in the political documentary category and achieved $461.6K in box office receipts.

34. Ward Harkavy, "Perceptive Talking Heads Can't Redeem a Sloppy Cinematic Blog," *Village Voice*, 18 August 2004, 58. See also Dave Kehr, "Revisiting the Road to Iraq War, Step by Step," *New York Times*, 20 August 2004, 16(E); Wesley Morris, "Too Many Experts Almost Spoil 'Uncovered'," *Boston Globe*, 20 August 2004, 4(C); Jay Weissberg, "Uncovered: The War on Iraq," *Variety*, 11 August 2004, 33.

35. Peter Travers from *Rolling Stone*, criticism found at www.metacritic.com/video/title/whywefight.

36. Kevin Crust from the *Los Angeles Times*, criticism found at www.metacritic.com/video/title/whywefight.

37. Ty Burr, *Boston Globe*, criticism found at www.metacritic.com/video/title/whywefight.

38. Roger Ebert, "Why We Fight," *Chicago Sun-Times*, 17 Feburary 2006, 30(NC).

39. Bauerlein, *The Dumbest Generation*; Ravitch, *What Do Our 17-Year-Olds Know?*; Hirsch, *Cultural Literacy*.

40. Among their findings: 39 percent of college graduates cannot name the three branches of government; 32 percent believe the president (not Congress) has the power to declare war, and while 56 percent can name Paula Abdul as a judge on *American Idol*, only 21 percent could recognize a key phrase from Lincoln's Gettysburg Address. See "Our Fading Heritage."

41. David Ansen, "Why We Fight; directed by Eugene Jarecki," *Newsweek*, 23 January 2006, 65.

42. www.dmoz.com/News/Media/Watchdog is a website that lists more than thirty sources that regularly track biases in news reporting. Another excellent monitor is www.niemanwatchdog.org that is part of the Nieman Foundation for Journalism at Harvard University.

43. Ned Martel, "Turning a Critical Lens on Television News," *New York Times*, 4 February 2005, 22(E1).

44. *Fire over Afghanistan* is a rare action film and one of the few fictional features to address Afghanistan instead of Iraq. Jeff Walker (Fred Dryer) is a pilot who is shot down over Afghanistan. He teams up with a beautiful journal-

ist (Jordan Baynes) and together they track down an Afghan warlord who is putting bounties on American soldiers. It is a poorly done, cheap action film, that is cranked out in the same vein as much of Terence Winkless's other dubious films, such as *Get a Clue*, 1997; *Rage and Honor*, 1992; and *Bloodfist*, 1989.

45. Schecher has won numerous awards for television documentaries, but in a media with less strenuous production demands.

46. *Last Letters Home* is the story of ten military personnel killed during Operation Iraqi Freedom and the memories family members have of their loved ones as they read their last letter. It is likewise open to interpretation: conservatives will see the film as a tribute to fallen heroes; liberals will see their stories as a tragic loss in an unnecessary war.

47. Robert Koehler, "The War Within," *Variety*, 17 October 2005, 48.

48. Owen Gleiberman, "The War Within," *Entertainment Weekly*, 14 October 2005, 28.

49. Teresa Wiltz, "'The War Within': The Making of a Mild-Mannered Terrorist," *Washington Post*, 14 October 2005, 5(C).

50. A platoon from the 2/3 "Gunners" was also being followed by photojournalists from *Time* magazine, which picked "The American Soldier" as its 2003 Person of the Year.

51. Dreamland is the facetious name the soldiers dub their base near Fallujah.

52. Andrew M. Lindner, "Among the Troops: Seeing the Iraq War through Three Journalistic Vantage Points," *Social Problems* 56, no. 1 (2009): 21–49.

53. Lindner, "Among the Troops," 38. See also Michael Pfau and others, "Embedded Reporting and Occupation of Iraq: How the Embedding of Journalists Affects Television News Reports," *Journal of Broadcasting & Electronic Media* 49, no. 4 (2005): 468–87; Shakuntale Banaji and Ammar Al-Ghabban, "'Neutrality Comes From Inside Us': British-Asian and Indian Perspectives on Television News after 11 September," *Journal of Ethnic and Migration Studies* 32, no. 6 (2006): 1005–26.

54. See Jonathan Foreman, "How Not to Write About Iraq," *Commentary*, 126, no. 3 (October 2008): 42–45; Michael Fumento, "Covering Iraq: The Modern Way of War Correspondence," *National Review* 58, no. 20 (6 November 2006): 42–46; Karl Zinsmeister, "They're in the Army Now—Not Really: Most 'Embedded' Journalists are Fish Out of Water," *National Review* 55, no. 7 (21 April 2003): 32–34.

55. Deborah Scranton revisited her subject by giving minicams to another Guard Unit, the Bad Voodoo Platoon, which led to a one-hour PBS Frontline feature, *Bad Voodoo's War* (2007).

56. See Paul Arthur, "Iraq in No Particular Order," *filmcomment* (September–October 2006): 19–22.

57. Malcolm Turvey, "Iraqis under the Occupation: A Survey of Documentaries," *October*, no. 123 (Winter 2008): 234–41.

58. See Dana Stevens, "Voices of Iraq: For the Iraqis Interviewed, Daily Life is Better Today," 29 October 2004, Imdb.com (accessed 3 November 2009).

59. Ty Burr, "A Lucid Look at Al-Jazeera," *Boston Globe*, 11 June 2004, 1(D). See also A. O. Scott, "Film Festival Review; A Portrait of Al Jazeera, Reporting the War Its Way," *New York Times*, 2 April 2004, 15(E.1); Roger Ebert, "Control Room," *Chicago Sun Times*, 11 June 2004, 43.

60. Scott, "Film Festival Review."

61. Robert D. Kaplan, "Why I Love Al Jazeera," *Atlantic*, October 2009, 55–56.

62. Herbert J. Gans, *Deciding What's News: A Study of* CBS Evening News, NBC Nightly News, Newsweek *and* Time (New York: Random House, 1979).

63. Kaplan, "Why I Love Al Jazeera," 56.

64. See Mohammad El-Nawawy, *Al-Jazeera: The Story of the Network That Is Rattling Government and Redefining Modern Journalism* (Cambridge, Mass.: Westview, 2003); Hugh Miles, *Al-Jazeera: The Inside Story of the Arab News Channel That Is Challenging the West* (New York: Grove Press, 2005); M. Lynch, *Voices of the New Arab Public: Iraq, Al-Jazeera, and Middle East Politics Today* (New York: Columbia University Press, 2006).

65. See Kaplan, "Why I Love Al Jazeera"; Josh Rushing, *Mission Al Jazeera: Build a Bridge, Seek the Truth, Change the World* (New York: Palgrave Macmillian, 2007).

66. Al Jazeera often devotes fifteen minutes or more to a story. An in-depth story on any of the nightly news in the United States runs about two minutes and seldom exceeds five. See Kaplan, "Why I Love Al Jazeera."

67. Ebert, "Control Room," 2004. See also Bill Stamets, "Channeling Democracy: *Control Room*," *Senses of Cinema* 36, no. 3 (August 2004), www.sensesofcinema.com/2004/feature-articles/control room; Scott, "Film Festival Review"; P. Kennicott, "In *Control Room*, The Splitting Image of War Coverage," *Washington Post*, 16 June 2004, 1(C).

68. "Reel time" is used purposefully since the film, which depicts events in March 2003, was not released until 2004.

69. The name is even more telling today. The Mac (Mc) part of MacWhite[ness]'s name conveys a banalization and massification of consumer products (fast food) and services (education, religion, government) in American society that characterizes the growing preponderance of trite, low-quality products and services that are enthusiastically embraced by the public. The

"Mc"iffication of society was evident, but nowhere near as prevalent, when Lederer and Burdick wrote the novel in 1958. See George Ritzer, *The McDonaldization of Society: An Investigation into the Changing Character of Contemporary Social Life* (Newbury Park, Calif.: Pine Forge Press, 1993); John Drane, *The McDonaldization of the Church* (Macon, Ga.: Smyth & Helwys, 2008); Dennis Hayes, and Robin Wynyard, eds., *The McDonaldization of Higher Education* (Westport, Conn.: Bergin & Garvey, 2002).

70. The two exceptions are the cranked-out fictional film, *Fire over Afghanistan*, and the British documentary, *The Liberace of Baghdad*.

71. See chapter 1, endnote 1 for details about this movie.

72. Zidane was born in France (1972) of Algerian parents. He is a retired World Cup football player.

73. Roger Ebert "Movie Review: 'Turtles Can Fly'," *Chicago Tribune*, 14 April 2005, www.rogerebert.suntimes.com (accessed 16 October 2009).

74. Deborah Young, "The Tiger and the Snow," *Variety*, 12 October 2005; Kevin Thomas, "'Tiger' Loses Its Stripes with Dumb Antics," *Los Angeles Times*, 29 December 2006, 12(E).

75. One of the "silences" in these films is the failure to depict the increased number of females who are joining the ranks of suicide bombers. This silence may simply be that the phenomenon is fairly recent, but it is clear that not only are the numbers growing but that the motivation for becoming a suicide bomber is much different for women. See Karen Jacques and Paul J. Taylor, "Male and Female Suicide Bombers: Different Sexes, Different Reasons?" *Studies in Conflict & Terrorism* 31, no. 4 (2008): 304–26; Anne Speckhard, "The Emergence of Female Suicide Terrorists," *Studies in Conflict & Terrorism* 31, no. 11 (2008): 1023–51.

76. See Claude Berrebi, "Evidence about the Link between Education, Poverty, and Terrorism among Palestinians," *Peace Economics, Peace Science and Public Policy* 13, no. 1 (2007): 1–36; Riaz Hassan, "Global Rise of Suicide Terrorism: An Overview," *Asian Journal of Social Science* 36, no. 2 (2008): 271–91.

77. See Alan B. Krueger and Steven Lerner, "The Estimation of Choice Probabilities from Choice Base Samples," *The Journal of Economic Perspectives* 17, no. 4 (2003): 119–44; Rex A. Hudson, and Marilyn Lundell Majeska, *The Sociology and Psychology of Terrorism: Who Becomes a Terrorist and Why?* (Washington, D.C.: Federal Research Division, Library of Congress, 1999); Charles Russell and Bowman Miller, "Profile of a Terrorist," in *Perspectives on Terrorism*, eds. Lawrence Zelic Freedman and Yonah Alexander (Wilmington, Del.: Scholarly Resources, 1983), 45–60.

78. Berrebi, "Evidence about the Link between Education, Poverty, and Terrorism among Palestinians," 8.

79. Brian Glyn Williams, "Mullah Omar's Missiles: A Field Report on Suicide Bombers in Afghanistan," *Middle East Policy* VX, no. 4 (2008): 26–46.

80. The 9/11 terrorists were all educated and Osama bin Laden, as most everyone knows, came from an extraordinarily wealthy family. Hassan, "Global Rise of Suicide Terrorism"; Russell and Miller, "Profile of a Terrorist."

81. Mohammed M. Hafez, *Manufacturing Human Bombs: The Making of Palestinian Suicide Bombers* (Washington, D.C.: U.S. Institution of Peace Press, 2006). See also Mohammed M. Hafez, *Suicide Bombers in Iraq: The Strategy and Ideology of Martyrdom* (Washington, D.C.: U.S. Institution of Peace Press, 2007); Mohammed M. Hafez, *Why Muslims Rebel: Repression and Resistance in the Islamic World* (Boulder, Colo.: Lynne Rienner Publishers, 2003); Hassan, "Global Rise of Suicide Terrorism"; Williams, "Mullah Omar's Missiles."

82. In Pape's study, the leading instigator of suicide attacks between 1990 and 2001 were committed by the Tamil Tigers in Sri Lanka, a radical nationalist group whose members are from Hindu families but are adamantly opposed to religion. See Robert A. Pape, *Dying to Win: The Strategic Logic of Suicide Terrorism* (New York: Random House, 2005); Jacques and Taylor, "Male and Female Suicide Bombers"; Hassan, "Global Rise of Suicide Terrorism."

83. See Raphael Patai, *The Arab Mind* (New York: Hatherleigh Press, 2002); Enis MacEain, "Suicide Bombing as Worship," *Middle East Quarterly* 16, no. 4 (2009): 15–24.

84. Patai, *The Arab Mind*, 101–12.

85. Pape, *Dying to Win*; Hassan, "Global Rise of Suicide Terrorism."

86. See Hassan, "Global Rise of Suicide Terrorism," 286.

87. Scott Atran, "The Moral Logic and Growth of Suicide Terrorism," *Washington Quarterly* 29, no. 2 (2006): 127–47.

88. Shortly thereafter, and with this scene still fresh in the audience's mind, we learn that there are strings attached to the money. Bahta is informed that he has to do what he's told because "I gave you money."

89. Marc Sageman, *Understanding Terror Networks* (Philadelphia: University of Pennsylvania Press, 2004).

90. Roger Ebert, "Paradise Now," *Chicago Sun-Times*, 11 June 2004, 43.

91. "NATO Directive Limits Night Raids," *USA Today*, 15 February 2009: 8(A).

THE DIALECTIC RAGES ON

Documentary Films 2006–2010

The dialectical process suggests a reciprocal discourse. This certainly was seen in the thesis/antithesis cinematic dialogue in the last chapter where antithetical films outweighed those that took the administration's stance by a margin of close to 2:1, with seven films weighing in on the side of the war while ten, including Michael Moore's film, weighed in against the war. At first glance, the thesis/antithesis arguments that took place in the second half of the decade look less skewed. There are four thesis films in this period and four general antithesis films that access Iraq, with two more taking a critical stance toward the war in Afghanistan. But if the antithesis films are broadened to encompass the Abu Ghraib prison scandals and the Guantanamo facility, the ratio of antithesis films increases by almost a 3:1 margin.

Thesis
No Substitute for Victory: From Vietnam to Iraq (2006)
The Hunt for Zargawi (2006)
The Surge (2007)
The Iraq War (2008)

Antithesis: General

Iraq for Sale: The War Profiteers (2006)
No End in Sight (2007)
War Made Easy (2007)
Bush's War (2008)
The Tillman Story (2010)
Behind Taliban Lines (2010)

Antithesis: Abu Ghraib/Guantanamo

The Prisoner, or, How I Planned to Kill Tony Blair (2006)
My Country, My Country (2006)
The Road to Guantanamo (2006)
Taxi to the Dark Side (2007)
Ghosts of Abu Ghraib (2007)
Standard Operating Procedure (2007)
The Oath (2010)

The thesis films of this period are not dramatically different from those from 2004 and 2005. *No Substitute for Victory* simply repeats, intact, an earlier narration by John Wayne who explains the domino theory in Southeast Asia and why American troops need to be there. There is no connection to Iraq except that Iraq has been added to the title in a crass attempt to cash in on the Iraqi angle. The argument promoted by Wayne and the other featured player, Staff Sergeant Barry Sadler, for American involvement in Vietnam has strong parallels to that which the Bush administration relied on to justify American intervention in Iraq, which is why it is likely to be embraced by conservative viewers. Wayne's mantra was "the Commies are coming, the Commies are coming"; Bush's was "the terrorists, the terrorists."

The other thesis films at least are relevant to the current conflict, even if they add little. *The Hunt for Zargawi* retools the hunt for Saddam Hussein films with similar results. The most wanted al-Qaeda terrorist in Iraq, Abu Musab al-Zargawi, was killed by two 500-pound bombs. Technology triumphs again, as it also does in *The Iraq War*, a rather late entry by the History Channel that continues the glorified spectacle of war by parading America's decisive military victory in Iraq as a direct result of its sophisticated weaponry. *The Surge* at least makes a contribution to the thesis stance because it is the only one to justify the rationale for the military buildup in Iraq long after the war was officially over.

The more general antithesis films that focus on Iraq also do not significantly add to the dialog. Indeed, *War Made Easy: How Presidents and Pundits Keep Spinning Us to Death* had been raised in just about every antithesis film in the 2004–2005 period. *War Made Easy* simply lays the root cause of all wars since World War II at the deceptive footprint of Washington elites. Sean Penn, who provides sporadic narration, is surprisingly dull, or, in the words of Jeannette Catsoulis with the *New York Times*, evinces "all the personality of a potato."[1] The movie can be similarly characterized. Much the same can be said for *No End in Sight*. *The Tillman Story* and *Behind Taliban Lines* stand up because as the war winds down in Iraq after 2008 attention is turned to the Afghan campaign, though neither adds markedly to the storehouse of public knowledge about events in Afghanistan.

Like *War Made Easy*, *No End in Sight* offers little substance. The reason for Iraq has likewise been made before. It simply (re)points an accusative finger. The primary decision makers were a bunch of armchair warriors without military experience. It may be true that these Washington insiders did not have military experience, but much the same can be said of Lincoln (Civil War) and Johnson (Vietnam), who each had only one year of active duty experience (1832 and 1942, respectively), and, of course, neither Wilson (World War I) nor Roosevelt (World War II) had any military experience—indeed, it is surprising that no thesis film has developed this point to rebut this recurring criticism of antithesis films.[2] The movie argues, somewhat more convincingly, that this lack of experience was aggravated by the administration's failure to listen to ranking military advisors. But like Kennedy with the Bay of Pigs, the people who advise tend to have a lockstep mentality that William Whyte called groupthink: individual creativity, uniqueness, and independent thinking are lost in the pursuit of group cohesiveness by group members who try to minimize conflict and reach consensus.[3]

Despite JFK's military experience, he *wanted* to invade Cuba, and because of his predisposition, his advisors went along and did not present a strong case for not invading in the now infamous debacle.[4] In the Bay of Pigs fiasco one of Kennedy's advisors, Arthur Schlesinger, who was opposed to the invasion, later lamented, "I bitterly reproached myself for having kept so silent during those crucial discussions in the cabinet room. . . . I can only explain my failure to do more than raise a few timid questions by reporting that one's impulse to blow the whistle on this nonsense was simply undone by the circumstances of the discussion."[5] The same can be said with George W. Bush. Hindsight inevitably leads to the *correct* conclusion. After a decade of war in Iraq, it is now conventional wisdom that invading Iraq was the wrong decision, but at the time many ranking politicians and military personnel thought it was the right one. Bush's problem with Iraq was not the war, which militarily ended rather quickly, but in failing to extricate America's forces from Iraq after the war was officially over—which meant to Bush that Saddam had been deposed. This point is crucial to why American troops remain in Iraq. The problem, only tangentially touched on in the film, was that George W. Bush, unlike his father, had virtually no international expertise and therefore did not fully grasp the implications of Saddam's removal. This is the reason there is no end in sight. It is also the reason that the most frequently used adjective (56 percent) to describe President Bush is "incompetent."[6]

No End, like many thesis and antithesis films critiqued in the last chapter, covers too much territory too perfunctorily and thus fails to provide any significant insights. It is further hampered by traveling familiar territory. *Iraq for Sale: The War Profiteers* also covers familiar ground but is saved because it does it more thoroughly than predecessor films that, at best, only briefly touch on the issue. It is cinematically also lifted above the other antithesis movies in this section because it is done by seasoned filmmaker Robert Greenwald who did *Outfoxed* (2004) and both *Uncovered* films (2003, 2004). Here Greenwald tackles Halliburton and Blackwater, as well as other corporations contracted to provide services in Iraq, such as DynCorp (police training), Transatlantic Traders (surveillance aircraft) and TITAN (interrogators). Halliburton and Blackwater justifiably bear the brunt of Greenwald's attention because they were among the largest and most profitable of the various companies in Iraq, and Greenwald musters an impressive array of graphics to make this point; of course, Vice President Cheney's former association with Halliburton is mentioned, as it always is, because it inevitably raises a nepotistic eyebrow.

As an antithetical film, it does not explore the driving rationale that led to the use of contractors to provide services once the realm of the military, but it does convincingly underscore how the profit motive can lead to the failure of providing adequate services. The big bad corporation, in the best David and Goliath tradition, is always, and often deservedly, a popular theme. It is also one that Greenwald had some success with the previous year when he assailed Wal-Mart in *Wal-Mart: The High Cost of Low Prices*. In a sense, Greenwald simply marries two successful former films: *Outfoxed*, which raised many of these issues but not in this detail, and *Wal-Mart*, which set the pace for assailing corporate greed, transferring the theme from rural Arkansas to Iraq.

Bush's War is also an antithesis film. It is a compilation of some "40-plus hours of documentary footage and 400 interviews" of preexisting PBS tapes that are repackaged for the PBS Frontline series in 2008 to commemorate the fifth anniversary of the Iraq invasion. It runs four and a half hours. It's all been done before. Nevertheless, it is an excellent overview for anyone not familiar with the political machinations that led, in the aftermath of the attack on the WTC, first to the invasion of Afghanistan and then justified the incursion into the tar baby of Iraq. It is told from the perspective of 2008 and not 2003 or 2004. The result is a clearly antithetical interpretation of events that reflects the mood of the country after five years of escalating American casualties. The chapter heads can be interpreted positively or negatively, but in this case they are all negative: Cheney's Focus: New Wartime Powers (subverting Congress); Cheney's Secret Plan for Handling Detainees (circumventing the Geneva Convention); Working in the Shadows (ignoring human rights); Rumsfeld: Hardball In-Fighter (bull in a china shop; won't listen to advice); Tough New Interrogation Techniques (appraised negatively); Powell Makes the Case for War at the United Nations (based on misleading information from the White House); Plans for Postwar Iraq Quickly Go Awry (because Rumsfeld rejected the need for more military *after* the war than was needed to fight the war); No Weapons of Mass Destruction; Things Are Getting Bad, Fast; and the Insurgency Rages (leading to more, rather than less troops being committed).

ABU GHRAIB ON THE BIG SCREEN

The body of antithetical films addresses the Abu Ghraib scandal. Abu Ghraib came to light between January and May 2004. It received considerable media attention and is a key reason why 76 percent of Americans were aware of the abuses that took place there.[7] This awareness can be attributed to the graphic photographs of torture that appeared in the press and on the news throughout 2004 and 2005. The initial question was whether this was an isolated incident conducted by a few errant military personnel, the side the administration promoted, or whether it was fostered, if not officially sanctioned, by administration policy that viewed torture as a sometimes necessary means to end terrorism. A number of earlier dialectical films (2004–2005) briefly addressed these points. There were two films on the thesis side and three on the antithesis side. *Buried in the Sand* dismisses Abu Ghraib by giving it short shift, passing over it as if it were of no consequence; *Voices of Iraq* laughs it off by having an Iraqi say that Saddam Hussein's torture was much, much worse. This is countered by *Soldier's Pay* when retired Marine Corp Major General J. Michael Myatt says that the behavior that took place at Abu Ghraib was "the darkest cloud to descend on the military in my lifetime"; it is raised in *Return to the Land of Wonders* when an Iraqi man the director is interviewing tells of his unjust imprisonment at Abu Ghraib. The only film that dwells on the issue is the fictional film *The War Within* that is set in New York City. It is a strong indictment against the Bush administration's use of torture, even though no connection to Abu Ghraib is made, because the protagonist's abduction and torture directly leads to his terrorist affiliation.

It is really not until 2006 that documentary films focusing on Abu Ghraib begin to be released. This lag is partially attributed to the year-plus it usually takes to put a film together. But it is just as likely that the dust had not settled in 2004 as to exactly who was responsible for the incidents or just how extensive they were: the Senate hearings that commenced in May did not conclude until near the end of 2004. By 2005, it was becoming clearer that the incidents at Abu Ghraib were fostered by the administration's stance toward torture and that the pictures depicted not just a few isolated instances of abuse but exposed a much deeper pathology.

Ghosts of Abu Ghraib, which aired on HBO, is a good, solid film (1:18) by Rory Kennedy (daughter of Robert) who won an Emmy for her 2007 documentary. It does not significantly add to the public knowledge of Abu Ghraib reported in the news, but it does nicely weave the isolated news material into a coherent narrative and is the first to do so. It also strongly underscores the administration's bureaucratic virtuosity in handling the scandal that it was responsible for creating: the viewer learns that the secretary of defense is not happy with the results of the interrogations at Abu Ghraib, which are nowhere near as productive as those that have taken place in Guantanamo, and so Major General Geoffrey Miller is "sent to Iraq to 'Gitmoize' the situation." Despite the apparent collusion from higher-ups, only a handful of noncommissioned officers (NCOs) who regularly appeared in the photographs were charged, found guilty, sentenced to serve time, and dishonorably discharged. The film suggests that their only real guilt is that they followed orders. This dubious point will be examined more closely after critiquing the next film, but it is cogently made by the way this movie is framed. *Ghosts* opens and closes with file footage from Dr. Stanley Milgram's famous obedience study at Yale in 1961. Milgram is shown in a white lab coat urging ordinary men to give electric shocks to people simply because he urges them to do it. The reason they comply is that Milgram is imbued with authority, otherwise the subjects would not have inflicted electric shocks past the danger point, 450 volts. The implication is obvious: the everyday soldiers at Abu Ghraib would have never done what they did unless they were ordered to. The fault, then, *Ghosts* boldly states, is not with the rank-and-file guards at Abu Ghraib, but with those higher in the chain of command. Stanley Milgram's conclusions are left ringing in the viewer's ear as the film closes. He states that his findings are "disturbing [because it shows that] human nature cannot be counted on to insulate men from brutality and inhuman treatment at direction of malevolent authorities. Substantial numbers of people [simply] do what they are told to do." The film fades out as George W. Bush is seen signing the Military Commission Act (HR-6166) in October 2006 that authorized military commissions to try alien unlawful enemy combatants as suspected terrorists, "further eroding rights granted under the Geneva Convention."

Standard Operating Procedure (SOP) is a feature film documentary (1:50) released in 2008 by Sony Pictures. It is produced and directed by virtuoso documentarian, Errol Morris (*The Thin Blue Line*, 1988; *The Fog of War*, 2003). The title takes its name from a comment by a former police officer who was charged with analyzing the pictures, and who, remarking on the sequence of events depicted, indicated that the torture of prisoners at Abu Ghraib was obviously standard operating procedure.

Morris attempts to understand why the pictures were taken. Less blatantly than *Ghosts* and the other films that address Abu Ghraib, he only hints that higher-ups were culpable. Early in the film former Brigadier General Janis Karpinski, who oversaw the Military Police Brigade in Iraq,[8] says that she was told by General Miller that she was too soft on the prisoners: "You have to treat the prisoners like dogs. You have to let them know you are in control." The brass is not mentioned during much of the film, but at the very end, after hearing the concluding comments of those who were court-martialed, the viewer is reminded that "no one above the rank of Staff Sergeant has served any time in prison for abuses at Abu Ghraib." The statement is true but misleading because while no ranking officer "served any time in prison" Brigadier General Karpinski was demoted to colonel, effectively ending her military career.[9]

SOP focuses on the pictures themselves, which are shown in a montage throughout the film, interspersed with commentary by five of the seven MPs who were court-martialed. J. Hoberman, critiquing the film for the *Village Voice*, feels that the director "cuts the Abu Ghraib MPs some slack" because he doesn't specifically condemn their actions.[10] This may be true, but Morris allows them to condemn themselves. The pictures were taken by Sabina Harmon, who boastfully sent them home to prove how they were abusing the terrorists because no one "would believe [it] if [they] didn't see [it on tape]." The interviewees are naturally resentful that they had to pay the price; they are the sacrificial victims that are necessary: "[we're] how they'll cover it up." They don't get it, though. They seem to feel their only crime was taking the pictures: "The whole thing would've gone away without those pictures." Private Lyndie England, who appeared in many of the photographs, says they "only did what we were told to soften them up for interrogation." Besides, she says elsewhere in the film, "We didn't kill them. We didn't cut their heads off." Referring to the infamous leash picture that she appeared in, she admits it "might have been unorthodox, but he wasn't hurt." Another laughs as he fondly recalls that they deprived the prisoners of sleep by pounding them with loud music: "they got used to Metallica guitars . . . then I played country music. That worked. They couldn't stand it." Indeed, one of the most unsettling aspects of the interviews in *SOP* is how fondly many recall some of the fun they had.

The telltale camera from *Standard Operating Procedure*.

The behavior of those at Abu Ghraib and of some of the attitudes and behavior of the grunts at the front that is often remarked on in these films is how young, and hence how impressionable, many of those recruits are. This is compounded by the lack of training they were given to prepare them for the task at hand. But there are some old hands in all these events, too: Sergeant Granner at Abu Ghraib, for instance, was fifteen years older than England, who turned twenty-one while she was at Abu Ghraib. Age is too simplistic an explanation. One of the

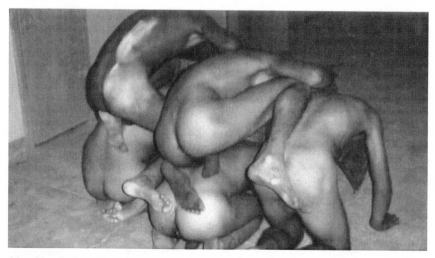

Abu Ghraib from *Taxi to the Dark Side*.

Abu Ghraib from *Taxi to the Dark Side*.

interviewees who was at Abu Ghraib inadvertently explains the driving rationale for their behavior: When he arrived, he says, he found the behavior at the prison "unusual, weird, and wrong . . . [but] that's the way it was, [so] it was okay."

Going alone with others is more than groupthink, though groupthink plays a part in the process. Groupthink becomes pronounced when

Explaining aberrant behavior in *Standard Operating Procedure*: "I was blinded by love."

Explaining aberrant behavior in *Standard Operating Procedure*: "Yeah, we're really not supposed to do that, but . . . "

people are immersed in what Erving Goffman called a total institution, which is defined as "a place of residence and work where a large number of like-situated individuals, cut off from the wider society for an appreciable period of time, together lead an enclosed, formally administered round of life."[11] An institution where one is cut off from the wider society and which has twenty-four-hours-a-day, seven-day-a-week control over an individual is relatively rare: prisons and locked psychiatric facilities are common examples of total institutions. An extended tour in Iraq or Afghanistan where one interacts almost exclusively with other like-minded soldiers, like Abu Ghraib, could qualify as a total institution. At the very least, a combat tour in Iraq and Afghanistan would cause what I call a social eclipse, which takes place when one is cut off from outside stimuli, but some degree of contact nevertheless remains with the social world of orientation—letters from loved ones, telephone calls, television shows, and so forth.[12] The more people are cut off from their social world of orientation, the more severe the social eclipse, which is to say, the more they may be affected by those they are around and consequently change some of their attitudes and behavior. It is the total isolation that took place at Abu Ghraib that, while it did not necessarily cause the behavior to occur, does explain why it quickly became standard operating procedure.

VARIATIONS ON ABU GHRAIB

The other three films that touch on Abu Ghraib or related events have a more distinct approach to the topic than either *Ghosts* or *SOP*. *Taxi to the Dark Side* relies on the docudrama format to tell its story about similar events in Afghanistan; *The Prisoner, or How I Planned to Kill Tony Blair* is about Abu Ghraib, but told from the point of view of a prisoner falsely incarcerated in the infamous prison; *Road to Guantanamo*, as the name suggests, tells the tale of three young British citizens of Pakistani origin who decide on their visit to Pakistan to check things out for themselves and travel to Afghanistan where they were detailed by Northern alliance forces before undergoing what is called "extraordinary rendition" to Guantanamo (see *Rendition*, 2007; *Extraordinary Rendition*, 2007).[13] The films are critiqued in chronological order.

The Prisoner, or How I Planned to Kill Tony Blair

The Prisoner's length, seventy minutes, makes it one of the shorter featured film documentaries. The length works in the film's favor by making it more focused. It is also helped by the seasoned writer-director team of Michael Tucker and Petra Epperlein who were responsible for the critically acclaimed *Gunner Palace*. It is the story of Yunis Khatayer Abbas (and his two brothers) who was a freelance journalist who was proximate to a house that was raided by military personnel because they had information that a terrorist cell might be making a bomb that would be used to kill Prime Minister Blair during his Iraqi visit. Yunis happened to be at the wrong place at the wrong time, and so was rounded up with other suspicious terrorists and carted off to be interrogated. The scene is reminiscent of the one shot by the filmmakers when they followed American troops to make *Gunner Palace* in 2003. They picked up Yunis's story eighteen months later to make *The Prisoner*.

A military spokesman says the raid, called Operation Grab Ass, was "a quite simple [one]," and while they found no bombs, they got the bomb makers. They are sure Yunis is a terrorist because he talks back to them and won't shut up when told to. He tells the viewer that when his interrogators ask him where the plans are and he tells them he is innocent, they bark, "You're a liar." Shortly thereafter he is transferred to Camp Ganci, a tent city enclosed by barbed wire at Abu Ghraib with 4,000 others of "no intelligence values." The rest of the story is his experiences there and his attempts to gain his freedom. After nine months, he is brought before the camp commander and told, "We don't know why you're here. . . . Sorry." Yunis is understandably upset with the apology that took away nearly a year of his life. "Sorry?" he says. "That's it? Nine months!" On May 2004 he takes a taxi home and he and his brothers celebrate the end of their ordeal. The prison pictures that the viewer might be familiar with are given an Iraqi face, and that makes this picture stand out from the crowd. It is the first to give the Iraqi perspective in any detail.

Road to Guantanamo

Abu Ghraib received its share of attention largely owing to the graphic photographs that make it all too evident what took place there. Guantanamo had been in the news long before many stateside ever heard of Abu Ghraib, but because no unauthorized military personnel had access to the base in Cuba, few were aware of what took place. Abu Ghraib connected the dots because General Miller was specifically re-assigned to Abu Ghraib from Guantanamo to "Gitmoize" interrogations at Abu Ghraib. *Road* is the first to focus extensively on the base. It is also one of only a handful of docudramas relating to events surrounding 9/11 (see *9/11 Commission Report*). A thin line separates docudramas from fictionalized features based on true events. The latter tells a dramatic story about something that took place, but the director is free to improvise the thoughts, words, and deeds of those whose story is being told. Good examples of 9/11-related films that fall into the fictionalized depiction of actual events would include *World Trade Center*, 2006; *Valley of the Wolves*, 2006; *Battle for Haditha*, 2007; and *The Hurt Locker*, 2009. Docudramas, on the other hand, act out the events of the principals involved. It dramatizes their story by putting their actual words into the mouth of actors; their actions may be intercut with file footage of events they are discussing or voice-overs that tell some aspect of the story being enacted. It is also common to have experts appear, in the best documentary tradition, to lend credence to parts of the story being told.

Road revolves around Asif (Afran Usman) whose mum in Tipton (Birmingham) wants him to go home to Pakistan to find a wife. He is accompanied on his trip by three friends, Fuhel (Farhad Harqun), Shafiq (Riz Ahmed), and Monir (Wagar Siddiqui). There, they decide to see for themselves what is going on in Afghanistan. They are surprised at how easy the border is to cross, a point that underscores the permeability of the Pakistan-Afghanistan border for Westerners who are used to more clearly delineated separations between countries. This early part is largely travelogue. It allows one to see the normalcy of activities in Afghanistan as people go about their everyday business; it also emphasizes the primitiveness of the country. They are not particularly happy with their sojourn, finding their journey around Afghanistan arduous, the situation unpleasant ("this is the middle of nowhere"), and the Nan tasteless. They also suddenly find themselves in the middle of a war, which is decidedly unlike wars they've seen in the movies: "Fucking shit," one says when bombs start to drop, "it's terrifying." In the confusion, Monir is separated from his friends. He is never seen again.

The remaining three are able to escape the conflict in Kunduz province, and a day later arrive in Mazar-e-Sharif. There they are arrested and taken to Sheberghan Prison in Northern Afghanistan, where, we are told in a television news bite, "hundreds of Afghani and foreign fighters are being held. . . . These Taliban fighters are presumed highly dangerous." It looks like things are going to turn out all right, however. They are pulled from their cell and stood before an army interrogator, who learns they are from Tipton: "You're from England, asshole? Why here? It's okay, you're in U.S. custody now." But the interrogators are not looking for terrorists so much as "detainees we can use for collecting intelligence." This is why, suddenly, their heads are hooded and they, along with numerous other detainees, are marched lockstep into the belly of a cargo plane. Their destination—Guantanamo.

At the airbase in *Dr. Strangelove*, Kubrick mocks the mentality of the Cold War by having the slogan, "Peace at Any Price," embossed over the gate (see also *Make Peace or Die*, 2006). At Camp Delta in Guantanamo, the three are greeted by the slogan, "Honor Bound to Defend Freedom." The remainder of the film very effectively shows the harshness of how they and the other prisoners are treated, and the sham tribunals the military was forced to set up in the face of the Supreme Court's decision that detainees had a right to a trial (see also *The Oath*, 2009). The viewer learns just how General Miller "Gitmoized" the base. In the end, they are told, like Yunis in *The Prisoner*, "Okay, we made a grave mistake. . . . Congratulations, you've been cleared." They are released and

Arriving at Guantanamo Bay in *Taxi to the Dark Side*.

treated like "three kings: burgers, pizza, television." Then they are told, "We want you to work for us." Their obstinate refusal ("Fuck you, man") leads to three more month's detention: "No, fuck you. Now, you're not going home." In the end they do, thanks to pressure from the British government to release them. As we watch a plane take off with the three aboard, the concluding crawl informs the viewer that 750 prisoners were held at Guantanamo and that 500 are still there. "Only ten ever charged. None ever found guilty of any crime."

Taxi to the Dark Side

Taxi focuses on the story of one Afghan young man, Dilawar, and his imprisonment, torture, and death in Afghanistan. This film completes the cycle of abuse: the detention and treatment of innocent people is standard operating procedure wherever U.S. forces have a presence (see also *The War Within*). This Oscar winner for best documentary is directed, written, and narrated by Alex Gibney, who also made *Enron: The Smartest Man in the Room* (2005) and *Casino Jack and the United States of Money* (2010).

The "dark side" in *Taxi* is not just what happened to Dilawar, but the attitude of the government. A clip in the film with Vice President

Dick Cheney on *Meet the Press* shortly after 9/11 enunciates just how dark the dark side is going to get: "A lot that needs to be done will have to be done quietly without any discussion about sources [using whatever] methods that are available to our intelligence agencies . . . that's the world these folks [terrorists] operate in." In short, any means are justified to prevent another attack on the United States. *Taxi*, to quote Robert Ebert (2008), is not a movie about "anything I learned in civics class."[14]

Dilawar is the family pride and joy. The family members are peanut farmers and they proudly encourage his upward mobility: He wants to move to the city and become a taxi driver. He and his three passengers suddenly disappeared one day; we learn later that they were fingered by an Afghan guerilla commander in an attempt to ingratiate himself with American military personnel to deflect attention to his own culpability in a recent rocket attack on their base. Five days after Dilawar is taken to Bagran Air Base, an old, abandoned Soviet base that now "holds thousands of suspected Taliban," he was dead, despite being designated a PUC, a person under control. The parallel is explicitly made to Abu Ghraib: "Captain Caroline Wood, the officer in charge of investigations at Bagran Prison, was awarded the Bronze Star [for services in Afghanistan] and shortly after the Iraq invasion, she and her intelligence unit were given a new assignment—Abu Ghraib." Her sworn statement is shown that explains that because of the pressure she was under, she found it necessary to utilize otherwise unauthorized techniques: dogs, nudity, sleep deprivation, and stress positions.

Dilawar's death surfaced only after an investigation was prompted by a story in the *New York Times*, after the investigative journalist discovered Dilawar's death certification that stated his death was a homicide (box checked) that was "caused by blunt force trauma to legs." Similarities to Abu Ghraib pepper *Taxi*. One MP who is interviewed says that "strikes on Dilawar became amusement"; another says he "didn't want to go against my fellow soldiers." Gibney suggests, with a montage of pictures of higher-ups, that the policies at the prison were prompted from Washington: the vice president strongly pushed this means to gain his end, and John Woo, legal counsel to the Department of Justice, and Attorney General Alberto Gonzales were responsible for finding legal grounds to abandon policies against torture in the Geneva Convention.

In the end, we see President Bush signing a bill that prevents himself and all members of his administration from being held accountable for torture of detainees. This, Gibney states, is disgusting: "At least President Nixon had Gerald Ford do his dirty work. . . . Bush is trying to pardon himself." In a scene reminiscent of both *Ghosts* and *SOP*, we learn from one of the guards midway through the film that "someone had to be held responsible [especially after Abu Ghraib]," and at the end, over a roll call of those punished, the viewer is not surprised to find the punishment meted out to only the NCOs who administered the punishment to Dilawar. The closing is dedicated to the director's father, Frank, who died the year before this film came out, but who was a World War II Navy interrogator. His comments ring in the viewer's ear as the movie goes dark: "[I] cannot believe [members of the administration] didn't know. . . . Really destroyed my faith in the American government."

VIEW FROM THE FRONT: PERMUTATIONS ON A THEME

These films generally redeem the men and women who serve. They do not necessarily portray those on the front lines in heroic terms, but neither do they characterize them as malevolent. Indeed, one absent film in this group is the decidedly abhorrent killing of civilians by military personnel in Haditha when Marines went on a rampage and shot anyone they came across because they were incensed that some of their own had lost their lives (this *is* addressed in the next chapter in the fiction film, *Battle for Haditha*; see also *Redacted*). In general, members of the military serving on the front lines are portrayed in these documentaries much as they were in earlier films: ordinary men and women caught up in situations beyond their control and doing what they have to do to survive.

The Grunt's View

Make Peace or Die (2006)
The Short Life of José Antonio Gutierrez (2006)
Combat Diary: The Marines of Lima Company (2006)
Operation Homecoming: Writing the Wartime Experience (2007)
Soldiers of Consciousness (2007)

Alive Day Memories: Home from Iraq (2007)
Inside the Green Berets (2007)
This Is War: Memories of Iraq (2007; critiqued in chapter 2)
Full Battle Rattle (2008)
The Corporal's Diary: 38 Days in Iraq (2008)
Lioness (2008)
Brothers at War (2009)
Restrepo (2010)

The Reporter's View
War Feels Like War (2006; critiqued in chapter 2)
The War Tapes (2006; critiqued in chapter 2)
Bad Voodoo's War (2007; critiqued in chapter 2)
War and Truth (2007)

Roughly half the films in this category repeat the view of the grunt that was seen in chapter 2. One of these films does inadvertently touch on the macabre: *Make Peace or Die: The First Days of the War in Iraq*. This documentary was shot by Sergeant Sam Hunter, who is given co-producer credit; he also did most of the interviews of his fellow soldiers with the 1st Battalion, 5th Marine.[15] The 1/5's claim to movie fame is that they were the first to take casualties in Iraq. The macabre is the unit's slogan, from which the film takes its title. The opening shows a bare-chested Marine with the slogan tattooed across his chest. No one seems to appreciate the irony of the slogan (see also *Road to Guantanamo*, 2006). The film is otherwise pretty basic: soldiers telling of their combat experience interspersed with scenes of combat. Much the same can be said of the National Geographic special, *Inside the Green Berets*, though it is one of the few to give the grunts view from Afghanistan. Similarly fated to cover familiar territory are *Brothers at War*; *Combat Diary: The Marines of Lima Company*; and *The Corporal's Diary: 38 Days in Iraq*. The film *Restrepo* (2010) is a retelling of the grunt's perspective in Iraq, but the perspective is nevertheless refreshing if only because it is one of the few to depict their lives in Afghanistan. The other films that tell the grunt's view do so by trying to give a new insight into an aspect of their life. Some are more successful than others.

Alive Day Memories: Home from Iraq

The subtitle would suggest this film would be better placed in the Home Front section in this chapter that examines the adjustment issues returning veterans confront. This is raised in the opening, when we learn that this is a "new generation of veterans; it's the first time 90 percent of the wounded survived, but with amputations [and] traumatic brain injuries . . . 50 percent have posttraumatic stress symptoms." A couple of the veterans interviewed do have adjustment issues. Corporal Jernigan was blinded; Staff Sergeant Jones has flashbacks when he sees a van because he lost both his legs in a roadside bomb. Corporal Michael Jernigan was blinded and has terrible dreams, often awakening in the middle of the night, saying, "Wow! What's wrong with me?" Sergeant Eddie Ryan is his mother's miracle man because he should not be alive: He was shot twice in the head and has serious frontal lobe damage and has to be strapped to his wheelchair so he doesn't fall out of it. Poignant as these stories are, the focus of the documentaries is really on they're alive day, the day they narrowly escaped death on the battlefield: "Yeah, [it's] burned into my memory," says one of the ten interviewed; another remarks, "I feel like I'm not supposed to be here. My best friend was behind the door, and he lost his life"; another quips, "I got a second chance." James Gandolfini of *Sopranos* fame is the executive producer of the film and does the interviews. He remains unobtrusive throughout; he is heard asking the question but the camera is positioned behind him so the focus is not on him but the soldier being interviewed. Their stories describe some of the events that have been seen on the other films in the last chapter under Grunt's View. Nevertheless, the film makes their experiences more real than the isolated incidents of combat because each of the ten have ten minutes to tell their stories. The lingering scars of their alive day memories makes their stories particularly affecting.

Operation Homecoming: Writing the Wartime Experience

This film was prompted by a grant from the National Endowment for the Arts (NEA), which provided funds to allow distinguished authors to present workshops at military bases across the country to teach soldiers the therapeutic value of writing. The NEA project would eventually be compiled to make the *Operation Homecoming Anthology*. But it is the established authors who appear intermittently throughout the film who generally make a more cogent argument for writing of their wartime experiences. This is because they are more articulate at conveying their feelings to an audience, whereas the young soldiers are really writing for themselves. The writing experience that the young men and women undertook was undoubtedly cathartic for them (see also *The Corporal's Diary: 38 Days in Iraq*), but struggling to articulate their motivation to write and reading their works on camera does not make for a riveting film.

Soldiers of Consciousness

The moral qualms some soldiers have about the war have been glimpsed in some of the Grunt's View films in the last chapter. Here those moral qualms that lead one to declare conscientious objector status become the focal point of the film.

The film opens by establishing the patriotism of the soldiers: "I made it easy on the recruiter. I told him I just want to shoot a machine gun and jump from a plane. He said, 'sign right here'"; "I was raised on apple pie"; "[I wanted to] defend my country"; "I'm a patriotic son-of-a-gun"; "[My] family's been in [the] military since there's been a country." It is one thing to be patriotic; it's another to take a person's life. This is not conveyed in most of the other grunt movies, where the front-line soldiers are always talking about the need to be callous and do what has to be done to get home in one piece, no matter what it takes: "I will kill anyone here who will keep me from going home without even thinking about it," says one of the men in *Off to War*; in *The Ground Truth*, discussed in the Home Front section of this chapter, one soldier says, "Told if someone gets in front of [your] truck, run over 'em. And that's what [I] did"; another says, "Everyone is considered hostile. If one guy shoots at you and you cannot find him, [you] blanket the whole area." In *No End in Sight* one soldier is bemoaning their orders not to shoot at Iraqis while the camera pans the street from behind the jeep's bullet-ridden windshield: "Oh, but we cannot use deadly force. Fuck you!"

The reason so many are quick to take another's life is because boot camp has trained them to kill. This is boldly stated over a picture of re-

cruits getting pumped up by chanting, "kill, kill, kill." This is the purpose
of boot camp: to strip one of his former identity (and morals) and to get
the recruit to learn to follow orders without hesitation. The boot camp
footage is interspersed with scenes from Iraq, frequently showing soldiers kicking in a door, pushing people to the floor while pointing their
weapons threateningly, and screaming at them: "Should I shoot him in
the leg?" one Marine yells over his shoulder while pointing his weapon
at a cowering man who ostensibly has done nothing.

In many films this behavior is depicted as standard operating procedure, even if sometimes some of the men might question the legitimacy
of treating Iraqi civilians this way: "Cannot blame them for not really
wanting us here," says one soldier in *Operation Dreamland*, "gotta admit, we're pretty fuckin' intimidating when we roll in, weapons pointed
. . . [guess] they have to fight back"; another in *Dreamland* says that
rounding up and taking women and children into custody is "indecent." In *Soldiers of Consciousness*, this kind of behavior is what often
gives rise to the soldier's conscientious concerns. "My father [a WWII
veteran] tried to tell me war is not that glamorous," one conscientious
objector says while the viewer is shown soldiers who have burst into a
house in the middle of the night, their weapons raised and pointed at
two children who are holding their hands up and crying, which leads
him to ask, "Why are we doing this anymore"; another reflectively asks,
"Why am I carrying an M1 [sic] in the Garden of Eden [cradle of civili-
zation]?" It is their combat experience that has led to the conscientious
objector status; "[killing someone] is not like in the movies." This is followed by an often-depicted grunt's view scene of a night vision scope
of a man seeming to simply walk down the street and being shot by a
soldier as his comrades cheer him. There's "nothing honorable in killing," says one conscientious objector.

The viewer learns that conscientious objector status was among the
first laws passed by the Constitutional Congress. Still, a spokesperson
for the military says, one cannot just pick and choose what war you are
going to approve of and what one you are not going to support. Besides,
says Major Pamela Stephens with public affairs, one "cannot have discipline if [soldiers] don't obey orders." And so, to send a clear signal that
this kind of behavior is not sanctioned by the military, these men, we are
told by one's defense attorney, must pay the price. The military needs

to send a strong signal, the public defender says, "don't do this." Those that attempt to declare themselves a conscientious objector pay for their pacifism: they have all been demoted, incarcerated, and dishonorably discharged. The movie, however, is framed to suggest that some men, in the process of serving their country, gain morality, and thus have a right to object. The defense rests, somewhat idealistically: "we've done away with human sacrifice, and slavery, [now we] need to get away from [war] altogether." The American flag waves in the breeze over the closing credits, reinforcing the fact that these men are patriotic Americans and have a right to object to a war that more and more people in the public sphere by 2007 were beginning to view as unjust.

The Short Life of José Antonio Gutierrez

The film opens as an older veteran sets white wooden crosses in the sand near a pier. The camera pulls back for a long shot to show rows of white crosses stretching across the beach of the "thousands who have been killed." It comes as no surprise that the viewer is going to be told the story of one of those fallen. The one picked is distinct because he was another first: the first U.S. casualty in Iraq. What makes the story unique is that he was killed by friendly fire from members of his own squad. This, in itself, would justify a documentary investigation, but it is not the focus of the film. The director is out to trace the story of José who, though serving in the U.S. Marine Corps, was not an American citizen.

Immediately after the crosses are shown, the viewer sees a picture of a flag-draped coffin; a newscaster remarks on José's sacrifice: "He came to the United States at 14 [illegally] and always wanted to be a Marine." The orphanage director in Guatemala where José grew up, Patrick Atkinson, says the newscaster's remarks were "pure propaganda, and unnecessary since [the] real story is so powerful." Later we learn the propagandistic aspect of the story is that José's desire to become a Marine was sparked fairly recently when another Guatemalan young man broached the idea because it was a means to gain amnesty. The viewer is later told that George W. Bush promised green cards and fast-track naturalization to Latinos who served in the military. Thirty-two thousand Latinos joined.

The story is not about how José died, though that is touched on in the film as a tragic accident that the director takes at face value; nor does the film tackle the Latino issue, which would have given the film more substance and would be more in keeping with the director's motivation for doing the film. "This film" idea, the Swedish director says at the Sundance Film Festival, "is the result of intensive involvement with the history of Latin America and the social realities of the continent . . . as well as the need to contribute to changing these realities."[16] This is not accomplished by the singular focus on José, whose story, while interesting, is the story of many Mexican and Central American immigrants, though not all were caught in the Indian genocide that raged in Guatemala during the 1970s and which indirectly led to his growing up in the streets of Guatemala City.

To trace José's life, the director went to Central America to basically, so she says, "shoot a road movie." And that's how the film comes off, and the reason it falls flat. We never get the real feeling for the tragedy of "growing up in one war, and dying in another." The story of Guatemala's war, which killed over two hundred thousand people, is much more convincingly told in *When the Mountains Tremble* (1984). A few comments from the director about the war do not suffice to depict the difficulty young José must have faced. Her road trip through Mexico likewise fails to capture the danger of the trip for illegal immigrants. Heidi Specogna does talk to a young woman at the House of Migrants in Tapachula, who laughingly shows her how to jump on a moving train, and who mentions some of the problems faced by illegals crossing Mexico by train: rape, bandits. The film *Sin Nombre* (2009) much more forcefully depicts the horrors of the journey. Had the director intercut some scenes from these movies into her film, or delved into the wealth of file footage about the Guatemalan wars and the ardors of the train trips many illegals undertake to reach the United States, her film would have been greatly strengthened. Similarly, had she used José's life to underscore the broader story of Latinos serving in the military, a much more powerful documentary might have been made. The film also raises a point that has gone largely unaddressed: there have been no documentaries that examine friendly fire incidents in Iraq. This documentary raises the issues, but it is addressed only as a sidebar to explain his death, which, in turn, is used to justify the director's Mexican road trip.

Full Battle Rattle

This film, along with the next one that closes this section, *Lioness*, depicts an aspect of life at the front not even hinted at in films to this point,
which, in itself, causes these two documentaries to stand out from the
crowd. The name, *Full Battle Rattle*, makes it sound like it is going to
depict, full throttle, a battle at the front line. In reality, it depicts a commendable attempt by the military to prepare men and women going to
Iraq for situations they will confront and attempts to teach them how to
handle situations between themselves and locals in a humane manner.

The film opens with what one would anticipate from a "full battle"
film "at the front." There is an attack taking place in an Iraq village:
Muslim women are screaming, shots are being fired, a door is kicked
in, a man lies in the street grasping his bloodied leg. Then suddenly a
voice says, "Leave your bandages on!" A woman asks, "Are we done?"
The camera pans as the crowd moves to queue up before an ice-cream
truck on the road. Welcome to Fort Irwin, a U.S. training facility that
spans one hundred acres in the middle of the Mojave desert where
thirteen Iraq villages are simulated. The Army employs three hundred
Iraqi Americans to play the role of Iraqi citizens; some three thousand
soldiers go through the simulations monthly. This is the story of one of
those villages in the fictional country of Medina Wasl.

Azhar Cholagh is one of the Iraqi Americans who is identified as Iraqi
Role Player Number 4491. He says the whole simulation is "sorta [like] a
large reality television show." Iraqi Role Player Number 3214 elucidates
that one "gets into" the role: role players eat, sleep, and live in the village
just as they would in Iraq. The role players are also given a family tree
so they can relate to the character they play: some have histories where
they are hostile toward Americans because a family member was killed
by a soldier; another might have a family member that was tortured
under Saddam's regime and looks at the Americans more benignly. The
newly arrived soldiers are told by the role-playing company commander
on their arrival that "We're committed to helping [Iraqi] people with
their basic needs."

The soldiers stay for two weeks. They know it is a simulation, but
take it seriously because, the "CO [commanding officer]" says, "by [the]
second [or] third day, training [aspect] disappears. Soldiers get into the

reality of what they're doing. It gets real. They get lost in the scenario." The problem, however, is that the scenario is unrealistic; it certainly has not been seen on any of the documentaries that address the conflict in Iraq. In one extended scene, for example, the mayor's son was killed by a soldier, so a meeting has been set by the company commander to address the "collateral damage" that the scenario depicts. The CO calmly listens to the angry role-playing mayor as he lambastes the CO because "innocent people are being killed"; off to the side, a Muslim female role player weeps. The CO says, "It was his fate" (Allah's will), and peels some bills off a large wad to compensate for the loss of those killed. This certainly reflects the American mind-set that money cures everything— and here it seems to work. Later, the mayor is further appeased because the CO has arranged a few hundred thousand dollars to be invested in the village to build a water storage and treatment plant as well as other infrastructure needs. The mayor is pleased: "I will be [your] friend and cooperate with you."

Little fighting is depicted. Everything works out because people communicate and work together.[17] But battles do happen, even in Medina Wasl. They too are unrealistically tinted, even if the wounds "inflicted" look real. In an almost ludicrous battle scene toward the end of the simulation, a Muslim woman on her knees in the street screams into the air as bullets from insurgents fall around her: "For the sake of Allah, spare the Americans." One would have to search diligently through all the documentary footage to find a parallel real-life scene. This point is inadvertently made by a role-playing soldier who has served two tours in Iraq when he comments on the uprising that just took place that supposedly killed eighteen and wounded another fifteen: "There'd be so much collateral damage [caused by military personnel], the town [would] be fuckin' destroyed" (see *Battle for Hadith*). Fifteen insurgents were rounded up after the attack. They apparently were not sent to Abu Ghraib.

The ending crawl indicates that after fifteen months deployed, five from the battalion that trained at Medina Wasl were killed in Iraq. Despite their deaths, the film hints that things are getting better in Iraq. The Iraqi village simulations are no longer needed. The U.S. government is spending $15 million to expand Medina Wasl and transform it into an Afghan village.

Lioness

A female soldier has occasionally been caught on a documentary, but they are often in the background. Here they are foregrounded (see also *G. I. Jane*, 1997). Female military personnel are not supposed to serve in front-line combat. The PBS documentary *Lioness* shows that they are. They might never have been sent into battle, a military spokesman says, but sometimes battles came to them. Five of the twenty women from the First Engineering Battalion are interviewed who volunteered to search Muslim women because male military personnel could not do so. They were not supposed to be in combat, but the nature of their charge—searching women during house-to-house raids and related intelligence-gathering missions—often put them in front-line areas when combat erupted. One, Specialist Shannon Morgan, a crack shot from rural Arkansas, was attached to a Marine combat patrol in Ramadi during one of the war's bloodiest battles. She and the others comported themselves exceedingly well considering their lack of combat training. They pay the same price as the men too; many suffer from post-traumatic stress syndrome: "she cannot sleep," Shannon's mother says, "remembering what was seen in the war . . . [she] talk[ed] of suicide when she first got home"; her uncle, a Vietnam veteran, says, "told her, and now she understands . . . no one will understand what you have to remember. [The] lucky ones are dead."

It is a tribute to the filmmakers that a film about these women was made at all. Meg McLagan and Daria Sommers became interested in the women's role in the Iraq war after the media attention toward Jessica Lynch, who was captured at Nasiriyah in 2003 (see *Saving Jessica Lynch*, 2003; *Control Room*). "The film started with a question, 'What's going on here?'" McLagan says about the Jessica Lynch story in the news. "We felt this historic shift was going on with the contribution women were making, and once we started contacting people, we came to this story."[18] It is a story, Jesse Ellison remarks in *Newsweek*, "that otherwise might be lost to history."[19]

The women themselves are not appreciative of how their contribution has been overlooked. At a reunion of the lionesses in July 2006, one of the women is shown slipping a tape from the History Channel into the VCR. It is about the heroism of those on the front lines, told, the nar-

Women warriors in *Lioness*.

rator says, "by the men who were there." The women all roll their eyes. One says, "[It's] like they went out of their way not to mention us." There might be some justification for the military cover-up since these women (1) were not supposed to be in a combat situation, and (2) being in a combat situation, the women were given no training to prepare themselves for what they might encounter.

Excised from history in *Lioness*.

The need of military personnel to search Iraqi women for possible weapons is an obvious one. Male personnel searching women is always problematic, and it is especially problematic in a Muslim country. Lieutenant Colonel Richard Cabry, Commander of the 1/5 Field Artillery, makes this clear: "Culturally, male soldiers could not search women with their hands, but we had to make sure they didn't have weapons or contraband." The fact that these women went on raids greatly assuaged the sensibilities of both Iraqi men and women. In one scene, for example, we see the soldiers on a raid. When the inhabitants refused to open the door, a military vehicle was used as a battering ram. The soldiers rush in, weapons raised; the women and children are put in one room, the men in another. One lioness indicates the relief women felt at having another woman in the room: "The women and children were panic stricken. . . . We took off our helmets. Once they saw we were women, they tried to talk to us. . . . I felt like the Gestapo." Another comments on the raids: "Hard to imagine these families fighting against us. . . . Just had to trust Intel [reports] that these people are doing wrong."

A number of lionesses were in Ramaldi when the Marines went in because the city was known for training insurgents. It was in Ramaldi that the four Blackwater contractors were killed in a car bomb attack. One of the lioness's remarks in her diary on seeing their charred bodies hanging from a bridge: "They don't want us here. I wonder what would happen if we left? It's going to be a *long* five months." The significance of Ramaldi is further addressed by Lieutenant Colonel Cabry: "Ramaldi is in Al Anbar province and because of its size, if [you] control that area, [you] control Iraq."

The lionesses were not sent into battle, but a battle erupted while they were there, and they were in the middle of it. It was a hell of a battle and the women handled themselves admirably. In the midst of the battle, Shannon suddenly found herself detached from her unit, alone in the middle of the street. She explains that the Marine behind you is supposed to tap you on the shoulder when the unit is withdrawing because one often cannot hear the order to pull back because of the din of battle. No one tapped Shannon on the shoulder. When she got back to the squad, she says she "kicked [the squad leader] in the nuts" for leaving her like that. The lionesses were fortunate not to have taken any casualties. Their lack of training could have cost lives—theirs and the members of their team. "There was a TOW [anti-tank] missile on top of the Humvees," one of the lionesses says, but she didn't know how to shoot "our most powerful weapon; if no one else could [use it], I couldn't because I had no training." The need to tactically train women if they are going to face combat situations is one of the specific points the directors say they wished to convey in this film.[20]

Like many of the men who have been seen in the other documentaries that depict life on the front lines, killing is not easy, but, as one lioness says, "you hesitate, then fire. . . . Something you learn to deal with; don't regret [it], but wish it hadn't happened." Another lioness makes a good point: women deal with it [killing] better than men because they can show their emotions. But even though they might be able to cope better than men, they still bear the scars at what they have done, just like the men. It would help though, Shannon says, if people realized they were there. Her wish is this film! And while the directors insist *Lioness* takes no stand regarding women in combat, it certainly shows they can acquit themselves quite well. Indeed, there are some staunch conservatives who feel it is inappropriate to send women into combat. Republican Congressmen Duncan Hunter (CA) is one of them. He pushed the secretary of defense to respond to the 1994 policy that women should not be in direct combat. Pressure from the military hierarchy forced Duncan to back down. Congress was told not to push this earlier directive, otherwise they would have to withdrawal most of the women in Iraq and Afghanistan and "our ability to wage these wars would fall apart." It seems, to paraphrase Bob Dylan, "the times are [still] a-changing."

REPORTER'S VIEW

War and Truth is the only one of the four films in this period that was not critiqued in the previous chapter. It is saved from contention for the Roland Hedley award because it does recognize some of the problems journalists face when reporting from the front lines; it also acknowledges that many journalists are more concerned with promoting themselves than the news story. In spite of this, *War and Truth* still reveals that journalistic standards are becoming increasingly difficult to maintain in contemporary war journalism.

The journalistic heritage is established from the outset by linking contemporary journalists with those of old. The viewer is told that "Reporters [are always] there to witness [wars]" as a roll call of distinguished war correspondence is shown: Ernie Pyle, Ernest Hemingway, Edward R. Murrow, Walter Cronkite. The connection to Iraq is quickly made. The viewer is told that journalists are the eyes and ears of the American public and that, thanks to them, the truth is laid out. This is ironically stated over a picture of one of the most notoriously staged events during the Iraq war: the tumbling of Saddam Hussein's statue in Firdos Square.

The Iraq material is intercut throughout the film by reports about how journalists covered other wars. In fact, the first twenty minutes of the film lingers over the heroic reporting of previous wars: Joe Rosenthal's famous photograph of the flag being raised at Iwo Jima; Joe Galloway's coverage of Vietnam that led to the book he coauthored with Harold Moore,[21] *We Were Soldiers Once . . . and Young*, which, the narrator mentions, was made into a film starring Mel Gibson. This foregrounding suggests that while some reporters put themselves at the center of the story in Iraq (a picture of Geraldo Rivera is shown) most do their best to cover the war. And it is a dangerous job. Sixty-five journalists have died in Iraq over a three-year period; later, the number rises to 102. Interspersed between these two statistics is the famous photograph by Eddie Adams from 1968, "Murder of a Vietcong," that shows a (also staged) Vietnamese officer executing a Vietcong in the streets by shooting him in the head. The connection between this picture and the bookended statistics is puzzling. Nor is the viewer told that precious few of the journalists killed were Americans (see Table 2.4 in chapter 2). Indeed, the film suggests they were mostly American by immediately talking about the tragic death of the American journalist from the *Boston Globe*, Elizabeth Neuffer, who lost her life in an automobile accident in Iraq. The issue of embedding and its effect on the journalist tradition is raised but not substantively developed.

The reporters who appear in this film do, in fact, follow the classic journalistic tradition and are critical of some of the grandstanding that took place in Iraq. They also realize that some of their more graphic pictures of suffering and death are sanitized back home. Coming from the old school, they are critical of how instant news networks, like CNN and FOX, force a reliance on pictures that have no context and stories that do not stimulate the viewers to reflect on what they are seeing or hearing. Danny Schechter, who did *WMD: Weapons of Mass Deception* for this studio (Cinema Libre; see also *Soldier's Pay, Outfoxed, Uncovered*), offers insights into the showbiz nature of Iraq war coverage that he found in his analysis of the major networks and how it ultimately was little more than a packaged Pentagon production.[22] Joe Galloway, commenting on General Sanchez's remark that Iraq is not another Vietnam, closes the film by reflecting on his own Vietnam journalistic experience, sidestepping some of his own cheerleading coverage of the Iraq war that was seen in the last chapter.[23] It is important for people to understand that unlike Vietnam, he says, "people came to hate the war . . . but they also came to hate the warrior." Galloway's point is that those back home need to understand the soldier, even if they do not approve of the war.[24] He is suggesting that the soldier's point of view has not been expressed in the news. He is probably right. This does not mean that the soldier's story has not been told, however. The soldier's point of view has been well documented on film.

SAVING LIVES

These films continue to depict life at the front, but from an entirely different perspective. It addresses the medical aspect of the war. Most follow the *M*A*S*H* (1970) tradition and show medical staff working to save the lives of injured soldiers. They are very successful: *Baghdad ER* tells us that that 90 percent of American soldiers wounded in Iraq survive and that this is the highest rate of war survivors in U.S. history. These films explain just how this achievement is accomplished. The other film in this section, *Motherland Afghanistan*, spins the medical by showing the struggles of a physician couple to improve medical conditions for the locals in Afghanistan.

Heroes in Scrubs

There are three films in this section that are thematically similar in their approach. *Life and Death in a War Zone* is carried over from 2004; it is a ninety-minute NOVA special that is the first to address how medical personnel attempt to treat the combat wounded (see also *Alive Day Memories*). The other two are *Baghdad ER* (2006) and *Fighting for Life* (2008). All three films present a remarkably consistent face. *Life and Death* follows the medical staff of the 10th and 21st CaSH unit (Combat Support Hospital), who, the jacket sleeve indicates, are "prepared for everything from chemical and biological attack to mass U.S. casualties. . . . [It's] an intimate story of survival in a combat hospital." *Baghdad ER*, the film's opening crawl states, "is a tribute to the heroism and sacrifice of the soldiers who are the patients and staff of the 86th Combat Support Hospital." *Fighting for Life* "captures the compelling scenes of doctors and nurses treating wounded victims at combat support hospitals, on medevac flights, and [in] . . . military hospitals." The thematic parallel of these three documentaries justifies a detailed analysis of only one of the films. *Baghdad ER* is selected simply because it is sandwiched between the other two.

A frantic scene of injured military personnel opens *Baghdad ER*: a man on a stretcher is seen with severe burns on his face and legs, another is brought in who has been shot by a sniper, "while handing out candy to Iraqi children." The viewer is introduced to Colonel Casper P. Jones III who is the commander of the 86th CaSH. Then the viewer follows the medevacs as they take off in a Blackhawk helicopter on a rescue mission 134 miles south of Baghdad. Here we see why the grunts often expressed concerns about IEDs; it is the leading cause of death in Iraq: "some dip-shit strapped explosives to [his] body and walked into a crowd and pulled the pin." Later IED alley is discussed: a five-mile stretch of highway from the airport to CaSH in the Green Zone, "the most dangerous stretch of highway in the world."

The 86th, like the medical personnel in *M*A*S*H*, do not do major surgery. Their job is to stabilize the wounded so they can be flown to better-equipped military hospitals in Germany, and then stateside (see *Fighting for Life*). Their operating room, however, is ready 24/7 and is always going "900 miles per hour, from breakfast to dinner." Their gallous humor is a way to deal with the horrors they daily face: "Probably shouldn't," one doctor says, then shrugs, "[but] it keeps us sane."

One story will suffice to convey the multitude of stories that this and the other medical documentaries depict. This one takes place the day after "MD cigar night." Cigar night occurs once a week. It is when the doctors in their green scrubs lounge in rooftop lawn chairs as they watch the sporadic night flashes from IEDs that dot the cityscape while they smoke cigars. It's "the closest to normality you're going to get here," one comments. The norm, however, takes place the next day when seventeen casualties are brought in after the parking lot next to the PX was hit by a mortar shell.

It is not a pretty sight, and the filmmaker does not flinch from showing the graphics. The viewer watches as a pin is driven into the flesh by an electric hand drill "to stabilize the fracture . . . makes [it] a lot easier when transporting a patient [than old plaster casts]." Another patient, we learn, "turned twenty-one today; hell of a way to celebrate a birthday." It is the shrapnel that poses the biggest problem because "little shrapnel wounds go everywhere." A medic comments that "they [patients] often want to see" what they've been hit with. This is told over a graphic picture of someone with a serious stomach wound. A nurse says that she often whispers to them when they are on the operating table, "You'll wake up in Germany. Have a beer for us," to which someone else quips, "Some aren't even old enough to drink."

On July 4 one of the medics make a wish: "No dead soldiers today." He got his wish—four Iraqis were brought in who had been wounded by an IED. On July 5 the chopper brought in two that didn't make it. The film ends with a Marine on the table as the medics work feverously to save his life. Ultimately they have to turn off the monitors and stand by somberly as he is carried off on a gurney. Not everyone makes it. And as we'll see in the next section, Home Front, some have made it but they pay a heavy price trying to adjust back home.

Motherland Afghanistan

The director, Sedika Mojadidi, follows her obstetrician father, Dr. Quidrat Mojadidi, and her general practitioner mother, Dr. Nafisai Mojadidi, on their return to Afghanistan in 2003 from their middle-class home in Virginia. The Mojadidis fled Afghanistan in 1972 but have sporadically returned to the border area to provide medical care. This trip is the first time they have been able to get inside Afghanistan to provide medical assistance since the Taliban takeover of the country. Dr. Quidrat, along with five other physicians, will be training sixty Afghan physicians at Rabia Balkhi Hospital in Kabul. His wife, Nafisai, is not part of the U.S.-sponsored team but is going along; she will be rendering medical assistance at a nearby family-planning clinic.

This is not the first film where a daughter taped the exploits of her father. Maysoon Pachachi followed her diplomatic Iraqi father, Adnan Muzahim Amin al-Pachachi, home in *Return to the Land of Wanders*. This film is more successful because the topic is more cinematic. Sedika films her father visiting hospitals, treating patients, which holds the viewer's visual attention more than watching Adnan al-Pachachi ponder his plans and penning drafts of the new constitution. *Motherland* is also more of a visual treat simply because the viewer has not been overexposed to Afghanistan and so it is not another familiar trek through the streets of Baghdad. The director's previous experience is particularly notable in conjunction with 9/11 documentaries. She was in Kabul making *Kabul Kabul* in 1996 just as the Taliban was taking over. The film was her graduate school thesis, but it is interesting to note that her attempts to get it distributed met with little success until September 11 and Afghanistan entered the public consciousness.

The need for medical care, and for Dr. Mojadidi's presence, is made forcefully by statistics given at the outset of the film: Afghanistan has one of the highest maternal mortality rates in the world; it has the second highest infant mortality rate in the world and 18 percent of newborns won't live to see their first birthday. One can immediately see why. The conditions Quidrat encounters at Rabia Balkhi are horrendous. "The smell in the hallway," her father says, "is unbearable." The viewer can readily believe it: one shot shows a *filthy* toilet (see *Trainspotting*, 1996), another shows a sink that is clogged and overflowing with polluted water. The hospital lacks even rudimental equipment: Quidrat has to buy his own soap to wash his hands before surgery; patients must bring their own bandages. The staff, Quidrat says, shaking his head, has "no clue on how to do anything, probably because no one has shown them." He is there to do just that, but it is very basic stuff, Surgery 101: "don't make the sutures too tight," he explains as he works on a patient, "[the] swelling can break them."

Quidrat's ire at hospital conditions is inflamed because the Department of Defense supposedly spent $300,000 on renovations before his arrival. Letters pleading for supplies and concerns about hospital conditions Quidrat's written to Health and Human Services (H&HS) go unanswered. But he does receive a (standardized) letter from the Secretary Tommy Thompson at H&HS saying what a wonderful job he is doing. His tour up, the Mojadidis return to the states.

Six months later they are returning to Afghanistan, but disgusted after his experience with H&HS, they are now employed by the United Nations High Commission for Refugees. On their way to the hospital in Jaghori, an eight-hour drive from Kabul, they visit Rabia Balkhi. Quidrat is surprised at the tremendous changes that have taken place. The viewer is also since before we see the hospital we are told that H&HS allocated $2.2M and this was contracted out to International Medical Corps. Other films, notably *Iraq for Sale: The War Profiteers*, would suggest any government subcontract would lead to abuses. This is decidedly not the case here. Dr. Quidrat finds the facility clean and fully stocked. No longer do patients have to bring their own bandages. But rather than give credit for this change to the contracting agency, he gives credit to the staff physicians. They may deserve some credit, but Quidrat fails to appreciate the funds allocated from the United States that allowed for these improvements to be implemented. In fact, he remains critical because he learns at the time of his departure that the Corps has postponed the OB/GYN training program.

The second sequence is shorter than the first. Jaghori hospital is clean and well stocked. The physicians still lack basic skills, but that is why he is there—to train them. They are anxious to learn. The whole staff lines up to greet him on his arrival. There are some patients seen, but because this has already been well documented in the first part of the movie, more time is spent filming Quidrat's visits to other facilities: the orphanage and the girl's school. We also see Quidrat interacting more with the locals outside the hospital in this final sequence.

Dr. Quidrat's dedication to helping those in his motherland is commendable, but there is a touch of Twain's *Connecticut Yankee in King Arthur's Court* in his approach to things. Like Twain's Yankee, Morgan, Quidrat is transported back to a more primitive time. And like Morgan, he relies on his superior knowledge to help to poor benighted folk (see also *Manderlay*, 2005). Quidrat's solution to medical problems he encounters is to utilize advanced technology. In Jaghori, for example, the viewer sees boxes of oral contraceptives stacked on the shelves in the hospital and is told that the women are given a year's supply. The impression is that the problem of unwanted pregnancies will now be solved. This makes sense to Westerners, but it is problematic to rural villagers who are largely illiterate and do not understand how technology works—the same problem confronts those who are uneducated in the United States: they often forget to take their medication and don't realize that missing a day here and another day there will result in the medication failing to work. The lack of education of many he treats is remarked on by the doctor, but he doesn't connect the dots that advances in modern medicine are not necessarily the solution for rural villagers. It might be more productive to teach the locals how to utilize the resources that are available, rather than to promote a dependence on resources that they either do not have access to or might subsequently become unavailable.

In a similar vein, Dr. Quidrat relies on money to solve his problems—supplies, supplies, supplies—and like a contemporary Yankee, he is often unappreciative when that money is forthcoming. Another contemporary Yankeeism is the cleft between attitude (praising the pristine landscape) and action (despoiling that same landscape). In a concluding scene, the viewer sees him bonding with the locals. He is on a picnic in the countryside and lauds the unpolluted beauty that surrounds him. The camera announces the majesty of the scene by lovingly dwelling on the clear running creek that cuts a swatch through the mountainous region. The irony, however, is that his attitude doesn't match his actions. Right after his announced appreciation of his motherland's beauty, he is seen firing a shotgun in the air with the locals. He hasn't done this in a while, he says, but we see he's a pretty good shot: he plugs one of the many water bottles that are being tossed into the air. It lands in the once-pristine creek.

HOME FRONT

Film is often at the forefront of telling the veteran's story because it gives a face to the issues they confront. News reports may touch on the veteran's plight, but they seldom portray the in-depth, multifaceted look that is necessary to pull the viewer into their story.

Film was quick to address the problems World War II soldiers faced in postwar America. *The Best Years of Our Lives* was released in 1946 and depicted the story of three veterans and the different problems each confronted as they tried to reintegrate into society. The double amputee Harold Russell played Homer, the veteran who actually lost both his hands in the war. He stole the show, winning two Oscars for his performance: one, an Honorary Oscar, was given to Russell because he wasn't a professional actor and he was not expected to win one for his role, but the academy wanted to honor him "for bringing hope and courage to his fellow veterans"; however, his performance stunned everyone and he also won the Oscar for Best Supporting Actor. A number of Korean War films addressed one of the pressing social concerns that confronted the returning vet: the aftermath of Communist indoctrination on their postwar adjustment (*The Rack*, 1956; *Time Limit*, 1957; see also *Prisoners of War*, 1954; *The Manchurian Candidate*, 1962). Then there was Vietnam where Jon Voight won an Oscar for his role in *Coming Home* (1978) playing the embittered paraplegic Luke Martin (see also *The Deer Hunter*, 1978).[25] It seems nothing has changed. This is a new crop of film addressing the same issue in another war. But more have survived their injuries in this war, and more suffer for it. Many of the films that depict military personnel touch on the veteran's plight. The films in this section are much darker because they delve more deeply into the issue.

Poison Dust is addressed first because it is a carryover from 2005 but fits more snuggly here. It is the first to make the connection between what is going on over there and how returning veterans are affected stateside. The use of Agent Orange during the Vietnam War was highly controversial. More than 77 million liters of the chemical dioxin were sprayed over Vietnam between 1961 and 1971.[26] It is reputed to have killed or seriously deformed nearly one million Vietnamese; a lawsuit by Vietnam veterans against companies for the personal injury it caused them was dismissed because Agent Orange was not considered a poison under international law when it was used. This time, Agent Orange is Depleted Uranium (DU): 375 tons of DU was used in Gulf War I in 1991; 22,000 tons, according to this film, had been used by 2004 in Gulf War II.

Poison Dust can be divided into two uneven parts. The first 60 percent of the film addresses the effects of poison dust on Gulf War I and

II victims. The consequences of DU in Operation Desert Storm are carried by three minority veterans (African American and Latino). They tell of their headaches, sinus infections, and related problems. This is the result of their exposure to DU in Iraq. Interspersed throughout their commentary are pictures of the opening shock and awe salvo on Baghdad and file footage of tanks and other military vehicles being destroyed by missiles. Medical personnel misattribute the victim's illnesses to benign causes, or dismiss their concerns as psychosomatic.

One man's daughter was subsequently born with a stumped right hand because of DU. The physicist's comments are interspersed with tedious graphics that attempt to show how DU affects the body. The graphics and their presentations are more fitting to a classroom lecture and do little to provoke viewer interest. Much the same can be said of the three veterans. A broader veteran base would have been much more effective in showing the extent of the problem. The real connection in this part of the film is made by veterans of Gulf War I, especially when the film replays the pictures that ran in *Life* magazine entitled, "Tiny Victims of Desert Storm," showing seriously deformed children. It is shortly after this segment that we get an inkling that this film is not really about the war in Iraq, but against the use of radioactive material by the military, starting with the dropping of atomic bombs on Hiroshima and Nagasaki.

Slipped Procrusteanly into this section is a segment about atomic testing that took place in the United States during the 1950s at a time—conveniently not raised—when the long-term harm of radioactive material was not clearly established: the men in the file footage from a test site in the Nevada desert in 1956 are simply told to put on goggles or turn their heads away so they will not be temporarily blinded from the flash. It is suggested that the government lied to them. A Los Alamos report is held up that "revealed Army documents recommending [a] cover-up." The document, when freeze-framed, bears a date from 1991. No excerpt from the fifty-six-page document is read to support the assertion.

It is in the second part of the film that the People's Video News Network's real purpose becomes clear. Footage is supplied from vested interest groups across the world—Korea; Yugoslavia; Vieques, Puerto Rico—that are opposed to the American military's presence in their country, ostensibly owing solely to the military's use of DU in their country. There is nothing wrong with this; in fact, had the historical issue of poison dust been developed without treading first through the Gulf Wars, it might have been a successful film addressing a serious issue. It falls flat, however, if it is examined as a film that sheds light on the injuries inflicted on veterans and civilians in Gulf War II.

The other films in this group look at the injuries sustained as the direct result of combat in Iraq during Gulf War II. The weakest of this group is *Between Iraq and a Hard Place*, narrated by Martin Sheen.

Between Iraq and a Hard Place purports to "put you inside the mind and hearts and boots of [the] Marines [who served]. The more we understand what our returning troops feel and think, the better equipped we will be to help them transition back to normal life." Hemingway admirably achieved this in "Soldier's Story" because he focused on how a solider felt; this film spends too much time with Lieutenant Commander Ronald Ringo, a chaplain and psychologist with the U.S. Navy. The result is that the viewer is provided secondhand information about returning veterans. The film's talking heads are other clinicians. A social worker mentions the flight or fight response then notes that Marines must fight or fight without really relating how the two responses are different and with what results. We get no more insight to the horrors of war than that provided in any of the grunt's view films. Says one veteran in *Between Iraq and a Hard Place*, "I just remember doing my job, seeing my buddies killed and wondering why am I still here"; says another; "Just hell . . . RPGs (rocket propelled grenades) flying everywhere"; "Chaos" quips another veteran, "First time any of us [had] been in a situation like that."

Body of War is produced by Phil Donahue; *Home Front* is a Showtime Independent Film. They are more successful in conveying the consequences of war because they get their information firsthand. Both feature the plight of one solider: *Body of War* tells the story of Thomas Young, who left for Iraq a "gung-ho soldier . . . [and] returned home paralyzed"; *Home Front* tells the story of small-town boy Jeremy Feldbush and how he and his family have attempted to cope with his injuries (see also *Johnny Got His Gun*, 1971, 2008).

Body of War is slightly less successful in appraising the plight of veterans because it tends to stray from Tom. It starts with Tom as the focus: He is lying in bed, struggling to put his pants on over his artificial limbs.

But then it veers away from Tom and turns its cinematic lens onto Senator Byrd (D) from West Virginia who reads a statement on how easy it is to lead people down the garden path by simply "denouncing the pacifist for a lack of patriotism and exposing the country to danger. It works the same in every century." It is then that the viewer learns that these words were not spoken by a member of the administration but by Hitler's chancellor Hermann Göring in a speech he made as president of the Reichstag in 1934. Senator Byrd opens and closes the film. He links Göring's comment with the Bush administration's manipulation of the public mind-set after 9/11 and the false WMD scent that was a prelude to the Iraq war.[27] He proudly holds up a list of "the immortal 23" at the end of the film: 23 members of the senate who didn't fall lockstep into the Iraq war procession. Senator Byrd's role may be commendable but it pulls the viewer away from Tom's story, even if the film does not focus on Byrd. The film ends with a roll call of those voting yea and nay for sending troops to Iraq. The ending to *Home Front* is much more provocative: It is a montage of the twenty- to twenty-one-year-olds (model age) who have returned with lost limbs or disfigured faces.

Home Front gives a view of not only how soldiers suffer and cope but the issues and problems confronted by the family of the injured veterans (see also *Operation Homecoming: Stories from the Heart*, 2008). The pressure on the family to cope with their returned loved ones has been remarked on in any number of films, but here it is the focus of attention without—as was the case with Senator Byrd's insertion into *Body of War*—detracting from the coping strategies used by the veteran.

The film nicely unfolds with the viewer constantly getting new pieces of information about the extent of Jeremy's injuries. The viewer is told in the opening crawl that more than twenty thousand American soldiers have been wounded in Iraq, and "this is one man's story." He is twenty-four and was born in a small coal-mining town in western Pennsylvania, population 3,400. Jeremy has a bachelor's degree in biology from the University of Pittsburgh and signed up in March 2003 at the outset of the war. The viewer sees a night vision battle and we're told in a voice-over, "My first memory after being hit by the shrapnel was waking up in the hospital. It wasn't a dream." Jeremy was blinded when the shrapnel, the physician says, went under his goggles and "played ping pong in his head."

After a homecoming parade—the irony of his blindness and inability to observe the warm welcome is not lost on the sighted viewer—we see him struggling to adapt and to live a normal life. He refuses to capitulate to his handicap and is learning to read Braille. He misses the simple things: "seeing beautiful women, being able to drive, [the] scenic mountains" of his hometown. His father describes the autumn trees over the lake on their walk and tells him that "lots of people [are] better off for what you did." Jeremy is not comforted: "Enough of the song and dance, Dad. We've talked about this before."

He wants a beer, and his mother reluctantly goes along because she wants him to "feel human." She is concerned, however, because she fears the alcohol with the medication might lead to violent outbursts. He often awakes screaming in the middle of the night and is prone to grand mal seizures. The implication is that the seizures are a direct result of this wound, which, in a later scene, we learn is more severe than simple blindness. He is shown on the beginner's slope learning to snow ski. The viewer immediately admires his tenacity. But his mother is concerned, and she is not just being overprotective, afraid that he might run into a tree and injure himself. People don't understand, she explains, "that he has a metal plate in his head." His simple fall could cause severe damage! She has a right to be concerned, and now, enlightened, the viewer shares her very legitimate concern.

Because this film *focuses* on Jeremy's injuries and slowly reveals just how extensive they are, the viewer has more empathy with him than with Tom in *Body of War*. Both films end similarly, however. Tom and Jeremy independently become involved with veterans groups that are against the war (see *Born on the Fourth of July*). Jeremy has become involved with the Wounded Warriors Project. Tom, who was initially put off by Cindy Sheehan's antiwar protests, reconsiders his earlier stance. He visits her in Crawford, Texas, then goes to Washington, D.C., where he meets Bobby Muler, who founded Vets for America after returning a paraplegic from Vietnam. Back home, Tom watches men and women on television arriving at a black-tie dinner for correspondences in Washington. President Bush is a guest and gives a lighthearted speech to the group as a video shows him in the oval office searching for WMD. "Nope, not here," he quips, "maybe over there. . . . " Everyone at the dinner laughs. The viewer doesn't. Tom's wife enunciates the feeling the clip promotes: "They're isolated."

Ground Truth is the last home front film and attempts to go where the others haven't, into the psychological repercussions of the war for returning veterans. The psychological devastation of the war is a point that has been made innumerable times by any of the films that allow the soldiers to remark on their experiences. Here it is the reputed focus of the film. It is only partially successful because it relies too much on well-established visual depictions on the war.

The film can be roughly divided into thirds. After the introductory comment from James Hillman's book, *A Terrible Love of War*, that "[t] he return from the killing fields is more than a debriefing . . . it is a slow ascent from hell," the film then goes into a lengthy depiction of why the soldiers in the film joined up and their boot camp experience. The next third takes the viewer to Iraq and we hear the men tell of their combat experience: "Until you get a kill, they [other guys] make fun of you"; says another, "I remember laughing after I blew up the truck. Burning flesh. None of us talked about [it] after. It was done!" It is only now, in the last third of the seventy-eight-minute film, that the viewer gets any hint of the psychological damage done that is the focus of the film. Family members tell us, "Part of him died over there"; a wife says, "Every day he wakes up he's kinda like a different person. Today, will he be happy Robert, or distant Robert?" The returning vets mention their horrors: "We're all casualties of war . . . completely changed"; "PTSD (post-traumatic stress disorder) gets a lot of press but [it's really] not that frequent. More common [are] obtrusive thoughts—every day"; "All sucks. I don't know what it is but I have a lot of it. I think I need therapy." None of their comments really convey the depth of their anguish.

One point was clearly made at the end of this film, however. While it failed to convey the extent of the returning veterans' psychological distress, it did clearly show the lack of empathy for their condition. Right after the one vet is quoted above as saying, "I think I need therapy," another vet reveals how his attempt to get therapy was thwarted when he sought help at the Ashville veterans hospital: "I told her [the psychologist] that I killed lots of civilians and [was] having problems dealing with [it], and she looked at me and said, 'Staff Sergeant, I cannot help you.'

I asked why, and she said, 'I don't deal with conscientious objectors.' I [kinda] lost it."

THAT'S ENTERTAINMENT

The United Service Organization (USO) was established in 1941 to provide entertainment to American troops stationed abroad. USO clubs and facilities were closed after World War II (1947) only to be reactivated during the Korean Conflict in 1951. They are perhaps best known to Americans over fifty years old because the Bob Hope tours were rebroadcast on national television. His first Christmas tour was to Vietnam in December 1964 (see *Apocalypse Now Redux*, 1979). In January 2003, the USO launched Project Salute, which was its first large-scale entertainment tour to the Persian Gulf since Operation Iraq Freedom. Though none of these films are about the USO per se, one, *Graham Elwood*, is about a comedian who brings his one-man show to the troops. The other four are about either how the troops or the locals seek to entertain themselves in the midst of war.

> *Soundtrack to War: The Movie* (2005)
> *Graham Elwood: Live from Afghanistan* (2006)
> *Heavy Metal in Baghdad* (2007)
> *Afghan Star* (2008)
> *Sadr City Soccer* (2008)

The *Graham Elwood* tape is an embarrassment as a film. The comedian simply positions a camera on a tripod behind the troops in the room—the back of their heads figuring prominently in many of the takes—and records his half-humorous bit. Once or twice the viewer gets the feeling that he is, on occasion, part of a larger entertainment troupe, but it is his film and any competing entertainers are excised. His shtick is not particularly funny, either. He seldom gets more than a few chuckles now and then from his often sparsely attended performances. It might be commendable that he is trying to entertain the troops, but one gets the feeling from his DVD and its tagline, *Live from Afghanistan*, that his trip was a way to make and market a film about himself that otherwise would not have generated much interest.

Soundtrack to War and *Heavy Metal in Baghdad*, as the titles suggest, both focus on music, but take divergent approaches. *Soundtrack* examines the music the soldiers listen to, write, and sing. *Heavy Metal* is the story of a group of young Iraqi men who enjoy a form of music not often appreciated by the ruling elites in Iraq.

Soundtrack is directed and produced by the Australian filmmaker George Gittoes, who also functions as his own cameraman because, he comments in the film's DVD extras, it negates the need for a crew and this makes his interaction with military personnel more up close and personal (see *Man with a Movie Camera*, 1929). The body of the interviews appears to be shot at one location while the soldiers are enjoying R&R. In actuality, Gittoes made four separate trips to Iraq: one before the invasion, one during it, and two after Iraq was occupied, one in October 2003 and one, Gittoes says, in 2004 "when everything [had] gone to shit." It was unfortunate that Gittoes did not analyze how the songs sung and written might have changed during these very distinct periods, but Gittoes is a filmmaker interested in the music the troops listen to and not a sociologist who might be interested in how social conditions gave rise to different music lyrics.[28] The reason for the focus on music, Gittoes explains, is that it is the first time the military allowed personal music to be played on the battlefield. Music became a way for the MTV generation "to deal with the horrors of war."

Many of the men picked soundtracks to pump them up for battle. Two battle-ready favorites are "Angel of Death," the opening track from Slayer's 1986 album *Reign in Blood*, and "Raining Blood" the final track from Slayer's CD. In the Abrams, CDs could be inserted into the tanks' intercom and the music could be pumped directly into the soldier's helmets. "It's the ultimate rush," one soldier says. It is impossible to listen to their comments without thinking of Robert Duvall's character in *Apocalypse Now* as the choppers soar toward the beach with Wagner's "Ride of the Valkyries" blaring from loudspeakers as napalm explodes over the jungle. Fiction has become reality!

The overriding favorite genres are rap, especially Tupac, 50 Cent, and Eminem. Heavy metal is also widely popular, especially among thirty-somethings who enjoy Metallica, AC/DC, and Guns N' Roses, particularly the driving energy of "Civil War." Country music also gets a nod: Toby Keith's "Courtesy of the Red, White and Blue" is a patriotic favorite, and one female solider mentions the Dixie Chicks' song "Traveling Soldier," and cannot wait "to be the soldier that goes home."

Soundtrack is enhanced by the bonus material. It is one of the few documentaries where the extra material, similar in length to the feature, makes a significant contribution. Its contribution lies largely in enunciating the filmmaker's reasons for using the documentary style and his cinematic techniques (see also *Capturing Reality: The Art of the Documentary*, 2008). In fact, many of the comments by Gittoes that are noted in the examination of *Soundtrack* were taken from the interviews with the director. Gittoes remarks on some of the scenes he shot. The ones from Fallujah remind him of Goya's sketches. He is referring to the dark, ghoulish, and distorted faces from Goya's famed Caprices series, which reviewer Matt Halburn remarks, after touring the new exhibit that opened in Madrid, made him "feel as though he [were] entering an authentic chamber of horrors."[29] There is certainly a grotesque parallel. The director mentions seeing a burned car alongside the road in Fallujah with a clearly visible charred corpse sitting behind the wheel, was made all the more surreal by a well-dressed man in a coat and tie dancing on the hood of the car.

He also discusses his filmmaking techniques. One of the soldiers asked Gittoes when he was about to interview him if he should look straight at the camera. "I said, 'I don't give a shit' . . . [Later] when I showed the film at film school,[30] some students felt threatened, just like [artists] felt threatened by Marcel Duchamp when he did the readymades [such as "Fountain" which was a porcelain urinal]. . . . Traditional filmmakers [are] threatened because [today] they can make films without a crew, without even a budget, and without all the ancillary stuff: caterers, production managers, and so forth." Gittoes's comments on the modern documentary are exemplified by many of the films made by independent filmmakers who made the documentaries about aspects of the Iraq and Afghanistan wars.

Heavy Metal in Baghdad also unfolds over a lapse of some years. The directors, Eddy Moretti and Suroosh Alvi, intended a film about four young men who had formed a metalhead band in Iraq before the war started. The band, Acrassicauda (Latin for "black scorpion"), performed

three shows before the war started and three after over a period of
five-plus years. The directors, both metalhead fans, had arranged one
of the prewar concerts at the Al Fana Hotel in Baghdad and were on
their way to meet the group when plane connections caused them to
miss the show. It would be another two years before they would get to
meet the band in Baghdad. Their love of metal music was an immediate
bond; they talked about Iron Maiden's CD *Death on the Road* and one
of the director's comments that the cover art for the album is "What it
looks like here."

Eddie Cockrell, writing a review of the film for *Variety* (2007), said
that it is a "unique cable buy and [a must for] ancillary fan acquisition."[31]
Nevertheless, Cockrell finds the film says little about life in war-torn
Iraq: "bassist Firas al Lateef, whose firm rejection of the existence of
sectarian violence—he's a Sunni, his wife is a Shiite—reps [represents]
the deepest political bonds here." The focus is clearly on the band's
tenacity to follow their musical heart in the face of resistance to metal
music, which Muslim (and some Christian) clerics link to satanic worship. Insights into conditions in Iraq pepper the film, however. The
viewer learns that not just metal is banished but "music-filled parties
and all kinds of singing is banned." The war has taken its toll in more
ways than circumscribing musical performances, however; seventy-five
singers have been killed in Iraq since the invasion and another "65,000
Iraqis have died." The musicians also point out that "2.4 million Iraqis
have fled the country: 750,000 are in Jordan, 1.2 million [live] in Syria,
[only] 466 have been allowed into the USA." This means that "3,000
Iraqis flee their country every day." But it is not the everyman who is
fleeing. Those who are getting out are those with education and money.
It is, one of the Iraqi metalhead remarks, "a young brain drain." This
"brain drain" has not been brought up in any other documentary and
will have serious repercussions for the restructuring of Iraq when U.S.
troops withdraw and one that deserves greater attention.

The film also confirms another silence, the "tarnished" view of reporters that we saw in the last chapter. Moretti comments that "We haven't
seen any journalists around. [There are] two camera crews [at the hotel]
but they've [only] been filming inside the hotel. So [when something
happens in Baghdad] they send out Iraqi camera crews to film an acci-

dent, then the Western journalists just talk over it: 'Twelve people were killed when a bomb went off in the market'."

The band members later find themselves refugees. They escape to Syria. Their families tell them, "Baghdad is worse. [They] tell me, don't come back; horrible here." Still, they want to return because while "life is safer [in Syria], it's not a happy place. Have to start over and have less than zero—no friends!" They do manage to cut three songs in Syria in a makeshift studio with funds provided by the directors. Life remains difficult, however. The ending crawl notes that six months after the film was shot the group had to sell their instruments to pay the rent.

Afghan Star looks at how the civilian population in Afghanistan is coping with the war on the other front. Though the film does not point it out, there is a burst of new broadcast media in Afghanistan: no less than seventeen private television stations have surfaced in Kabul since the country was liberated from under the restricted thumb of the Taliban. *Afghan Star* is typical of the shows. It is a variation of *American Idol*.

Auditions are conducted around the country. Thousands of young men line the streets for the chance to compete. The turnout is understandably strong. The prize is $5,000, a hefty amount in a country where the per capita income is $800. This purse brings out a lot of people that have limited talent. The judges, mimicking those on *American Idol*, sometimes roll their eyes or stick their fingers in their ears to show their displeasure at the musically impaired. The show makes sure it represents the country; contestants are picked from each province. The four from the final ten that are followed in this film come from across Afghanistan: Rafi, a nineteen-year-old young man, is from Mazarj-e-Sharif in the north; Lenna, a twenty-five-year-old female, is from Kandahar Province in the south; Hameed, a twenty-year-old male, is from Kabul in the east; and Setera, a twenty-one-year-old female, is from Herat City in the west. The geographic diversity ensures wide popular appeal. But it is clear the fix is in (see *Quiz Show*, 1994). Of the thousands of contestants, only three were women, two of whom made the cut. It is not all glitz and glamour, however. The women, in particular, are often criticized for going beyond the bounds of propriety. Lenna, a Pashtun woman from Kandahar where the Taliban remains a strong presence, is often criticized for not covering herself—her hair peeps through her veil and she uses heavy makeup: the viewer sees blush and eyeliner being applied before she goes on stage. She is also secretly taking voice lessons and still continues to hide her songbook at night. Setara's dance steps and hip sways likewise receive some critical attention, even death threats. Still, their families are proud of their singing and all four of the contestants survive: one contestant's provocative behavior on *Afghan Model*—striking poses, according to Kim Barker (2010), like a dancer in a Madonna video—was cut off from his family as soon as he joined *Model*; another was shot dead one night.[32]

The success of *American Idol* would suggest that *Afghan Star* will garner some attention in the United States. Fans of *Idol* will find *Star* similarly entertaining, much as sports enthusiasts will enjoy its Iraqi counterpart, *Sadr City Soccer*. *Star*'s real value, Ann Hornaday rightly suggests, more likely lies in the "snippets of Afghan life [the director] gathers to create a lively, textured depiction of a beautiful if confounding country."[33]

POTPOURRI

The five films in this section stand outside the classificatory scheme used in this chapter. They look at the situation in Iraq from the Iraqi perspective. In this, they are similar to the quasi-foreign documentaries and foreign fictive feature sections in the last chapter which tells of the Iraqi experience from their side of the looking glass. The difference here is that only one of the films is made by a quasi-foreign director, none is made by an Iraqi, and the most successful insider takes are made by Americans.

My Country, My Country (2006) was an Academy Award nominee by American filmmaker Laura Poitras. It is part of her planned "New American Century" trilogy about post-9/11 America. The second in this series focuses on Guantanamo, *The Oath* (2009); the third will be on the 9/11 trials that are scheduled to take place in 2011 at a to-be-determined location after opposition to them being held in New York City forced the government to reconsider New York as the site for the trials. The first film, *My Country, My Country* focuses on the January 2005 elections in Iraq, the first to be held since the U.S. invasion.

The documentary focuses on Dr. Riyadh, who Poitras initially met in July 2004 at Abu Ghraib while he was conducting an inspection of the facility. Dr. Riyadh runs a free clinic in Adhamiya, a Sunni section of Baghdad, and has decided to run for the Baghdad City Council. The intercutting by the director works well to pull the viewer into Riyadh's otherwise staid story: Dr. Riyadh is shown feeding the chickens at home, pondering whether he should run for office; then we are in the Green Zone where an Election Security briefing is taking place—U.S. Assistant Secretary of State Richard Armitage is saying he is here to make sure the "show" (election) is run right; after this scene, Poitras cuts to Dr. Riyadh outside the fence of Abu Ghraib. A man wants Riyadh to take his name and help get him out of there; he is innocent. Dr. Riyadh shakes his head sadly and tells him, "We are an occupied country with a puppet government." Riyadh is then seen at home watching the offense taking place in Fallujah on the television with his family; then he is at the clinic where a group of concerned males solicit his help to bring medical relief to Fallujah where they cannot gain access. Dr. Riyadh informs the viewer of the serious refugee situation: 109,000 have fled to Amiriyya; demonstrations outside the Abu Hanifa Mosque in Baghdad are shown as a fighter plane soars overhead while a protestor carries a placard, "Our hearts and homes are open for the people of Fallujah." Dr. Riyadh comments: "If free, this wouldn't happen."

Free elections in Baghdad are problematic. This is indicated from the opening when the viewer is told that voting is dangerous: "just the other day there was an attempted assassination of a minister who was shot and whose bodyguard was killed." Dr. Riyadh sardonically comments that this is the "fruits of democracy" (see also *Control Room*). Now, six weeks before the election is to take place, the viewer watches Dr. Riyadh working at the dining room table at home. The television is on in the background. The news announces that four election officials have just been killed. Right after this, a female patient comes to invite him to a wedding. Dr. Riyadh quips, "There isn't much to be happy about."

On the other hand, we do get the feeling that there is something to be happy about. There is a strong turnout on Election Day; people want to participate. Long lines are shown winding around polling booths. "Oh, My Country" is optimistically sung as people are shown voting: "Oh, my country, may you have a happy morning / Reunite everyone; heal your wounds / I yearn to see you smile someday / When will sadness set you free?" The ending crawl announces the results: "58 percent of Iraqis voted on January 30, 2005," even though "44 people [were] killed at polling sites." Unfortunately, the "majority of Sunnis boycotted the election; turnout in Fallujah was two percent." The Sunni boycott had consequences: Dr. Riyadh was not elected.

Iraq in Fragments (2006) by James Longley, who did Gaza Strip (2002), was also nominated for an Oscar (see also Sara's Mother and Other Stories, 2006).[34] Fragments is divided into three parts. Each part focuses on a young boy in a different part of the country: the first section appraises the harshness of life on the streets in Baghdad; the second takes the viewer to the Shia south where Muqtada al-Sadr is rallying his ultraconservative Islamic militia; the last sojourns to the Kurdish northern region of Iraq.

The film is a bit disjointed but this is done purposefully. It is not a neat, cohesive, linear story. But then neither is the situation in Iraq. Langley purposefully tells the story in fragments. Iraq is now splintered, perhaps irrevocably. There are distinct geographical and political differences. This is made clear by the father telling his young son at the conclusion of part three that the voting that will soon take place is "better than 100 bombs, 200 bullets," but it will divide the country more than ever: "Now it will be hard for Kurds, Sunni, and Shia to live together. The future of Iraq will be in three pieces." The scene fades out over a darkened landscape.

Fragments is so named because it is a story told in fragments. The fragments include perceptive takes on a potpourri of issues: the importance of literacy; how young boys mimic, for better or worse, their elders; parallels connecting Muqtada's abuse of power to Saddam's (see The Blood of My Brother); the ubiquity of America in the international arena; and the importance of voting, among a host of related fragments. The structure of Fragments may, as Ella Taylor put it, make the film "unmarketably complex."[35] Among the initiates, however, the film was applauded: it won for directing, cinematography, and editing at Sundance. One reason for this, Nathan Lee writes in the Village Voice, is because "it's characteristic of the film to pun and layer meanings."[36] Langley achieved what he set out to do: "I didn't just want to bring the viewers into Mohammed's neighborhood [Part I]—I wanted to put them inside his head."[37] One can only wonder how Robert Koehler, writing for *Variety*, could dismiss the film so cavalierly as "superficial."[38]

Meeting Resistance (2007) by first-time filmmakers Molly Bingham and Steve Connors is not as solid as the other two. The topic is certainly interesting: one-on-one interviews with Iraqi insurgents. The directors selected the Adhamija neighborhood in Baghdad because they identified *one* person from that area to be an insurgent. They ended up interviewing eight Iraqis. The interviews were conducted over a ten-month period in 2003; the film was released in 2007. It might have been timelier had it been released sooner. In the aftermath of films depicting the abuses at Abu Ghraib and related films that showed how American troops treated locals, the insurgent's motivation for wanting to expel the occupying forces was pretty clear. They also fail to accomplish their stated intention to get an intimate portrait of the insurgents. Anthony Kaufman with the *Village Voice* sums up their failure: the directors do "a remarkable job of [accomplishing] the opposite. Instead of individualizing the jihadists, the film shows a series of characters who are blurred, faceless, nameless, and generalized non-personas, with monikers like 'The Teacher,' 'The Warrior,' and 'The Imam,'"[39] none of whom, it might be added, say anything not already well known.

The Making of an Army (2006) is also a first-time film for the Norwegian journalist, Sigurd Falkenberg Mikkelsen. It takes as its focus the four weeks of training recruits who want to be part of the new Iraqi army. Precious little training is actually shown. Mostly, the viewer is treated to scenes of American military personnel going about their business rounding up locals in identity checks in nearby cities while someone watches behind a window and identifies suspected insurgents. The recruits apparently tag along to see how it is done, but they are seldom seen. The viewer does learn that the group of recruits Mikkelsen is following are unusual because they are a mixture of Arabs and Kurds—most other training areas separate the two because of the language barrier. A lot of time is lost translating what the American instructors say. Sometimes, they don't actually translate. One Iraqi translator says that if the drill instructor (DI) tells the recruit to "'Get up, mother fucker,' we tell him, 'please, get up.'" The focus of the film is less on the Iraqis than how American military personnel try to train them to Marine standards. One DI goes ballistic when he sees the recruits drinking water out of water bottles and not canteens (in almost all the grunt films, American military personnel are also drinking out of water bottles). The film clearly shows the disparity between American and Iraqi standards. The result is that, purposely or not, the Americans come off looking culturally insensitive. This is clearest at the end of the film when, now graduating, all the new Army initiates must have their beards cut and hair shaved. "This," one Iraqi says, "is not normal to Arabs." Doesn't matter: a Marine at the barber shop shouts, "[We] can do this the easy way or the hard way," to one Iraqi who resists the obligatory shave and haircut, "but you're getting your hair cut. Sit!"

It is surprising that the one film made by an Iraqi-American is the weakest of the group. The problem, as with the other two, is that the director of *Nice Bombs*, Usama Alshaibi, has no cinematic credentials. The result is that there is no real focus in the film. The only rationale for making it is that he is an Iraqi and curious "what his family in Baghdad was experiencing." The first ten minutes give his background. Soon thereafter, he enters Baghdad with his expatriate father and is warmly reunited with his family, which he hasn't seen in more than a decade. Snapshots of his childhood are interspersed throughout the rest of the film. Life in Baghdad, however, is unrelated snippets, real fragments. The following is an illustration of the unconnected wandering of our naïve young director.

We learn his family has a long lineage in Iraq and that his family's name is inscribed over the entrance to the al-Kadhimiya Mosque where members of his family are still employed as custodians. This gives him unprecedented access in the neighborhood. Rather than explore any unique insights this might give him, we jump to another family reunion where we see the picture of his mother in cap and gown holding her diploma. Then, suddenly, Usama wants to try to get into the Green Zone. He is just curious what will happen—well, you could get *killed*, dude (see *Gunner Palace*; *Occupation: Dreamland*). After all, he's an American citizen. At the entrance to the Green Zone he's told that he and his wife, who both have passports, can enter, but not his Iraqi driver, even if he is family. When asked who his sponsor is, Usama has no answer. He says he was told to report to the American Consulate upon arrival in Baghdad. The disembodied voice on the intercom says he'll find out where the Consulate is. Well, "that was fun," he says, back home with members of his family, a lavish banquet is spread out in the background while men in the foreground dance. The family scene ends as abruptly as it started, and the next day Usama says he wants to go to the old market where they still make handcrafted goods. One picture that lasts a millisecond is shown of a man hammering an object, then we're back with his family. On one of his wife's rare appearances in the film, she comments on how friendly Iraqis are (compared to standoffish Americans), then, without realizing the irony of what she says, mentions offhandedly that "everyone [here] has a gun." Shortly thereafter Usama takes a video of a mangy cat on the street and says that his aunt told him "all stray cats got sick and died after Gulf War I" (see *Poison Dust*). None of this goes anywhere. No dots are connected. No insights are offered. It is too bad: *Nice Bombs* could have been a good film had Usama done a little homework.

CONCLUSION

At first glance, the cinematic thesis/antithesis divide arguing the war appears only slightly more skewed than those in the earlier 2004–2005 period: four films weigh in on the conservative side, six on the liberal side. This changes dramatically when the six documentary films that dissect Abu Ghraib and Guantanamo Bay are added to the antithesis side. These later films raise those that are against the war by a three-to-one margin. The split is even more pronounced when one takes a close look at the thesis films, which are extraordinarily weak, much more so than those made by conservative documentarians prior to 2006. The retooled John Wayne Vietnam homily, *No Substitute for Victory*, looks particularly pale next to *Michael Moore Hates America* or *FahrenHYPE 9/11*. The only connection *No Substitute* has to Iraq is the subtitle of the film: *From Vietnam to Iraq*. *The Hunt for Zarqawi* is similarly attenuated and is little more than an updated hunt film in the style of those films that searched for Saddam Hussein and Osama bin Laden. *The Iraq War* also falls flat by repeating the now-stale story of how technology triumphed in Iraq. Only *The Surge* adds new insights as to why combat troops need to be in Iraq.

This should not suggest that antithetical films outside the Abu Ghraib scandal are particularly strong. They, too, add little to the dialogue. *No*

End in Sight has little to do with the rationale driving America's continued presence in Iraq and simply recounts the lockstep mentality of the administration that led to war. *Bush's War* follows much the same path. *Iraq for Sale: The War Profiteers* plows familiar territory, too. *The Tillman Story* and *Behind Taliban Lines* simply move the criticism of the Iraq war to Afghanistan. The antithetical point of view is saved by the new insights the Abu Ghraib scandal provided to documentary filmmakers. *Ghosts of Abu Ghraib* is noteworthy because it threaded the unconnected stories that appeared in the public press into a coherent narrative, and *Standard Operating Procedure* gives a face to those who were charged with criminal misbehavior by letting the guards give their perspective on events that took place at the prison. *The Prisoner, or How I Planned to Kill Tony Blair* varies the Abu Ghraib story by presenting the Iraqi view. The other two films employ the docudrama format to examine events at the Guantanamo facility. The docudrama has not been extensively used. It was necessary in this case because the filmmakers lacked the photographic evidence that was so pronounced at Abu Ghraib. *Taxi to the Dark Side* and *Road to Guantanamo* (see also *The Oath*) are particularly effective since they expose conditions that had to this point only tangentially been raised in the public arena. They are also instructive because they are among only a handful of documentary films that take us beyond events in Iraq.

Grunt-view films move beyond the dialectic, which generally posit a "for" or "against" view of the war. The films in these later years (2006–2010) are dramatically different from those previously encountered. Earlier grunt films often inadvertently depicted the behavior of those serving in a less than heroic light. Documentarians in these later grunt films turn their lens on little known facets of the war. The people making these films are filmmakers, not military personnel with cameras taped to their helmets or reporters with minicams taking pictures of everything and then later trying to make sense of what they filmed. In this crop of grunt films, the filmmaker sets out to tell a specific story about those serving that purposely taps into an aspect of the war that might be of cinematic interest. These films tend to portray military personnel in a positive light: Latinos who served, and died, in the hope of gaining citizenship; women at the front in combat zones who comport themselves extremely well in the face of hostile fire; soldiers who became conscientious objectors after being deployed, and not as a way to avoid serving; the meaning and importance of an "alive day" for those who were fortunate enough to have one; and how writing about their wartime experiences proved cathartic in grappling with inexplicable, and sometimes conflicting, emotions.

Another face of the war is also seen, or seen in greater detail in films made during this period. This war has witnessed the highest survival rate of any war in history. *Life and Death in a War Zone*, *Baghdad ER*, and *Fighting for Life* looks at the medical personnel on the front lines who are responsible for this phenomenon. They do what the film *M*A*S*H* did for an earlier generation by attempting to "capture the compelling scenes of doctors and nurses treating wounded victims at combat support hospitals, on medevac flights, and [in] . . . military hospitals." The difference is that in these films what medical teams are doing is not fiction and unfolds as it takes place—real life in reel time.

The end result of the medical interventions that takes place in these wars is that more lives are saved. The survivor films examine close up the injuries that have been sustained that the viewer has only caught fleeting glimpses of in those documentaries that the grunts at the front filmed. The films focus on the adjustment these men and women confront daily after surviving their alive day. *Between Iraq and a Hard Place* is not as successful as *Body of War* or *Home Front* because the former spends too much film footage with secondhand sources, unlike the latter two that follow the adjustment issues two veterans faced at home. By focusing on the plight of Tom in *Body of War* or Jeremy in *Home Front*, the viewer gets to relate not just to the struggles encountered by the survivor but the pain and trauma that affect their families as well. *Ground Truth* goes beyond the physical injuries military personnel have suffered and tackles the psychological effects the war has had on those who have returned. This trauma too has been touched on in any number of films, but here it is subjected to greater scrutiny.

The subject matter of these films has been noticed in other films. Documentaries now begin to more closely dissect their subject matter. This also holds for those films that fall into the entertainment category.

There is a lot of downtime wasted waiting for a mission to start. Grunt movies often show some of this time listening to music. The role of music in the troop's lives moves to the foreground in *Soundtrack to War*.

Soundtrack shows not only the musical preference of those at the front but how music is often used to "pump up" the men in the field as they roll into action. *Soundtrack* is also unique because it is one of the few films where the director's commentary provides significant insights into the role of a documentary filmmaker and how his personal ideology affected the content of this film. Other films in the entertainment group reveal how the locals entertain themselves. *Heavy Metal in Baghdad* depicts the trials and tribulations a group of metalheads had in performing under Saddam, but whose ability to play their chosen brand of music has not dramatically changed with the liberation of Baghdad, and may, in fact, have become even more problematic—conditions in the city have forced the group to disband. The liberation of Afghanistan, however, has changed things. The rigid restrictions of the Taliban lifted, *Afghan Star*, a variation on *American Idol*, has recently debuted. Some of the musical contestants are followed and the viewer learns that the show, like its American counterpart, may thrust some into the limelight, but in some parts of Afghanistan their "Western" behavior raises eyebrows and can even lead to more trenchant forms of censorship—one contestant was killed and others have been threatened with physical punishment if they continue their lascivious behavior.

There is, finally, a group of films that defy ready classification. This fact alone underscores how varied the films during this period are compared to those that preceded them. These films are different because they look at the situation in Iraq from the Iraqi perspective, but only one, *Nice Bombs*, was made by an Iraqi American. In the last chapter, films made by the locals or what we've dubbed quasi-foreign were among the more successful films because they gave a hard look at things from a perspective not often seen in the West. Curiously, the weakest film in this group was the one made by a quasi-foreign Iraqi. This also indicates that the dialogue has moved solidly away from the conservative camp as more Americans make films that appreciated the perspective from the other side.

One of the strongest in this group is *My Country, My Country*. Its strength may reside as much in the fact that the filmmaker, Laura Poitras, is making a career of films that examine the war from the other side. *My Country* is the first of her three-part series. The other, *The Oath*, was made after *My Country*. Here, her lens follows a local, Dr. Riyadh, who runs for office in the first free election in Iraq. *Iraq in Fragments* by James Longley is also a strong film, though it received mixed reviews because of its wandering structure. But Longley's three-part fragmentary development is precisely what makes this a strong film. It not only gives a close-up view of the Iraqi experience—itself fragmented—but the structure of the film reflects this fragmentation of the local populace toward the war and America's presence. *Meeting Resistance* continues the Iraqi lens by interviewing insurgents, and *The Making of an Army* provides insights into the men who comprise the new Iraqi Army and how they are being trained.

In the final analysis, films after the initial dialectic phase (2004–2005) provide some solid, in-depth insights into events taking place in Iraq that its predecessor films only covered in a very cursory manner. Despite this, there are a few events that took place in Iraq that escaped the documentarians' lens. These films fall under the purview of fictive directors to address. Fictive features also extend the parameters of cinema by tackling wider issues. Fictive features did not try to follow the trail cut by documentarians, but blazed their own cinematic path. The path fictive feature directors took is examined in the next chapter.

NOTES

1. Jeannette Catsoulis, "War Made Easy," *New York Times*, 14 March 2008, 12(E).

2. One could go further and suggest that some of those with military experience did not make sound military decisions simply because they had military experience.

3. William Whyte, "Groupthink Reconsidered," *The Academy of Management Review* 14, no. 1 (1989): 40–56.

4. Irving L. Janus, *Victims of Groupthink* (Boston: Houghton Mifflin, 1972).

5. Janus, *Victims of Groupthink*, 74.

6. "Bush and Public Opinion: Reviewing the Bush Years and the Public's Final Verdict," Pew Research Center, 18 December 2008. www.people-ress .org/report/478/bush-legacy-public-opinion (accessed 24 February 2010).

7. "America's Image Slips," Pew Research Center, 13 June 2006, www .pewglobal.org/2006/06/13/americas-image-slips (accessed 24 February 2010).

8. The 327th at Abu Ghraib was part of the 800th Brigade that General Karpinski commanded.

9. General Karpinski appeared as a talking head in a number of antithetical films that were critiqued in the last chapter; her insider command rank gave her "credentials." It is only here that the viewer becomes aware that she was demoted because of the way things were handled under her command in Iraq. This now explains the reason for her bitterness and her caustic criticism of the war.

10. J. Hoberman, "Get Out of Jail Free: Earl Morris Cuts Abu Ghraib MPs Some Slack," *Village Voice*, 23 April 2008, 60.

11. Erving Goffman, *Asylums: Essays on the Social Situations of Mental Patients and Other Inmates* (New York: Basic Books, 1961).

12. John Markert, "Social Eclipses and Reversion to Type: Sexual Issues Confronting Postmodern Men and Women Working in Strongly Patriarchal Societies," *Theory in Action* 2, no. 1 (2009): 86–109; John Markert, *Sexual Harassment: A Resource Manual for Organizations and Scholars* (Spokane, Wash.: Marquette Books, 2010).

13. These films and the act of rendition, which basically means to kidnap, will be discussed in the next chapter.

14. Roger Ebert, "Taxi to the Dark Side," *Chicago Sun-Times*, 7 February 2008, www.rogerebert.suntimes.com (accessed 11 February 2010).

15. The director, Valerian Bennett, falls into the dubious Reporter's View category, if only because he essentially takes directorial credit for editing a film shot largely by the members of the 1/5.

16. Heidi Specogna, interview with IndiWire at Sundance Film Festival, 23 January 2006, www.tagtraum.de/pages/de/produktionen/rezensionen/32.htm (accessed 16 March 2010).

17. Mockenhaupt discusses the use of simulations as a means to train military personnel in how to work with Iraqis; he comes to a similar conclusion about the unrealistic expectations that these exercises engender. Brian Mockenhaupt, "SimCity Baghdad: A New Computer Game Lets Army Officers Practice Counterinsurgency off the Battlefield," *Atlantic*, January/February 2010, 26–27.

18. Gary Strauss, "'Lioness' Documentary Hunts Down Women's Role in Iraq War," *USA Today*, 12 November 2008, www.usatoday.com/life/televsion/news/2008-11-12-lioness (accessed 3 April 2010).

19. This film is a tribute to women serving. It does not look at some of the related problems women on the front lines confront, such as rape and the complexities of living with the enemy, as well as the challenges of long-distance motherhood. These issues are addressed by Laura Browder and Sascha Pflaeg-

ing in their book, *When Janey Comes Marching Home*. See also Riverbend, *Baghdad Burning: Girl Blog from Iraq* (New York: Feminist Press, 2005); Jesse Ellison, "Back from the Lion's Den," *Newsweek*, 10 November 2008, 6.

20. Strauss, "'Lioness' Documentary Hunts Down Women's Role in Iraq War."

21. Moore's coauthorial contribution is not cited in the film.

22. This is discussed in chapter 2.

23. See chapter 2.

24. Galloway supports the troops he was embedded with and also, it appears, the war, judged by his effusive comments made in other films he appeared in. See chapter 2.

25. Jane Fonda took home the Oscar for best actress in the same film.

26. Caroline D. Harney, *Agent Orange and Vietnam: An Annotated Bibliography* (Lanham, Md.: Scarecrow Press, 1988); Phillip Jones Griffiths, *Agent Orange: 'Collateral Damage' in Vietnam* (London: Trolley, 2003).

27. The "Patriotic Police" at FOX, discussed in chapter 2, were quick to follow Göring's lead by "denouncing the pacifist for a lack of patriotism and exposing the country to danger."

28. See John Markert, "Sing a Song of Drug Use-Abuse: Drug Lyrics in Popular Music—From the Sixties through the Nineties." *Sociological Inquiry* 71, no. 2 (2001): 194–220; Richard A. Peterson and Janet Kahn, "Media Preferences of Sexually Active and Inactive Youth," *Sociological Imagination* 32, no. 1 (1995): 29–43; John Ryan, Legare Calhoun, and William Wentworth, "Gender or Genre? Emotion Models in Rap and Country Music," *Popular Music and Society* 20, no. 2 (1996): 121–53; Cathy Schwichtenberg, ed., *The Madonna Connection: Representational Politics, Subcultural Identities, and Cultural Theory* (Boulder, Colo.: Westview, 1993).

29. Matt Halburn, "Goyas: More Grotesque Than Ever," *Wired*, 20 September 2001, www.wired.com/techbiz/media/news/2001/09/46615 (accessed 30 April 2010).

30. Gittoes received financial assistance from the Australian Film Commission. This is probably part of the "payback" for the stipend.

31. Eddie Cockrell, "Heavy Metal in Baghdad," *Variety*, 1 October 2007, 93–94.

32. Kim Barker, "Kabul Makeover," *Atlantic*, March/April 2010, 19–20.

33. Ann Hornaday, "In Afghanistan, a Feel-Good 'Star' Search," *Washington Post*, 17 July 2009, 4(C). See also Ty Burr, "From Repression to Expression: 'Afghan Star' Offers a Powerful Look at Post-Taliban Talent Show Performers," *Boston Globe*, 31 July 2009, 8(G); Ella Taylor, "*Afghan Star* Documents *American Idol* Translated to a Closed Society," *Village Voice*, 24 June 2009, 46.

34. *Sara's Mother* is a spinoff of the *Iraq in Fragments* feature.

35. Ella Taylor, "Sundance in Fragments: Festival's Documentaries Offer a Survey of Global Disorder," *L.A. Weekly*, 2 February 2006, www.laweekly .com/film+tv/film-reviews/15027 (accessed 13 March 2010).

36. Nathan Lee, "Style Offense: Poetic Construction Makes Film Not Just Another Iraq War Doc," 8 November 2006, 74. See also Bilge Ebiri, "The Ravages of War and Occupation: An Interview with James Longley," *Cineaste* 32, no. 1 (Winter 2006): 38–41.

37. Kenneth Turan, "'Iraq in Fragments': Iraq War Documentary Amounts to Ravishing Portrait," *L.A. Times*, 17 November 2006, www.calendarlive.com/ movies/reviews/ol-et-iraq7nov17 (accessed 20 March 2010).

38. Robert Koehler, "Iraq in Fragments," *Variety*, 12 February 2006, 23.

39. Anthony Kaufman, "Meeting Resistance," *Village Voice*, 23 October 2007, 182.

4

FICTIONAL
FEATURES BELATEDLY APPEAR

The films for most of the decade (2001–2010) were overwhelming documentaries. There were twenty films that depicted the villains Osama bin Laden or Saddam Hussein; twenty-three revolved around the WTC. Another 153 dealt with the ground wars. Even if the many television specials that subsequently appeared in DVD format that assessed America's "heroes" and "villains" are excised, close to 75 percent of the documentaries directly related to the wars in Afghanistan or Iraq.

There was a smattering of fictional features before 2006. Most of these either related to the attacks that took place on September 11 (n = 9) or were foreign releases that made it to America (n = 6). Domestic fictive features make an appearance in 2006 (n = 4) and begin to drop off in 2009 (n = 4). The body of fictional films occurs over a very narrow time frame: eleven are released in 2007, another seven appear in 2008, with a handful (n = 5) of films where terrorism is the central conceit peppering the second half of the decade. In all, only twenty-seven fictional treatments of events in Iraq and Afghanistan and the war on terror appeared in the first decade of the twenty-first century. This means that domestic fictional features between 2001 and 2010 that assessed post–9/11 related events accounted for less than one-fifth of all post-9/11 war-related movies, and two-thirds of these didn't appear until the second half of the decade. Nevertheless, almost any of the big budget films featuring Hollywood stars that were released were likely viewed by more people than the combined audience for all theatrically released domestic war-related documentaries, with the exception of Michael Moore's *Fahrenheit 9/11*.

Fiction Features
Home of the Brave (2006)
The Insurgents (2006)
Southland Tales (2006)
Cavite (2006)
Grace Is Gone (2007)
Extraordinary Rendition (2007)
Battle for Haditha (2007)
In the Valley of Elah (2007)
Day Zero (2007)
The Kingdom (2007)
Lions for Lambs (2007)
Redacted (2007)
Rendition (2007)
The Kite Runner (2007)
Generation Kill (2008)
Stop Loss (2008)
Traitor (2008)
Harold and Kumar Escape from Guantanamo Bay (2008)
War, Inc. (2008)
Body of Lies (2008)
The Lucky Ones (2008)
Taking Chance (2008)
The Hurt Locker (2009)
The Messenger (2009)
Brothers (2009)
Green Zone (2009)
Dear John (2010)

The first crop of fiction was largely dismissed by critics. Some, like *Southland Tales*, were justifiably panned as bad films. Others, notably *Lions for Lambs* that was produced, directed, and starred Robert

Redford, were viewed as bleeding-heart films because they so blatantly flagged their liberal biases toward the war (see also *War, Inc.*). The most frequent justification for dismissing some of these early films was their low gross. This did plague some of the films and these box office failures will be taken up in the next section in the chapter: many deserve their fate, but some do not. A number of other films broke even (± $1 million), and thus were often viewed as unsuccessful, a sign, some conservatives would argue, that served as a bell weather indicator that the public was not going to pay to see their ideals trashed. Preliminary box office receipts would indicate that many of these movies were a failure, but there are precious few *Avatar*s, and even *Avatar*'s receipts are not finalized until both domestic and foreign box office grosses are calculated, *and*, importantly today, DVD sales are accounted for: *Home of the Brave* only achieved $43,753 in gross box office receipts but pulled in $4.7 million from domestic DVD sales with another $4 million added after computing international DVD sales. Even a film that breaks even with the combined box office and DVD sales can be considered a winner because not counted is the clear profit that subsequently comes from DVD rentals and television rights, even after other costs, such as ads for the film, are taken into account.

In fact, there was only a handful that broke even. More made money than lost. For example, *Southland Tales* was a box office disaster. It cost $17.8 million to make (inclusive of print and ad costs) and took in only $364,600 at the box office—domestic and international. Another $5.4 million was garnered from domestic DVD sales; $4.2 million more would be added to this number once international DVD sales were taken into account. Combined domestic and international box office receipts and DVD sales are just shy of $10 million, so it still looks like a financial disaster with nearly $18 million in production costs. But now the money starts coming in: $18.8 million is added from domestic video rentals, a cost that alone surpasses the production costs of the film, and another $14.7 million comes from international video rentals, with some loose change ($1.7M) added to the pot from domestic and international television rights and ancillary fees.[1] Even those that at first glance seem like clear losers, such as *War, Inc.*, that cost $10 million to make but only grossed $2 million (inclusive of DVD sales), is seen, if we use only these sales indicators, by more people than many of the high grossing

Table 4.1.   Revenues and Budgets

Film	Total Receipts* (In Millions)	Production Budget** (In Millions)
Day Zero	$.088	$8
Cavite	$.378	$.007
Battle for Haditha	$.620	$1.5
Redacted	$1.1	$5
War, Inc.	$2.1	$10
The Lucky Ones	$2.7	$14
Grace Is Gone	$5	$4.1
Home of the Brave	$5.7	$12
Southland Tales	$6.6	$17
Stop-Loss	$15.9	$25
Rendition	$26.4	$27.5
Valley of Elah	$27.7	$23
Traitor	$41.1	$22
Brothers (USA)	$43.3^	$25
Harold and Kumer Escape from Guantanamo	$67.2	$12
Hurt Locker	$68.6	$15
Lions for Lambs	$72.4	$35
Kite Runner	$73.2	$20
The Kingdom	$120.5	$72.5
Body of Lies	$130.1	$67.5
The Insurgents	$.023†	$8
The Messenger	$4.6	$6.5
Dear John	$137.8^	$25
Home of the Brave	$5.2	$12
The Green Zone	$107.3	$100^
Restrepo	$2.9•	$1

* Domestic and foreign theatrical gross plus domestic DVD sales through 2010. International DVD sales tend to be in the same range as domestic DVD sales, plus/minus 10 percent.

** Hard production costs. Does not include ad and print costs. Figures are rounded for convenience.

† No box office receipts; film went straight to DVD.

• DVD sales not calculated since did not go to DVD until late 2010.

^ These three films are worth special note because of the generous gross from television and ancillary rights. *Brothers* added $10.2M from these sources; *Dear John*, $23M; and *Green Zone*, $20.1M.

Source: Nash Information Services, www.the-numbers.com.

top 100 documentaries (see Table 2.3). Some that appear to have made money when the cost of production is compared to receipts didn't because inflated advertising budgets cut into the profits: *Rendition*'s advertising budget of $24.8 million is almost the cost of the film's production, as is *Brother*'s $23 million ad campaign.[2] Table 4.1 is a partial list of box office winners and losers, if winners and losers are figured solely on how much the film generates in box office receipts and DVD sales compared to the cost of making it.

PROBLEMATIC FILMS

War is not funny. *Catch-22* and *M*A*S*H* managed to succeed because they were both dark comedies. Neither went for belly laughs but had lighthearted humorous moments sparingly interspersed throughout an otherwise serious story about war. Nor were either about the war in progress. Joseph Heller's novel, written in 1961, was made into a movie in 1970 and depicted military life of a small group of flyers in the Mediterranean during the latter stages of World War II; *M*A*S*H* (1970), though it too was released as a film at the height of the Vietnam War, was set during the Korean Conflict twenty years earlier. While there were obvious parallels to the Vietnam War that the audience couldn't escape, by removing the satires to another, more distant war, it muted some of the direct criticism of the ongoing conflict. In addition to the satiric, dark comedic element, both films had strong storylines and solid performances turned in by polished actors. None of this can be said for *Southland Tales*, which explains its dismal performance at the box office.

Southland Tales is not a film noir, as it is billed. Noir is characterized by dark shadows; small, bleak hotel rooms (*The Killers*, 1946), and dark, impersonal offices (*Double Indemnity*, 1944). Even in towns with wide open spaces, the lighting is toned down and the streets have a claustrophobic feel (*Panic in the Street*, 1950; *Red Rock West*, 1993; *L. A. Confidential*, 1997). In contrast, *Southland Tales* is brightly lit and the settings spacious. There are precious few chuckles in noir; *Southland Tales* consistently goes for belly laughs (see also *Harold and Kumar Escape from Guantanamo*).[3] The jokes are often crude and tasteless, belying its juvenile humor: references to pornography abound, buxomly women displaying an abundance of cleavage dot the film, Bud Light flows freely, and the number sixty-nine appears frequently for no apparent reason other than to raise a chortle from the young adolescent males the film is marketed toward. The male character, played by Dwayne "The Rock" Johnson, is typically shirtless to display his honed biceps, which keeps the audience focusing on his well-endowed physique, camouflaging his lack of acting ability.[4] Only Manohla Dargis, writing in the *New York Times*, found Richard Kelly's film a "funny, audacious, messy and feverishly inspired look at America and its discontents. . . ." Dargis even dismissed the rakish boos that greeted the film when it premiered at Cannes in 2006, reminding the reader that even such luminaries as "Sofia Coppola was booed, as were Antonioni and Bresson."[5] More indicative of the critical response is Roger Ebert, who wrote that even the twenty-minute streamlined post-Cannes film, which "loops off a couple of characters and a few of the infinite [infantile] subplots," still remains "a mess" and that it would be better if Kelly "keep right on cutting until he whittles it down to a ukulele pick."[6] Ruthe Stein with the *San Francisco Chronicle* concurs that it is "a mess" which "fails to come together" and that its 144 minutes passes "with the speed of molasses."[7]

The film's dystopian premise is solid and has worked in other films (see *Logan's Run*, 1976; *Brazil*, 1985; *Dark City*, 1998; *The Road*, 2009), and one appraising an apocalyptic, post-9/11 world could be thematically poignant. The film opens promisingly in Bush country (Abalone, Texas) in 2005. Neighbors are celebrating with a Fourth of July barbeque in the street when a mushroom cloud appears in the distance signaling the beginning of World War III. This is followed by Justin Timberlake misquoting the final stanza from T. S. Eliot's poem, "The Hollow Men" (1925), so that the explosive ending would fit the movie: "This is the way the world ends / This is the way the world ends / This is the way the world ends / Not with a whimper but a bang."[8]

Fast forward to Venice, California, in the near-future (2008), a key area in the southland is under lockdown because of the war, which now includes, besides Iraq and Afghanistan, other Bush pariah nations: Syria, Iran, and North Korea. The draft has been reinstated, but this is never developed (see *Day Zero*). In fact, the rest of the film after the five-minute opening is little more than a series of romps by the Mad Hatter on Spring Break in Venice Beach, replete with The Rock, whose character has somehow been transported from a nuclear rift in the fourth dimension, hoisting a six-pack of beer and, lofting it high over his head, pouring the contents down his mouth and over his body. Visual effects are supplied throughout by well-endowed, seminaked women prancing around preaching free love. It misses just about every opportunity to make political commentary on where post-9/11 events could take the country. But, then, that wouldn't be a comedy.

While *Southland Tales* attempts to exhort belly laughs from the audience, *War, Inc.*, another film clearly in the casualty box, is more of a satiric attempt to comment on the war. But satire is tougher than comedy. Comedy merely mocks and makes light of things that are readily related to by the audience. Satire takes itself more seriously and while it may mock the subject it is seldom lighthearted; it typically uses irony and sarcasm to express moral indignation at a state of affairs.[9] The reason satire is more problematic than comedy is that it requires the audience to be more informed of the topic and be able to recognize often fleeting, witty references; in contrast, comedy tends to beat the audience over the head with the scene. For satire to be effective, the audience has to pay close attention. It appears that many critics didn't.

In the opening of *War, Inc.*, Brand Hauser (John Cusack) bellies up to a bar in the Yukon and suddenly shoots the three rough-looking men drinking whiskey next to him, then saunters out to a plane which is going to take him to his new assignment. The opening serves to establish him as a hit man; the plane exchanges show that he has a conscious, however, and is plagued with increasing doubts about his career path. His next assignment, given by Dan Aykroyd—who talks out of the side of his mouth and is obviously meant to resemble Dick Cheney—is to go to Turaqistan (rhymes with Afghanistan) and eliminate Omar Sharif (Lubomir Neikov) who is thwarting Tamerlane's (Halliburton's) plans of exploiting that country's natural resources (see *The Oil Factor*, 2005; *Syriana*, 2005). In Emerald City (the Green Zone), two women enter his life: Yonica Babyyeah (Hilary Duff) provides the eye candy and plays the role of a misunderstood (and oversexed) Middle Eastern pop star that would never be allowed to appear in *Afghan Star* garbed as she is and gyrating as she does in this movie[10]; Natalie Hegalhuzen (Marisa Tomei) is the liberal journalist who acts as the hero's foil and love interest. Ben Kingsley plays CIA head Walken,[11] "the Viceroy," who gives the hero his nefarious assignments.

The plot is simple enough, but satire doesn't need much of a plot (see *Catch-22*; *Animal Farm*; *Fahrenheit 451*); its success rests with its vituperative condemnation of status quo situations and its quick, Benny Hill–like wit.

Numerous analogies are quite obvious: Dick Cheney; the Green Zone; Halliburton, and its next logical step, the outsourcing of the entire war; oil as a self-serving motivating factor for intervening in a country's internal politics; and the branding of America—Coca-Cola signs are regularly seen in the background and Popeye's Chicken outlets appear in the most unlikely places. But satire goes beyond the blatantly obvious and *War, Inc.* has some fleeting gems. One, which critic Roger Ebert puzzled over, was the main character's penchant for constantly shaking hot sauce into a glass and drinking it until perspiration dots his forehead. The protagonist typically took his dose of Nitrogen when he was lapsing, which in this context means that he showed momentary humanizing feelings and this was his way to expunge them. His hot sauce "feats" are also reminiscent of G. Gordon Liddy, a former FBI agent who was involved in the Watergate scandal under the Nixon administration: Liddy liked to show how tough he was at parties and is reputed to hold his hand over a candle flame to show how much pain he could endure without flinching.

The hero arrives at the Green Zone in Turaqistan to set up a trade show to market American products. There are a number of fleeting but significant war-related references while he is setting up the trade show. Scrawled on a bombed-out building is "Thank you USA" and locals run up and greet his arrival warmly. He is met by Marsha Dillon (as in Marshall Dillon from *Gunsmoke* fame who between 1955 and 1975 weekly "cleaned up" the city of Dodge); here "the Marsha" is Hauser's Communication and Interrogation Specialist. Over the doorway a barebacked man is seen for a split second hanging a welcoming sign; tattooed across his back is his real attitude toward the locals, and one widely expressed by many documentaries that depict the grunt at the front: "Fuck Haji." This attitude is reinforced when Hauser has Marsha Dillon rearrange the stage to face east rather than west, otherwise the Muslims in the audience will be turning their backs on the stage [America] five times a day for prayer. "Cultural sensitivity," he says, "that's what it's about, baby." The film is replete with such scenes. Three others are particularly noteworthy as commentary on the war.

The first brief scene takes on particular significance after having witnessed the dubious involvement of journalists that was seen in many documentaries and critiqued under the Reporter's View in chapter 2 and which was apparent in the documentary *Heavy Metal in Baghdad* that was discussed in chapter 3. Reporters enter an arena to be briefed, under a banner that reads "Coca-cola presents . . . the implanted journalistic experience." A guard at the door gives shots to those who enter. Natalie waves off the shot, "Allergies." The guard tells her, "You're sure? You won't get the full experience." The experience is a Disney-like themed event where the journalists, wearing virtual headgear, get to watch the war taking place out there as their chairs rock to simulate riding in a jeep over rough terrain. The childlike visage on the reporter's face tells it all: "Wow! Way cool" (see *War Feels Like War*). Only Garry Trudeau's journalist, Roland Hedley, who reports on the war "at the front" in his comic strip *Doonesbury*, comes close to this level of invective.

A second scene has Hauser, after giving the secret word by the way he orders his meal at Popeye's, jumping over the counter of the fast-food restaurant and riding an elevator down to the lower depths, à la Maxwell Smart in *Get Smart*, where he gets his orders from the disembodied voice of the Viceroy. This setup is critical because at the end of the movie we see Hauser again going to his secret rendezvous in the bowels of Popeye's, but now the Viceroy is revealed. It is basically the Wizard of Oz: his previous powerful voice is really machine-made and the Wizard, now in the guise of the Viceroy, is a bitter and helpless paraplegic. And like at the end of *The Wizard of Oz*, he is reveled onscreen to the masses, who are struck that they've feared this obviously unassuming figure: "*That's* the Viceroy?" Unmasked, the Viceroy races away in his motorized wheelchair, ranting, as missiles are about to be launched on Emerald City: "Tamerlane's weapons are precision guided to minimize collateral damage. Not only is our technology the most advanced in the world, but also with a smart missile system we can launch a matchstick in Milwaukee and stick it up the ass of a termite in Tehran." This has been heard before, and with similar results: the missile, instead of striking Hauser at the wedding reception, hits and destroys Popeye's where the Viceroy has taken cover. The Navy commander, watching from the submarine that launched the missile, has a simple Baghdadian disclaimer: "Shit happens."

The movie could just as easily end here, but Cusack, who also cowrote and coproduced the film, has one final scene that harkens back to the start of it all. The former vice president who now heads Tamerlane makes a televised announcement to the public. Tamerlane (Halliburton) has been given the contract to fire on Iran because of the incident that took place in Emerald City (Popeye's) "cannot be tolerated" and intelligence has determined the Yakastanees—recall this all started with Brand going to eliminate Omar Sharif because he was not predisposed to allow access to his country's oil reserves—are developing a nuclear arsenal and we "cannot let [the] smoking gun come in the form of a nuclear cloud."

A lot of the satire in this movie works, and it is dead-on commentary about the war that had gained widespread social currency by the end of the decade. Unfortunately, the satire is too sporadic and the movie gets tangled up with banal subplots. One subplot, and the reason Hauser could never be enticed by the lascivious Yonica, is that Yonica is his daughter who was kidnapped by the Viceroy as a toddler to take revenge on Hauser who pushed him into the back of a garbage truck crippling him in the decaying Pax Roma theme park when they had a rendezvous. Other subplots revolve around comedic relief that often turns *Southland* juvenile: the call from the plane from Hauser to the former vice president who has to hang up because he's "taking the crap of all time" on a commode; a cartoonish (and unnecessary) James Bond–like martial arts scene where he wreaks vengeance on a group of thugs; a plan by the husband-to-be to make and market a pornographic video of his wedding night with Yonica. In the end, the final verdict is perhaps summed up by *USA Today* critic Claudia Puig (2008) who found that the movie sometimes just tried too hard, but was nevertheless fast-paced and entertaining.[12]

Cavite, on the other hand, didn't try at all. Its poor gross may hide the fact that it didn't lose that much money because it didn't take any money to make it; the film cost only $7,000 to shoot. The critics mostly praised the film, despite the fact that, writes Stephen Holden (2005) in the *New York Times*, it "suffers mightily from the fact that Mr. Gamazon [the lead] can't act."[13] This is a rather serious flaw, considering that

Gamazon is the focal point of the entire film; nevertheless, Holden still finds *Cavite* "a gripping no-budget political thriller."

Widely applauded is the gorilla-style, jiggling handheld camerawork.[14] The film camera technique and low budget is akin to *The Blair Witch Project* (1999) which the critics also loved and whose glowing reviews were largely responsible for its financial success. This time the public was not buying. The subject matter didn't help.[15]

The film is made by two Filipino Americans, Ian Gamazon and Neill dela Llana, with Llana doing the shaky camerawork and Gamazon performing by running through the streets in Cavite City, a province in the Philippines.[16] The protagonist, Adam[17] (Gamazon), is employed in a dead-end job as a night watchman in San Diego harbor, where he is clearly bored to tears as he makes his rounds. In his dreary San Diego apartment, Adam receives an ominous phone call summoning him to return to his homeland in the Philippines. The first fifteen to twenty minutes of the eighty-minute movie follow Adam as he sits around his apartment, and then ostensibly stands around at different airports waiting for his plane—no other people are seen in any of the airports, all of which are identified by their name in the lower part of the screen to indicate his trek home: Bradley International at LAX, Chiang Kai-shek International in Taipei, Taiwan, and finally Aquino International in Manila. On arrival in Manila, he receives another call that informs him that his mother and sister have been kidnapped, after which the viewer has to ride through various small towns and villages before finally arriving at his destination. The tedious trek to Cavite City is held together by what might be called tourist visuals: a lengthy cockfight scene and visits to the local market.[18] The omnipotent eye of the kidnapper appears to follow his every move, communicating with him initially through a cell phone and then from an earpiece. This technique effectively leaves the viewer watching Adam all the time, and having his actions explained by the kidnapper's voice.

The connection of this film to post-9/11 events is the terrorist angle. The kidnapper goads Adam for failing to be a faithful Muslim (he's never visited Mecca) and later launches into a lengthy diatribe of "atrocities against Muslims by the [Philippine] government": the Manila massacre where seventy-nine Muslims were shot, point-blank range when in a mosque; the Tacub massacre that took sixty innocent Muslims;

the Tago-ig massacre where ten schoolgirls lost their lives; the Colong-colong massacre that left seven hundred Muslims dead. The film is interesting, if not particularly gripping, but it is disappointing that, in the end, Adam returns essentially unchanged to his humdrum San Diego existence. The film fleetingly suggests he might be somewhat reawakening spiritually—a central motif repeated throughout the movie. It is noteworthy that the film closes with Adam in bed muttering his declaration of faith (*Kalima*) from the Shahada: "I bear witness that there is no God but the Almighty God and that Mohammed is the Messenger of God." The recitation of this oath is considered the most important of the Five Pillars of Islam. The recitation is repeated as the movie fades out over a close-up of Adam's face reciting the *Kalima* to the slow, hypnotic ticking of a clock. This scene (and the movie) could be quite provocative, but the director's commentary disavows any political message in the film: "We are not pro this or pro that." It is precisely this failure to commit that causes the film to drift. There is no message because there is no message, consequently there is no film because there is nothing to say. One could say that saying nothing is a message, but the directors' disavowal would indicate they are not going in this direction either.

GRIM REALITIES, DISQUIETING THOUGHTS

The films in this category may be problematic also, in the sense that many were not profitable films. *Battle for Haditha* and *Redacted* are clearly box office failures, which indicate they were not seen by many people. The same holds for *Extraordinary Rendition*. On the other hand, *Rendition* had a respectable gross, though it was not earthshaking. Still, *Rendition*'s gross would indicate it garnered a fair-sized audience. Nevertheless, this film is also considered problematic because it was not warmly received by the critics. The problem for all these films is that they deal with grim realities and evoke disquieting thoughts at a time that such social reminders were themselves problematic.

At the height of the depression, and throughout World War II, Hollywood films received their warmest embrace by the public. People flocked to the movies. There are many reasons for Hollywood's success during this period (1930–1945), but one key factor was that people wanted to escape from the harsh social realities confronting them and lose themselves in the movies, which is the only explanation for the absurd popularity of Busby Berkeley musical extravaganzas (see *Footlight Parade*, 1933; *Gold Diggers of 1933, 1935, 1937*). The audience also wanted to be informed during World War II of events taking place at the front, and one of the main visual depictions of the war could be seen weekly in *Movietone News* clips. But while wishing to know what was taking place over there, the audience was at the movies to be entertained, which is why the short newsreel preceded the feature film. The film clips also invariably portrayed anything involving the troops in a positive light. This was done to keep up the spirits of those on the home front, but it was as also done for much the same reason as the cute, lighthearted story that closes the nightly news: disturbed viewers might not be able to enjoy the lighthearted entertainment to follow if they cannot shake disconcerting images.

The economy was problematic throughout most of the first decade of the twenty-first century. The sharp stock market decline in 2001–2002 was offset by the looming terrorist threats that the Bush administration hardly had to push, but nevertheless helped to fuel fears in the aftermath of 9/11. The stock market remained shaky and took another sharp downward spiral in 2008, shortly after the United States officially declared that it had entered a recession in December 2007.[19] Layoffs and the housing crisis acerbated economic concerns for Americans long after the recession was officially declared over in July 2009. People had enough problems in their daily lives; they did not want to go to the movies to be reminded of how bad the war was going, which is what the features in this group did with a sharp, pointed prong.

Battle for Haditha is a film with a very sharp prong. Made in 2007, it aired on British television in March 2008. It is the true story of an incident in Haditha that took place in November 2005 when a team of Marines, after losing one of their own after a roadside bomb struck a Humvee, went on a rampage and killed twenty-four Iraqis, at least fifteen of whom were noncombatants, including five girls killed in one house who were ages fourteen, ten, five, three, and one. The Marine Corps initially reported that the civilian casualties were collateral damage: the Marines were attacked by insurgents and returned fire. The death of the civilians, said Lieutenant Colonel Michelle Martin-Hing, spokesperson for the Multi-National Force in Iraq, lies squarely with the insurgents who "placed noncombatants in the line of fire as the

Marines responded to defend themselves."[20] *Time* magazine, however, received a video of the shootings and in March 2006 ran a story alleging a massacre had taken place. This caused the military to open an investigation. The probe concluded that two women and five children were killed by Marines and not by an insurgent's bomb and that no insurgents were in the first two (of three) houses the Marines raided.[21] Charges were subsequently brought against eight Marines in the 3rd Battalion, 1st Marines in December 2006.

A former Marine critiqued this film on Netflix. He first establishes his credentials to address what happened, and they are formidable: seven years as a Marine, three tours in Iraq, two purple hearts. Additionally, his first day in Iraq was in Haditha, in a convoy near where the incident took place; in fact, he says that he showed a PowerPoint presentation to his Colonel regarding the incident the day after it occurred, "not months later like the movie suggests." This is because "Every kill in Iraq is analyzed immediately since the theatre has become mature." He adds correctly that the movie fails to give a postscript that all the Marines were cleared of all charges in 2008 and signs off, "Semper Fi!"

This Marine reviewer is correct but not exactly accurate. At the time the film appeared (March 2008) charges against some of the Marines held directly responsible for the killings were still pending. Charges had been dropped against five Marines by the end of 2007; this still left charges pending against three others. In March 2008 charges against Lance Corporal Stephen Tatumges were abruptly dismissed "on the eve of the trial with little explanation," wrote Dan Whitcomb for Reuters.[22] But while charges had been dropped against six defendants in Article 32 proceedings (the military equivalent of a grand jury hearing) only one had actually been found not guilty, and the "ringleader," Staff Sergeant Frank Wuterich, still awaited trial in 2010; at least three other officers had also received official reprimands for failing to properly report and investigate the killings at the time they occurred. Any crawl that made the distinction between charges dropped and acquittal would only serve to suggest to the viewer that they were guilty and the military was covering it up. The disclaimer could also point out that the United States paid $2,500 to family members for each of the fifteen dead civilians; the fact that they steadfastly refused to pay remuneration to nine others who they identified as insurgents could be interpreted as a backhanded confession of culpability.

The Marine reviewer on Netflix, like many in the Corps, is no doubt a good Marine and does not condone the action that took place. He does not want to believe that a fellow Marine could do such a deed. There is also the concern that blaming a few may lead the public to sanction all. Events depicted in the movie, however, closely follow the reports that have surfaced, which lead to the inevitable connection to the My Lai Massacre that took place in Vietnam (1968) when an Army patrol killed between 347 to 504 unarmed civilians. In both cases it can be argued that the military personnel simply lost it. This does not excuse the behavior but it does explain it. The men on the ground in Haditha had much more rationale for doing what they did than the twenty-six soldiers in My Lai, all of whom, with the exception of Lieutenant Calley, were never convicted.[23]

At My Lai, the soldiers that participated clearly knew what they were doing in a rampage that unfolded over two days.[24] In contrast, Haditha was a direct response to a mortal injury to a comrade and the rampage quickly burned itself out. To fully appreciate how things happened at Haditha, it is necessary to delve further into groupthink since it is more than simply following along. The following are well-documented elements of group behavior and groupthink dynamics,[25] most of which have been seen in the multiplicity of documentaries that have been examined in the previous two chapters.

Group behavior is most likely to flourish under the following conditions:

1. Group newcomers will model their behavior on what old-timers do.[26] Old-timers often act as mentors by developing close personal ties with newcomers to help them be successful in the group. Close personal ties are enhanced even more so when the group is immersed in a total institution.
2. Many groups develop problem-solving strategies very quickly. In combat situations, the overriding problem-solving strategy is to stay alive *at all costs*.
3. Groups have two types of roles: instrumental and expressive. Instrumental roles focus on achieving the task at hand; expressive roles provide emotional support and maintain morale. Males are more likely to engage in instrumental roles, and in hyper-masculine

military organizations, such as the Marines, Army Rangers, or Navy SEALS, expressive roles are disdained as feminine (see *The Lionesses*).

4. The relationship between group cohesiveness and group performance is stronger in smaller (Squad level: 8–13 individuals) than larger groups (Platoon: 26–55 military personnel; Company: 80–225). This relationship is ever more intense when tasks require interdependence: group members must interact, communicate, cooperate, and observe. The military is the classic example of an interdependent group, and the documentaries, time after time, basically promote the theme, "you watch my back and I'll watch yours."

Groups that fit these conditions are more likely to develop a groupthink mind-set.

Groupthink behavior is most likely to flourish under the following conditions:

1. Members maintain an illusion of invulnerability and an exaggerated belief in the morality of the group's position.
2. Members rationalize the correctness of the group's actions and believe stereotypes about the characteristics of out-group members.
3. There is strong pressure to sustain group cohesiveness. Group members censor their own thoughts and acts if they are deviant from those of the group.

Additionally, there are two environmental cues that intensify the loss of control among group members.

1. Accountability cues: When accountability is low, those who commit deviant acts are likely not to be caught or punished. This may cause people to engage in gratifying but usually inhibited behaviors.
2. Attentional cues: The person's self-awareness declines, causing a change in consciousness. In the "deindividualized" state, the person attends less to internal standards of conduct and reacts more to the immediate situation with little regard to long-term consequences.

In this state, the individual is more likely to act on impulse because
their behavior is not being monitored.

To varying degrees, all these behaviors have been seen in the documentaries. One that is clearly, and repetitively, seen in the grunt's view
documentaries is the tendency to demean the Iraqi people. This is aptly
captured in the opening of *Battle* and strongly harkens back to those
documentaries that depicted the grunt at the front: "Only thing fighting
for is to get home without getting killed. I don't know why we're here";
"I've seen women with—what do you call it? A burka?—pull an AK from
under her skirt start [and start] spraying"; "Man, woman, child, if they
pick up a gun, they're combatants. Marines kill"; "[It's] just like hunting
. . . [this war is the] ultimate style of hunting"; "Iraq's a giant butt
hole."

This kind of attitude was also seen at My Lai: the Vietnamese were
not seen as human beings. There is a necessary side to debasing the
enemy. It allows military personnel to sometimes do unpleasant tasks.
Nevertheless, such verbalizations also serve to reinforce and strengthen
a negative mind-set, which makes actions against those who fit the stereotype easier to carry through with. The circulatory of the argument
is never clear, since only the one side is ever seen: "if they do shit to
us," one Marine says early in the film, "we should do more of them."
Pick a documentary at random and this characteristic attitude will be
on display. Added to this mind-set is the necessary, and extraordinary,
cohesiveness of combat units. This is compounded by the constant stress
military personnel are under in a combat situation. Going through a
door where insurgents may lurk, grunt's view documentaries constantly
remind us, weapons are raised and any movement, even a peripheral
one, may result in a perspicuous squeeze of the finger. In modern weaponry the result is not just a spent bullet but a burst of twenty rounds in
a fraction of a second. This all comes together in Haditha for the worst-
case groupthink scenario: a group of strongly bound individuals whose
lives depend on each other and who are in a highly stressful situation
with a common, extremely hostile view of the enemy—which is considered to be everyone of the same broad category. This can be laid out
syllogistically: Iraqi insurgents are everywhere in Iraq, Iraqi insurgents
are the enemy, therefore the enemy is everywhere.

The Marines are already pumped up; they know Haditha is a hotbed of insurrection: "Remember the fifty Marines who got slaughtered before we got here?" one Marine cautions as they roll out of the compound in the film. Then something happens to one of yours by one of them. This is followed by a long moment of perplexity, indecisiveness, unbelief—aptly captured in the film *Battle*; then a strong, authoritative person reacts (Sgt. Wuterich) and everyone instinctively, and unthinkingly, follows. This would mean that if Sgt. Wuterich screamed, "Everyone in your vehicle and outta here. Now!" They'd be gone. In this case, Sgt. Wuterich appears to have directed the men to go after "them." The insurgents were in one of those houses—they were seen running in that direction. The Marines hit house one, then two, then, in three, they nail the insurgents. Immediately thereafter (and this separates Haditha from My Lai) what one has done is suddenly realized—and stops, almost as quickly as it started. But the deed is done. At just about any other time, in any other place, the deed would not have taken place. The realization of this helps to rationalize the cover-up that follows. Remorse may be felt but it is quickly stymied by the group in a "We-only-did-what-we-had-to-do" attitude. It's combat. High command wants to believe, so they accept the statement offered at face value; besides, the explanation of collateral damage has occurred all too frequently so unless there is some extenuating reason not to believe (the article by *Time* magazine), high command believes.

This is exactly how the film *Battle for Haditha* indicates the event happened. The film also clearly shows this was not a celebratory moment and that there was remorse for what took place by many who participated. Nor does the film place the blame solely on the 3/1. The first part of the film shows the recruitment of two Iraqi civilians to plant and detonate the roadside bomb. They are not doing it for some greater good, but for the money. They once had a good job with the Iraqi army, not, they say, out of love for Saddam, but for the country. However, policies promoted by the Bush administration led to the disbandment of the army and swelled the ranks of the unemployed. For planting an IED, they will be paid $1,000 (half before, half after the act is successfully carried out). This amounts to a handsome sum in post-Saddam Iraq. They are also politically quite naïve. Watching events unfold from the rooftop after the bombing, one says, "We're killing our own people." They had anticipated that the Marines would "just shoot in the air." Now, they wish they hadn't done it. Still, their jihad recruiter says when they first met that the goal is to make "Haditha an Islamic city," regardless of any collateral damage. The jihadist recruiters lose no sleep over the death of their countrymen when told of events that took place after the bombing: "We're proud of you. . . . Now the world will see how Americans behave." Had the Americans not behaved the way they did (e.g., had they returned to their barracks), the recruiter would have kept planting roadside IEDs until the desired response was obtained.

The film also recognizes there were some propagandistic nuances behind the film that eventually made its way to *Time. Battle* shows one young girl being prompted to correctly phrase her statement, "Say the Americans hit you," to indicate that the damage to the right side of her face that is covered by bandages is their doing. The television announcer frames the injured girl's appearance on television: "This is a symbol of what the Americans are doing." The Sheik, who might be likened in the Western world to the local mayor, takes political advantage of the situation. Earlier, the two bombers went to him to discuss their concerns and were simply advised to pray. Now the Sheik is on television and, with his audience in mind, says, "Americans killed her whole family." The zealots who instigated the whole thing are pleased: "The Americans have lost the battle of Haditha. Everyone has joined us, and [soon] we will control the city." But the two naïve bombers have come to realize something: "I'm afraid that after the Americans leave we will get worse than Saddam Hussein, and he will burn Iraq more than it burns now."

Battle for Haditha is a more complicated film than simply depicting a small group of young Marines who temporarily lost it. It is the logical conclusion of the grunt's view seen in the documentaries that the grunts themselves filmed. The critics considered it a much better film than *Redacted*,[27] but it is not an entertaining one. Sometimes, however, films have to be made that address serious issues. The world, and especially the world at war, is not a perfect place.

Not only do innocent people die in war, but women are raped (see *Two Women*, 1961; *Apocalypse Now Redux*, 1979; *Rape of Nanking*, 2007; *The Greatest Silence: Rape in the Congo*, 2008). These things have always happened and they have always been brushed into the backroom. A new level in linguistic hygienics may have been reached in the present war, however. The killings of innocent civilians are passed over as collateral damage, as are other unsavory incidents, such as rape. These incidents are redacted. Redact means to edit or revise; here it means to sanitize an otherwise abhorrent incident by transforming (editing) the incident into an innocuous phrase—collateral damage. A related but misleading word that will be examined shortly is "rendition"—a euphuism that means, oxymoronically, to legally kidnap.

The Sapir-Whorf Hypothesis addresses the issue of language. It was formulated by two linguistic scholars, Edward Sapir (1884–1939) and one of his students, Benjamin Whorf (1897–1941). They did not themselves formulate the hypothesis but others, leaning on their work, coined the term after their deaths. Simply stated, the Sapir-Whorf Hypothesis suggests that the structure of language affects the perception of reality of its speaker and thus influences their thought patterns and worldview. In short, the language that is used in the social group affects how people perceive reality. The theory is controversial because it suggests people are the prisoner of their language; however, from the vantage point that is it employed here, it is a rather straightforward linguistic assumption: calling someone an African American is much different than calling the person a nigger. Similarly, saying one has murdered or raped conjures up a completely different image of what took place than saying collateral damage occurred. The redaction that is taking place today is nothing new; the government has often sought to edit reports from the front. The concept of redaction has likewise been previously employed: "friendly fire" deaths are familiar jargon from previous wars. It's also been raised in fiction and is at the heart of George Orwell's 1948 novel, *1984*, where he labeled it "newspeak." Newspeak is the language Orwellian-envisioned government employs to control what people think by getting them to talk, and consequently think, about things differently. Collateral damage and rendition are contemporary newspeak terms that the government and military find much more palatable than murder, rape, and kidnapping.

Redacted is a French-backed film[28] by Marc and Francois Clement that is directed by Brian De Palma who has a long and distinguished career as a moviemaker: *Carrie*, 1976; *Blow Out*, 1981; *The Untouchables*, 1989; *Mission Impossible*, 1996; *Femme Fatale*, 2002; *The Black Dahlia*, 2006. The critics have widely panned *Redacted* as a remake of his earlier film, *Courage under Fire* (1989), which is about a group of soldiers in Vietnam who take a young girl from her village and rape and murder her. *Redacted* relocates the plot to Iraq. *Casualties* had a very strong cast, which included Sean Penn and Michel J. Fox, and this might help explain its box office appeal: it grossed $18.6 million at the box office. *Redacted* was not only critically dismissed, it was also a box office bomb: it took in a paltry $65,000 at the box office. *Casualties'* success is also related to its audience-friendly narrative structure. Not only is the topic more problematic in *Redacted* because it is set in the here and now, but De Palma utilizes a disturbingly real documentary format, making the here and now even more immediate. This makes the true story on which it is based more unsettling than the parallel event that took place "back then" in Vietnam.

The plot of *Redacted* is similar to *Battle for Haditha*. The first part of the film establishes the characters: they are seen intermittently interacting in the barracks or manning a checkpoint. Character development is oversimplified, reminiscent of World War II films: there is the egghead, whose nose is always buried in a book, in this case John O'Hare's *Appointment in Samarra*[29]; the old-hand, three-tours-of-duty Sergeant; the dreamer, who is going to win fortune and fame back home once the war is over, in this case with his video of life at the front that he is shooting; the joker, who is always interjecting ribald comments and kidding around; and the uneducated redneck Southern hicks, here pointedly named Bubba and Flake, who are invariably "reading" skin magazines and who are responsible for instigating the central crisis in the film, the rape of a fifteen-year-old girl. When not in the barracks, the viewer observes the men performing their duties at a checkpoint, routinely stopping cars and searching civilians with the ever-present sense of threat that something can happen at any moment. The second part of the film revolves around "the incident."

The incident is precipitated by two events: the soldiers have just learned they are being stop-lost; this means their tour of duty has been extended, which adds to their discontent. The second is an IED that explodes and severs a limb from one of the men in their unit—the IED is payback for their killing of an innocent woman and child at the checkpoint. That night, the squad goes on a house raid looking for explosives. In one of the homes is a comely fifteen-year-old girl, recognized by

Flake as someone he has enjoyed "frisking" at the checkpoint. Back in the barracks, fueled by their drinking, the rednecks want payback and return to the house where the adolescent is to claim their "spoils of war." To cover up what they've done, they kill her and her family and burn the house. One of the men is already having pangs of conscious-ness after witnessing the rape, but is told threateningly, "What happens in Vegas, stays in Vegas. You understand me, soldier!" It was less a question than a statement. As in *Battle for Haditha*, a news report of the deaths, in this case by a French reporter, leads to a formal inquiry. The investigation comprises the remaining third of the film. Flake, who is giving a video deposition, sums up the logic behind their subsequent acquittal in a rather lengthy self-serving speech:

> We went back to the house cause [we] knew they were hiding weapons and shit. [The] old man tried to shoot me with an AK-47 . . . and after everything we've done for these niggers: got rid of Saddam, planted de-mocracy, given up our lives to keep them safe from their own insurgents. . . . This is bull shit. Doing [this] for the folks back home. . . . We're keep-ing Arab scum off their doorstep. [We] shouldn't be in here answering this crap. . . . [We] should be out doing our job, boots on the ground, finding the bad guys and putting two in the heart and one in the head, keeping America safe, making sure the motherfuckers [are] dead. . . . [And] you prosecute guys like us.

As with *Battle for Haditha*, there is no clear and unequivocal proof that the men charged did the act, and American law for a capital offense requires that if there is *reasonable* doubt the accused must be acquit-ted. But movies try and convict because the proof *is* clear in the way the evidence is presented to the jury. The men are responsible, and they got away with it. This makes for a very disturbing film. It is much preferable to pretend the world is a lovely place and that Americans do not commit reprehensible acts of this kind.

Historically remote disquieting incidents may have some chance of success because they are rooted to a bygone time (see *Courage under Fire*, 1996; *The Accused*, 1988). This allows the audience to recognize that society has not always been perfect, but by locating it historically it also allows the audience to delude itself that the world is now cleansed of past sins.[30] The more recent the disturbing behavior that is depicted on film, the greater the chance that it will fail commercially. But commercial success alone is not why some films are made (see also *Lions for Lambs*; *War, Inc.*). Indeed, De Palma's stated purpose in making this film is to rock people's orderly worldview; the people, he says, "are not seeing the [disturbing] pictures that we saw during Vietnam."[31] The movie's dubious box office answers critic David Ansen's question: "Perhaps the real question is: do we want to see those images?"[32] The answer is no, but that does not mean we shouldn't or that the film should not have been made.

The theme of *Redacted* is clearly disturbing for the audience, but the critics have more of a problem with the film style. De Palma is making a fictional movie using the documentary style of storytelling with its ancillary method: jerky camera; odd angles; grainy, often hard to distinguish, low-resolution images. The central conceit of the movie is that one can never escape the prying eye of the camera. This is made obvious from the plethora of documentaries from the front. However, if one is not familiar with these documentaries, De Palma's film aptly captures this reality. The film opening sardonically promotes the central conceit. Angel Salazar (Izzy Diaz) is filming the men in the barracks, hoping that his video will launch him on a Hollywood film career and make him famous. Angel pans the barracks and asks the men the camera alights on to speak into the camera. While Angel is filming his video, another in the barracks is filming him. Angel is being filmed, filming the men, while De Palma is filming them filming. Lovely! And in the end, Angel gets his wish: The jiggling helmet cam also captures the men rushing into the houses at night, and then returning to rape the young girl, which, because he filmed it, puts him there and makes him culpable. He's now (in)famous!

The biggest problem the critics had was with the acting. Kaufman calls it "ham-handed acting,"[33] Scott dismisses it as "clumsy,"[34] Ebert finds it "curious."[35] Most fault the amateur status of the actors who often play to the camera. Gleiberman complains that they are not acting like real soldiers: "the soldiers don't sound like soldiers; they sound like the cast for *Rent* acting like roughnecks."[36] But that's the point. This is how soldiers (people) act when a camera is stuck in their face: they "play" to the camera; their natural poses suddenly become hamlike. For soldiers playing to the camera, they'd want to sound tough, like they'd imagine soldiers would act. This is exactly what De Palma says he wished to achieve: "the actors are often playing to the camera. They're self-conscious."[37] Only Ebert seems to have found this incongruity to work: "[The] edge of inauthentic performing paradoxically increases the effect—moments seem more real because they are not acted flawlessly."[38] The reason this works is because De Palma made sure his actors felt the experience. Rob Devaney, who plays Lawyer McCoy in the film, says that they spent two weeks in a Jordanian boot camp with "a military advisor who put us through our paces," so by the time they were shooting *Redacted* they had learned proper military language, hierarchy, protocol, and, most important, what it feels like to wear armor-plated vests and to tote "20 to 35 pounds of gear around in 95-degree heat. . . . That affects you emotionally. So does the monotony of the sand and rocky desert."[39]

The treatment of rape by De Palma also needs to be addressed. A. O. Scott with the *New York Times* feels that the acting and filming technique "rarely hits the audience with genuine shock or a clarifying insight. It churns through a set of ideas and emotions that . . . are unpleasant, to be sure, but also, by now, dispiritingly familiar."[40] Gleiberman goes further and says that "De Palma trivializes wartime atrocity by reducing it to the level of a sick hothead getting his payback."[41] This is the reason Elley feels the movie fails: "There isn't the faintest trace of any moral or ethical complexity visible onscreen."[42]

Rape is all too dispiritingly familiar. More than 90,000 rapes are reported every year in the United States.[43] This is widely considered underestimated because many women do not report rape.[44] It is, nevertheless, a subject that is rarely treated in popular film, and yet another off-putting reason the movie did not succeed at the box office. As abhorrent as rape is, it is not that complex either. Rape is a very straightforward act; indeed, the act itself should be sufficient to make it a moral issue—even more so when it is committed upon a fifteen-year-old girl.[45] It is also performed at the individual level, more often than not by those with traditional, condescending views toward women. These views can be found among men at all social levels.[46] It is particularly pronounced among those men with a high school education or less,[47] which is more than 50 percent of the male population in the United States.[48] Even the Southern prototype depicted in *Redacted* has some validity: the majority of documentaries depict reserve units from the southern states, notably Arkansas and Texas, and the South has a disproportionately high number of individuals who have dropped out of high school.[49]

In short, the depiction of the rapist that is found in *Redacted* is accurate. The only inaccurate depiction in this film is the alcohol. One of the biggest complaints in the documentaries by grunts at the front is that the Muslim country in which they are based complicates their access to alcohol; many cannot wait to get home and have a beer. Nevertheless, alcohol is frequently a catalysis to committing the act of rape and is often an excuse for rape, as in "I would have never of done it if I hadn't been drinking."[50] Indeed, alcohol serves to inflame conduct toward individuals who are viewed by the rapist as "pussy."[51] This denigrating view of women as "meat" is clearly set up in the film because it is Bubba and Flake who are the ones talking about women in this manner and are often seen reading skin magazines. The alcohol in the film acts as a catalyst, then, to explain the "why now" aspect of the event. The background and behavior of Bubba and Flake explain *why* it happened. For anyone not familiar with how others join in on the fun or stand idly by and do not intervene, Jody Foster's *The Accused* (1988), about a true-to-life gang rape that happened to a young woman at a bar in New Bedford, Massachusetts, is recommended, though disturbing, viewing.[52] An appreciation of Foster's movie helps explain the ending of *Redacted*, where one of the men, on leave back home, is with his friends who urge him to tell a war story. His war story: "I went on a raid [where] two men from my unit raped and killed a fifteen-year-old girl . . . and I didn't do anything to stop it." Those at the table applaud. They don't get it. They are out to celebrate the return of their hero. "Come on," they say, "smile [for the camera]." They don't want to be made aware of the seamier side of war. Apparently, neither does the public.

The seamier side of war continues in *Rendition* and *Extraordinary Rendition*, which also continues to linguistically neutralize the occurrence that takes place. Both terms refer to another dark side of the war: taking someone without due process and confining and torturing them because they are *suspected* terrorists. The act of rendition has been documented in *Road to Guantanamo* (2006), *Taxi to the Dark Side* (2007), and *The Oath* (2010); it was also the motivation for the terrorist suicide bombing of Grand Central Station that was depicted in the movie *The War Within* (2005).

Both *Rendition* and *Extraordinary Rendition* were released in 2007. *Rendition* is clearly the better of the two films. It is helmed by Gavin Hood whose directorial credits include *King Solomon's Mines* (2004) and *Tsotsi* (2005), which won the Academy Award for Best Foreign Language Film in 2006; the film is also supported by a strong cast that includes, among others, Jake Gyllenhaal, Reese Witherspoon, Alan Arkin, and Meryl Streep. In contrast, the director for *Extraordinary Rendition*, James Threapleton, has no previous directorial experience and, though the cast turns in a satisfactory performance, only Andy Serkis has any solid movie credentials. *Rendition* also has more time to develop the characters than *Extraordinary Rendition*: the former runs 122 minutes, the latter a scant 77 minutes. The shorter length of *Extraordinary Rendition*, which also relies on opening and closing visual crawls to drive home the film's theme,[53] instead of letting the storyline speak for itself, gives it the feel of a made-for-television movie. For this reason, the forgoing analysis focuses on only *Rendition* since the plots are the same: An Egyptian-born chemical engineer (Omar Metwally) disappears on a flight from South Africa to Washington on his way home to Chicago, presumably because his cell phone has been called by a terrorist group that is responsible for a recent bombing in North Africa that killed an American CIA operative. The engineer's American wife, Isabella (Reese Witherspoon), desperately tries to track down her husband. Meanwhile, the CIA analyst (Jake Gyllenhaal), who's been assigned to monitor the rendition of an American citizen at a secret location in North Africa, begins to question his role in the torture he is forced to witnesses. Supporting roles in *Rendition* are played by Alan Arkin (the senator) and the senator's aide, Alan Smith (Peter Sarsgaard), who is Isabella's old boyfriend and to whom she turns for aid.

First the names, which seem to have escaped critical attention. This may be because they are so obvious, but subtlety is not something American moviegoers tend to appreciate. The CIA analyst is Douglas Freeman. He is not a trained operative but fills in because the other was collateral damage in the terrorist bombing that had targeted the local chief of police, Abasi Fawal (Igal Naor). Todd McCarthy at *Variety* dubs him "conscience" because he so conspicuously represents the morale side of the tale.[54] The character fulfills his destiny by, in the end, being the man who frees the wrongfully imprisoned engineer. If Freeman is the conscience, his nemesis is CIA Director Corrine Whiteman, a name that is reminiscent of Harrison MacWhite in the *Ugly American*.[55] Even without that connection, the name, and arrogance, of Streep's character is sufficient to convey the dominant white woman or man rule mentality. The nice guy, don't-rock-the-boat everyman is personified by the common moniker (Adam) Smith, who, when forced to choose—"Please don't be one of those people who turn away" Isabella pleas—turns his back on her and walks away.

The film acknowledges that rendition measures were initiated under the Clinton administration, but makes sure the "blame" is laid at the feet of the Bush administration. In a walk, fittingly along the Potomac, Alan explains it to Isabella: extraordinary rendition started under Clinton and was supposed to be used under very extraordinary conditions, but "after 9/11 [it] took on a whole new life." Secret prisons outside the United States are mentioned, and soon the viewer is in one of those prisons witnessing, along with Douglas Freeman, waterboarding taking place. This leads to didacticism: the engineer "breaks" under torture and gives them the names of other terrorists. It turns out the names he gave were of members of the soccer team he was on just before he left Egypt almost two decades ago. When this comes to light, Freeman quotes Shakespeare to Abasi: "I fear you speak upon the rack where men enforce do speak anything." Should the audience miss the Shakespearian passage, Freeman says more clearly, "Torture one person, create 10, 100, 1,000 new enemies."

Many critics were lukewarm to the film. McCarthy says of Witherspoon's performance that she is a person who is "normally the most spirited of performers [and] who can inject even limited characters and blah scripts with her own spark, [but she] can do little but mope around and search for a different way to look worried. A limited acting exercise, to say the least."[56] But how spirited would a normal housewife be who cannot understand what happened to her husband and has to contend with the unbending bureaucracy in Washington? She most likely would mope around, which is to say, she'd be gloomy and brood. If there is any weakness to the film, it is in its ending. It is all wrapped up too neatly in what might be called the American ending. There is no room for doubt, everything is resolved, the good guys win, the bad guys pay, and the fourth estate plays its pivotal role. A European ending would have left things hanging: maybe he got away (Freeman pondering whether to free him), but maybe he didn't (did Freeman have the courage to act?). And things in Washington would not have changed: the CIA director would be ordering another act of extraordinary rendition, and the viewer would be left to wonder about the state of the very pregnant Isabella when she collapses at the airport as she dejectedly leaves D.C. Instead, the viewer is left with a "happily ever after" closing of the engineer pulling up to his middle-class suburban home in a taxi to embrace his wife and see his newborn son, effectively washing away the sins that have been committed against him.

ON THE FRONT LINES

There are only a handful of films in the second half of the decade that depict troops at the front lines, if the stinging *Battle for Haditha* and *Redacted* are expunged from the list. Three address the war in Iraq: one is the seven-episode, seven-hour HBO miniseries, *Generation Kill*, that examines the early days of the war; another is the Oscar Award–winning *The Hurt Locker*; and the third, though chronologically the first of the three, is the Turkish film *Valley of the Wolves* (2006), which will be critiqued later in this chapter. There is only one film that assesses the situation in Afghanistan, though the one is actually two films: the original Danish version of *Brothers*, made in 2005, and the American remake, which debuted in 2009. This film is of particular interest in the way the American version has been reframed for a domestic audience. There are a host of other films that appraise aspects of the war, but these either focus on the aftereffects of the war on those who served or their families or assess the continued threat of terrorism today.

The War in Iraq

Generation Kill sidesteps any contemporary debate on the war by focusing on the First Reconnaissance Battalion's initial surge across the line from Kuwait into Iraq through the fall of Baghdad. This period has been the subject of innumerable documentaries and is familiar to anyone who watched news reports of the surge into Baghdad. *Generation Kill* provides a fictionalized view of the war by closely following the exploits of the Bravo 2 Platoon. This allows the viewer to get to know the grunts more intimately than is achieved in the documentaries. They do resemble the grunts in many of the documentaries in their coarse jokes and crude language, but *Generation Kill* fails to capture the "humdrum, confusion and unvarnished hilarity of the lost hours waiting for combat" that critic Jonathan Finer (2008) finds to be one of the finer points of the film.[57] There is *far* too much action to capture the humdrum of life at the front—even when there is no action, there is action: the opening assault which turns out to just be a dress rehearsal; the assault on an airfield that turns out to have been abandoned by the enemy. Finer also finds the film to be "as authentic as it gets"[58]; in large part, this is because "[v]iewers will see more mangled bodies of Iraqi *civilians* in each episode than in a month of network newscasts" [author's italics].[59] Finer is correct. Most of the mangled bodies are not the result of combat but are collateral damage, which, more often than not, is lightly tossed off by those inflicting the damage, despite some reminders, studded throughout the seven hours, to take care not to kill civilians:

> As Bravo Company 2 rolls toward Nasiriyah, bodies litter the road. One of the dead "civilians" is shown with an RPG in his arms. Next to him is a little girl with both her legs missing. The juxtaposition of these two indicates that war is hell and sometimes innocents die.
>
> As the men move to assault an airfield, ostensibly held by the Republican Guard, they are told that all Iraqis in proximity to the objective should be treated as hostiles. One Marine says the CO has lowered the bar; another retorts, "Hell, he's removed the bar." Because the airfield has been abandoned, no casualties occur. The attitude, however, undercuts the early concern by the CO to minimize civilian casualties since he effectively said if they are there, they're dead.
>
> Moving toward another town, one of the men shoots a man and his camel who are just standing beside the road. Shortly thereafter a woman moves toward the platoon carrying a little girl. The men realized that the bullet ridden body was shot by one of their own, the same Marine who shot the man and his camel. "He's a psycho," one says of Corporal Trombley, to which another retorts, "[He] may be a psycho, but he's our psycho." The episode is appropriately entitled "Screwby."

One of the men is looking at a house in the middle of nowhere. Through his field glasses, women and children are seen standing around; no men are visible. Suddenly, a missile lands and the house evaporates. We learn that the CO ordered the attack on the "village" because it was occupied by hostiles. "Maybe we don't have the full picture," one says; "Maybe [hostiles are] inside." The bucolic scene negates such an "assessment." In a subsequent scene in another episode another town is blown away by a Navy bombardment in what one of the men refers to as "Precision Guided Whoop Ass." There is no indication that the town was harboring Iraqi military personnel. It appears to be shown simply for the visual (bombardment) effect.

Manning a roadside checkpoint, one of the men fires a smoke bomb at a car coming toward them. "What was that for?" "The idea," the shooter says, is to "scare [them] off; if the car keeps coming, [we] still have a chance to fire. [It] gives civilians a chance." A moment later an approaching car is fired on; the smoke bomb this time tears through the windshield and blows the car and its occupants away. The Marine who fired is reprimanded by another, "You're supposed to fire a warning shot first!" Oh, well.

At another checkpoint in another episode, a car approaches while a mass of refugees stream away from Baghdad, flanking the oncoming vehicle as it moves toward the checkpoint. One of the Marines fires at the car from the back of his vehicle. Rather than hitting the oncoming car, he blows away the back of the head of one of the civilian refugees. "What the fuck!" someone exclaims. "Roll on," he's told. They do. A head lies in the middle of the street; "watch the head," the driver is told. He swerves around the head; the vehicle rolls over the decapitated body.

The death of civilians is a tragic occurrence of war. It is probably more pronounced in Iraq than previous wars where the bad guys wore uniforms clearly demarking them as bad guys. The point of this lengthy tragic scroll is not that civilians die in war, but that their deaths become a central motif of the film, casually dismissed.[60]

The authenticity of the film rests on a three-part series in *Rolling Stone* entitled "The Killing Elite" that was written by Evan Wright, an embedded journalist with the 1st Recon, whose previous writing credentials, he tells the men on his arrival to impress them, was penning the "Beaver Hunt" column in *Hustler*. The award-winning story is promoted in the opening of the first episode where the viewer is informed that the film is a "fact-based dramatization [though] some [sic] events [are] fictionalized for dramatic purposes." But as Nathaniel Fick, a former platoon commander in the 1st Recon, pointed out in an interview with Finer (2008), *Generation Kill* is "an interpretation of a book, which is itself an interpretation of events." Fick, who wrote his own different account of the 1st Recon in *One Bullet Away: The Making of a Marine Officer*,[61] goes on to say that if some of the behavior exhibited by ranking officers had actually taken place, the officer would have been relieved of command. Wright's "warts and all" tell-all book, then, served as a sales tool to authenticate the film, even though one of the coauthors of the script stated emphatically, "we were rigorous about not re-reporting [Wright's] work."[62]

Alessandra Stanley (2000) writes that *Generation Kill* is about troops "raised on hip-hop, video games and *South Park* . . . a generation desensitized to violence [who are] captive to pop culture . . . [less] preoccupied with the latest BBC report [than] with rumors that Jennifer Lopez, or as they refer to her, J.Lo, has been killed."[63] Stanley is probably right.[64] This is why this movie is perfect for an HBO audience—actually, any television audience because television has to be visually stimulating to maintain attention, otherwise people will surf to another channel. It is appropriate as an HBO production (pay television) because it can get away with more questionable dialogue and graphic violence than network TV and this is likely to appeal to a young male audience similarity raised on hip-hop, video games, and *South Park*. This explains the need for an episode entitled "Combat Jack." The episode opens with a man standing in the field masturbating. The unit suddenly has to deploy: "damn," the Marine says, after pulling up his pants and jumping into the back of a vehicle, this "ruined my first good combat jerk." This kind of bathroom humor peppers *Generation Kill*.

One of the most recurring themes of the grunt documentaries is the overriding desire to just survive. This is only mentioned twice, and in passing, during the entire seven hours. One time it is excused because the person screaming, "I don't want to die," is a newly arrived reservist, and he's not even in any imminent danger. The other time survival is an issue is a scene in the same episode (Part VI: "Stay Frosty") when the men are huddled together watching the night bombardment of Baghdad and one of the men says that he's glad they're "out of it" [not involved in the assault] because as a reconnaissance unit they really aren't trained for combat, which is a rather unusual thing to say because at the time of the Iraqi invasion, Marine Reconnaissance meant that the unit would be the first on the ground and thus had to be prepared for direct action.[65] He is rebutted by another who says that to not be in on the assault is an affront to his warrior spirit, which seems to be more in keeping with the 1st Recon's never-shown shoulder patch: a skull and crossbones encircled by three succinct words: swift, silent, deadly. The word "stupid" does not appear on the battalion's insignia, which is the only way to characterize the scene where one Marine stands up in the middle of a firefight and, afterward, explains his unorthodox action: "I wanted to see what it [would] be like to be shot."

The filmmakers are proud of their attention to detail. Sergeant Eric Kocher, one of the men in the 1st Recon, was hired to make sure the small things were done right: "pant legs are bloused and sleeves rolled, per Marine style . . . [and] the men all keep their rifles trained diagonally toward the ground."[66] "I wanted to make sure Marines could watch this without laughing at how many things are wrong," Kocher said in an interview with Finer.[67] This attention to details, notably the grousing and profanity, is generally applauded by lay reviewers who have seen combat in Iraq. This attention to all the little things suggests *Generation Kill* got the big picture right. The "big picture" is scary.

Among the rank-and-file NCOs, only Sgt. Brad Colbert (Alexander Skarsgard), who's known as the Iceman, seems to have any military savvy. The Sergeant Major is portrayed as a nitpicky, by-the-books senior NCO who is more worried about appropriate protocol than combat preparation. He is met in the first episode giving the men in the field a hard time because some have their shirttails out; he reams out another grunt because his mustache is a millimeter beyond regulation length. As the Sergeant Major takes the troops to task, a Marine goose-steps by in the background with one hand over his upper lip, mimicking a Hitler mustache, while his other arm is raised in a Nazi salute. One Marine quips as the Sergeant Major stomps away, "We all have our jobs to do, and the Sergeant Major's job is to be an asshole, and he excels at it." The point about discipline that is missed is that appropriate protocol is a standard means to instill discipline to make men sharp for combat: if you are slovenly "here" you will like be slovenly "there" and slovenly "there" can get you killed. It would seem appropriate, then, that the Sergeant Major is trying to instill discipline in his men while they are sitting around killing time, waiting for the word to go. Told from the point of view of the "foot soldier," however, any superior who enforces needless regulations is not going to be looked on favorably. The Sergeant Major appears only now and then throughout the film, inevitably to rant about some minor breach in military attire: one time he raves at a Marine for losing his helmet, another time at a Marine for not having his helmet on. The implication: he's still being needlessly petty. It is standard procedure, however, to wear your helmet when on the front line, and failure to do so can be deadly. These scenes could be reframed to show the Sergeant Major's concern for those in his charge by suggesting that he is being petty for a reason. As it is, he is made to look like an ass. This is pretty much how the officers are depicted.

Three officers are central to the film: the Lieutenant, who is in charge of the Platoon; the Captain, who is in charge of the Company; and the Lieutenant Colonel, who is in charge of the Battalion. In numerous scenes Lieutenant Fink (Stark Sands) is shown trying to explain things to his men: "We made a mistake today," he says in one episode. "[We] need to see past the huts, the camels, the clothes they wear . . . [if you] take [a] shot, [you] need to know what [you're] shooting at. Their family might lose their son; shoot their camel—a camel could be a year's income to them." This reasonable statement to his men does not serve him well. He's depicted as a well-meaning but generally incompetent officer. In one scene, the Lieutenant asks his men how they feel about his leadership. "Speak freely," he says. Okay, says one of the men, "You're incompetent." The Lieutenant defends himself: "I'm doing the best I can." He's rebutted: "Sir, not good enough."

If the lieutenant is incompetent, Captain Craig "Encino Man" Schwetje (Brian Patrick Wade), called Captain America by the men, is just crazy. In one scene, the company is attacking an airfield that, unbeknownst to them, has been abandoned by the Republican Guard. On the runway Captain America jumps out of his vehicle and starts to charge. Sgt. Colbert observes this behavior sardonically, "For Christ's sake, he's got a bayonet on his rife . . . shooting scraps of metal"; another remarks, "He thinks he's Rambo." The Captain runs to the men, yelling, "Engage those buildings!" He's told, "They're too far. [They're] over 3,000 meters [which is] way beyond range of our weapons." In any event, he's told, they're not military buildings, they're civilian huts. In another episode, he purposely kills a civilian, in another he attacks a civilian who has been captured and beats him; after he's pulled off the man, the Captain says boastfully, "I fucked his shit up good, didn't I?" At the end of the film, the reporter asks the Colonel why he never relieved the Captain of command and is told that the Captain "walked [a] fine line but [always remained] within the box of acceptable behavior." The reporter raises a quizzical eyebrow, "Two attempted bayonetings?" The Colonel rejoins that nevertheless, "No Iraqi *prisoners* [were] actually wounded" (author's italics).

Lieutenant Colonel Stephen Ferrando (Chance Kelly) is called the Godfather by the men, not out of any respect for the title, but because the Colonel refers to himself in the third person as the "Godfather." This is because his raspy voice is similar to the one affected by Marlon Brando in *The Godfather*. But it is just as likely that the Colonel likes the moniker for the imbued "godlike" qualities that are associated with Brando's character. He is constantly saying, "Godfather wants this . . . "; or "Godfather wants that. . . . "; never "I want you to . . ."

The Godfather's only desire is to bring glory to himself. He is constantly trying to get the General to get him (back) into the action, despite any number of missteps that take the battalion out of the action—getting lost a number of times being one of them. In one early episode Bravo Company accidentally goes off the main road. A town lies ahead that, we learn, "isn't even on the map." A local indicates a way around the town, but the Godfather wants the men to proceed directly through the heart of the town where they "get lit up." Despite the firefight down the main street running through the town, Bravo takes no casualties. The reason Godfather insisted on this course of action, he says, is to show the Iraqis that "Americans won't back down from a fight." That's a reasonable explanation. But later the Godfather is talking to his staff and gives his real reason. He says he could put his decision in terms of tactics, in terms of strategy, but he'd be misleading them. The reason he put his men at risk is because "My biggest fear, my darkest hour, I sometimes fear. . .," he pauses for dramatic effect, "that I will do something the General won't like." This leads him to later tell the General, misleadingly but accurately, after taking the abandoned airfield: "We've seized the airfield, captured several tanks [that were sitting there abandoned]. . . . Appears we've overrun the entire 255th mechanized regiment. Zero casualties." The General is pleased: "Outstanding!" The fact is, the Lieutenant says to another Marine, had the Republican Guard been there and defended the airfield with the tanks, "[We'd] be dead before we ever saw them."

Nothing has changed at the end of the film. The men complain about their inability to help the Iraq people. One says, "We've rolled through this country fucking things up and now we have to show these people what we liberated them for." The next scene depicts the Marines' sensitivity as they repel down the side of a building and smash through a window into what was once a government office. They immediately become vandals: a computer is smashed for no good reason, art is stolen off the wall, and one urinates on the papers they have strewn about that now litter the floor. The Godfather, likewise, figuratively pisses on the men under his command. He sends Bravo 2 out to help defuse a minefield. A Marine quips, "At night? [That's] against [regimental] orders." Doesn't seem to matter; they're doing it because that's what "Godfather wants." An explosion is heard: "Man down. Correction, two men down." This scene is followed by the Godfather explaining his actions to the reporter who is about to go home; he's laying it on, and we know this because none of his actions match his words: "Terrible feeling sending men into combat. Terrible feeling!" Godfather shakes the reporter's hand. As the reporter walks away, Godfather adds, "But then there is always the excitement—of getting shot at. [I] hadn't anticipated that. And you?" The reporter turns and looks at the Colonel strangely, then leaves to climb aboard a waiting helicopter, taking a seat across from a wounded Marine that is being medically evacuated.

The closing credits roll over Johnny Cash singing, "When the Man Comes Around." In this case, the man is now the American military raining down death and destruction. It is a fitting, if ironic, conclusion to the movie, the last stanza of which is, "And I looked and behold [in the midst of the four beasts]: a pale horse. And his name, that sat on him, was Death. And Hell followed with him."

The acting is solid in *Generation Kill*, but miniseries are often too long, which forces the director to "fill up" time that might be more convincingly conveyed with a tighter (i.e., shorter) script. Miniseries are also under time constraints and tend for the most part to be filmed both quickly and economically. The end result is often a mediocre and not particularly memorable film, which means, in the best television tradition, that one watches it with half an eye, enjoys the fleeting images, and then quickly forgets the program. This is the fate of *Generation Kill*. The film relies far too much on visual images and sound bites, and these take precedent over storyline. The Godfather's "war is cool" platitude falls flat at the end of the film since he's not the focal point of the story and his words are disconnected from any exhibited behavior. This is not the case with *The Hurt Locker*.

Attitude and behavior are consistent throughout *The Hurt Locker*. The Academy Award–winning film focuses on three men who are members of the Army's elite Explosive Ordinance Disposal (OED) unit: Staff Sergeant William James (Jeremy Renner), Sergeant J. T. Sandborn (Anthony Mackie), and Specialist Owen Eldridge (Brian Geraghty). The opening quote sets the tone for the film: "The rush to battle is often a potent and lethal addiction, for war is a drug." The scene fades with the last clause visually lingering. There are no titles, no credits, just an identifier to root the time: Baghdad 2004. This, plus the opening shot of a moving camera catching the ground as it goes by, then shopkeepers, followed by troops in the street, gives the movie a strong documentary feel. The camera, of course, is not on a Humvee or other military vehicle; it is from the eye of remote-controlled miniature probe. In similar documentary fashion, we see, as the probe falters, Sergeant Matt Thompson (Guy Pearce) suit up and march down the cordoned-off street to defuse the bomb. An Iraqi in the doorway of a butcher shop watches the soldier's movement. He starts to punch in a number. The men in the foreground scream a warning to the Sergeant who takes off just as the bomb explodes. He didn't make it; the next scene shows his dog tags being placed in the box with his belongings. The new man arrives, Staff Sergeant William James; it is he who lives on the edge and who gets a rush from his job, not because he's crazy, but because, for some, war is a drug. The "some" is critical to the success of the movie because it establishes that most—the other two featured players—just do the best they can because it's the job they have been given, but their overriding concern is to avoid being sent to the hurt locker and get home in one piece.[68] James, therefore, is an anomaly.

The (sexual) rush James gets from the job is shown in a subsequent scene, where, after a tense diffusion successfully takes place, James marches purposely back to a waiting vehicle, gets in, slams the door, takes a hit from a water bottle, throws it to the floorboard, pulls out and lights a cigarette, lets out a rush of smoke, and exclaims, "That was good!" Should anyone miss the point, a Colonel comes up and applauds him: "You're a wild man. . . . How many?" Considering James's actions after defusing the bomb, it remains a moot point whether the Colonel is asking James how many bombs he's defused or how many sexual conquests he's had. In either case, James says that he doesn't know: it is "ungentlemanly" to keep score. The Colonel nudges him, and James quickly relents: "873, Sir." The Colonel exclaims, "Wow. You *are* a wild man. That's hot shit." James's wild man status clearly established, the question, and tension, which dangles for the rest of the movie, is whether James will make it home. He does, as do the other two. The others were just doing their job; they didn't get the rush out of it that James did. They are glad to be going home. James is too, but boredom quickly sets in as he wanders through the endless aisle of consumer products, overloaded with superfluous choices, doing the mundane things that constitute everyday life, like cleaning the gutters. It is not surprising, given the opening crawl and his humdrum life at home, that Jones needs the excitement of doing what he is good at. The last scene shows him stepping off a helicopter in Baghdad. The closing crawl: "365 days for Delta Company rotation."

There are few films that upon delivery are viewed as instant classics. They are any number of things that make this movie work: excellent directing by Kathryn Bigelow; a strong cast, including a supporting role by Ralph Fiennes; outstanding story by Mark Boal, who was embedded with a bomb squad during the war; and stunning camerawork by Barry Ackroyd. This led A. O. Scott (among a legion of other critics) to consider it "the best American feature film yet made about the war in Iraq,"[69] though veterans of the war often faulted the film because, Brandon Fiedman writes in *VetVoice*, that "if you know anything about the Army, or about operations or life in Iraq, you'll be so distracted by the nonsensical sequences and plot twists that it will ruin the movie for you."[70] Another veteran of the Iraq war, Alex Horton concurs but adds an important caveat: "the way the team goes about their missions is completely absurd"; nevertheless, he still says the film is "the best Iraq movie to date."[71] There are two other aspects that make this film of public interest and a commentary on the war. The first is the same thing that Katherine Bigelow says initially attracted her to the film: It is an aspect of the war seldom recounted. The movie, therefore, succeeds in its dualistic purpose—it not only entertains, it informs. The other thing of interest as commentary on the war, perhaps more subliminally appreciated, is that it focuses on lives saved and does not remind the public of how many American lives have been lost, or how many innocent Iraqi lives have been taken.

The War in Afghanistan: *Brothers* versus *Brothers*

There were two *Brothers* films. The 2005 Danish one, directed by Susanne Bier, and the American version, released in 2009 and directed by Jim Sheridan. Critics generally accord the Danish version to be superior, though reviewers at *Entertainment Weekly* gave them both a C+.[72] There are two reasons the Danish version won the Sundance Dramatic Audience prize, even though Sheridan might have a stronger directorial career: he was nominated for an Academy Award for *My Left Foot* (1990), which did win an Oscar for Best Actor (Daniel Day-Lewis) and Best Supporting Actress (Brenda Fricker) while *In the Name of the Father* (1993) was nominated for nine Oscars, including best picture.

First, the Danish film was the original screenplay, making it fresher, especially given that it tackled the war five years before Sheridan. And second, the performances were stronger, especially the role of Sara, played by Connie Nielsen—Laura Kern, reviewing the American version, captures the general critical consensus when she says, "Natalie Portman [as Sara] attempts the impossible: filling the shoes of Connie Nielsen, who was so real, so heartbreaking, and who grounds a film ostensibly titled after two men."[73] The Danish version may, perhaps, be the better film, but Sheridan's reason for remaking the film, he points out in the DVD bonus material, "Remade in the USA," is that the film has a timeless quality, but more importantly, many people would not have seen the original because it was a foreign film. Box office receipts would suggest Sheridan is right: U.S. box office gross for his version was

$28.5 million; another $8.3 million would be generated from international box office receipts, with another $8.1 million from DVD sales, combined, totals just shy of $45 million in total receipts. Sales revenue aside, the interest here is how the American version modified the film's message. To appreciate this, it is first necessary to explicate the plot. The Danish version is critiqued first.

Michael (Ulrich Tomsen) is a career officer in the Danish Army who is married to Sara (Connie Nielsen); they have two young daughters, Natalia and Camilla. He has fourteen hours before he ships out to Afghanistan as part of the Danish contingent of a United Nations peacekeeping force. This time is used to establish the age-old sibling "good son–bad son" differences between the two brothers. In the car, the two brothers argue and the viewer learns that Michael is the responsible one who wants Jannik (Nidola Lie Iaas) to "patch things up" with a woman that he has caused problems for; later in the film what happened is revealed: he robbed a bank at gunpoint—the female teller still has the psychological "scars" from her experience—and has, when Michael picks him up, just been released from prison. Michael, the do-gooder, says he has apologized to the female teller in Jannik's behalf for the emotional trauma Jannik caused her. This irks Jannik; they argue and Jannik gets out of the car in the middle of nowhere. Later, he joins their parents who, with Sara and the girls, are hosting a send-off dinner for Michael. Here, and subsequently at Michael's grave, we learn the father's clear preference for Michael and his low opinion of Jannik, "Michael is the responsible one," the father says to Jannik. "You've never followed through with anything." At the funeral later, the father disowns Jannik: "That was my boy," he says, looking at the coffin in the ground. "[Now] I am left with nothing." The next day the two halfheartedly apologize for the exchange, but the viewer gets a glimpse of the cross Jannik has lived with and the reason for his heavy drinking: "I never could live up to Michael." His father doesn't give an inch and retorts, "You never tried."

The body of the movie revolves around a series of cross-cuts between what is taking place in Afghanistan and at home. The cross-cuts are nicely linked by connecting scenes: Michael riding in a helicopter, Sara riding in a train, both going off to work; later, after Michael has been taken prisoner, he is seen riding in the back of a transport truck while Sara is riding home from the funeral. Neither knows what the future holds.

Michael's helicopter is shot down shortly after his arrival in Afghanistan; he has been sent out to find a missing radio operator who might be injured after a Taliban attack on the team the previous day. Michael is one of the few aboard who was not killed by the surface-to-air missile. Naturally, he is presumed dead. A messenger arrives at first light to tell Sara that Michael has been killed. The funeral follows.

Jannik begins to redeem himself—he finishes the kitchen that Michael has started but left undone because of his deployment. A bond begins to form between Jannik and Sara: "I always thought you were a stupid bastard," she tells Jannik, who responds, "And I always thought you were a boring middle-class bitch." Jannik also begins to connect to the two daughters. The spark between Jannik and Sara is shown as potentially promising, but it never develops: in one scene, they tentatively kiss, and the following day, he apologizes; in another scene, Sara is showering; she knows Jannik is downstairs. The camera cuts to her, then Jannik, who starts to ascend the stairs. At the top of the steps, he hesitates, listens to the running water, then turns, descends the stairs and leaves.

In the meantime, Michael is taking his trip into the heart of darkness to face "the horror" that will plague him the rest of his life. He has been placed in a confined hut in the Afghan mountains with the missing radio operator. Michael's strong personality is contrasted to the young operator who has a wife and baby back in Denmark. Both suffer from their imprisonment. One day Michael is taken from confinement and faces the Taliban leader who wants to know how to fire the rocket launcher they recently acquired. In exchange for water for the dehydrated radio operator, Michael shows him how to fire the weapon. Back in the hut, Michael assures the whimpering radio operator that they won't die here and encourages him to be strong. Shortly thereafter, both are taken from their confinement; the Taliban chieftain wants Michael to shoot the radio operator who is of no value to them. Michael refuses, and throws the revolver to the ground. The Taliban leader tells him if he doesn't do it, they will both be shot. Amid chants to "kill, kill, kill," from the Taliban rabble, Michael pumps himself up, grabs a pipe, and beats the radio operator to death.

The next day, there's an assault by United Nation forces on the Taliban stronghold; Michael is discovered and rescued. Waking the next day in a military hospital, he's asked about others who might have been imprisoned with him and is shown pictures of missing men; Michael fails to identify the radio operator. Back home, his CO thinks he is suffering shock because of his hazy memory. At the end of their talk, just before Michael goes home on leave, he acknowledges to his CO that the radio operator was held at the same camp with him, but says he does not know his fate. Later, he visits the radio operator's wife. At first she thinks he's just one of the military personnel whose been sent to check up on her. Then she learns they were in the same camp. He tells her he doesn't know what happened to her husband because shortly before the rescue he was moved to another camp. He's raised her hopes, "Then he's alive." "Yes," Michael lies, "[he's] fine. He'll make it."

Michael is obviously not the same man he was after what he did. Most think his change is the result of his captivity; no one knows the cross Michael now carries. He is at first surprised when returning home that the kitchen has been finished by his brother: "You did this?" Noticing the closeness of Jannik and Sara, he becomes obsessed that they have had an affair, asking one, then the other, "Did you sleep with her? Did you sleep with him?" She acknowledges that they kissed, and Michael goes ballistic and chokes her. When he releases her she says, "*What* is wrong with you?" His outbursts alienate his children. After the choking episode, he looks outside for the girls the next morning and tries to entice them to come out, "Don't be afraid of me." They are. His wife continues to plea for an explanation: "What happened out there?" Michael never answers. At a dinner later for Camilla's birthday with the parents, he rebukes one of the girls, who responds, "You don't decide shit . . . You're just pissed because mom would rather fuck Jannik. . . . They fuck all the time."[74] Upstairs her mother asked why she said that: "I don't like dad [anymore]"; her sister agrees.

The film moves toward its closure after the daughters disown their father. At home, he goes on a rampage, destroying the kitchen his brother so thoughtfully finished. Sara calls Jannick. He arrives and helps Sara and the girls escape, and then goes to confront his brother. A fight ensues. The police arrive. Michael walks out of the house looking bloody and disheveled. The police wrestle Michael to the ground, during which time Michael manages to rip a handgun from an officer's holster. He wants to be shot, to be put out of his misery—suicide by cop! His brother puts his hand on Michael's outstretched arm, which holds the handgun, and lowers it. The dénouement follows. Some time has passed and Michael is visited by Sara; he's in a mental health facility. They take a walk on the grounds and sit next to each other on a bench. "Tell me," she says, softly. "No," Michael answers. "If you don't, I will leave you." There's a long, silent moment. He begins to tear up and puts his head on her shoulder. The camera pans out to a long shot and we hear him, choking back sobs, saying, "He had a little boy." The healing has started, but the viewer knows he has a long, long way to go.

The American version faithfully follows the basic theme of the Danish film. The names have been Anglicized, of course: Michael is now Sam (Tobey Maquire), Sara becomes Grace (Natalie Portman); Jannik doesn't work anymore and is changed to Tommy (Jake Gyllenhaal), the girls become Isabella and Maggi, the father is now Hank and is played by Sam Sheppard; the mother largely remains in the background in both films and acts primarily as peacekeeper. Some minor stylist changes are made that are of little consequence. The fourteen-hour period before Sam deploys is not played out in as much detail; we also learn immediately that Tommy was in prison and what for. The protagonist is a Captain now, not a Major, a demotion that best befits the younger countenance of the character in the American film. The shortened introduction is more in keeping with American film narrative, which has more of a "get-to-it" framework. Explosions are also de rigor in American film, and the helicopter scene is stretched out: the faces of the men are seen when the missile hits, the viewers see the plane going down, and the helicopter goes up in a graphic fireball.[75] There is a long, drawn-out scene after the crash where we witness Sam trying to save his men in the snow-covered mountains as the Taliban close in. The radio operator has been replaced with members of his team who have been captured with him. The messenger scene is similar as is the funeral, though Dad is now in his former Marine outfit and Sam's CO comes up to him and says, "Best Marine ever served under me." The period of time in both films from opening to the funeral is roughly fifteen minutes. The difference: in the Danish film a good ten minutes are devoted to establishing family tensions; this is shortened in the American version, which replaces the lost ten minutes with ten minutes of visuals where Sam and his men are fighting the Taliban before they are finally taken prisoner. The point: Americans put up a good (scenic) fight before they get captured.

They also *do not* help the enemy, and this is the crucial thematic variation. In the Danish version, Michael was shown the pictures of the radio operator's wife and baby; in the American version, the Taliban rabble are looking at them: they laugh, tear up the pictures, and throw them aside. Michael immediately acquiesces with a minor concession (water for the radio operator) when asked to show how to operate an RPG; Sam refuses and is beaten, but he's an American, and Americans (in American-made films) do not cooperate with the enemy. Then comes the critical scene where Sam has to kill one of his men. He's taken to the Taliban chieftain. We learn what an evil man the chieftain is because he points to one of his own men, tells Sam that they're related, then, because he betrayed them, shoots him in the head. He tells Sam he will do the same to him if he doesn't make a video statement saying that this is the Taliban's country and that America shouldn't be here. Sam refuses and is tied to a post where he spends a torturous night. The next day, they take the man with a wife and baby from the hut; Sam yells, "be strong." He isn't.

Later, Sam is shown a video where the man says what he was told. It is of little help. He is no longer useful and, similar to the Danish version, they want Sam to kill him, otherwise they will kill them both. Feverishly, Sam commits the deed. The next day he's rescued. The rescue scene is more drawn out in the American version with the Taliban chief shooting down in the pit where Sam is held trying to kill him. Bullets ricochet around Sam. The chief is riddled by bullets from the Marine rescue squad and falls into the pit, symbolically landing at Sam's feet. It is critical to the rest of the film that Sam commits the murder to explain his anguish back home. And while Sam is plagued by what he's done, and much of the rest of the movie plays out like the Danish version, there is one critical difference: Michael committed the act solely to preserve his own life; Sam did it because he was tortured and had what was once called "battle fatigue." Michael's anguish is the anguish of self-knowledge; Sam's is the result of post-traumatic stress disorder. Two minor, but important, post-rescue variations: Sam does not destroy the kitchen; Grace simply comes downstairs one night and finds him sitting in the dark, staring off into space. She asks him what's wrong and he says, "Do you know what I've done for you?" then goes crazy at the thought and destroys the kitchen. This is a necessary variation because the tension between Sam and his brother Tommy has not been developed to the same degree, so the destruction of the kitchen without the prompt would not be fully appreciated in the American remake. The ending at the mental health facility is likewise similar to the Danish version with one notable exception. When Grace says that if he doesn't tell her what the problem is, she will leave him, Sam blurts out, "I killed him." There are no tears. Marines don't cry!

The Danish version makes a strong, antiwar statement by showing how a good man, for no reason other than the war, has his life destroyed. The American version shows the protagonist in a more heroic light, his deed explained as a consequence of his abuse at the hands of his captors. The American remake may be interpreted by some as an antiwar statement, but if it is, it has been substantially toned down.

ADJUSTING

This section is similar to the Home Front section in the last chapter. But unlike Home Front, which dealt primarily with how military personnel cope upon returning from the war, this section includes other adjustment issues. The first, *Day Zero* (2007), is a spin on the usual postadjustment slant; it is three men who have to adjust to going off to war after receiving their draft notification. The second, *Stop-Loss* (2008), deals with another adjustment issue: the notice that their tour of duty has been extended. This film might have been slotted in the last section that dealt with grunts facing combat situations, except that *Stop-Loss* focuses on how the men handle this issue while they are on leave in the States. *Home of the Brave* (2006) and *The Lucky Ones* (2008) come closest to the traditional home front movies that assess how men and women who have served deal with combat injuries after they've been discharged. The other two deal with a similar but slightly modified home front theme. *In the Valley of Elah* (2007) is the story of how a father comes to learn, and comes to terms, with the loss of his son in combat, while *Grace Is Gone* (2007) focuses on how a husband not only has to deal with the loss of his soldier wife's death but how he has to tell his two daughters that their mother won't be returning home. The last film in this section is *The Messenger* (2009), which deals with delivery of the message that a loved one is not returning to surviving family members (see also *Taking Chance*).

Day Zero

This is a much more realistic near-future scenario than the nuclear holocaust of *Southland Tales*. It is one that may not be too far-fetched, given how stretched the military is for manpower as the wars in Iraq and Afghanistan continue to chew up personnel. The opening credits roll over three men who get their draft notice. The viewer learns from the television in the background of one of the men's apartments that for want of manpower the draft has been extended to those who are thirty-five-years old, so it is not just college students who are eligible, but corporate types too.

The story revolves around three men who open an envelope that informs them they have thirty days to report. It's countdown to day zero for three social prototypes: Aaron Feller (Elijah Wood) is a skinny, nonathletic geekish-type, whose claim to fame is having written a semi-successful novel; James Dixon (Jon Bernthal) is a blue-collar taxicab driver; and George Rifkin (Chris Klein) is a late twentysomething moving on up as a married corporate lawyer. Despite their distinct social status, they all went to high school together and grew up in the same area of New York, so they all know one another. The story lays out how each of them deals with the draft. Intermittently they meet to discuss their different approaches in dealing with their respective draft notices.

The "intellectual" is a caricature of the attenuated young man on get-in-shape ads from the '50s that had sand kicked in his face on the beach by a burly Atlas type. During his thirty days he becomes obsessed with news broadcasts of the war. He goes to the gym to get ready for his deployment and cannot even pick up a twenty-pound barbell. He makes a bucket list of things to do before he deploys. At the end of the film, after jumping to his death from a high-rise apartment, his bucket list flutters to the ground; it is things we've watched him do over the last thirty days: fuck a prostitute, visit a peep show, get a tattoo, shave head (he does,

Draft notification in *Day Zero*.

looking like De Niro in *Taxi Driver*), skydive (the jump to his death), and "serve with honor." He's done all of them but the last.

The "blue-collar" character represents the man-on-the-street. He's not happy about being drafted but he'll do what is expected of him, for God and Country. His boss approves and will be glad to hold his job for him while he serves. His story is stretched: during his thirty days he meets a young working-class woman like himself and falls in love. When she finds, at the 11th hour, that he's been drafted, she slaps him, mad that he waited this long to tell her. Nevertheless, she applauds what he is doing and says that she will wait for him.

The "corporate" character is upset that he's been drafted as it will interfere with his upward mobility at the legal firm where he is up for partner. He tries everything to get out of going. In one scene, he is drinking heavily in his apartment kitchen late at night to get up the nerve to cut off one of his fingers—he doesn't; he talks to his wife about going to Canada; he leans on his connected father to get help from a senator to obtain a deferment. It looks like the senator can do nothing, but at the last minute, his father calls him. The senator has come through. He doesn't have to go.

Much of the ideological tension is parlayed between blue-collar and corporate characters, obviously representing two ends of the social spectrum. Their meetings are always fraught with ideological dialogue. In one bar scene, the corporate character says, "The whole thing is so wrong. We're making new enemies every day. [We] cannot win." The blue-collar character rejoins in a long speech, paraphrased here: "You don't know that. I believe it is the right thing to do. If we don't stop them, then when they get a chance, they'll do it to us. . . . I know I'm a fuck up, but I believe in this place, all of it. We're in a fight for a way of life. That's what I know." There are numerous meetings between the old school friends; every meeting of the three dissolves into a similar ideological exchange.

Stephen Holden (2008) at the *New York Times* faults the film for being too cautious to take political sides. The fact that both sides are given does not mean that it doesn't take sides, however. The blue-collar character not only wins the verbal tête-à-têtes, he wins in the end. Day zero: it's 0700 and he's in Pennsylvania Station having coffee, waiting to leave. It looks like no one is going to join him. He understands, and gets up and walks out of the coffee shop. There's Corporate. He's come around. They look at one another, and then march off to serve their country. Blue collar has always come out ahead in the verbal exchanges, and the ending shows that his points have registered with Corporate, who despite having received a senatorial reprieve, goes off to do his duty. It is one of the few strong prowar statements in fictive movies during this period.

Stop-Loss

The opening of *Stop-Loss* strongly harkens to grunt documentaries: men are seen suiting up, singing, and carrying on. Their day at a check-point in Tikrit is about to start. It soon hits the fan. A speeding car opens up with a .50 caliber, but the soldiers don't return fire, "Not yet! Too many civilians!" The insurgents speed away. The soldiers give chase. It was all a setup. They've been lured into an ambush. An RPG hits their vehicle. Now it's house-to-house fighting and the visual dynamics so dear to fictional film kicks into high gear. A ten-minute fight-or-die battle skirmish follows, during which time the action hero, Sergeant Brandon King (Ryan Phillippe), runs down the alley shooting insurgents on the rooftop with dead-eye accuracy. Rounding a doorway, he blasts a man who is standing there; a grenade rolls from his hands as he falls to the floor so the viewer clearly knows he was a baddie. There is also a dead woman and child. Collateral damage; however, the clear implication is that if the insurgent was not hiding behind their skirts, they would not have been casualties. The Americans win the intense skirmish but Preacher is dead and another wounded.

Immediately after this intense opening the men, who are all from the same reserve guard unit, are about to get off a bus in Brazos, Texas. They've earned a well-deserved weekend at home: "Don't drink and drive," they are cautioned. "Pick up a lady and let her drive. Don't beat up civilians. Don't fuck anyone under age. See you 0700 at formation on Monday." Their small town gives them a hero's parade: cheerleaders twirling (and dropping) their batons, cheering crowds line the streets, young women run up and kiss the soldiers who are riding down Main on the back of a convertible. The mayor points out Brandon on the stand with the others from the squad and welcomes the Purple Heart, Bronze Star hero home. He's supposed to say something but chokes up. His buddy rushes up and pushes him aside and yells at the crowd, "We're over there killing them in Iraq so [you] don't have to kill them in Texas." Wild cheering greets this statement.

Homecoming parade in *Stop-Loss.*

Though the various members of the squad dot the long weekend, the story focuses on two: Sergeant Brandon King, who is the squad leader, and his buddy, Sergeant Steve Shriver. Their tour of duty is just about over and both are happy to be done with the killing. Various early scenes establish Steve has been at war too long. In one scene that takes place the night they return, they are partying at the Cattle Club. A man comes up and asks Michelle (Abbie Cronish), Steve's wife, to dance. She politely declines. He persists and is told by Steve, "My wife said no, you fucking deaf?" The guy quips, "Hey, no problem, you're the hero," and starts to walk away. Steve attacks him and the others from the squad have to pull Steve off him. Later that night Steve is in the front yard digging a hole: "Gotta dig in," he says. Brandon arrives and learns that prior to this Steve had hit Michelle. Michelle brushes it off: a backhand. Brandon excuses his behavior: "He's so drunk right now he thinks he's on a mission outside the wire." Monday is when the story actually commences. The setup, however, is important. These men are combat veterans, and Steve is suffering combat fatigue. Brandon is not as bad, but subsequent scenes show that he has brought lingering memories of the war home too.

At the base on Monday, Brandon is told he's being stop-lossed.[76] He goes to see his Colonel, who tells him, that according to "Subsection 12305, Title 11, by authority of the president, you've been stop-lossed." Discussion over. Not for Brandon, who argues that he's been on 150 combat missions and never complained; he's done the job he volunteered for, but he cannot do it anymore because in the last month he lost three men and almost his entire company [sic]. Besides, he nicely argues, stop-loss can only happen in time of war, "and the president declared the war over, so legally . . ." The Colonel interrupts, "You a lawyer, son?" An argument ensues. Brandon barks, "Fuck the president." The Colonel orders him confined to the stockade where he will be taken to a transport plane and sent back to Iraq. As the two MP flanking Brandon march him to the stockade, he breaks free, and speeds away in a vehicle by the side of the road.

Brandon is now officially AWOL. He and Michelle embark on a road trip to Washington where they hope to convince their senator to come to his aid. Much of the rest of the film revolves around the road trip where they meet, among others, blinded PFC Rodriguez, a member of the squad who's recuperating at a military hospital, an African American veteran who is on the lam as a conscientious objector, and some young thugs who broke into his car. In this latter scene, Brandon goes after the three who broke into his car and almost kills them. The scene serves to underscore his combat stress. In Washington, the senator won't see him because he's a fugitive. The road trip serves as an opportunity for the director, via Brandon, to state in some detail his objection to the war.

Brandon and Michelle go to New York City to a man they heard about in Memphis who might be able to help Brandon get to Canada. He's told that once he takes this step and gets a new identity, he can never come back. Just before leaving for Canada, Brandon calls his mother to say good-bye and learns that another in his unit, Tommy, has taken his life. He slips back for the funeral and watches the services from the shadows, only to emerge to pay his respects after everyone has left. Almost everyone. Steve appears and chastises Brandon for "running out on us and for coming back too late," which leads to a knockdown fight between the two. Both on their knees, exhausted from the fight, they embrace one another. Brandon tells Steve that he cannot deal with all the men he's gotten killed and is going to become a conscientious objector. The next night he is standing at the Mexican border and contemplating crossing; his mother and Michelle are next to him when he says his last line, "This war ain't never gonna be behind me." The next scene shows Steve on the bus as fresh-faced young soldiers board for their first deployment. Just before the bus pulls out, Brandon appears and takes the vacant seat next to Steve. They look at one another, then make up by shaking hands. It seems the war isn't going to be behind him.

The film was directed by Kimberly Peirce, whose debut film, *Boys Don't Cry* (1999), was widely applauded. More was expected of her by the critics. It moves forward rather nicely until the road trip, which is overdrawn and collapses into a series of tedious adventures that primarily serve to enunciate all the reasons the war is wrong. Given the overt didacticism of the long road trip, it is difficult to understand how A. O. Scott, reviewing the film for the *New York Times*, can say that the film "makes no argument beyond the recognition . . . [that the war's end] grows harder to imagine with every passing day."[77] Joanne Kaufmann with the *Wall Street Journal* may be more on target when she writes that "Brandon's troubles and the movie's troubles begin more or less simultaneously" given that his "stalwart sense of duty and almost saintly nature," so suddenly and inexplicably change course[78]; and, it might be added, swerve again so suddenly and inexplicably at the end. This seems to occur because the director is in a rush to launch into her antiwar diatribe, which takes up the body of the film. She appears to be more intent on this than with making a film, and her contempt for the audience is especially conspicuous toward the end of the film.

Peirce sets up the Mexican scene very nicely. In New York, Brandon is told that Canada, a place he's never been, is just like New York City. A country boy, this doesn't appeal to him; he says he'd be more comfortable in Mexico. It is not surprising, then, that after the funeral, Brandon now contemplates going to Mexico instead of Canada. When he gets out of the car on the American side of the border, a large floodlight behind him blinds the viewer. The floodlight is a film light that is meant to provide night illumination for the camera. In the DVD director's commentary, Peirce said she noticed this in the rushes and tells her cameraman, "You cannot let the film light shine into [the] camera." He asks her why not, after all, he says, the audience won't know what a flood light looks like, so what does it matter? Peirce pondered this for a millisecond and agreed, "We're like, yeah, you're right" and laughs, thinking it is a big joke she's put over on the audience.[79] If the director has no standards and looks down on the audience, it is not surprising that the film meanders and fails to connect. Her condescending view toward the audience helps explain why she felt it necessary to lecture them, rather than let the picture make the point she wants to get across.

The Injured Vet: *Home of the Brave* and *The Lucky Ones*

Home of the Brave was the first fictive treatment of the home front veteran and the issues of adjustment that the documentaries closely examined. It did not fare well. Critics and lay film reviewers alike generally gave it two stars and dismissed it as a nice but mediocre made-for-television quality film.[80] This explains its reasonable success when made available for the television market: it garnered $43,753 at the box office but netted $4.7 million in DVD sales.

The movie opens with the cheerful news that the National Guard unit in Iraq will soon be going home, but they are sent on one last humanitarian mission. This mission is the proverbial straw that broke the camel's back for three of the four soldiers who are irrevocably psychologically damaged. Will Marsh (Samuel L. Jackson) is a physician who increasingly hits the bottle after returning home and toward the end is no longer trying to conceal his drinking—he leaves a package store and starts pulling from the bottle in the brown paper bag. His life is further complicated by clashes with his pacifistic teenage son and his caring but increasingly estranged wife.

Tommy Yates (Brian Presley) just doesn't care anymore. The job that was supposed to be held for him while he served is gone. The small business owner just couldn't let the job go vacant so long, and now finds it inappropriate to fire an otherwise good employee because Tommy has returned. The real conflict with Tommy is with his blue-collar father, who pushes him to do something constructive with his life, and cannot understand why he doesn't move forward now that the war is behind him. When Tommy mentions in passing that he might need to talk to someone about things, his father berates him: "About what? Your feelings? Sound like your mother." At least wait, his father urges, "until [you] get the police job [a manly job his father's been pressing him to take] because they'll find out and you don't want them to think you're a pussy." One gets the feeling that the problems Tommy and Marsh are grappling with go well beyond the war. In the end, Tommy reenlists, essentially to prove his manhood to his father, though he wraps the reason up in a higher cause: he feels that he'll dishonor the memory of those who have sacrificed their lives if he doesn't return. Jamal (Curtis "50 Cent" Jackson) is similarly conflicted. His girlfriend leaves him because of his erratic behavior. Cast as an inner city street survivor, one cannot help seeing Jamal's problems with his more sophisticated girlfriend as rooted to other issues beyond the war. He flies off on violent tangents and in the end is shot by the police while holding some people hostage in the deluded belief that this will win his girlfriend back. The connection between the war and their issues is only tangentially made at the beginning of the movie and an occasional battle-related flashback is insufficient to provide justification for the extent of their psychological traumas.

Psychological trauma is difficult to depict on film. It can be done, but it needs to be more fully developed and less one-dimensional (see *The Spy Who Came in from the Cold*, 1965; *Equis*, 1977; *Looking for Mr. Goodbar*, 1977). *Home of the Brave* tries to convey the anguish of too many people too superficially with the end result that it gives insights into none. The only lingering refrain of *Home* is that war messes people up. The documentaries are much more successful in depicting the psychological consequences of war because they *focus* on the state of mind of the veteran (see *Ground Truth*).

Home of the Brave is somewhat more successful in depicting the difficulty soldiers have in adjusting to physical disabilities by showing how one vet, Sergeant Jessica Biel (Vanessa Price), tries to adapt after losing an arm. Biel adds little to what documentaries such as *Body of War* and *Home Front* say about the same issue, but she does reinforce the message of the documentaries to a wider audience. This is done by (1) showing her new physical limitations and the initial difficultly she has coping with her prosthetic arm, things she was used to doing more adroitly with the use of both hands; (2) depicting the psychological anger at being "helpless"; and (3) how, after a while, she adapts, accepts, and ultimately moves on with her life.

If there is any singular fault to be found with Biel's inabilities it is the lack of time devoted to her stay in the hospital. There is only one brief scene where she is wheeled into a ward with numerous other injured vets and another where she is told she has to receive counseling before she can be discharged. Immediately after these two brief points are noted, she is home. Even a few more minutes devoted to this critical adjustment phase would have strengthened the extent of her trauma, but then it would have moved the focus away from the other characters. The summary judgment by the critics is that the film adds little to what the documentaries have achieved. Still, it brings the picture of the problem to a wider audience, even if the picture is somewhat attenuated.

The Lucky Ones did not fare much better dealing with the same issue. It is another road trip movie in the style of *Stop-Loss* but it, along with *Home of the Brave*, is widely considered a much better movie by the critics. Neil Burger (*The Illusionist*, 2006), like the director of *Stop-Loss*, is also a relatively new director but lets his story unfold more naturally than Peirce. The three-person cast doesn't talk to the audience when in their car traveling across the heartland, but to each other. Indeed, the cast is generally viewed by the critics as carrying a sometimes meandering script.[81] The story focuses on three "lucky" veterans who are returning to the States for thirty days of R&R because of injuries sustained. Sergeant Cheever (Tim Robbins) sustained a back injury, the occupants of the car learn, when a Port-O-Let that was being unloaded fell on him; his tour of duty up, he will soon be discharged and, unlike the other two, doesn't have to go back in thirty days. Sergeant T. K. Poole (Michael Peña) was shot in the upper thigh near the groin and is now impotent; he's on his way to Las Vegas to hook up with a prostitute and see if he can be cured before he goes home to Texas to see his fiancée. Private Colee Dunn (Rachel McAdams), who both film critics and lay movie commentators alike laud for her performance, is on her way to her "new" family in Vegas, a family that doesn't know she exists; her "fiancé" (possibly imagined) was killed in the firefight that also injured her, and having no family of her own fantasizes that when she takes his guitar to them as a memento and they learn that she was engaged to their son, they will embrace her as family.

The three don't know one another but are seatmates on the plane home, so pass the time in idle chitchat. Arriving stateside, they find that all planes on the East Coast are grounded, the result of a blackout on the eastern seaboard, which means it could be days before they can make their respective plane connections. Cheever decides to rent a car to get to his home to St. Louis; the others ask to ride along, figuring that flights are not grounded in the Midwest. There is a long queue in the car rental line and no cars are left. The car rental agent hears them talking to one another and asks if they've been "over there." When he learns that they are combat veterans, he gives them the one car that is still available, the one that he's supposed to be holding back for his manager. The reason he's doing this is that he "really appreciate[s] what you're doing." They thank him, to which he rejoins, "No! *Thank you!*"

The road trip to Vegas—Cheever goes all the way with them after learning his wife is divorcing him—is a typical road trip movie, which is to say, it is a means to get to know the individuals involved and entertain the audience with various adventurous side trips. The film is particularly noteworthy as commentary on the war because it exposes the multifaceted attitudes of civilians toward the war and those serving.

Many films indicate that the "home" reception is largely negative, or turns negative after the initial welcome home parades. This movie reminds us that many Americans are warmly predisposed to those who serve. The car rental agent is one good example of this, and there are a number of other positive assessments by the public that dot this film, including two sex workers the group encounters on the road who waive their fee when they learn of T. K.'s injury and patriotically agree to attempt a cure.

A number of other scenes are of interest for what they say about aspects of the war. One shows the short-term time warp. Dunn has to go to the bathroom, so they pull over and stop at a local bar. After finishing her business, she stands behind a group of college coeds and is mesmerized at what everyone is watching so intently on television. It's an *American Idol* clone. "What's that?" she asks some Indiana college women. They look at her like she's from Mars. She tells them she's been overseas and, explaining her limp, says that she took a bullet in the leg. They don't believe her and mock her injury. She gets mad at their dismissive attitude and starts a fight. Before it turns into a full-scale brawl, the other two have her back, and they edge out of the bar.

In another scene, they get locked out of their car. The cell phone is on the seat, so they hike down the road until they find a place where they can use the phone to call for assistance. It turns out to be a Hummer dealership and the owner takes them back to their car where he will use a Slim-Jim to unlock it. The car dealer does most of the talking on the short ride to their car and is impressed because they got to ride in a real Humvee. He has lots of customers that would be mightily impressed; indeed, many want a Humvee just like they have and order ones with special camouflage paint, though theirs, of course, has air-conditioning, a state-of-the-art stereo system, and cupholders.

In another scene, they are invited to a barbeque party of a well-off man they met in town. It is obvious the man is influential as the eye roams the grounds behind his home: "This guy has some serious dough." The party is an opportunity to display the requisite liberal-conservative argument: a middle-aged conservative male applauds them for what they are doing, a young liberal takes them to task. The liberal's wife leads him away while he continues to rant about the war. The conservative gets to have the last word. "Lot at stake over there," he says. "Yeah," Cheever retorts, "money." "So," the conservative asks, "what are you guys doing over there?" The answer: "Just trying to stay alive." This is not the patriotic response the civilian expects, or appreciates: "Well, if that's your answer, no wonder we're losing." The point is that neither the liberal college students nor the conservative businessman understand the war. The only one that does is a police officer who, when Dunn chastises him for not understanding where she is coming from, says that he was in the military and "Know[s] just what it's like."

This film does one thing few other fictional films achieve, though it is one the veteran documentarians persistently point out: military personnel are people and no one can understand their war and their feelings. The film is as critical of liberals as it is conservatives. It depicts vets that have been wounded and are coping with the injuries. They are not bitter and display a wry sense of humor. The characters are not heroes, just ordinary men and women who do their duty because it is their duty. There is no "shell shock," though T. K. doesn't really want to go back—still, he does. There is little war-bashing, but neither is there a clamor to arms. In the end, they all are back at the base waiting to board their respective flights to destinations unknown, each going their own separate way. Cheever has joined them, even though his term of enlistment is over. He reenlisted. But not out of any higher cause; he needed the bonus money to help send his son to college. Besides, there's nothing for him stateside now, so, basically, shrug of the shoulders, why not? The movie ends as the plane lifts off into the rising sun, symbolically signifying the start of a new life.

In the Valley of Elah

The name probably didn't help the movie. The Valley of Elah, the protagonist, Hank Deerfield (Tommy Lee Jones) tells us as the film unfolds, is where David slew Goliath. It is a fitting story because Hank is cast as David who is going up against a Goliath, who alternately can be seen as "America" herself, the unbending bureaucratic system Hank is pitted against, or the apathetic people he constantly encounters in his search for "the truth." His quixotic quest is to learn the truth about what happened to his son, Mike. In an oddly refreshing way, his son was not killed in Iraq, but has gone missing near the base in New Mexico; he is later found dead but, in the end, the film comes full circle, bringing it back to Mike Deerfield's tour of duty in Iraq.

The military connection is strong. At the outset, when Hank gets the call that informs him his son is AWOL, the television in the background reports on the Sunni Triangle offensive. Hank, a retired NCO who served most of his time as an investigator with the military police and who now hauls gravel, cannot accept the fact that his son would go AWOL: "It's not like him." He makes the trek to the base in New Mexico to look into matters himself. The rest is basically a murder mystery, compounded because his son's body has fallen on disputed borders: was he killed thirty feet off the road on land that is a military reservation, which would allocate jurisdiction to the army, or was he killed, and dismembered, beside the road, which would make it a local police matter? Hank's investigative insights put the murder within the city's border, and his goal is to incite the local police, namely Detective Emily Sanders (Charlize Theron), to investigate the crime.

The plot is carried along nicely, largely by the presence of Tommy Lee Jones, who gives a solid performance as a weary, retired NCO, who has now lost his only surviving son; his first, coincidentally named David, was killed in a helicopter accident at Ft. Bragg ten years earlier. The murder mystery angle is of less interest to this analysis than what the film says about the war.

The film rests on a number of stereotypes. The first is encountered early in the film when Hank starts his long drive from Tennessee to New Mexico. Leaving town, he passes a school. The flag has just been raised on its pole, but it is upside down. Hank stops the car and walks to the custodian who has just raised the flag. He's Hispanic, and this is supposedly the reason he doesn't know flag protocol. Hank informs him that the flag displayed in such a matter is a distress call: "It means," he informs the viewer as much as the janitor in an overreaching metaphor, "we're in a whole lot of trouble so come save our asses cause [we] don't have a prayer in hell of saving ourselves." The custodian rights his wrong, but is again cautioned on protocol when lowering the flag: "Don't let it touch the ground." The scene may seem like an unnecessary sidebar, but it is important because it closes the film.

The other stereotype is that the female officer, who Hank eventually prods into following through with the case, is persistently mocked

Righting the flag in *In the Valley of Elah*.

by her two fellow male detectives in the squad room. This depiction is accurate: women in police work, largely viewed as a male profession, often encounter difficulty in being accepted. The stereotype is that she received her promotion because she slept with the boss. The film affirms this, perpetuating the stereotype that women only get ahead when granting sexual favors. Her outcast status is used by the director, Oscar winner Paul Haggis (*Crash*, 2005), as motivation to explain her ability to get the case assigned her rather than her dogged tenacity—she pressures the Sheriff, who she's had an affair with, to let her proceed with the case.

Another mistake, and one more central to a movie that depicts military events, is the incorrect enunciation of military procedures. This happens in any number of fictive features. Few directors rely on military consultants and often the mistake is of minor consequence. In this case, it is pivotal to the solution, the Hercule Poirot "Ah-ha" moment. Detective Sanders informs Hank that she has taken depositions from all the men in his son's unit. Not all, he corrects her. She's taken depositions from six of the men, another died in Iraq, plus his son, that makes eight men; there are nine soldiers in an infantry squad, he emphatically states, so she is missing a key statement. He knows this because he's former military. The point is that thirteen men typically constitute a squad. It might be fewer in the field if the squad takes casualties, but a squad of less than thirteen members would be considered too small according to the Table of Organization and would be "under T/O" and needing replacements. A squad, then, would never be a basic unit of nine.[82]

The film's strong statement about the war in Iraq revolves around what happened there, and whether that had any connection to his death. There are conflicting stories but it becomes increasingly evident that Mike was getting "really weird" over there and carried some of this baggage back with him. As did the others. The man who actually killed his son lost it and took Mike's life in a fit of Iraq-instigated rage; his own remorse at what he has done leads him to ultimately take his own life. The others were there when it happened and tried to cover it up by dismembering the body since one of the men had formerly worked as a butcher. The reason they didn't just bury the body is that they were in a hurry because they were hungry. The fast-food credit card receipt was critical to Hank in establishing a timeline that led to solving the mystery. Here it serves to show how calloused the men have become toward killing. This callousness is the direct result of the war, and Hank reflects on a phone call he received and how he ignored the cry for help. His son had pleaded, "You gotta get me outta here, Dad," and he brushed it off: "Just nerves talking."

Mike seems to have realized he was losing it by his behavior. Hank now learns the real reason for the men in the unit referring to his son as "Doc." They had arrested a wounded Hajji and were taking him back in their Humvee. Mike liked to place his hand in the wounds of prisoners and hear them scream. He'd pretend he was a medic, and ask, "Does that hurt?" The answer would invariably be yes, and then Mike (and the others) would laugh, and he'd push his hand back into the wound. This is the garbled videotape that Hank had received prior to his son's disappearance and that throughout the film he'd been trying to make sense of. It now fell into place: It was a tape of what he did in the back of the Humvee.

Hank was a military man and raised his kids to embrace the military. The film says that the military has changed. Heroism has become barbarisms. This is the curse that Hank must now live with. Home, he opens a package from his son that arrived late: it's a flag with a picture of the squad sitting atop a Humvee. Hank put the framed picture next to his chair and stares off into space to the song, "Memories to Keep By Your Chair." The movie did not end here. The director presses home the message by having Hank return the next morning to the flagpole outside the school and, the custodian next to him, duct tapes the ropes so the flag will not be taken down. As he drives off, the viewer sees the flag flying upside down in the breeze. The distress call is just as much about what is happening to American troops "over there" as it is to the indifference of those stateside to the war and the warriors.

Grace Is Gone

Grace Is Gone is another road trip movie but vastly different than *Stop-Loss* or *The Lucky Ones*. This road trip is Stanley Phillips's (John Cusack) bond time with his two daughters as he tries to figure out how to tell thirteen-year-old Heidi (Shélan O'Keefe) and eight-year-old Dawn (Gracie Bednarczyk) that their mother, Grace, has been killed while serving in Iraq.

Stanley's life is very basic: work, home, dinner with the kids, a little television, though coverage about the war is not permitted while Grace is in harm's way, bedtime, then up early to make sure the girls get a good breakfast, and off to work for another mundane day. He has a good, steady job but it's very ho-hum: he's a manager at a local big-box hardware store. We know he's proud of his wife serving her country, and later we find that he was briefly in the army, which is where he met Grace, but his poor eyesight led to his forced, early discharge. Shortly after the film establishes his love and admiration for his wife and his attempts to raise the girls in her absence, a messenger arrives after the girls have gone off to school with the news that Grace has been killed in a helicopter accident. We watch the clock tick off the hours as he just sits there, lost in a daze. The girls return and he tries to tell them but cannot. He takes them on a meal-time spree to Dave & Buster's. Still unable to break the news, he thinks it might help if they have something special to remember the day by, rather than their mother's death, so he takes them on a road trip to a place they've always wanted to go, Enchanted Castle, a Disney-like theme park that is a few days' drive. The older girl is suspicious: "Why are we doing this? Did you lose your job? Mom will be really mad if you lost your job." He assures them he hasn't.

The trip is largely spent bonding with the kids: he shares a cigarette with his older daughter who wants to try one; he relents and allows his youngest daughter to get her ears pierced. There is only one side trip that detours the bonding experience. In proximity to his mother's house, they stop for a visit. His mother isn't there, his ne'er-do-well brother is. The visit serves a number of purposes. There is the usual difference of opinion regarding the war, and his brother blasts it, and by default his sister-in-law. The purpose of this scene is shown later when Uncle John (Alessandro Nivola) is at a Dairy Queen with his nieces and explains that it is all right if people have different opinions; it doesn't mean they don't like one another. The scene also provides Stanley the first real opportunity to grieve. Initially, upon receiving the news that his wife was killed, he was too stunned to respond, then the girls came home and he was forced to put his "face" on and go on like nothing had happened. Now, with the girls gone, he cries! The anguish he's chocked back surfaces full throttle. It is a necessary and important part of the grieving cycle.

At the end, after the girls have had their day at the park, and on the way home, he pulls off on a beach road and they go for a walk: "[Your] Mother is hurt, hurt real bad. So bad," he says, "So bad, [they] couldn't fix her. . . . Sometimes they even die in battle." Tears well up, and they all cling to one another. The next scene shows them at the grave site where he tells the girl that Grace is gone but she will always live on for them: "[We'll] always think of you when we wake up, fall asleep, look at the ocean." The one girl asks, as they stand by the gravestone, "Is it time?" She and Grace had a special moment. Before Grace left for Iraq they set their watches so that no matter what they were doing, they'd have that special moment. Stanley looks at his watch, "Not yet." A few moments later, it is, and they all close their eyes and connect with her in the beyond.

Grace is a long way from Cusack's caustic look at the war in *War, Inc.* This is a very touching film about love, loss, and grief that doesn't deteriorate in the Hallmark moment embraced by *Dear John* (2010).[83] It focuses on an issue that, outside of documentary form, receives scant cinematic attention. It is not a pleasant film, which may be the reason it was not warmly received by the critics. The film may, in fact, be more fitting to the smaller screen. Roger Ebert, who otherwise favorably reviewed the film, inadvertently suggests this when he faults the film for looking "dingy" which causes it to seem as if "some life . . . [has] faded from it."[84] Stanley's life is just that—dingy—and the life that Ebert feels is bled from the film reflects the life that has been bled from Stanley. Mick LaSalle has hopes for the film's DVD release.[85] His hopes are warranted. *Grace* had respectable sales despite its box office failure: it took in just under $10 million in domestic and international DVD sales, twice its production cost, and generated nearly $35 million in domestic and international rental fees. Lay movie reviewers tended to view the film in a much more positive light than the critics, which may be why it won the Sundance Audience Award for best drama in 2007. The general public seems to understand Cusack's uninspired everyman character and more about the grieving process than some, like Lisa Schwarzbaum who doesn't understand either: "A fattened-up Cusack gives his character the trudging gait of a longtime resentful sad sack, suggesting the guy was no lighthearted spirit even in the best of times," which, she goes on to write with no justification since Grace is never seen, is probably the reason "he drove his wife a little nuts with his dour act." Nevertheless, she continues, now looking at his grief, "undone by grief and loss, Stanley can't find the words to break the news to his [daughters]. He stalls by plopping them in the car and whisking them off on a road trip to a theme park in a manic [sic] search for the balm of manufactured fun. . . . Who is this father who thinks he's shielding his kids from pain but is actually prolonging their agony? He's an actor's dream, that's who, an amalgam of arbitrary ac-tions," who she then says, "even gets to wear unattractive eyeglasses."[86] Schwarzbaum's choice of words is interesting, since amalgam means mixture; however, the word is typically used in a positive way, as in, "[he's] an amalgam of strength, reputation, and commitment to ethical principles." And in an ordinary way, that is just what he is: his lifelong wish was to be in the army but poor eyesight prevented him from serv-ing, and maybe, he explicitly says in the film, had he been in, he might have been the one to go to Iraq and die there instead of Grace, a not uncommon feeling among those who've lost a loved one. As it is, he is trying to make the best of an otherwise humdrum existence, and his life just got more difficult: not only does he have to tell his children of the loss of their mother, and now take on the sole burden of raising them, but he's lost one of the things (other than the girls) that gave his life meaning. It is a rare film because it not only deals with the sensi-tive subject of a family's grief, it also reminds the viewer that women serve and die today too. It has much more depth-displaying loss than *The Messenger*.

The Messenger

The messenger who brings news of a loved one's death to family members has been seen fleetingly in any number of films, but in *The Messenger* it becomes the focal point (see also *Taking Chance*). *The Messengers* would be a more appropriate title since the news is typically brought by two members of the military, as it is in this film: Captain Tony Stone (Woody Harrelson), aptly named for his stony demeanor when delivering his message, and Staff Sergeant Will Montgomery (Ben Foster). The bureaucratic mentality that spills over to the way the message is delivered is immediately established. The CO asks Capt. Stone how long the Staff Sergeant has been waiting in the outer office. Stone looks at his watch: "Seventeen minutes, Sir." As if that is sufficient time for a subordinate to have waited, the CO then says, "Okay! Send him in." The Staff Sergeant, an injured war hero, has three months before the end of his enlistment and will complete his tour of duty as a member of the Casualty Notification Team (CNT). The sergeant looks less than enthusiastic, which causes the CO to snap, "[Your] mission [is] not just important, it's sacred." Seasoned CNT leader Stone will show him the ropes.

Over coffee, the Captain explains their mission in very rigid terms that make the assignment anything but personal: "Stick to the script. Read the book. Don't say lost, expired, or passed away. . . . Say killed or died. Call each casualty by name; we honor [sic] them. . . . Hours of operation, 0600 to 2200." If the next of kin [NOK] is not available, "[We] come back later [and] don't touch NOK [sic]. It'll only get [you] in trouble," by which he means emotional trouble. The rules are there for a reason, primarily to steel the messengers from the message they have to deliver. The reason for some of the rules is delineated as the movie unfolds, but the driving rationale behind the rules, the necessity of distancing oneself from their onerous duty, is never fully developed. This distancing of the two messengers undercuts the honor that is ostensibly accorded the fallen; indeed, the Harrison character says that during Vietnam the NOK (a linguistic distancing strategy in itself) received notice by telegram and momentarily ponders whether their way of personal notification is an improvement.

Six notifications occur and most family members, understandably, are shaken to the core by the news, often blaming the messenger(s) for the message. Each notification takes about five minutes during the course of the nearly two-hour film. *The Messenger* is less about those who have been lost, than it is about the two messengers. The movie, then, rather than shedding light on the plight of surviving families does not, as Owen Gleiberman (2009) has it, move the death of those who've served to the foreground. It does shed light on the process of informing families, however.

Will Montgomery is the central character. The films opens with him meeting (and bedding) his old girlfriend upon his return; shortly after, they break it off. The staff sergeant is suffering from severe post-traumatic stress from his tour of duty. He has a hard time keeping it together and alone in his apartment at night often flies into a rage. Until he meets one of the widows to whom he delivers the message of her husband's death and falls for her. She takes her husband's death notification pretty well, and the captain thinks the reason for her calm demeanor is that she's "banging" someone else; later the viewer accepts the couples growing entanglement because she was estranged from her late husband. The staff sergeant is inexplicably attracted to her, perhaps, his failed relationship with his girlfriend and his personal demons suggest, because he has a desperate need to connect with someone. He will find little solace in company with the captain.

The captain is a puzzling character, though the movie shows him in a straightforward light: Laura Kern finds the captain "a hard-nosed womanizing military lifer who's a puppy dog at heart" and A. O. Scott finds the friendship and camaraderie that develops between the two men "remarkably nuanced and completely convincing."[87]

The captain is a puzzle, first, because he's a captain. Promotion from 2nd to 1st Lieutenant is usually automatic and tied to length of service, the promotion occurring within eighteen to twenty-four months. Subsequent promotions is based on merit, though the move from 1st Lieutenant to Captain often takes place within forty-eight to sixty months. The move from captain to major is much more competitive. Captain Stone says that he served during Desert Storm. This means he has been in the army twenty years, and is still a captain. His behavior may be one reason for his failure to move up the ranks. He is a coarse person, more representative of any of the enlisted grunts that have been seen in the documentaries than an officer—even the officers in *Generation Kill* exhibit more refinement than Captain Stone. It might be that the captain is an enlisted man promoted to officer rank, which would explain his age, rank, and behavior. There is no indication that this is how he rose to officer rank, so it must be assumed he entered the military as a lieutenant and spent most of his twenty years as a captain. The ribbons on his chest are correct for the time he served and the areas he likely served in. The correctness of his service awards and the absence of the Army Basic Training ribbon on his chest is a further indicator that he was not promoted from enlistment rank. The failure to rise in rank over a twenty-year career may have caused some of his bitterness but there is no hint of this in the film; in any event, it still doesn't explain his coarseness. He clearly has his own demons, however: He is an alcoholic, though has now been sober for the last three years, and he seems resentful that he's missed any opportunity to service in the present deployments, quipping in one scene that he served in Desert Storm and Desert Shield and that while "it wasn't much of a war" it served as his baptism, too. This fails to impress Montgomery, who later in the film says he's been in firefights that lasted longer than his war.

The camaraderie that fascinates A. O. Scott is likewise puzzling.[88] Fraternization between officers and enlisted personnel tends to be strongly discouraged. And this is more than congenial association—the two regularly hang out at dive bars, get drunk together (Stone falls off the wagon), and pick up women. In one highly unlikely scene, they stop to help an attractive young woman fix a tire on the highway and, after Stone learns that her husband is away, ends up with her at a cabin retreat in carnal embrace, while Montgomery and the woman's girlfriend pass the time outside chatting. Given the fact that both men have issues and seem to need to connect to another human being, their friendship is plausible, but the opposite is also true: they are oil and water and while that gulf may be bridged, it would normally tend to evolve over more months than the staff sergeant has remaining on his tour, especially given the social distance that separates them and which, in itself, would take some time to surmount.

Foster and Harrison are widely applauded for their strong performances, and Harrison was nominated for an Oscar for his supporting role. The story, nevertheless, strikes too many false notes. Suspending one's disbelief, it stands as a good film of two men who bond while doing an unpleasant task. But it offers no glimpses into those who have fallen, and shows only the immediate reaction of rage or disbelief of those who have lost a loved one without touching on the depth of their loss. In the end, the viewer is left with none of their pain and gets lost in the two messengers' hijinks of a road trip that commences with the pick up on the side of the road. The film is helmed by first-time director Oren Moverman. Laura Kern, finishing her review in *filmcomment*, says quite boldly that this is the root of the problem and holds that a more seasoned director "could have" made this film "after *The Hurt Locker*, the second best to date among the proliferating ranks of Iraq War-related films."[89]

THE VIEW FROM OVER THERE

The next, and last, section in this chapter addresses a potpourri of contemporary films that deal with the terrorist threat more than the wars in Iraq or Afghanistan. Indeed, contemporary terrorist films take the viewer away from the war while paradoxically and simultaneously justifying the two-front war. The two films in this section keep their eyes on the current conflict in Iraq and Afghanistan. *The Kite Runner* (2007) examines the war in Afghanistan. It is not really a foreign film but falls into the quasi-foreign classification previously utilized because the person making the film is an American citizen, but his birthright, and lens on the war, is Afghan. The other film is the Turkish movie, *Valley of the Wolves* (2006). It is included in this analysis even though it did not gain widespread circulation in the United States because of its unique slant on the war. The latter is addressed first because it is more distinctly foreign. The precipitous decline in foreign films released in the United States is most likely the result of a concomitant increase in domestic films that address the same issue.

Valley of the Wolves

The film opens with a Turkish general writing a letter to his brother, just before he commits suicide. He was in charge of the region in Northern Iraq and was responsible for the dishonor that befell his men, which was just as much of an affront "against [the] Turkish nation." The first part of the story revolves around that dishonor: the arrest and detention of ten Turkish soldiers the General ordered to lay down their arms to the Americans. The second part of the film focuses on the leader of the group who was arrested, Polat Alemdar (Necati Şeşmaz), and his revenge.

The film is of interest because it is one of the few fictive features to focus on private contractors in the war, the single exception being the satiric film *War, Inc. Iraq for Sale: The War Profiteers* (2006) was the most invective of the documentaries to tackle this issue, but *Valley of the Wolves* dramatically raises the vituperative bar. It also is an intense indictment on the use of quasi-military forces by contractors in Iraq, a slant that largely escaped scrutiny in the documentaries. Sam Marshall (Billy Zane) is the constantly smirking contractor who is a law unto himself, simply because he is an American. He is dismissive not only of the Turkish involvement in Iraq, but of the Turks: "The U.S. has been paying you [Turkey] the last fifty years. Hell, we even supply the elastic for your Goddamn underpants." Marshall heads a quasi-military force of thugs that has total disregard for human life or the rules of war. In one scene, an American officer objects to how one of the paramilitary personnel, Dante, who looks like Dog the Bounty Hunter, is mistreating prisoners: "We need to remember we are soldiers." The lieutenant is rebuked by the brawny, snarling civilian: "Don't ever talk to me again like that." The lieutenant says that what is taking place is not proper conduct and that he's going to place Dante under arrest. Dante responds by riddling him with bullets, then walks to the corpse and spits on him. In a related scene, just before all hell breaks out, Marshall is watching American troops check guests at a wedding from his Humvee; he nods at the commanding officer, then at his driver, who drives off. The impression that the viewer gets is that the American military are at the beck and call of civilian authority. Immediately after Marshall leaves, the military starts taking people at the wedding ceremony into custody. A shot accidentally rings out and the military opens up. This is the only direct scene involving American troops. Most violence is the result of the civilian contractor and the total disregard for human life by him and the pseudo-military personnel who are under his direct authority.

A major subtheme in the film is another that has received scant attention, both cinematically and in the mainstream media: the harvesting and selling of body parts. Body parts are shown being loaded into ice chests in the courtyard of an Iraqi prison compound. Their destination is clearly labeled on the lids: Tel-Aviv, London, New York. A seemingly concerned surgeon, his back to the audience, gives morphine to a donor: "This patient is going to be in pain for a while." Trucks wheel in more wounded. The "caring" medic screams, "What kind of bastard did this?" "Insurgents," he's told by Dante. The doctor turns to face the speaker. It is a manically looking Gary Busey, who knows it wasn't insurgents who wrought the damage to his new patients: "Stop lying to me. How many times must I tell you, these are people, not animals." His concern is short-lived and self-serving. He is as corrupt as the others: "If you don't quit killing my patients so I can remove their organs properly, I will kill you."

The second half of the film follows the traditional payback formula. The last sequence, in particular, is basically a Turkish shoot-out that is reminiscent of those that take place in American action films. The contractor's hired mercenaries open fire indiscriminately, not just with automatic weapons, but with missiles, killing civilians as they run from a mosque. Their total disregard is not just for the people, but their religion. In one earlier scene, when the "doc" is cleaning shrapnel from Mitchell's superficial wound, Mitchell says, "How dare they" [for firing at him]. "Don't they understand, [they're] not going to heaven without embracing our Lord, Jesus Christ," which, for him, justifies their slaughter.

There is also the love interest for the Turkish hero, Polat, and Leyla, who dies in his arms in the end. In the finale, Leyla stabs Dante, who killed her husband, with the knife her deceased husband gave her when they became engaged. Meanwhile, a lengthy knife fight takes place between Polat and Mitchell, which Mitchell loses. Leyla, having been shot twice before Mitchell expires with an I-cannot-believe-it look on his face, dies in Polat's arms. Her death has not been in vain: She dies with the knowledge that Mitchell is dead and is thankful that she's had the opportunity to know Polat. The ending is as hackneyed as any B-budget vigilante script, but the film is highly political and tackles a number of issues largely ignored in American film, in addition to showing that the Turks are in Iraq for more than just for show—not one film that touches on the Iraq issues acknowledges Turkish participation in the war. The political vein that runs through this film should not be surprising. In

Turkey, Adnan Khan said at the 44th annual Golden Orange Festival, Turkey's version of Cannes, "nothing is immune from politics," to which Turkish documentarian Cayan Demirel, added, "There is no art for art's sake in Turkey."[90] *The Valley of the Wolves* proves that.

The Kite Runner

The Kite Runner was favorably received. Both critics and lay film reviewers found it a warmhearted story, even if it was faulted for not having the cultural depth of the best-selling semi-autobiographical novel by Khaled Hosseini, who is Amir (Khalid Abdalla) in the film adaptation by Marc Forster (*Monster's Ball*, 2001; *Finding Neverland*, 2004). Large swatches of *The Kite Runner* take place in Afghanistan. Nevertheless, it is primarily a fictionalized story of the childhood guilt the protagonist carries with him and his subsequent adult redemption by righting past wrongs. The present analysis does not do justice to the film as film, since the focus here is on what the film conveys (or fails to convey) to the average viewer about the situation in Afghanistan.

The story is told through flashbacks. At the opening of the film, Amir, who came to America as a refugee with his father when he was a youngster, is a young adult. He has just published his first novel when he receives a telephone call beckoning him back to Afghanistan. The call hints at the redemptive aspect of the film: "You should come home," he's told. "There's a way to be good again."[91] The telephone call sets up the first flashback. The story is of Amir and his family in Kabul. The result is a very limited view of Afghan culture—the only real cultural awareness that Westerns learn from the film is the importance of kites among Afghans that bookend the movie's opening and closing scenes.

Amir's family in Kabul is influential and very affluent. Their social situation makes Afghanistan look like a first-world country that has been destroyed, first by the Soviets and then by the Taliban. There is little doubt that these occupying forces have done considerable damage to the country, but the impression is that its present backward status is the destructive result of these two occupying forces. This negates the problematic history of Afghanistan after King Zahir Shah was deposed in a bloodless coup that effectively ended Afghanistan's longest period of political stability (1933–1973) and ushered in a period of political turmoil that laid the groundwork for the Soviet invasion in 1979. In short, the period immediately preceding the Soviet entrance into Afghanistan was not the idealized land that is depicted in the film, except, perhaps, for a few (Pashto) insiders. It is also worth nothing that the United States is not an "occupying force." This is adroitly dealt with by the author and director by setting the era in the past: the Soviets roll in and the family, because of the father's outspoken opposition to the Soviets, leaves; Amir returns when the Taliban are still in power and before the country has been "liberated." The father, Baba (Homayoun Ershadi), makes one interesting observation before fleeing the country that is directed at the occupying Soviets, but is just as applicable to the Taliban and could equally be applied today to the U.S. presence: "Everyone [eventually] leaves. This country is not kind to invaders."

Continuing to use flashbacks, the story goes on to explore how the family has adapted to its refugee status in the United States. Then, returning to the phone call in the present that opened the film, Amir returns to Afghanistan in search of redemption to find his old friend, Hassan (Ahmad Khan Mahmoodzada). It turns out that Hassan is his brother from a secret, adulterous affair his father, a Pashto, had with an inferior Hazara, who was his servant. Hassan is dead, but he has a son, who, the viewer subsequently learns, is being sexually abused by a mullah. This, and a scene at the soccer stadium where an adulteress is stoned in a ritualistic Shari'a, depicts the extreme intolerance of the Taliban. Amir rescues the boy in a literal David and Goliath scene: He uses a slingshot to send a stone flying that fells Assef, who bullied Amir and Hassan as young boys and who is now a thuggish Taliban mullah. This allows Amir to escape with his nephew.

The time in Taliban Afghanistan shows the devastation to the city after nearly two decades of occupation. Amir sniffs the air upon his return, recalling the scent of lamb kabobs that once aromatically filled the market that is now permeated with the odor of diesel oil because the electricity is constantly going out. Immediately thereafter, he goes to the orphanage to learn of the sexual abuse of the children by a mullah who comes calling every month or so; the last time the mullah visited he took Amir's nephew. The next scene is Amir hunting for the mullah in the stadium where a Shari'a takes place. The focus on these two scenes, in particular, perpetuates the evilness of the Taliban. As if they were not evil enough, the movie connects them to two of the most heinous acts a person can commit in Western eyes: child sexual abuse and the stoning of a woman for adultery. The former tends to indict all Muslims, which is tantamount to indicting all Catholics for the behavior of few miscreant priests, and doesn't "contextualize" the punishment of the woman, instead implying it is a barbaric rite of a backward people, and for Westerners, one that is not just associated with Taliban extremists but with the subjection of women in Muslim society.

The viewer is left with the impression in *The Kite Runner* that now that the Taliban have been deposed, life is better, which it certainly is, but that does not mean that life is necessarily good—that is, like it was depicted in the opening of the film as a picture-perfect world before two occupiers destroyed the country. Since post-Taliban Afghanistan is not integral to the story, it is not necessary to go there. At the same time, by not going there it allows a more idealized image of Afghanistan to be drawn than might otherwise be challenged if contemporary post-Taliban conditions had been broached (see *Restrepo*, 2010).

There is one interesting scene at the end, which harkens to the quasi category that was used earlier to classify filmmakers who are expatriates. This classificatory scheme was used to suggest that Afghan and Iraqi Americans are sensitive to their culture of orientation but nevertheless are thoroughly Americanized. This Americanization helps the film (and book) succeed with an American audience because it does not challenge cherished extant beliefs.

Amir meets and falls instantly in love with Soraya (Atossa Leoni) who is the daughter of a Pashto general living in exile. Amir's father, Baba, tells his son that he should respect the general even though Amir has a dislike for him, for no apparent reason except the American one: respect must be earned and is not owed simply by birthright. This new-world-versus-old-world attitude is aptly captured near the end of the film when, now married to Soraya and at dinner with her family, the general, concerned with his "face," wants an explanation as to why an inferior Hazara boy is living with his daughter and son-in-law. Amir lays it out: "You see, General, my father slept with his servant's wife . . . that boy is my nephew. That's what you tell people. And one more thing, never refer to him as that Hazara boy in my presence. He has a name." His Americanized wife looks at him admiringly.

THE TERRORIST THREAT

Attitudes toward the war have clearly shifted. Bush's popularity surged after 9/11 when he sent troops into Afghanistan and Iraq. Almost a decade later, support for the war has dramatically eroded. A *Newsweek* poll conducted in mid-2010 showed only 36 percent of Americans were in favor of the war in Iraq[92]; a *USA Today*/Gallup Poll, also conducted in 2010, that appraised attitudes toward the war in Afghanistan found that only 42 percent were in favor of the war.[93] The latter poll also asked whether respondents thought that eliminating the threat from terrorists operating from Afghanistan is a worthwhile goal. The percent responding in the affirmative shot up nearly 20 percent: 61 percent support keeping troops in Afghanistan when the issue was connected directly to terrorism. The war may be unfavorable but the threat of terrorism continues to rank high, and has remained relatively consistent: 83 percent felt defending the United States against terrorism was a top priority in January 2002; in January 2010, it stood at 80 percent. Indeed, a public priority poll by Pew found that the three top priorities for 2010 were the economy (83 percent), jobs (81 percent), and terrorism (80 percent); social security was a distinct fourth priority (66 percent) despite the persistence of the latter as a long-standing social issue that has been under public scrutiny for at least twenty years.[94] This suggests that as the economy improves and people begin to feel more secure about their jobs, terrorism may become the top concern of Americans.

The terrorist fears are a bit surprising, considering there has been no major terrorist attack on the United States in almost a decade. Nevertheless, there continues to be considerable attention to potential acts of terrorism: in December 25, 2009, a Nigerian national tried to detonate explosives hidden in his underwear during a flight from Amsterdam to Detroit; in May 2010 a thirty-year-old Pakistani who had become a citizen of the United States less than a year earlier tried to trigger a car bomb in New York City's Time Square. Newspaper headlines and news reports acerbate the fear: "Al Qaeda," reports the *New York Daily News* in a headline story, "Poised to Try Major Attack in United States within 3–6 Months, Intelligence Chief Warns."[95] The terrorist threat remains a constant reminder for air travelers, who, despite some grousing, have come to expect and accept long security lines and intrusive searches.

The popular media also plays a pivotal role in perpetuating the terrorist threat. Terrorism is the raison d'être for HBO's series *Sleeper Cell* and FOX's popular *24*; it is also the driving plot device behind many episodes of *Law & Order*, *Criminal Intent*, and *NCIS*, along with the various dramatic spinoffs of these shows: *Law & Order: Criminal Intent*; *Law & Order: Special Victims Unit*; *CSI: Miami*; *CSI: New York*; *CSI: Crime Scene Investigation*; *Criminal Minds*; *NCIS: Los Angeles*; *Bones*; and the *Mentalist*. A large body of films also touches on the terrorist threat, if only obliquely. For example, *The Visitor* (2007) is a film about a disenchanted college professor who has lost direction in life until he finds two illegal immigrants in his seldom-visited New York apartment. The story focuses on how Walter's (Richard Jenkins) apathetic life is reinvigorated by the immigrant mother and son, only to have the young man unjustly picked up by the police, and, upon learning of his illegal status, deported. Walter's lawyer tells him there is little he can do. The reason: "Before 9/11 [illegal status] wasn't a big deal. Everything is now black-and-white [for the government]. You belong or you don't." *Lions for Lambs* is an even better example because of the way it addresses the present conflict, yet touches on the war on terrorism.

Lions for Lambs generated a respectable $72.41 million at the box office and from DVD sales, which is nearly twice its production cost. This is no mean feat, considering that it is the peachiest of the war-related films. It was produced and directed by activist Robert Redford, who also starred in the film, along with Meryl Streep and Tom Cruise. The name power of these three well-known Hollywood celebrities helped generate public interest in the film.

The film pivots around its three stars sitting around talking in two offices. Senator Jasper Irving (Tom Cruise) is being interviewed by seasoned journalist Janine Roth (Meryl Streep). The senator is cast as an ambitious up-and-coming young conservative politician; Janine plays the skeptical old dog, hard-nosed liberal reporter. A substantial portion of the story revolves around the ideological clash of these two and unfolds in the senator's office. The senator spends most of his time justifying his new Afghan plan that will not only help check the spread of "evil and terror" but it will also "win the hearts and minds of the Afghan people." The senator's plan is framed to fail: interspersed throughout the senator's pitch is satellite visual of two soldiers, one black, one white, who are caught in a firefight on a mountaintop in Afghanistan and who are clearly on the losing end. It turns out that the two soldiers were students of Professor Stephen Malley (Robert Redford).

While the senator rants on from his conservative position, the political science professor pontificates his liberal stance to an apathetic student in his office, Todd Hayes (Andrew Garfield). He asks his student rhetorically, "How can you enjoy the good life? Rome is burning, son. And [the] problem's not with people who started this. . . . The problem is with us, all of us." It's complacency. But the professor is better at talking than doing. At the end, he's on a couch watching the news. The television reporter is going on about a pop star who's getting divorced from her rapper husband while a crawl at the bottom of the screen (mis)reports on the war: "U.S. troops seizing high ground in surprise offensive." This televised report serves two purposes. One purpose is to underscore the nation's priorities: people are more interested in the personal lives of celebrities than real matters. The other point is to suggest the press "lies" about the war, a point the viewer cannot fail to miss after being exposed to the losing situation faced by the two soldiers in that "surprise offensive." The movie also inadvertently suggests that the professor, despite all his pontificating, is also complacent. He watches the news flash silently, contemplatively, but the news report washes over him and fails to engender any action. The right-leaning senator is all talk, but so too is the liberal-leaning professor.

The movie's title is vague, so it is necessary that it be explained. The professor does this in one of his long monologues to his student (the audience). The German generals in World War I, like the senator—and the professor, though this was a connection probably not intended— were far removed from events in the field. The men out there, the men on the front line, were lions, but they were led by lambs. Fearful that the connection to today might be missed by the audience, the professor makes it explicit: "Dead right on now!" But he too is a lamb. The two soldiers, who are on the mountaintop about to die, were his students, and he tried to talk them out of going; in a way, he wanted them to be complacent and do nothing. They refused to heed his advice.

The movie ends by returning to Streep's character. It appears that the two men stranded on the mountaintop are part of the senator's grand strategy to win the war. This point is made clear (to the audience) in an interrupted telephone conversation the senator takes as he is wrapping up his talk with Janine. She's skeptical of his whole sales pitch. She tells her editor that she won't run the story the way the senator wants: "It stinks. It feels bogus. . . . Cannot do it again, cannot just buy the whole program. Remember The Who, 'Meet the new boss, same as [the] old boss'?" She is told that this is not an investigative piece and to write the story as a straightforward interview. The editor's compromise, his complacency, is thrown in his face: "What happened to you, Howard? You were a good [reporter] once." But she doesn't get off. If she doesn't do what she's told, she'll be out, and this now has consequences: "You're fifty-seven, [your] mother needs twenty-four-hour care. . . . No one will hire you." She still cannot bring herself to compromise her principles. "Think it over," he tells her. She rides away in a taxi. This last chapter is entitled, "At a Crossroads."

There is no reason to believe, especially given her hesitation at the end, that Janine is going to stick to her old liberal principles. The professor's lengthy liberal pontifications also go nowhere; he *sounds* good, but he's never shown taking any action. The senator is no better; he is one of the lambs who directs the war from the comfort of his well-appointed office. The professor and the reporter are cast in a positive light in the film, the senator in a clearly negative one. Nevertheless, the only heroes in the films—the ones who do *something*—are the soldiers on the mountaintop who made a choice and are now about to die for something they believe in. In this sense, the film applauds the lions in the field. In presenting them in such a light, the film casts the war in Afghanistan and, by default, the war on terror, in a positive light as well. In a roundabout way, the film actually upholds the status quo it was meant to challenge. Only the self-serving senator is cast in a negative light; those who serve, the war itself, and the general war on terrorism—the evil and terror that is raised in the course of the film—are never negatively assessed.

In other films, terrorism moves to the forefront. Films where terrorism becomes the central motif help perpetuate the notion that constant vigilance by American agents and agencies is the only thing keeping terrorism at bay, which is a bit paradoxical since faith in the ability of government agencies is at a near all-time low.[96] The films in this section go a long way in explaining the paradox.

Numerous studies have found that the entertainment media is a major stimulant to raising feelings such as anger and anxiety in public life.[97] The media's impact is particularly strong with laypeople. Experts tend to assess risk based on quantitative data: mortality estimates and probabilities. Lay judgments of risk tend to be more qualitative; that is, subjective in nature. In other words, risk is socially constructed by most people: it is their feeling of what *might* happen and not, as it is with experts in the field, based on an informed analysis of the facts.[98]

The public's perception is predicated on what risk researchers call risk amplification.[99] Risk amplification focuses on those personal and social factors that create either a heightened or lowered sense of risk within a society. Films that focus on the terrorist threat are a social factor that amplifies the public's fear by indicating, as the films in this section do, that terrorists are posed to strike at any moment and are only thwarted by the vigilance of government agents and agencies. The silences in these films are just as important because they serve to amplify the central tenet of these films. Movies seldom raise the point that many terrorists are not particularly adept or well-organized, a point made in a recent article by Byman and Fair in *The Atlantic* in a proactively titled article, "The Case for Calling Them NITWITS"[100] (see *Four Lions*, 2010). Films, by failing to raise this "voice," amplify the threat of terrorism to an audience that gets precious little information from "legitimate" sources.

The Kingdom

The Kingdom preceded *Lions for Lambs* and was made by the same director, Peter Berg, though both were released in 2007. But while *Lions* covered every conceivable aspect of the war on terror, including the press's complicity in launching the wars and the Abu Ghraib scandals, as well as how al-Qaeda solicits recruits in Afghanistan by threatening to execute them if the young men don't join, *The Kingdom* is focused exclusively on terrorism.

The Kingdom is the Kingdom of Saudi Arabia. This is immediately made clear at the beginning of the movie should anyone think the reference is to the Kingdom of God. A crawl as the credits run establishes a timeline and is accompanied by newsreel visuals that start with 1932, the year the Kingdom of Saudi Arabia was formed, and end with the

Saudi connection to the 9/11 hijackers. The viewer is then informed that the FBI is the lead agency whenever U.S. citizens are attacked abroad. Shortly thereafter, a terrorist bomb kills a number of Americans playing softball in a U.S. compound in Al Rahmah, Saudi Arabia. This is the FBI's big chance "to put [our] boots on Saudi sand." This movie is extraordinarily ethnocentric in the way it promotes the backward Arabs (see also *Reel Bad Arabs*, 2007).

The FBI team is led by Special Agent Ronald Fleury (Jamie Foxx) who assembles an elite four-member group of experts to go to Saudi Arabia to hunt down and capture the terrorists responsible for the attack. The clock is ticking. The scene of the crime is only "hot" for thirty-six hours, so if they don't get there right away, they won't be able to successfully do their job. This lengthy setup consumes one-fourth of the film. It is dealt with in some detail to show how tenacious the FBI agents are and how much bureaucratic red tape they have to face just to do their job. Bureaucratic resistance does not just come from the Saudis, though the head of the Saudi investigative team, General Al Abdulmalik (Mahmoud Said) objects and resents their intrusion, but internally as well: a State Department bureaucrat objects to the FBI's intervention in Saudi Arabia's internal affairs because it's against "the rules, you know." In the end, Agent Fleury's tenacity wins out and the team is given final "clearance" by Prince Ahmed Bin Khaled (Omar Berdouni) shortly after they arrive in Riyadh.

The young prince assigns Colonel Al Ghazi (Ashraf Barhom), head of the police, to babysit the Americans, a role he resents. The prince, however, tells the colonel he is lucky to be involved in the investigation at all since the suicide bombers wore police uniforms, which is why the military, and not the police, will be in charge of the investigation. The rest of the movie follows the classic Hollywood action formula: the Americans, through rigorous investigation and over all obstacles, identify the terrorists and in the process uncover a more nefarious terrorist plot that they spoil in the de rigor car chase and gun battle in the film's lengthy finale where they kill all the bad guys before, literally, flying off into the sunset. Subsequent comments are confined to showing how the FBI is portrayed and what the ending conveys about terrorism.

The agents are thoroughly dismissive of the Arabs. They make no attempt to understand Arabic culture and wear their arrogance of Saudi ways on their sleeve. They are told by the colonel that the general has only cleared them to "walk" the crime scene. This is not satisfactory. Special agent Fleury *demands* to talk to the colonel's superior. The agents display a "you-cannot-tell-me-what-to-do" attitude throughout the film, implicitly, if not explicitly, saying, in effect, "We're Americans! We know everything!" They take the colonel to task as they survey the crime scene: "Your men are contaminating *everything*," then, with a sharp look and mocking tone, add, "Don't you understand evidence? Little things—like *clues*." Three related scenes are sufficient to emphasize American competency vis-à-vis their backward hosts.

In the first scene, a Saudi military guard refuses to allow the colonel and the Americans access to a house rooftop the agents want to examine. The colonel argues with the guard and the guard hits him. The guard is just about to take another swing when Special Agent Fleury (Foxx) intervenes and, using his martial arts skills, overcomes the guard, essentially rescuing the colonel.

The second scene takes place shortly after the first. The colonel and Americans gain access to the rooftop of the house. The locals have already examined it as a possible site where the terrorist might have lurked and found no evidence that he was there. It takes only a second for the sharp-eyed agents to emphatically pronounce that the terrorist was on the roof. The colonel is skeptical but agrees to look into it. The FBI agents aren't happy: "Fucking bullshit. . . . We're not tourists here." Slightly more diplomatically this same point is later made to the prince: "We're the good guys, let us help you."

The third scene shows the help they are able to render, and, again by default, the ineptitude of the locals. At the crime scene, Agent Grant Sykes (Chris Cooper), frustrated with the lack of progress, jumps into the mud pit where evidence may be buried, and, quite joyfully, wallows in the muck that the Arabs refused to climb into. The agent's willingness to do whatever is necessary, no matter how menial, leads to the clue that breaks the case. This is how Americans work: jump in, get your hands dirty, and get the job done. The Saudis (Arabs) are prima donnas; they don't want to get their hands dirty. The movie perpetuates the myth that Americans aren't afraid of a little hard work, ignoring the fact that the overwhelming majority of American citizens entering the workforce today want a white-collar desk job.

The four FBI agents perpetuate a number of professional characteristics, among them, hard working, resourceful, and tenacious. These attributes could be reflected in any film about the FBI set in the United States (see *The FBI Story*, 1959; *The Silence of the Lambs*, 1991), and are found regularly on the police dramas that proliferate nightly prime-time television. In these films and television programs, the key principals always know better than anyone else. There is, then, nothing, in itself, wrong with any of these attributes; they are well entrenched in the American ethos and often promoted in film. They appear particularly stark, however, when the social category being depicted is of "out-group" members.

Social categorization is when people are sorted into groups: men/women, Christians/Muslims, Americans/Arabs. The people in the group are stereotyped as behaving in certain ways. These stereotypes tend to be pronounced only for out-group members—those in a group to which one doesn't belong. This is known as the out-group homogeneity effect: perceivers assume that there is a greater similarity among members of an out-group than among members of one's own group. This effect engenders an "us" versus "them" mentality. Subtle differences among out-group members are not noticed because one doesn't interact with "them" that much, so they all "look alike." Even if a black or white Christian American knows some Arabic Muslims at work, and may have even spent some time socializing with them outside the workforce, they still don't know that many Arab Muslims. If the ones they know don't match the stereotype, it is because the people they know are different, not because the stereotype is inaccurate. This means that if a member of the audience is not an Arab Muslim, they are going to perceive Arab Muslims as "all" behaving the way they do in the movie, even if they are personally acquainted with one or two Arab Muslims who defy the stereotype. At the same time, the members of the in-group don't accept the stereotype of their group because they see the wide-ranging differences of people who belong to their group.

An excellent illustration of what we might call the homogeneity "exclusion" phenomenon is the colonel in *The Kingdom*. He is portrayed as a good guy throughout the film. This is established right away: the general is torturing someone falsely accused of complicity in the initial terrorist attack and in a separate scene the colonel states his abhorrence with the general's methods of interrogation. The colonel is an Arab Muslim but he's appreciative of the "American approach." This is partially explained in the film because the viewer learns that he went to school in the United States, so is at least somewhat "Americanized." He even, in the end, lays down his life to save one of the FBI agents. Despite the colonel's pro-Western leanings, he's the exception to the rule—all the other locals in the film are depicted in a negative light. That is why the FBI agents and the audience can embrace the colonel and yet never have their stereotypes challenged, since all the other characters in the Kingdom are benighted Arabs.

Further underscoring the difference between "us" and "them" is the depiction of gender relations. Most Westerners see Muslim women as second-class citizens who are subjugated by men. The media plays a critical role in perpetuating this perspective. A study by sociologist Gema Martin-Munoz underscores this point. Martin-Munoz found that 85 percent of the stories in the Western media tended to portray Muslim women as a victim of Islam.[101] The traditional Muslim veil or hijab, in particular, is often cited to show how Muslim women are subjugated.[102] Women's "rights" seem particularly backward from a Western perspective because most Western countries are now well into "third wave" feminism while the feminist movement in Muslim countries is still in its early incarnation. Nevertheless, it should be remembered that the second wave of feminism began in the United States during the 1960s and did not make substantial headways until well into the 1970s,[103] so the "backward" position for women in the United States is not rooted to some distant time, and there is still considerable argument today just how far women have come in society.[104]

The subordinate status of women is particularly pronounced in *The Kingdom*, even if there are only two brief scenes depicting the backward place of women in Saudi society. These scenes are particularly illustrative because they jointly take up only a few minutes and both could have been readily excised without detracting from the plot. In the first scene, the prince arrives at the crime scene to determine what progress is being made. An American diplomat admonishes the T-shirted, braless FBI agent (Jennifer Garner) in the group to "tone down the boobies" before the prince arrives. She uses a makeshift shawl to cover herself. This is apparently done for the prince's benefit because in subsequent scenes she is not appropriately attired. Her covering is portrayed as a bureaucratic rule to which she must (momentarily) acquiesce. The backward state of women is further enunciated when the female agent gains access to the bodies of those killed by the terrorist bomb to probe their wounds. She is immediately rebuked by the guard at the mortuary. She can instruct the colonel what to do, but she is prohibited by Muslim law from touching a male's body; she huffs off to examine the Western corpses in another room.

Then there is the final shoot-out. It is an action movie, so it is not surprising that the last thirty minutes is a Ramboesque kill-fest with bodies falling left and right. After an intense firefight in the film's finale, a noise is heard from another room in the apartment. Things are still tense. It turns out it is a simple family: a sickly old man lying on a bed, a woman, a young teenage boy, a little girl. No threat. A blood trail is noticed. Carefully, the agent follows it. It leads only to the dead, bullet-ridden body of one of the terrorists. The movie does not end here, however. It has something more to say. The young teenage boy suddenly opens up with an AK-47 and spews bullets everywhere. He's killed. It looks over, but it's not. One more critical scene needs to be depicted. The colonel reaches out his hand to the old man on the bed; "Let me help you," he says. The old man suddenly pulls out an AK-47 from under the bed linen and, screaming fanatically, begins blasting away. He kills the colonel just before he is shot by one of the agents. Dying, the old man gasps his legacy to his granddaughter, instructing her to carry on the jihad against the infidels. The battle was over before the old man's last stand. By concluding the film on this note, the viewer takes this final scene from the movie. There is only one possible interpretation: You cannot trust any Muslim! They are all would-be terrorists.

A. O. Scott with the *New York Times* remarks that *The Kingdom* is in some ways an antiwar movie, not because it makes an explicit statement against the war, but because it makes no mention of the war in Iraq.[105] But it does push the terrorist hot button and in doing so justifies the necessity of action against countries that harbor terrorists. That was, after all, the driving rationale for America's entrance into Afghanistan and Iraq. The movie, then, promotes a prowar mentality if the war is necessary to stop terrorism.

Traitor

Traitor is more of a thriller than an action film, though it certainly has a strong dose of the latter. The thread for *Traitor* is whether the lead character, Samir Horn (Don Cheadle) is a traitor. It is a strong directorial debut for Jeffrey Nachmanoff who cowrote the script with Steve Martin.

Samir's background is purposefully murky to move the plot forward. It is slowly unraveled by two FBI agents who keep popping up in the most unlikely places: Madrid, Nice, Marseille. They always appear to render unasked-for assistance to the benighted locals. This point is made crystal clear in one scene. The two agents are having difficulty in Marseille with a local French police officer who is not cooperating with them. They lay it on the line for him, in much the same way the agents did in *The Kingdom*: "We came here to stop an [terrorist] attack. . . . Let's cut the bullshit."

The more the agents learn about Samir, the more they are convinced that he is a terrorist. His father was Sudanese, killed by a car bomb when Samir was a child; it is not stated, but this early childhood experience may have had a traumatic effect on him. His mother is an American from Chicago, though when she is seen later in the film she is wearing Arabic clothing, suggesting her ties are more Arabic than American. He was kicked out of high school because of brawling, though it appears justified: he put two boys in the hospital for taunting a black female

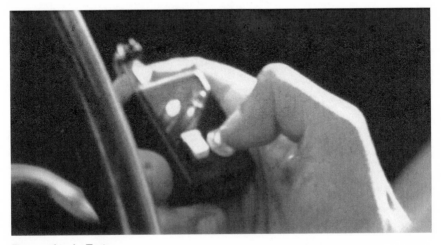

Detonation in *Traitor*.

student. That is when he enlisted. He was a staff sergeant with the Special Forces, trained in explosives, when he went to Afghanistan to help the rebels. He found religion while in Afghanistan, which is one of the reasons he stayed in Afghanistan and joined the mujahideen, rubbing shoulders, one agent says, with a "who's who of terrorists." If this is not enough to convince the agents (and audience) that he's a terrorist, the film enunciates his religiosity. He had a job in Chicago for a while but lost it because people complained about him wearing a skullcap. He is invariably seen wearing his religion on his sleeve. The strength of his Muslim religious beliefs is meant to suggest a connection to fanaticism.

Samir is praying in the courtyard of a prison where he has been incarcerated as a suspected terrorist. The terrorist connection is strengthened in this scene. He's accused of being a traitor to the cause by one of the Muslim inmates; he refutes the accusation by staying, "If I was a traitor [to the cause], would I be here?" He gets on the wrong side of one of the gang henchmen who runs the prison. In a courtyard scene, the man approaches Samir to finish what was started but Omar (Said Taghmaoui) intervenes with his gang: "[You] put a hand on one of my brothers [fellow Muslim], it'll mean your life." Samir and Omar become friends, and Omar takes Samir with him when he breaks out of prison.

Omar is a lieutenant in a terrorist organization. The others are suspicious of Samir so he has to prove himself. He plants a bomb at the U.S. Embassy that the news reports kills eight people. He's accepted into the group. It is here that the viewer learns that Samir is one of the good guys. In the night rain a car pulls up beside him on the street and the window rolls down. We learn that the deaths were accidental; "No one was supposed to get killed," Samir says. The section of the embassy where the bomb exploded, his handler tells him, was supposed to be empty; he was unaware that a local maintenance crew had been slotted to go there and make repairs while it was empty.

The movie is now quickly moving to its dénouement. Samir learns that a sleeper cell of fifty terrorists are going to board fifty buses and detonate their bombs across the heartland of America, all on the same day at the same time to strike fear across America. The cell has been slowly infiltrating the United States for years. A number of dramatic interludes forestalls the ending, before the de rigor finale shoot-out. Samir kills Omar, who, dying in his arms, gasps, "I thought you were my brother. How could you do this?" Samir tells him: "They used us, they used us for our religion." The FBI agent concedes his heroism: "The country owes you a large debt." Samir quotes the Qur'an: "If [you] kill an innocent person, you killed all mankind." To save forty-nine buses from the terrorists' bomb and countless lives, Samir had to sacrifice one bus, and the lives of those aboard it; it is Samir's curse to live with that knowledge. Lead Agent Roy Clayton (Guy Pearce), who was a minister's son and has a Ph.D. in Arabic studies, quotes the Qur'an back to Samir, offering him solace: "It also says that if you save an innocent person, [you] save all mankind." They shake hands, and part: "Shalom!" The closing shot in the film shows Samir in a skullcap kneeling on a prayer rug in a mosque.

The ending of the movie does try to present the Muslim religion in a positive light. It shows a religious believer who is not an extremist; moreover, he's an American Muslim who fights against the terrorists, indicating one can be a Muslim and still be a patriotic American. Samir, like the colonel in *The Kingdom*, is this film's homogeneity exclusion character. The final message is the terrorists *are* Muslim and, except for Samir, have been shown in a consistently negative light. They are also all out to destroy America. The terrorist threat looms large: it happened in the Sudan when Samir was but a child; it took the lives of innocents in the Costa del Sol, which is why the agents flew to Madrid; bombs were being assembled in Marseille, where, because a would-be terrorist boasted of his activities with a terrorist organization to his cousin, the young man had to be killed because "We don't allow liabilities." The terrorists ruthlessly pursue their single-minded goal: the destruction of the United States. The movie suggests terrorists are all around us; they are everywhere. They have been infiltrating the United States for years, passing themselves off as innocuous neighbors. They are just waiting for "the word" to rise up and take the lives of innocents. It could happen anywhere, anytime, except it won't because American agents and agencies remain constantly vigilant.

The Insurgents

The Insurgents adopts the tone of *Traitor* but is less successful. In fact, it is the lowest grossing of the fictive features (see Table 4.1). Studios sometimes feel that the movie is not up to standards and, rather than spend more money distributing and advertising the film, slot it directly to the DVD market. This appears to be the fate of *Insurgents*.

The Insurgents is the only film made by Scott Dacko. It jumps back and forth across time, which can pose some initial confusion in the viewer's ability to follow the plot. These time transgressions occur throughout the film, but they are less pronounced after the opening act and focus more on the here and now.

The story is right out of the 1960s and the contemporary insurgents could just have easily been the Weathermen, Students for a Democratic Society (SDS), or the Chicago Seven. The main characters are a group of disaffected young people who want to change "the system." The group is nudged toward its revolutionary goal by Robert (John Shea), a pseudo-intellectual college professor who, as the voice of the people, stands around pontificating the rationale for rising up. He could easily be mistaken for a radical college professor from Berkeley in the Sixties, relying, as he does, on Henry David Thoreau's essay on civil disobedience to justify action against the government. In his apartment, surrounded by mesmerized middle-class students, he rants on: "Need a group so disillusioned with the status quo [they're] willing to sacrifice anything to change it. . . . [The] harder the government cracks down, stronger the movement becomes. . . . .Without [the] occasional forest fire, [the] next generation of trees will never grow. . . . [I] need [some] to stand with me."

The three characters Robert recruits represent a cross section of Americana. Hana (Juliette Marquis) is a contemporary middle-class young woman, not unlike Patty Hearst, who immediately bonds with Robert at a bookstore lecture when she recognizes his quote from Voltaire's *Candide*. Marcus (Henry Simmons) plays the part of Eldridge Cleaver, the black activist who wrote *Soul on Ice* and who was a prominent member of the Black Panther Party. Cleaver came up the hard way on the street; Marcus came up the hard way in Iraq before he, too, had his eyes opened. In the '60s, Marcus would represent the angry, disaffected Vietnam War veteran. Here he is the angry, disaffected Iraq War veteran. The third recruit is James (Michael Mosey) who wants to belong but is always questioning whether the means justifies the end. The three steal a delivery truck, replace its contents with explosives, and plan to detonate its cargo in proximity to a government building in order to take their stand against the establishment. It turns out, however, that James works for a government agency, and joined the group to uncover and stop their nefarious plan. In the film's shoot-out finale, James kills Marcus just as he is about to detonate the truck; law enforcement agents cuff and take Hana into custody. Robert was killed just prior to this. He died with a deer-in-the-headlight look when he realized his plan would not succeed and that he'd been double-crossed.

The Insurgents spins a variation of the terrorist theme. The threat comes from within, not from without. Idealistic young people in the United States are susceptible to being turned into terrorists. The message, however, remains constant: America is at risk and it is only the result of constant vigilance by dedicated professionals that keeps the terrorist threat at bay.

Body of Lies

Body of Lies is directed by Ridley Scott (*American Gangster*, 2007; *Gladiator*, 2000) and follows the formula of some of Scott's earlier war-related films, *Blackhawk Down* (2001) and *G. I. Jane* (1997). The monitoring of terrorist activities in the international arena is here in the province of the CIA, since the FBI's jurisdiction is limited outside the United States. The framework of the movie is established at the outset of the film with a quote from a W. H. Auden poem: "Those to whom evil is done / Do evil in return."

The plot revolves around two diametrically different personalities within the CIA. Ed Hoffman (Russell Crowe) is a jaded, uncaring bureaucrat in Washington who heads the agency, or at least the section of the agency that oversees the protagonist. Hoffman observes international events from satellite feed to CIA headquarters in Langley. The American arrogance that won the day in *The Kingdom* doesn't play well in this film. In an early scene, he takes a call from the protagonist in his suburban home. His wife calls him to dinner. He'll be there momentarily, calling over his shoulder, "In a minute, I'm saving the world." He clearly thinks he is. Subsequent scenes show him pushing full-steam ahead despite whomever he has to step on.

His nemesis is a young field agent, Roger Ferris (Leonardo Di-Caprio), who is really saving the world because he is out there on the front lines and culturally attuned. The two are in constant communication, with Harris wanting him to plow ahead, head down, and Ferris trying to apprise him of cultural issues that need to be taken into account. The clashing will of agency opposites—bureaucrat versus field agent—is a driving force behind the Jason Bourne novels Robert Ludlum started writing in 1980, which have recently been made into a succession of successful movies.

The opening shows terrorists in Manchester watching a videotape on the television that is promoting random terrorist attacks across Europe. Outside, a British tactile team moves in. Those inside hear a noise, realize what is happening, and blow themselves up to avoid being caught. The scene jumps to Ferris in the desert. He's rendezvousing with an Arabic informant who gives him a disc, which he plays on his car system. It's the tape of "the White Whale"—Osama bin Laden. It's the same tape that the terrorists in Manchester were watching: "We will revenge the American wars on the Muslim world. We will come at them everywhere. We will strike at random across Europe." A subsequent desert rendezvous leads to a shoot-out. Ferris enters a hut where a terrorist looks up at him and smiles, then pushes a button detonating the explosives and demolishing the hut. Ferris leaps aside, barely escaping the blast. These two scenes establish the ruthlessness of the terrorists. They will do anything to accomplish their task, even if it means they must sacrifice their own lives to the cause. Their cause, and their goal to spread terror across Europe, is shown later in the film. Lest the viewer be left with the impression that they don't accomplish anything other than killing themselves, a newscast from Amsterdam later in the film shows their success: seventy-five dead! The newscast is being watched from the Middle East by the jihadist, Al-Saleem (Alon Aboutboul).

The newscast is also being watched from Jordan by the head of Jordanian intelligence, Hani Salaam (Mark Strong). Ferris has established a relationship with Hani that flushes out Al-Saleem. Al-Saleem, however, ends up taking Ferris prisoner whose fingers he breaks with a ball-peen hammer before putting him onto a "torture bed" that will lead to his death, at which moment Hani bursts in and rescues him. It turns out that Al-Saleem's driver is actually a security offer who works for Hani. This near-ending scene reinforces, once again, the vigilance of security agents and agencies to thwart terrorism.

The ending statement in *Body of Lies* is no different from the other action-themed cinemas that assess the war on terrorism. It is different, however, in the way it portrays Arabic culture. Ferris's relationship with Hani, as well as those that revolve around his love interest with Aisha (Golshifteh Farahani), an Iranian refugee nurse, are always treated respectfully. He knows the native language and the native culture. His cultural sensitivity is all the more striking when juxtaposed to Ed Hoffman's cultural arrogance. Ferris's relationships with these two people are peppered throughout the film. At least in this film, the beliefs and behavior of those who are different is not dismissed as backward or barbaric. The dual of cultural opposites is played out overtly in the end. Ferris quits the agency to stay in the Middle East. Hoffman criticizes the decision: "Nobody likes [the] Middle East. There's nothing there to like." The viewer has had a glimpse throughout the film that there are things there to like. Ferris walks out. Hoffman flings his parting shot: "Walk out on me, means you give up on America." Ferris retorts: "Be careful about calling yourself American."

Both men accomplished the end goal of thwarting terrorism, but they both used different paths. The audience is left to ponder, however fleetingly, just which of them is the better representative of the country. It is a question that few other films in the genre have raised.

CONCLUSION

Americans still supported the warrior in 2006 but their attitude toward the war had shifted. Public attitude against the war would become even more pronouncedly negative over the next few years, though it would never reach the antiwar hysteria of the Vietnam era. Fictive features pandered to this mind-set by attacking the war but seldom the warrior. Only a handful of these films, such as *Day Zero*, can even remotely be construed to represent the war in a positive light. Nevertheless, the first burst of fiction (2006–2007) would be dismissed by conservatives. Their claim was that these films were financial disasters and this showed that

Hollywood was out of touch with what people in the country thought about the war. The financial benchmark that conservatives relied on was correct but misleading. Many of the films did not recoup their cost at the box office, but there were more winners than losers after DVD sales and rentals were taken into account.

The first group of fictive features (2006–2007) was more problematic than those that came later (2008–2010). Some, such as *Southland Tales*, though it would turn a tidy profit once it went to DVD, had little to say about the war, which was used solely as a framing device for a juvenile plot marketed to an adolescent male audience. The juvenile market also clearly drove the financial success of *Harold and Kumar Go to Guantanamo Bay*, but it too had little to say about what was taking place at the Guantanamo facility or the policy of rendition. The same holds for *Cavite*. *War, Inc.* definitely addressed the present conflict. It did not do well at the box office either. It did make a number of sharp, caustic thrusts at events taking place, but its satiric jabs often got lost in its juvenile subplots.

There were also some big picture films that carried weight but which were not warmly embraced. *Battle for Haditha* and *Redacted* did not do well financially because their themes were problematic. People go to the movies to be entertained. This expectation is not as pronounced with documentaries, which, while they have entertainment value, are consumed more for their informative nature. The documentaries that fell into the permutations category in the last chapter are an excellent example of this, such as *Lioness*, *Full Battle Rattle*, and *Alive Day Memories* to mention just three. It is unlikely that the troubling themes that *Battle for Haditha* and *Redacted* addressed would have been successful as documentaries, but they become even more problematic as fictive features. This partially explains why De Palma in *Redacted* utilized the documentary style to fictively tell the true story about the rape of a young Iraqi girl and the subsequent murder of her and her family. This made the film a little too real for the viewer who was not expecting a documentary but a *film*, which is to say, they expected a fictional treatment of events to be entertaining, and there is nothing entertaining about these events. *Battle for Haditha*, though certainly likewise informative, is also not entertaining: no one wants to believe Marines would go on a rampage and vengefully kill innocent women and children. It did once occur in a far-off place called My Lai way back when (should anyone under fifty remember the incident), but that was a "bad" war. The war today may not be warmly embraced but it is one that does not vilify the troops. It is difficult for the public to support the warrior if the warriors are not worthy of support. The fact that these are isolated incidents gets lost when the focus is on the incident. The films needed to be done, but that does not make them popular.

A number of other big picture films touch on the seamier side of the war but place the blame not on the troops but with self-serving government officials. It is Meryl Streep's character in *Rendition* who circumvents the law when, as head of a government agency, she takes it upon herself, with no firm basis for her action, to order the act of rendition against an American citizen simply because he is of Middle Eastern descent. This film did relatively well at the box office, at least in part because it reflected a popular angst against the government. It also washed away the harm the act of rendition might inflict because the final scene wraps the film in the requisite happy ending, leaving the viewer untroubled by any lasting damage caused by the act of rendition. *Lions for Lambs* also had a respectable gross at the box office. In part, this can be attributed to its stellar cast—Redford, Streep, and Cruise— but it also did well because, despite its preachiness, it perfectly married the two attitudes that pervaded the public sphere: *Lions* trashed the war by depicting the senator (government) as self-serving, but still managed to depict the men who sacrificed their lives in the film as heroes.

The films that came later in the decade were more financially successful and more warmly embraced by the viewing audience. In large part, this is the result of a more action-driven movie that addressed the popular notion of lurking terrorism. *Traitor, The Kingdom, The Insurgents, Body of Lies,* and *Green Zone* are all action-packed movies that fight "the terrorist threat." *The Hurt Locker* and *Generation Kill* are visual, action movies that fight the war in Iraq; the American version of *Brothers,* more so than the Danish version, is its action counterpart in Afghanistan.

There is another category of films that continues to address the effect the war has had on military personnel and their families seen in home front documentaries in the last chapter. Two early ones, *Day Zero* and *Grace Is Gone,* are among the few that positively assess the ongoing conflict. Both were made in 2006, though not released until 2007. This may explain their prowar stance since the tide against the war in the public sphere had not fully shifted. The character dubbed "blue collar" in *Day Zero* carries the film by accentuating one's patriotic duty to serve. In a similar vein, *Grace Is Gone* is unequivocally prowar because, though Grace lost her life in the war, she is portrayed as serving proudly and died for her country.

The other fictive features in the home front category continue the "it's-the-war-not-the-warrior" theme. *Home of the Brave* (2006) is the first fictive treatment of the injured vet. It did not fare well, even with Samuel Jackson in one of the lead roles. *The Lucky Ones* also followed three veterans who had been injured and, despite a strong performance by Tim Robbins, did not fare any better than *Home of the Brave* at the box office. *In the Valley of Elah* with Tommy Lee Jones fared better, in part because it was a higher quality production than *Home of the Brave*, but it also did not dwell on the psychological toll the war had on military personnel. It was more palpable as a mystery-thriller, with the harm the war inflicted not revealed until the end of the film, negating, or at least minimizing, its disturbing effect on the viewer.

Two other thematic permutations in the home front category were *Stop-Loss* and *The Messenger*. Both address aspects of the war not previously assessed. *Stop-Loss* appraises the effects extended tours of duty can have on those serving. *The Messenger* is an interesting topic. It was the policy of the Bush administration to ban the face of death by excising body bags being shipped home from public scrutiny. *The Messenger* foregrounds the casualties that occur during war (see also *Taking Chance*).

The last fictive feature category is a very small one. Quasi-foreign and foreign fictive feature films had been a primary means of revealing a face of the war that was not addressed by domestic films. With the surge in domestic fictive features, fewer quasi- and foreign films were filtered into the American market. Hollywood distributors most likely stopped importing fictive features because they saw the domestic market now filling this niche.

The Kite Runner is the only quasi-fictive feature during this period. It was based on the best-selling book by an Afghanistan American. The success of the book helps explain its appearance in the fiction category. The movie was not about the war itself, but depicted life in Afghanistan under the Taliban. The film mainly reinforces the popular perception of Taliban fanaticism that, for many Americans, was sufficient justification in itself for sending (and keeping) troops in Afghanistan. The only classically foreign film available on DVD in the United States but not widely distributed is the Turkish film *Valley of the Wolves*. This film underscores the role of foreign films. It addresses three key areas that have escaped critical attention in the public arena: (1) the "harvesting" of body parts from prisoners in Iraq; (2) the "outside the law" arrogance of some paramilitary contractors in Iraq; and (3) the presence of coalition forces in the wars.

NOTES

1. All sales figures in this chapter were obtained from *Box Office Data: The Numbers*.

2. Most advertising budgets are more modest. Of the dozen films I have extensive data on, if *Rendition*'s and *Brothers*' exorbitant campaigns are excluded, the average campaign is around $1 million and these numbers are inflated because they include big but not excessive budgets for films such as *Stop-Loss* ($14.4 million) and *The Lucky Ones* ($4.7 million). More often than not, the budgets range between $22,000 (*Battle for Haditha* and *Day Zero*) to $700,000 (*Grace Is Gone*).

3. This is a follow up to their first successful movie, *Harold and Kumar Go to White Castle* (2004). The movie is simply a vehicle for the comedians to perform their irreverent humor. There is no serious analysis of terrorism. They are arrested on a plane when the marijuana bong is thought to be a terrorist bomb; the fact that it is clearly established that it is not a terrorist bomb assuages any real threat. They are shipped off to Guantanamo and escape in record time—the base not being particularly funny. It is interesting to note that while they escape from the prison the "real" terrorists who are confined there and are involved in the escape are captured. This keeps the focus on the two comedians without raising undue concern among the audience as to the security of the base.

4. The Rock looked particularly uncomfortable in those scenes where he wore a coat and tie and, forefinger to pursed lip, tried to affect a thoughtful countenance.

5. Manohla Dargis, "Apocalypse Soon: A Mushroom Cloud Doesn't Stall 2008 Electioneering," *New York Times*, 14 November 2006, 1(E).

6. Roger Ebert, "*Southland Tales*," *Chicago Sun-Times*, 16 November 2007, www.rogertebert.suntimes.com (accessed 3 May 2010).

7. Ruthe Stein, "To Live and Die Appolaytically in L. A.," *San Francisco Chronicle*, 16 November 2007, 8(E).

8. The last line in Eliot's poem reads that the world ends, "Not with a bang but a whimper." The line was "recast" to fit the bang-up ending in the movie. Only the reviewer for the *New York Times* connected this line to Eliot, but didn't seem to recognize that it was incorrectly quoted.

9. Satire is subdivided into two types, each named for the Roman satirist who popularized the distinct styles: Horace, who wrote in the first century before Christ and Juvenal, who wrote in the first century after Christ. Horatian satire playfully criticizes some social vice through gentle, lighthearted humor. It tends to rely on exaggeration and self-deprecating humor to make fun of someone. Juvenalian satire portrays the social vice using scorn and ridicule and is much more abrasive. It relies on irony, sarcasm, personal invective in attacking its subject. Juvenalian satire is particularly popular today.

10. While female anatomical displays are common today in pop culture, the reader should recall that it was not that awfully long ago when audiences were aghast at the display of Barbara Eden's midriff in *I Dream of Jeannie* (1965).

11. Names mean everything in satire and it is unfortunate that the director chooses Walken for his lead character, not Walker. William Walker was the nineteenth-century American adventurer who became dictator of Nicaragua (see *Walker*, 1997).

12. Claudia Puig, "'The Lucky Ones' Takes Long Way Around," *USA Today*, 26 September 2008, 8(D).

13. Stephen Holden, "A Cell Phone Rings, and That Voice Is Calling the Shots," *New York Times*, 26 May 2006, 10(E).

14. Desson Thomson, "'Cavite': Cheap Thrills." *Washington Post*, 27 July 2006, www.washingtonpost.com/wpp-dyn/content/article/2006/07/27/AR2006072700429 (accessed 15 May 2010); Robert Koehler, "Cavite" *Variety*, 11 July 2005, www.variety.com/review/VE1117927625.

15. *Man Push Cart* (2005) focuses on a Pakastini man who sells coffee and bagels to busy New Yorkers from his sidewalk cart. This film was made for a similar amount, but is a much stronger film, so a low-budget film like *Cavite* does not preclude the ability to tell a story. Still, *Cavite* was widely praised by the critics who were more-often-than-not fascinated less by the storyline than with the style of filmmaking—much as they were with *The Blair Witch Project*.

16. Cavite is pronounced *Kabite*; it is located on the southern shores of Manila Bay, roughly thirty miles south of Manila. Cavite is one of the original

provinces that rose up in arms against Spanish domination in 1896; its critical role in the Philippine Revolution remains murky in the film.

17. The name Adam, representing as it does "first man," would be provocative if one ventured to give the filmmakers imaginative credit.

18. There is one nice local scene where, in the market, Adam is directed to savor the local delicacy, *balut*: a fertilized duck egg with a nearly developed embryo. This could be an effective critique on American consumerism—Adam's culinary habits in NYC appear to be confined to fast food; unfortunately, the director found it necessary to stick a severed finger (of the kidnapped victim) into the egg, undercutting any potential critique on American culinary tastes.

19. The recession officially ended after nineteen months in July 2009, which was the longest in twenty years. At the beginning of 2011, when this book was being finalized, few Americans would find economic comfort in that tenuous statistic.

20. Tim McGirk, "One Morning in Haditha," *Time*, 19 March 2006, 22–24.

21. McGirk, "One Morning in Haditha," 22; Ellen Knickmeyer, "In Haditha: Memories of a Massacre," *Washington Post*, 30 May 2006, 1(A).

22. Dan Whitcomb, "Charges Drooped against Marine in Haditha Case," *Reuters*, 18 June 2008, www.news.yahoo.com/s/mm/20080617/us_nm/usa_iraq_haditah (accessed 12 July 2010).

23. Lt. Calley was convicted and given a life sentence. He served only three years under house arrest.

24. Wikipedia is not always the most reliable source for information, but in this case it does give a good summary of what happened. For more details see Kendrick Oliver, *The My Lai Massacre in American History and Memory* (Manchester, England: Manchester University Press, 2006); Michael Belknap, *The Vietnam War on Trial: The My Lai Massacre and the Court-Martial of Lieutenant Calley* (Lawrence: University of Kansas Press, 2002).

25. Group dynamics and groupthink behavior are discussed in detail and documented in great length in any social psychology text. In this case, I have relied extensively on Sharon S. Brehm, Saul M. Kassin, and Steven Fein, *Social Psychology*, 5th ed. (Boston: Houghton Mifflin, 2002).

26. The reader might remember what one of the guards said upon his arrival at Abu Ghraib in *Standard Operating Procedure*: When he arrived, he said, he found the behavior at the prison, "unusual, weird and wrong . . . [but quickly learned] that's the way it was, [so] it was okay."

27. Robert Koehler, "Battle for Haditha," *Variety*, 17 September 2007, www.variety.com/review/VE1117934755 (accessed 28 July 2010); A. O. Scott, "Redacted," *New York Times*, 16 November 2006, 1(E); Anthony Kaufman, "Rage, Fear and Revulsion: At War with the War," *Village Voice*, 6 May 2008,

52; Manohla Dargis, "'Battle for Haditha': The Killing of Innocents Faces a Dry-Eyed Dissection," *New York Times*, 22 September 2007, 7(E).

28. This explains a reliance on French backdrop props, which are sometimes inadvertently seen in the background—French pornographic magazines, for instance, are lying on the table when Bubba and Flake are reading them. It also explains the reliance on a French television network to break the story.

29. John O'Hare's novel, itself based on a retelling of the Babylonian story by W. Somerset Maugham, is about the inevitably of death (fate; in Arabic, *qisma*—hence *kismet*—or *maktb*). The protagonist, Julian English, runs into Death in the marketplace in Baghdad. Thinking Death is looking for him in the city, Julian flees to Samarra. However, Death's surprise at seeing him in the marketplace was because Death had a rendezvous with him later that night in Samarra.

30. News events that show discrimination in the 1950s tend to make the audience feel that things are so much better today, which, in a sense is true, but the audience's assumption is that discrimination no longer exists, which is decidedly not true.

31. David Ansen, "The Hollywood War Front," *Newsweek*, 8 October 2007, 66.

32. Ansen, "The Hollywood War Front," 66.

33. Anthony Kaufman, "Hearts and Minds," *Village Voice*, 7 May 2008, 52.

34. A. O. Scott, "Rage, Fear, and Revulsion: At War with the War," *New York Times* (16 November 2007): 1(E).

35. Roger Ebert, "Redacted," www.rogertebert.suntimes.com (25 July 2010).

36. Owen Gleiberman, "War Is Hell. . . . ," *Entertainment Weekly*, 21 November 2007, 116.

37. Simi Horwitz, "Acting 'Redacted,'" *Back Stage East* 48, no. 47 (22 November 2007): 32–33.

38. Roger Ebert, "Redacted."

39. Horwitz, "Acting 'Redacted,'" 33.

40. A. O. Scott, "Rage, Fear, and Revulsion: At War with the War."

41. Gleiberman, "War Is Hell. . . "

42. Derek Elley, "Redacted," *Variety*, 10 September 2007, 89.

43. *Statistical Abstract of the United States, 2010*, www.census.gov/compendia/statab (16 July 2010).

44. Stephen T. Holmes and Ronald M. Holmes, *Sex Crimes: Patterns and Behaviors*, 2nd ed. (Thousand Oaks, Calif.: Sage, 2002), 179–89.

45. The girl who was raped was Abeer Qasim Hamza al-Janabi. Robert Ebert was the only reviewer to give the victim a "face" by giving her a name.

46. John Markert, "Social Eclipses and Reversion to Type: Sexual Issues Confronting Postmodern Men and Women Working in Strongly Patriarchal Societies." *Theory in Action* 2, no. 1 (January 2009): 86–109.

47. Holmes and Holmes, *Sex Crimes*, 182.

48. *Statistical Abstract of the United States, 2010*, www.census.gov/compendia/statab (16 July 2010).

49. *Statistical Abstract of the United States, 2010*.

50. Martin L. Lahumiere, Grant T. Harris, Vernon L. Quinsy, and Marnie E. Rice, *The Causes of Rape: Understanding Individual Differences in Male Propensity for Sexual Aggression* (Washington, D.C.: American Psychological Association, 2005), 138–40. See also Maria Testa, "The Impact of Men's Alcohol Consumption on Perception of Sexual Aggression," *Clinical Psychology Review* 22, no. 8 (2002): 1239–63.

51. Actually, "cunt" would be the word Bubba or Flake would use.

52. One Netflix reviewer found Jody Foster's movie to be an excellent film but faulted the male characters for being flat and one-dimensional. But that's the point: males who commit rape are often one-dimensional. There is not a lot of depth to the act of rape or the psychological characteristics of the rapist. See A. Nicholas Groth, *Men Who Rape: The Psychology of the Offender* (New York: Basic Books, 1979).

53. The opening crawl quote in *Extraordinary Rendition* is from Dick Cheney: "Men without conscience are capable of any cruelty the human mind can imagine." The closing crawl belabors the point that the administration supported the CIA's activity: "Since 9/2001 more than 1,000 people [have been] illegally transported by the CIA to countries which practice torture. European prosecutors have 39 outstanding arrest warrants for known CIA agents charged with Extraordinary Rendition in European Union countries."

54. Todd McCarthy, "Rendition," *Variety*, 7 September 2007, www.variety.com/review/VE1117934646 (accessed 26 June 2010).

55. See the discussion about this book and movie in chapter 2, as well as endnote 69 in this same chapter.

56. Todd McCarthy, "Rendition." See also A. O. Scott, "Redacted"; Ann Hornaday, "A Lackluster 'Rendition,'" *Washington Post*, 19 October 2007, www.washingtonpost.com/wp-dyn/content/article/2007/10/18/AR2007101800664 (accessed 20 August 2010); Claudia Puig, "'Rendition' Fails to Turn Over Interest," *USA Today*, 19 October 2007, 8(E).

57. Jonathan Finer, "'Generation Kill' Captures War's Lulls and Horrors," *Washington Post*, 11 July 2008, 1(C). Finer's phrasing sounds like the ending of *M*°*A*°*S*°*H* when, as the antiheroes Hawkeye (Donald Sutherland) and Trapper John (Elliott Gould) drive away, the loudspeaker proclaims, "Tonight's movie

has been MASH. Follow the zany antics of our combat surgeons as they cut and stitch their way along the front lines. . . ."

58. Jonathan Finer, "'Generation Kill' Captures War's Lulls and Horrors." See also Ken Tucker, "Generation Kill." *Entertainment Weekly*, 11 July 2008, 59.

59. Finer, "'Generation Kill' Captures War's Lulls and Horrors."

60. It been argued elsewhere that combat troops often have to steel themselves to the deaths they inflict. Nevertheless, the documentaries often show at least fleeting remorse at what they had to do. Home front documentaries also show that many are subsequently plagued with the face of their victims long after their tour of duty has ended.

61. Fick's book acknowledged some of the confusion and disarray of Bravo Company, but his book is absent of any of the officer-bashing that takes place in *Generation Kill*.

62. Finer, "'Generation Kill' Captures War's Lulls and Horrors."

63. Alessandra Stanley, "Comrades in Chaos, Invading Iraq," *New York Times*, 11 July 2008, 1(E).

64. Stanley may be right that in the sense the pop culture immersion of "these Marines would [make them] virtually unrecognizable to their forebears in the 'Greatest Generation.'" After establishing the difference between this generation of warriors and preceding ones, Stanley then contradicts herself in the next sentence by saying they're the same: "Warriors don't change that much from one conflict to the next. The men who fought at Guadalcanal and the Battle of the Bulge would probably feel right at home" with the way the troops in Iraq acted.

65. Direct action (DA) operations are now the preview of the U.S. Marine Special Operations Command. Reorganization in 2006 dissolved the direct action platoons (DAP) that had heretofore been an integral part of Force Recon companies. Nevertheless, if Special Ops forces are unavailable, Force Recon units must still be prepared to engage in direct action. At the time of the Iraq invasion, Recon Companies would be expected to not only gather critical intelligence but be prepared for direct action since they would often be the first unit into enemy territory.

66. Finer, "'Generation Kill' Captures War's Lulls and Horrors."

67. Finer, "'Generation Kill' Captures War's Lulls and Horrors."

68. Specialist Owen Eldridge is the earnest, eager-to-please young soldier whose on-the-edge job has reduced him to a bundle of frayed nerves; Sergeant J. T. Sanborn is the accomplished professional who does everything by the book in the hopes that protocol and procedure will get him home alive.

69. A. O. Scott, "Soldiers on a Live Wire between Peril and Protocol," *New York Times*, 26 June 2009, 1(C).

70. Katie Holt, *"The Hurt Locker* Doesn't Get This Vets Vote," *The Huffington Post*, 4 February 2010, www.huffingtonpost.com (accessed 7 July 2010).

71. Alex Horton, "The Hurt Locker," www.army of Dude.bogspot.com (accessed 7 July 2010).

72. Gleiberman's C+ is equivalent to the 2½ stars he accorded the American version; curiously, Schwarzbaum gave it a C+ also, but assigned the Danish version 4½ stars, which would be the equivalent of a B+/A-. See Owen Gleiberman, "Brothers," *Entertainment Weekly*, 12 December 2009, www.ew.com/ew/article/o,,1060091,00 (accessed 8 July 2010); Lisa Schwarzbaum, "Brother," *Entertainment Weekly*, 11 May 2005, www.ew.com/ew/article/0,6115,1060091_1_0_,00 (accessed 8 July 2010).

73. Laura Kern, "Brothers," *filmcomment* (November–December 2009): 72.

74. She actually says "shag," which in the United States is the same as saying fuck. I use the coarser American expression to convey how she came across at dinner. This translation is made clear in the title and marquee for the movie *The Spy Who Shagged Me*, which never lifted an eyebrow. There would have been quite a furor over the title had it conveyed its European linguistic equivalent, *The Spy Who Fucked Me*.

75. In the Danish version, a missile is seen launched from the ground; Michael's face is seen when the missile hits, then darkness. The next scene with him in it shows him in the back of a truck as a prisoner.

76. Stop-loss is another linguist euphemism that has arisen from the present combat experience. In the past, one was told that their enlistment has been extended. The meaning was clear: you are not getting out. The lengthy meeting between Brandon and his CO is to explain stop-loss to the audience, who might not be familiar with contemporary military parlance.

77. A. O. Scott, "Back from Iraq, on a Road Going Nowhere," *New York Times*, 28 March 2008, 1(E).

78. Joanne Kaufman, "'Stop-Loss' Lets Clichés Swamp Iraq War Story," *Wall Street Journal*, 28 March 2008, 1(W).

79. Mistakes happen in many pictures and they are often missed until the final cut when it is too late to do anything about it. The problem in this film is that the director recognized a scene problem that could have been readily fixed but didn't bother.

80. Stephen Holden, "After Iraq, Struggling on the Home Front," *New York Times*, 15 December 2006, 32 (E); Nathan Lee, "Home of the Brave," *Village Voice*, 13 December 2006, 100; Sam Adams, "Home of the Brave," *Los Angeles Times*, 15 December 2006.

81. Owen Gleiberman, "The Lucky Ones," *Entertainment Weekly*, 30 October 2008, 52; Peter Hartlaub, "Come Home with Plenty of Baggage," *San*

Francisco Chronicle, 26 September 2008, 12(E); Claudi Puig, "The Lucky Ones," *USA Today*, 26 September 2008, 8(D); Roger Ebert, "The Lucky Ones," *Chicago Sun-Times*, 25 September 2008, www.rogerebert.suntimes .com (accessed 27 July 2010).

82. To be fair to the director in this film, Hank is wearing his old Marine uniform at his son's funeral and the Vietnam service ribbon is prominently displayed, which would be correct given his age and his length of service.

83. *Dear John* touches on the war but is not critiqued in this analysis. The war in this film is simply a mechanism to separate two lovers and draw out their relationship. The geographical separation could just as easily have been the hero going off to college in a distant state or the heroine going to Europe for an extended vacation.

84. Roger Ebert, "Grace Is Gone," *Chicago Sun-Times*, 14 December 2007, www.rogerebert.suntimes.com (accessed 27 July 2010).

85. Mick LaSalle, "Few Saw This Film, But Now You Can," *San Francisco Chronicle*, 25 May 2008, 26(N).

86. Lisa Schwarzbaum, "'Gone' Astray," *Entertainment Weekly*, 10 December 2007, www.ew.com/ew/article/0,,20164469,00.html (accessed 27 July 2010); Scott Foundas, *"Good Grief!" Village Voice*, 5 December 2007, 68.

87. Laura Kern, *"The Messenger," filmcomment* (September–October 2009): 72; A. O. Scott, "Delivering Bad News and Truths about War," *New York Times*, 13 November 2009, 1(E).

88. A. O. Scott, "Delivering Bad News and Truths about War.

89. Laura Kern, *"The Messenger."*

90. Adnan R. Khan, "And the Award Goes to . . . No One: A Controversial Batch of Docs Comes to Turkey's Version of Cannes," *Maclean*, 19 November 2007, 130.

91. Manohla Dargis, reviewing the film for the *New York Times*, finds it difficult to believe that the narrator, who was "born and bred" in Afghanistan, would ask the caller, "Is it as bad as I hear?" This is one reason Dargis finds the film adaptation by David Benioff a "clumsy screenplay." The point, however, is that while the narrator was born in Afghanistan, he has not been there in close to two decades, so it is a legitimate question. One hears all kinds of things; it would be natural for him to ask the caller, who is in Afghanistan, if it really is as bad as he's heard. Manohla Dargis, "Apocalypse Soon: A Mushroom Cloud Doesn't Stall 2008 Electioneering," *New York Times*, 14 November 2006, 1(E).

92. *"Newsweek* Poll: Iraq," PollingReport.com (2010), www.pollingreport .com/iraq (4 July 2010).

93. *"USA Today*/Gallup Poll: Afghanistan," PollingReport.com (2010), www .Pollingreport.com/afghan (29 June 2010).

94. "Distrust, Discontent, Anger and Partisan Rancor: The People and Their Government," Pew Research, 18 April 2010, www.people-press.org/report/606/trust-in-government (accessed June 30, 2010).

95. John Marzulli and James Gordon Meek, "Al Qaeda Poised to Try Major Attack in Untied States within 3–6 Months, Intelligence Chief Warns," *New York Daily News*, 3 February 2010, 1.

96. "Distrust, Discontent, Anger and Partison Rancor," 2010.

97. Darrell M. West and Marion Orr, "Managing Citizen Fears: Public Attitudes toward Urban Terrorism," paper presented at annual American Political Science Association conference, Washington, D.C. (1 September 2005); John Hibbing and Elizabeth Theiss-Morse, "The Media's Role in Public Negativity toward Congress: Distinguishing Emotional Reactions and Cognitive Evaluations," *American Journal of Political Science* 42, no. 2 (1998): 475–98; John Hutcheson, David Domke, Andre Billeaudeaux, and Philip Garland, "U.S. National Identity, Political Elites, and Patriotic Press Following September 11," *Political Communication* 21, no. 1 (2004): 27–50; Michelle Slone, "Responses to Media Coverage of Terrorism," *Journal of Conflict Resolution* 44, no. 4 (2000): 508–22.

98. Clinton M. Jenkin, "Risk Perception and Terrorism: Applying the Psychometric Paradigm," *Journal of Homeland Security Affairs* 2, no. 2 (2006).

99. N. Pidgeon, R. E. Kasperson, and P. Slovic, *The Social Amplification of Risk* (Cambridge: Cambridge University Press, 2003).

100. Daniel Byman and Christine Fair, "The Case for Calling Them NITWITS." *Atlantic*, July–August 2010, 106–108.

101. Martin-Munoz focused on images of Muslim women in the Spanish press. Of a total of 332 photographs of women that appeared, 34 percent portrayed Muslim women: 18 percent on the front page and 68 percent on the inside news pages. She states that 14.9 percent did *not* portray women as a victim; I simply reframed this statistic to indicate that most images *did* portray women as a victim of Islam. See Gema Martin-Munoz, "Islam's Women under Western Eyes," *OpenDemocracy*, 8 October 2002, www.opendemocracy.net (accessed 4 July 2010).

102. Martin-Munoz, "Islam's Women under Western Eyes"; Fareena Alam, "Beyond the Veil," *Newsweek International*, 27 November 2006, ww.msnbc.msn.com/id/15789437/stit/newseeek (accessed 30 July 2010); Dominic McGoldrick, *Human Rights and Religion: The Islamic Headscarf Debate in Europe* (Oxford: Hart Publishing, 2006).

103. First wave feminism sought to extend the right to vote to women. This was achieved when the Nineteenth Amendment to the Constitution was ratified in 1920. Having achieved what they set out to do, the feminist movement

was eviscerated. Second wave feminism was "reborn" during the social ferment of the 1960s. The formation of the National Organization for Women in 1966 is typically looked at as a milestone in the rejuvenation of the feminist movement in the United States.

104. I've traced the international development of feminism. I place the United States and a number of European countries in the more "advanced" Tier IV category. It is worth noting that in this paradigm gender equity is achieved when a country reaches Tier X status, which suggests that even the more advanced countries have a long way to go before reaching gender equality. See John Markert, "The Globalization of Sexual Harassment," in *Advances in Gender Research, Volume 9—Gender Realities: Local and Global*, ed. Marcia Texler Segal and Vasilikie Demos (Amsterdam: Elsevier, 2005), 133–60; John Markert, "Social Eclipses and Reversion to Type: Sexual Issues Confronting Postmodern Men and Women Working in Strongly Patriarchal Societies," *Theory in Action* 2, no. 1 (2009): 86–109.

105. A. O. Scott, "FBI Agents Solve the Terrorist Problem," *New York Times*, 30 November 2009, 17(E).

⑤

CONCLUSION

It is not a startling revelation to say that movies reflect the social world in which people live. They do not reflect it perfectly, however. This becomes apparent when the reflective aspect is put under the microscope, as it is in this analysis. The first set of films that deal with 9/11-related events may come closest to being purely reflective.

The collapse of the Twin Towers is probably one of the most filmed tragedies in history. The event took place mid-morning in a major city bustling with pedestrians. Advances in technology meant that many of the people near Ground Zero had ready access to video equipment, so they could "capture the moment." Organizational features also played a role. New York City is the hub of network news-gathering organizations, and these organizations and their satellite stations in and around New York and New Jersey could muster a video crew at a moment's notice to follow events as they unfolded. This was facilitated by the time lag. Crews were assembled to investigate what was taking place after the first tower was hit, which means they had time to get there before the towers collapsed and could record the event as it unfolded. They were strategically in place to record subsequent rescue activities. The abundance of film shot that day meant that documentaries could be hastily assembled to reprise events. Indeed, the early onslaught of documentaries were little more than televised footage that was threaded together to go beyond the isolated clips of events shown on the nightly news. There was little remarkable material in many of these early documentaries.

However, there were two notable cinematic exceptions to the early documentary that were shot at Ground Zero. They are of a higher order than most films that detail events that day because they were shot by professional documentarians who happened to be in the process of making documentaries, coincidentally, of the two groups who spearheaded rescue operations. *9/11* is about New York firefighters, and the filmmakers just happened to be following a probie who was assigned the station house proximate to the WTC; and *Twin Towers* is about the elite ESU of the New York police department, who, because of their "special" designation, were the first police unit to respond to events that day. Both documentary filmmakers were on the ground that day and could record events with greater insight than news crews or pedestrians who overly focused on catching shots of the towers aflame. They could also add "depth" to their films by situating the police officers and firefighters who responded by giving them a "face." They are both solid films. In fact, *Twin Towers* won the Oscar for best documentary in 2002 if only because *9/11*, which would have been a strong contender, was excluded from Oscar competition because it originally aired on CBS.

The wealth of film shot that day, and those taken of the rescue efforts by news organizations in the weeks that followed, is explained, in part, by technology and, in part, by organizational features: the prominence of major network news organizations in the Big Apple. This explains why there are so many images of Ground Zero. It does not fully account for the surge in documentaries. Industry structure helps here.

Industry structure refers not so much to the size of the organization but the relationship to other organizations in the industry. Media organizations today are more interconnected than ever. This was not always the case. Indeed, the television industry and the movie industry were once, not that long ago, characterized by an antithetical relationship. Today they are bedmates: ABC is owned by Disney, which in turn owns Disney Studios, Pixar International (Films), and until mid-2010, Miramax; CBS and Viacom are both owned by media mogul Sumner Redstone, and through these two companies Redstone also owns MTV and BET Networks, Paramount Pictures, and DreamWorks; NBC

Universal, as the name implies, is the NBC network that is now married to Universal Pictures, which, until 2010, were divisions of General Electric; Time/Warner owns New Line Cinema and HBO, as well as Turner Studios, whose divisions include TNT, TBS, CNN, and TCM; and media mogul Rupert Murdoch owns the Fox network, along with FX and CW networks, as well as Fox Movie Channel, 20th Century Fox, and Fox Studios.

Televised news footage is no longer proprietary to the network, even if it might remain proprietary to affiliated companies. This relationship facilitated the transformation of televised images to cinematic films. Many of these early films were never released in theaters, but the DVD market vastly extended their lives. Anyone who wanted to glean more information about the World Trade Center's uniqueness as a historical structure could watch the Art and Entertainment (A&E) Network's retooled *World Trade Center: In Memoriam*. If they missed it when it first aired on A&E, it was readily available at rental outlets.

These films familiarized Americans with nuances of the WTC disaster that they might not have been exposed to on television. The films often went beyond the fleeting, fragmented images that appeared on television by tying the movie to a particular person or situation that could be explored in greater detail. The films also allowed people to revisit aspects of the events surrounding the fall of the Twin Towers that had disappeared from television because it was "old news." A decade later, they also serve as misleading historical artifacts because of their decidedly nonreflective aspects—the silences. Any disturbing, less than heroic depictions of events that took place that day have been excised. Indeed, two types of events that took place at Ground Zero are not caught in any of the documentaries. One is the self-aggrandizement of firefighters who impeded rescue operations by constantly stopping activities to honor *their* dead. The other is the fisticuffs that erupted between firefighters and police. It may simply be that the incident is still too fresh in the hearts and minds of Americans to tolerate *any* disparaging images, which is why there was so much antagonism across the country in 2010 when New York Muslims indicated that they wished to build a (new) mosque just a few blocks from where the Twin Towers once stood.

There were two thematic variations surrounding what happened that day that emerged later in the decade and which similarly reflect changing social attitudes. One was the increased public scrutiny of why the government failed to prevent events on 9/11 that began to percolate in society a few years after the attack. These "voices" are seen in films such as *9/11: Press for Truth* and *The 9/11 Commission Report*. Fictive features dealing with events that took place at Ground Zero extended the parameters of the documentaries by turning a lens on other dimensions of the tragedy: *WTC View* (2005) looks at the effect the event had on someone living in New York but not directly affected by the collapse of the Twin Towers; *Reign Over Me* (2007) looks at the effect on someone who lost loved ones that day and how their life is affected years later.

There was less film footage of the attack on the Pentagon, since the area was restricted, and no footage of what took place on United 93. This explains why it was left to fictive features to portray these events. *DC 9/11: Time of Crisis* was a hastily assembled, fictionalized account that appeared in 2003. It presents the president, members of his cabinet and military officials at the Pentagon, proactively taking charge of events. The film does not reflect what actually happened so much as it reflects what the public wanted to believe took place: there was no confusion the day of the attack and responsible leaders in government took direct, forceful steps against the attackers. Films depicting events that took place aboard Flight 93 were more reflective, in part, because they were helmed by seasoned filmmakers who had time to put together solid films, but they were also more reflective of events because there were so many telephone transmissions that took place that day by passengers aboard the plane to enable a fairly accurate portrait of events to be depicted. Fairly accurate is a key reflective point here. Susan Faludi presents strong evidence that the women aboard United 93 took a more proactive role in battling the terrorists than either of the films depict. Their disappearance in film tends to reflect the budding "masculine" mythology that Faludi saw coalescing around 9/11 activities.

The incursions into Afghanistan and Iraq, at least as they surrounded the hunt for Osama bin Laden and Saddam Hussein, were certainly reflective of events, to a point. Early films about Osama bin Laden devoted more time to background information since the hunt would not be successful for nearly a decade, and roaming desolate mountainous regions with a camera does not really hold the viewer. One of the silences in these historical details about bin Laden that negates the purely reflective dimension of film is the complicity of the United States in bringing him to power. Films touch on this relationship fleetingly, when they touch on it at all. One of the more pronounced silences in films surrounding the futile search for Osama bin Laden is the *failure* of technology to pinpoint his whereabouts. This technological silence is particularly stark when placed beside films that accentuate America's technological sophistication in bringing Iraq to heal so quickly.

People often hold diametrically opposite beliefs: I want a calorie-bursting Whopper but I want to lose weight. People are often unconscious of these polar-opposite cognitions, which is why the person eats the Whopper with a diet soda. Cognitive dissonance occurs when people become aware that they have conflicting attitudes. This realization is disturbing, so they must reconcile the inconsistent thoughts. This can lead to attitude change, which itself can be traumatic, especially if it requires a reassessment of long-held, cherished beliefs, like the American belief in its technological superiority.[1] Cognitive dissonance did not occur with the technological issue because its failure in Afghanistan is never raised. It is true that two later films did question the role of technology, but both did so fleetingly so it never "forced" the viewer to recognize the disparity in one's beliefs. The failure of technology to find bin Laden is the rationale that spurs Morgan Spurlock's quest to find bin Laden himself, but it is never revisited in *Where in the World Is Osama bin Laden?* It is a satiric antidote at the end of *War, Inc.* The fact that the only two films that raise the technological issue are lighthearted looks at the war further diminishes their ability to raise dissonance among viewers. More than likely, now that bin Laden has been located and eliminated, a television documentary will delve into the role of the Navy Seals and a made-for-television fictive feature will depict the exploits of Seal Team VI, no doubt lauding the sophisticated technology that ultimately located him in Pakistan, silently passing over the decade-long failure to ferret him out.

Roughly the same number of films devoted to bin Laden and to Saddam Hussein exist. The latter cinematic journey tends to be more compelling, however. This is because early films capitalized on the already entrenched public animosity toward Saddam that was widespread in society after Gulf War I and the decade-long controversy surrounding

Iraq's WMD. The journey also has more staying power because there is a historical progression that appealed to the public: the hunt, capture, trial, and subsequent execution of the former Iraqi leader.

It soon became apparent after the fall of Baghdad that no WMD existed. The political rhetoric following the invasion shifted away from the focus on the WMD and began to accentuate Saddam's dictatorial abuses. It was an easy sell. Despots are generally perceived in a negative light by Americans. And Saddam's abuses of power already had wide social currency. Saddam's irrational bent was enhanced by images of Saddam's crazy look when he was pulled from his hole and by his subsequent hysterical outbursts during his trial. Films that dealt with Saddam marched in lockstep with the pervasive social views of the mad Iraqi dictator. The general consensus was that he was crazy. The implication of this mental state suggested that though he might not actually have had WMD, he was capable of acquiring them—and crazy enough to use them if he ever got his hands on them. Removing Saddam was therefore an appropriate course. This comes across very poignantly in the HBO production *House of Saddam* (2008). These movies, then, reflect a popular mind-set, but in doing so perpetuate the false memory that Saddam actually had WMD.

Films that depicted events surrounding what took place on 9/11, and those that focused on Saddam Hussein and Osama bin Laden, are peppered with small silences that challenge the notion that films merely reflect events.[2] Still, they tended to reflect social attitudes more than they refracted a point of view. Refraction occurs when the filmmaker deliberately sets out to change people's ways of seeing the social world. This was Michael Moore's stated intention when he made *Fahrenheit 9/11*.

Social attitudes in the immediate aftermath of the 9/11 attacks were solidly behind the president. Cheers went up across the country when within weeks of the incursion into Iraq the president proclaimed the war won and by default, over, and on the Afghan front that the Taliban had been routed. Attitudes began to change over the coming year when it was apparent the war was not quite over in Iraq and Taliban forces were still causing problems in the southern region of Afghanistan. This was acerbated in Iraq when no WMD were found and in Afghanistan when troops failed to ferret out Osama bin Laden. People began to voice concern over the withdrawal of troops as the body count climbed; others started to question why the United States was in Iraq in the first place. Support for the president's agenda started to change between 2004 and 2005. It had not turned against the war, but it was moving in that direction. Public opinion was split roughly 50/50 over America's continued presence in Iraq, which received the lion's share of attention because reporters were embedded there and not Afghanistan, and because there was a clear target with troops entering Baghdad that could not be as clearly delineated in Afghanistan. Film cannot be shown to have changed people's opinion, but it certainly helped inflame the debate. It did this simply by keeping the issue alive in the public arena.

The first major cinematic salvo against the war was fired by Michael Moore, who received considerable attention because of his status as a popular documentarian. This meant that those in the middle, those who were not firmly entrenched in the liberal or conservative camp, might see the movie and possibly contemplate what it had to say. It clearly pontificated a liberal stance, but the two rebuttal films pontificated a strong conservative stance. The difference is that Michael Moore's film was seen by a much larger audience than either of the other two, and while this might reflect changing social mores toward the war, it must also be seen as stimulating the debate as to the rationale behind the war, which is the film's central theme.

It is impossible to state that a film changed social attitudes. It is clear in this case, however, that films preceded the change in public attitudes. If social attitudes in 2004 and 2005 were evenly split, films were decidedly split against the war by a 2:1 margin, if one counted only domestic features, and by a 3:1 margin, if one counted those quasi- and foreign films released in the United States. It is unusual to see such a clear demarcation between a film's presentation of events and the public's distinctively different interpretation of those same events.

The cinematic dialectic during this crucial two-year period revolved around Saddam's WMD. Conservative filmmakers enunciated that they were there, somewhere; they just hadn't been found yet. Liberal filmmakers posited that there were no WMD and focused on how the president used this as a pretext to sell Americans on the war in Iraq. This dialectic was gaining wider social currency at this time in society. Cinema added fuel to the social debate in two ways. First, it kept the issue alive. More importantly, its decided leaning toward the liberal camp would mean that more people were exposed to that idea than its counterpart, increasing the chances that it would be given greater weight, if only because it was the dominant cinematic perspective.

Films that focused on the war itself were also changing. Coverage of the Iraq war far outweighed coverage in Afghanistan. A major reason for this, though clearly not the only one, is that there were a substantial number of reporters embedded with the troops in Iraq. The issue of embedding was very controversial when it was first proposed. A key concern was whether journalists could remain impartial and report objectively on events. Subsequent studies would show their objectivity was seriously compromised. The military brass picked up on this immediately, however, which is why their initial skepticism veered sharply after the results were witnessed. A hard, critical look at the films covering the incursion into Iraq and the fall of Baghdad would reveal the positive biases the military hierarchy was quick to recognize. It can be seen in the glowing adjectives used to describe the troops, the emphasis on the "amazing" shock and awe technology that lit the Baghdad skyline, and how the film was framed to emphasize the positive attributes of the troops while casting the enemy in an unflattering light. The most blatant illustration of this bias is the televised images of Saddam's statue being toppled, which inevitably appears in any of the documentaries of the fall of Baghdad.

This early prowar cinematic depiction of Iraq would shift after the fall of Baghdad. Ironically, it was film shot by the troops that would, quite inadvertently, undermine the positive depiction of the unfolding war.

The "true" face of the war was captured by the troops. This would be the first time the grunt in the field had access to sophisticated technology in the guise of helmet-mounted cameras or small, handheld video cameras. The images they captured could be electronically, and instantaneously, transmitted to family and friends back home. Later they would be assembled into documentaries. These are basically home movies and would otherwise have been shown like home movies—at home to friends where events that were depicted could be contextualized. They are "upscaled" into documentaries because (1) a market existed—people stateside were interested in the men and women serving; (2) the "filmmaker" had access to relatively inexpensive, easy-to-use online editing technology; and (3) they could go straight to DVD, which circumvented the filtering process (editing) that typically occurs when a movie is made for mainstream distribution.[3] The contextualization that would take place when showing the films among friends is lost in these documentaries. The result is that the home movie quality of the films presented a less-than-flattering face of America's finest that was not seen on the nightly news or in documentaries that followed the troops into Baghdad. Ranking military might have taken steps to control access to the new technology had they realized this would occur; for example, they could have prohibited bringing video equipment into a combat zone. No one anticipated the tainted face of the warrior that would be exposed in these films.

One thing that immediately becomes apparent is their motivation for joining, and their attitudes toward the war. Some joined to serve their country in the patriotic fervor that swept the United States in the aftermath of the 9/11 attacks. Often, their rationale for joining is more self-serving. Many enlisted because they had limited life chances: they either were stuck in a dead-end job or couldn't find gainful employment, or they were in the guard to pick up a few extra dollars and never anticipated being deployed, or they figured that the military was the only way they would ever get enough money to someday go to college. They also regularly question the "higher cause" of the war. These faces appear particularly stark in the documentary because they are not the faces the viewer was used to seeing on the nightly news or in documentaries by embedded journalists.

The face that was portrayed in films like *Gunner Palace* and *Operation: Dreamland* was not "bad," but these films do not frame things as neatly as films that were shot by journalists or professional documentarians. Two activities dominate the grunt's perspective. One is the downtime—the time in the barracks; the other is their "combat" role. The lack of context in which these two daily activities unfold makes their depicting somewhat "unsettling." Barracks time overaccentuates the grousing; combat footage shows them knocking civilians around, often for no clear reason.

At the beginning of these films, the camera is intrusive and those being video recorded wave the filmmaker away or tell them to turn it off. The ubiquitous camera is soon forgotten, however. The result is that people are not as guarded in their intimate backstage comments as they might be when they present their face to the public. Some of the attitudes and behaviors that are bantered about in the barracks among understanding others toward the Iraqi people are very benighted, or at least appear so when the focus of the camera overaccentuates these comments. The attitudes are understandable, given the average grunt's educational level (high school) and limited world experience—many of them have never traveled beyond their hometown's boundaries. The problem is that this gets lost in the film and the viewer only sees some crude generalization about the indigenous population.

These attitudes carry over to the field. Though a substantial amount of time in the field is dead time—time spent guarding a gate, patrolling the streets, manning checkpoints—this is seldom documented; it is not very cinematic. Instead, a disproportionate amount of film is devoted to showing more "action" moments, mainly kicking in doors in the middle of the night and rousting unarmed civilians. At least, this is how it often appears since the civilians are often not armed and no weapons may be found. The viewer seldom gets the background behind the reason for the raids. Grunt films may sometimes say the people in the house they are raiding are dangerous or pose a threat, but we seldom see it. Instead, we see women and children being mishandled but don't appreciate how these same innocents may be a real threat to the soldiers. It is important to remember that women in the Middle East are increasingly being recruited as suicide bombers because they defy the stereotype and thus have a greater chance of accomplishing their mission, and children ages twelve to fourteen in some parts of the world comprise a very dangerous part of the fighting forces in a country.

Despite some depictions that might appear to "trash" the troops, they come off as they have historically: average Joes and Janes who are, overall, pretty good guys and gals, doing a difficult job, and trying to make the best of a bad situation. The same cannot be said regarding many journalists. They might look good when seen reporting on the war, but when the lens is turned on them, they come off rather poorly.

The reporters seem to think of themselves in "heroic" terms, but they like their creature comforts too much to venture too far beyond the Baghdad Hilton.[4] And even there, we saw in a casual aside in *Heavy Metal in Baghdad*, they rely on Iraqi nationals to shoot film of events taking place in the city. They then reframe the story with themselves in the picture to give the impression that they are following the famed footsteps of World War II journalist Ernie Pyle, who lost his life in the closing days of the war on a remote island (Ie Shima) off the coast of Okinawa. Nor is Pyle's modest, unassuming personality seen in those few reporters who do venture out of the city in search of a story, since the story is often centered more on them than the men and women whose lives they are reputedly chronicling. There were certainly journalists in Gulf War II who followed the high tradition of journalism and took their charge seriously. They are just not found in any of these films. It is a lens on the war that has otherwise not been exposed, and is exposed here quite inadvertently.

The dialectic continues in documentary film in the second half of the decade. There are three thesis films and three antithesis films, none of which are particularly remarkable. The Abu Ghraib scandal that broke in 2004 starts to garner the attention of documentarians in 2006, and these films are solidly on the antithetical side of the debate. Their darker assessment of behavior by military personnel in Iraq skews the cinematic debate and challenges the president's stance that the isolated incidents were due to a few "bad apples." This group of film also includes a number of exposés of conditions in Guantanamo. It is cinematically noteworthy that films exploring the Guantanamo facility relied on the docudrama format. This is because there were no photographs to present a "face" to show what took place there and, unlike Abu Ghraib, no one person or group of people could be identified to interview about conditions.

Films portraying the grunt likewise change in this later period. We move away from footage shot in the field by military personnel as professional documentarians begin to take a closer look, not at the war per se, but at those who served. Some of these films are dark, too, but it is a different "darkness." It is the darkness of their plight—the physical and psychological toll the war has taken. The injuries veterans have sustained were raised in the Michael Moore film, but here it moves center stage. Other films explain why so many injured survive in this war. These films focus on the medical efforts in the field that save so many today. The heroic efforts by medical personnel, however, are offset when these films are watched with those films that depict the physical and psychological tolls the war has taken on survivors, and those that decry the lack of government services for the veteran once home. Other films in this group, such as *Lioness* and *Full Battle Rattle*, turn their lens on nuances of the war that otherwise have escaped public scrutiny, while still others look at how the troops entertain themselves.[5] These films appeal to the broader public, but judging from reviews on lay movie sites and online blogs, they are also of some appeal to those who have served, and the families of those who are serving.

The documentary tide had clearly turned against the war in 2004 and 2005 and, if nothing else, nudged society to give deeper consideration to the rationale for continuing the wars. Documentaries in the second half of the decade were more in line with newly emerged social attitudes. Films during this later period are interesting because one can see how the issue was framed. The antiwar sentiment never touched the troops. Even the Abu Ghraib MPs are not castigated; it is, rather, the end result of policies formulated in Washington, so the guards are not culpable. The fact that the guards did what they did (and don't seem to appreciate what the fuss is about) is passed over.[6] Fictive features pick up this standard of fault finding and, in some cases, go beyond the documentaries by coming down forcefully on some issues that have escaped the documentarian's lens.

Fiction appears relatively late. The lumbering structure of large organizations helps explain their late entry. Expense is a key factor for large, profit-oriented organizations, and fiction is considerably more expensive than most documentaries. There are more intricate occupational layers involved in the making of a fictive feature. These layers are particularly stark when one examines the handful of people who might have been involved with making a documentary compared to the lengthy screen credits at the end of a mainstream fictive feature. The cost aside, it still remains a major undertaking just to get all these people lined up to participate in the making of a movie. Larger organizations are also more concerned with identifying the market for the film to ensure a profit, and the market size for a fictive feature has to be much larger than for a documentary in order for the studio to recuperate production costs. Studios are also careful to not ruffle social feathers since that could hurt the film's gross sales. These issues, while not solved in 2006, were less problematic. Social attitudes against the war started to rise sharply in 2006 and continued to climb through the remainder of the decade. This meant that a market of some size existed and people were more amenable to hearing about issues relating to the war.

The first crop of films to appear in 2006 is more problematic than later ones. *Cavite* is a low-budget film of no particular cinematic quality, made by two Philippine Americans and with a handheld camera with a production budget of $7,000. The fact that it was picked up by Magnolia Pictures, a major film distributor, indicates the studios were beginning to recognize a shift in attitude about the war was starting to take place and wanted to take advantage of the emerging market. Two of the other pictures, *The Insurgents* and *Southland Tales* are less about the war "over there" than terrorism. Both films are more polished than *Cavite* but neither makes a contribution to the dialogue about the war. Indeed, the war is incidental to *Southland Tales* because its juvenile plot is clearly marketed to an adolescent male filmgoer.[7] The only mainstream fictive feature in 2006 that assessed the war was *Home of the Brave*, about the difficulties three Iraq war veterans have adjusting to civilian life. It too is a problematic film. Its strong cast does not turn in a credible performance. The "rush" to say something in fictional film about the returning veteran may have hurried the film's production. Fictive features after 2006 got there a little later, and this, in itself, is a factor that makes them stronger films.

Despite the questionable cinematic merits in this first batch of fictive features, they all share postmodern characteristics. Postmodernism is distinguished by two primary characteristics. Thematically, postmodern cinema depicts considerable disenchantment with social arrangements and takes a more critical, alienated worldview. Structurally, postmodern cinema is more fragmented and tends to relay multiple viewpoints, rejecting the dominant metanarrative of modern filmmakers. Postmodern elements dot some of the documentaries. Film shot by military personnel in the field clearly shows their disenchantment and reflects a certain amount of angst. Their films are also fragmented, but they generally lack alternative points of view. The docudramas that appraise conditions at Guantanamo clearly fall into the postmodern cinematic tradition, as does *Iraq in Fragments*, and some of the foreign fictive features, such as *Turtles Can Fly* and *Paradise Now*. The launch of domestic fictive features that begins in 2006 roots post-9/11 films more firmly in the postmodern tradition.

Fictive features at the end of the decade are solidly against the war. Only two films can be said to have strong prowar sentiments: *Day Zero* and *Grace Is Gone*. Film has returned to its reflective roots: self-serving bureaucrats and narrow-minded politicians are at fault for any issues surrounding the wars; America should extricate itself from a no-win situation; nevertheless, the troops who serve are patriotic and are held in high esteem. *Lions for Lambs* is an excellent example of how the postmodern filmmaking method is married to the reflective. The film jumps back and forth between the senator's office and the professor's, with sporadic glimpses of men courageously sacrificing their lives in the mountains of Afghanistan as Taliban forces move in for the kill—and the connection to the men in the mountains and the other pivotal characters only becomes clear toward the end of the film. The senator is sanctimonious, willing to sacrifice the lives of patriotic warriors if it advances his political career; the professor gives voice to the public's view by questioning why the United States is involved in Iraq and Afghanistan, in effect, condemning the continued deployment of American troops, but explicitly praising his two former students who followed their conviction and joined the military, and who, the viewer knows, are about to meet their death; the journalist acts as a foil to the senator, the student to the professor, but both of their "futures" are left dangling at the film's end.

Fictive features at the end of the decade make a number of thematic contributions. Two films, *Battle for Haditha* and *Redacted*, take a closer look at two, distinctly dark faces of the war in Iraq. The former dealt with the "rampage" of a Marine squad that resulted in the senseless murder of fifteen women and children; the latter, the rape of a young girl and the murder of her and her family by an Army squad to cover their crime. These were not popular films, but they dealt with issues that were disseminated by news outlets and put a face to the two tragedies that took place, which were not raised in other films. The public seems to have rejected these films because they tarnished the image of the troops in the field. This explains why these films were not embraced but those that showed acts of rendition against innocent civilians did not meet the same fate: first, they were civilians, and second, those responsible were self-serving bureaucrats who overstepped their authority. Another thematic contribution of other fictive features, such as *Rendition* and *Extraordinary Rendition*, as well as *Stop-Loss*, is to expose facets of the war that had escaped the documentarian's lens: the kidnapping and torture of suspected terrorists and the effects on the lives of men and women who serve by extending their tour of combat duty beyond reasonable limits. Still others, like *Green Zone*, fictionalize events documentarians have addressed, such as the failure to find WMD. This is a topic that would have been problematic in 2003 but which had wide social currency by 2010. By fictionalizing it, however, it reaches a wider audience than any of the half-dozen documentaries on the topic, and, in the process, reinforces the perception that WMD never existed, while challenging the beliefs of a shrinking minority that still hold Saddam had WMD.

On August 31, 2010, President Obama announced the withdrawal of the last combat brigade in Iraq. He hedged his announcement by calling it a milestone rather than saying the war was won, or even over. His wording was precise and implied that things had improved sufficiently in Iraq so that American troops could now come home. Still, 50,000 military personnel and 4,500 special force members remain deployed in Iraq. It will be interesting to see how film covers Iraq in the coming decade.

Film about Iraq peaked in 2007and 2008. These dates coincide with the October 2007 surge, when troop commitment reached its peak of 170,000. The 2010 "end" was the culmination of a steady troop downsizing in Iraq that began in late 2008. The war has moved to another front, and with it, social concerns, and film.

Cinematic attention has only glanced at Afghanistan outside the hunt films. Suddenly, film has discovered what has been called the forgotten war. *Restrepo* (2010), for example, is the first documentary to follow military personnel into the mountains and give us a close-up view of the men fighting in the same vein that *Gunner's Palace* and *Occupation Dreamland* did with the grunt at the front in Iraq. Pat Tillman lost his life in a friendly fire incident in Afghanistan in April 2004. His former status as a professional football player helped generate a certain amount of media attention at the time. It was not until 2010 that a documentary was made about the event. The Tillman documentary followed the tradition of many Iraqi documentaries by casting a jaundiced lens on how the military attempted to cover up his death by laying blame on the Taliban. Cinema's discovery of Afghanistan reflects society's, and just like Iraq, the concern is over the rising death toll. Military fatalities in Iraq have dropped from a high of 961 in 2007, to 322 in 2008, 150 in 2009, to 60 in 2010. In contradistinction, more troops have been committed to Afghanistan and fatalities have been steadily rising: 232 in 2007, 295 in 2008, 521 in 2009, and 711 in 2010.[8] This would suggest that cinema will intensify its dissection of activities on the Afghan front in the near future, and perhaps longer, since the Taliban's presence remains strong. The Taliban, for example, recently ordered the stoning of a couple in northern Afghanistan who defied local conventions by having an affair and trying to elope, they warned residents in Logar province not to watch television, and in Jalalabad, they threatened to bomb music shops if they did not stop selling decadent Western music.[9]

Greater attention on Afghanistan will keep the terrorist fires burning in the public's eye. The Taliban represent one of the most vivid reminders of the strong enmity radical fundamentalists have toward the West, and their terrorist "solution." It is in this area that film seems to be moving.

Terrorism is a recurring theme on many television dramas and dots many mainstream films.[10] One-fifth of the fictive features examined in the last chapter that were produced between 2006 and 2010 explicitly revolved around the threat of terrorism. These films were also the money winners. The prevalence of this theme is likely to increase in the future, in part because the wars in Iraq and Afghanistan are winding down, and in part because terrorism is a popular topic that is not geographically bound to Iraq or Afghanistan and lends itself to graphic visualization. Paradoxically, the cinematic lens on terrorism primes the social mind-set to accept the need for military intervention even as the public wants troops pulled back from Iraq and Afghanistan.

NOTES

1. The "technological imperative" was clearly and strongly established in the American psyche at the outset of the twentieth century. See Leo Marx, *The Machine in the Garden: Technology and the Pastoral Ideal in America* (New York: Oxford University Press, 2000); Henry Adams, *The Education of Henry Adams* (Boston: Houghton Mifflin, [1918] 1973).

2. The silences can be seen in Saddam's trial, which glosses over the packed tribunal, and his execution, which shows the Iraqi dictator going to his death with more dignity than initially reported in the American press and behaving more civilly than those who gathered to watch his execution.

3. See Richard A. Peterson and John Ryan, "The Fate of Creativity in Country Music Writing," *Sage Annual Review of Communication Research* 10: 11–32.

4. The lack of creature comforts in Afghanistan must be considered a factor in the lack of coverage on the Afghan front.

5. Plenty of entertainers traveled to Afghanistan and Iraq to entertain the troops. There has been no substantive coverage of these shows, which is surprising given how popular USO shows were with the American people in former wars.

6. This also applies to those soldiers in *Soldier's Pay* who were cashiered from the army for stealing money found under the floorboards of one of the raided houses.

7. The difference between the juvenile antics in *Southland Tales* and those in *Harold and Kumar Escape from Guantanamo* is that the antics in the latter film are toned down and there is a strong female presence to broaden the audience base to encompass juvenile females.

8. Source for fatalities, icasualties.org.

9. Hashim Shukoor, "Taliban Try to Stop the Music Again," *The Tennessean*, 12 September 2010, 2A.

10. See Robert Cetti, *Terrorism in American Cinema: An Analytical Filmography, 1960–2008* (Jefferson, N.C.: McFarland, 2009).

SELECTED BIBLIOGRAPHY

Abelman, Robert, David Atkin, and Michael Rand. "What Viewers Watch as They Watch TV: Affiliation Change as a Case Study." *Journal of Broadcasting & Electronic Media* 41, no. 3 (1997): 360–82.

Adorno, Theodor. "On Popular Music." *Studies in Philosophy and Social Science* IX (1941): 17–48.

The Agent Orange Coverup: A Case of Flawed Science and Political Manipulation (12th report). Washington, D.C.: House Committee on Government Operations, 1988.

Alam, Fareena. "Beyond the Veil." *Newsweek International*. www.msnbc.msn .com/id/15789437/stit/newseeek. 2006 (accessed 12 March 2010).

Allen, Jody T., Nilanthi Samaranyske, and James Albrittain Jr. "Iraq and Vietnam: A Crucial Difference in Opinion." www.pewresearch.org/pubs/432 .2007 (accessed 23 November 2009).

Arnove, Anthony. "Cautionary Tales: Documentaries on the UN Sanctions and War with Iraq." *Cineaste* 28, no. 2 (Spring 2003): 21–23.

Arthur, Paul. "Iraq in No Particular Order." *filmcomment* (September–October 2006): 19–22.

Atran, Scott. "The Moral Logic and Growth of Suicide Terrorism." *Washington Quarterly* 29, no. 2 (2006): 127–47.

Auster, Albert, and Leonard Quart. *How the War Was Remembered: Hollywood & Vietnam*. Westport, Conn.: Praeger, 1988.

Barker, Kim. "Kabul Makeover." *The Atlantic* (March 2006): 19–20.

Baudrillard, Jean. *Simulacra and Simulation*, trans. by S. F. Glaser. Detroit: University of Michigan Press, 1995.

Bauerlein, Mark. *The Dumbest Generation: How the Digital Age Stupefies Young Americans and Jeopardizes Our Future*. New York: Tracher/Penguin, 2008.

Bellamy, Robert, and James R. Walker. *Television and the Remote Control: Grazing on a Vast Wasteland*. New York: Guilford, 1996.

Berrebi, Claude. "Evidence about the Link between Education, Poverty and Terrorism among Palestinians." *Peace Economics, Peace Science and Public Policy* 13, no. 1 (2007): 1–36.

Black, Joel. *The Reality Effect: Film Culture and the Graphic Imperative*. New York: Routledge, 2002.

Boggs, Carl, and Tony Pollard. *A World in Chaos: Social Crisis and the Rise of Postmodern Cinema*. Boulder, Colo.: Rowman and Littlefield, 2003.

Bourdieu, Pierre. *Distinction: A Social Critique on the Judgment of Taste*. Cambridge, Mass.: Harvard University Press, 1984.

Brehm, Sharon S., Saul M. Kassin, and Steven Fein. *Social Psychology*. 5th ed. Boston: Houghton Mifflin, 2002.

Bruni, Luigino, and Luca Stanca. "Income Aspirations, Television and Happiness: Evidence from the World Values Survey." *KYKLOS* 59, no. 2 (2006): 209–25.

Byman, Daniel, and Christine Fair. "The Case for Calling Them NITWITS." *Atlantic* (July–August 2010): 106–9.

Carnes, Mark C. *Past Imperfect: History According to the Movies*. New York: Henry Holt, 1995.

Carr, Steven Alan. "Mass Murder, Modernity, and the Alienated Gaze," in *Cinema and Modernity*, edited by Murray Pomerance, 57–63. New Brunswick, N.J.: Rutgers. 2006.

Chesebro, J. W. "Communication, Values, and Popular Television Series—A Twenty-Five Year Assessment and Final Conclusions." *Communication Quarterly* 51, no. 4 (2003): 367–418.

Cook, Deborah. *The Culture Industry Revisited: Theodor W. Adorno on Mass Culture*. Lanham, Md.: Rowman & Littlefield, 1996.

Cressey, Paul G. "The Motion Picture Experience as Modified by Social Background and Personality." *American Sociological Review* 3, no. 2 (1934): 230–44.

Dardis, Frank E. "Marginalization Devices in U.S. Press Coverage of Iraq War Protest: A Content Analysis." *Mass Communication & Society* 9, no. 2 (2006): 117–35.

Davis, Ronald L. *Celluloid Mirrors: Hollywood and American Society since 1945.* Ft. Worth, Tex.: Harcourt Brace, 1997.

DeFleur, Melvin L., and Mary M. Cronin. "Completeness and Accuracy of Recall in the Diffusion of the News from a Newspaper vs. a Television Source," *Sociological Inquiry* 61, no. 2 (1991): 148–66.

Dick, Bernard. F. *The Star-Spangled Screen: The American World War II Film.* Lexington: University Press of Kentucky, 1985.

"Distrust, Discontent, Anger and Partisan Rancor: The People and Their Government." Pew Research, 2010. www.people-press.org/report/606/trust-in government (accessed 30 June 2010).

Dixon, Wheeler Winston. "The Endless Embrace of Hell: Hopelessness and Betrayal in Film Noir." In *Cinema and Modernity*, edited by Murray Pomerance, 38–56. New Brunswick, N.J.: Rutgers, 2006.

Doherty, Thomas. *Projections of War: Hollywood, American Culture, and World War II.* New York: Columbia University Press, 1993.

Dommermuth, William P. "How Does the Medium Affect the Message?" *Journalism Quarterly* 51, no. 3 (1974): 441–47.

Dunlap, Celina. "My Lai: Legacy of a Massacre." *BBC News* (15 March 2008).

Eagleton, Terry. *Marxism and Literary Criticism.* Berkeley: University of California Press, 1976.

Early, Emmett. *The War Veteran in Film.* Jefferson, N.C.: McFarland, 2003.

Ebiri, Bilge. "The Ravages of War and Occupation: An Interview with James Longley." *Cineaste* 32, no. 1 (Winter 2006): 38–41.

Ellis, Jack C., and Betsy A. McLane. *A New History of Documentary Film.* New York: Continuum, 2005.

El-Nawawy, Mohammad. *Al-Jazeera: The Story of the Network That Is Rattling Government and Redefining Modern Journalism.* Cambridge, Mass.: Westview, 2003.

Faludi, Susan. *The Terror Dream: Fear and Fantasy in Post 9/11 America.* New York: Metropolitan Books, 2007.

Fitzgerald, G. J. "Chemical Warfare and Medical Response During World War I." *American Journal of Public Health* 98, no. 4 (2008): 611–24.

"Foreign Policy Attitudes Now Driven by 9/11 and Iraq." 2004, www.people press.org/report222. (accessed 12 March 2009).

Foreman, Jonathan. "How Not to Write About Iraq." *Commentary* (October 2008): 42–45.

Fumento, Michael. "Covering Iraq: The Modern Way of War Correspondence." *National Review* (6 November 2006): 42–46.

Fussell, Paul. *The Great War and Modern Memory.* London: Oxford University Press, 1975.

Gans, Herbert J. "Popular Culture in America: Social Problems in a Mass Society or Social Asset in a Pluralist Society?" In *Social Problems: A Modern Approach*, edited by H. Becker, 549–620. New York: Wiley, 1966.

———. *Deciding What's News: A Study of* CBS Evening News, NBC Nightly News, Newsweek and Time. New York: Random House, 1979.

Getlin, Josh. "All News Channels First Big Audience." *Los Angeles Times*. www.latimes.com/news/custom/timespoll. 2003 (accessed 20 November 2009).

Gitlin, Todd. *The Whole World Is Watching: Mass Media in the Making and Unmaking of the New Left*. Berkeley: University of California Press, 2003.

Goldsmith, David. A. *The Documentary Makers: Interviews with 15 of the Best in the Business*. Switzerland: RotoVision, 2003.

Griffiths, Philip Jones. *Agent Orange: 'Collateral Damage' in Vietnam*. London: Trolley, 2003.

Grossberg, Lawrence. *Bring It All Back Home: Essays on Cultural Studies*. Durham: Duke University Press, 1997.

Hafez, Mohammed M. "Suicide Bombers in Iraq: The Strategy and Ideology of Martyrdom." Washington, D.C.: U.S. Institution of Peace Press, 2007.

———. "Manufacturing Human Bombs: The Making of Palestinian Suicide Bombers." Washington, D.C.: U.S. Institution of Peace Press, 2006.

———. "Why Muslims Rebel: Repression and Resistance in the Islamic World." Boulder, Colo.: Lynne Rienner Publishers, 2003.

Harney, Caroline D. *Agent Orange and Vietnam: An Annotated Bibliography*. Lanham, Md.: Scarecrow Press, 1988.

Hassan, Riaz. "Global Rise of Suicide Terrorism: An Overview." *Asian Journal of Social Science* 36, no. 2 (2008): 271–91.

Heeter, C. "Program Selection with Abundance of Choice: A Process Model." *Human Communication Research* 12, no. 1 (1985): 126–52.

Herber, Lori, and Vincent F. Filak. "Iraq War Coverage Differs in U.S., German Papers." *Newspaper Research Journal* 28, no. 3 (2007): 37–51.

Hess, Frederick M. "Still at Risk: What Students Don't Know, Even Now." *Common Core* 110, no. 2 (2009): 5–20.

Hibbing, John, and Elizabeth Theiss-Morse. "The Media's Role in Public Negativity toward Congress: Distinguishing Emotional Reactions and Cognitive Evaluations." *American Journal of Political Science* 42, no. 2 (1998): 475–98.

Hilburn, Matt. "Goyas: More Grotesque Than Ever." *TechBiz: Media* www.wired.com/techbiz/media/news/2001/09. 20 September 2001 (1 May 2010).

Hirsch, E. D. *Cultural Literacy: What Every American Needs to Know*. Boston: Houghton Mifflin, 1987.

Hodges, Adam. "The Political Economy of Truth in the 'War on Terror' Discourse: Competing Visions of an Iraq/al Qaeda Connection." *Social Semiotics* 17, no. 1 (2007): 5–20.

Hogan, David J. *Science Fiction America: Essays on SF Cinema.* Jefferson, N.C.: McFarland, 2006.

Hudson, Rex A., and Marilyn Lundell Majeska. *The Sociology and Psychology of Terrorism: Who Becomes a Terrorist and Why?* Washington, D.C.: Federal Research Division, Library of Congress, 1999.

Hutcheson, John, David Domke, Andre Billeaudeaux, and Philip Garland. "U.S. National Identity, Political Elites, and Patriotic Press Following September 11." *Political Communication* 21, no. 1 (2004): 27–50.

Jacques, Karen, and Paul J. Taylor. "Male and Female Suicide Bombers: Different Sexes, Different Reasons?" *Studies in Conflict & Terrorism* 3, no. 4 (2008): 304–26.

Jameson, Fredrick. *Postmodernism, or, The Cultural Logic of Late Capitalism.* Durham, N.C.: Duke University Press, 1991.

Jarvie, Ian. "Film and the Communication of Values." *European Journal of Sociology* 10, no. (1969): 205–19.

Jenkin, Clinton M. "Risk Perception and Terrorism: Applying the Psychometric Paradigm." *Journal of Homeland Security Affairs.* Vol. II, no. 2 (2006): 1–14.

Kahn, Jeffery. "Postmortem: Iraq War Media Coverage Dazzled but It's Also Obscured." 2004, www.Berkeley.edu/news/media/releases/2004/03/18_iraq media (accessed 7 August 2009).

Kaplan, Robert D. "Why I Love Al Jazeera." *Atlantic* (October 2009): 55–56.

Kasdan, Margo, Christine Saxton, and Susan Tavernetti. *The Critical Eye: An Introduction to Looking at Movies.* Dubuque, Iowa: Kendall Hunt, 1998.

Kehr, Dave. "Revisiting the Road to Iraq War, Step by Step." *New York Times,* 20 August 2004, 16(E).

Kohut, Andrew. "Trends in Political Values and Core Attitudes: 1987–2007." The Pew Research Center, 2007, www.peoplle-press.org/trends-in-political values-and-core-attitudes-1987-2007 (accessed 4 November 2009).

Krueger, Alan B., and Steven Lerner. "Education, Poverty and Terrorism: Is There a Causal Connection?" *Journal of Economic Perspectives* 17, no. 4 (2003): 119–44.

Langewiesche, William. "American Ground: Unbuilding the World Trade Center, Part I: The Inner World." *Atlantic Monthly* (July–August 2002): 45–79.

———. "American Ground: Unbuilding the World Trade Center, Part II: The Rush to Recover." *Atlantic Monthly* (September 2002): 47–79.

————. "American Ground: Unbuilding the World Trade Center, Part III: The Dance of the Dinosaurs." *Atlantic Monthly* (October 2002): 94–126.

Lehmiller, Justin J., and Michael T. Schmitt. "Intergroup Attitudes and Values in Response to the U.S. Invasion of Iraq." *Peace and Conflict* 14, no. 2 (2008): 259–74.

Lentz, Robert J. *Korean War Filmography*. Jefferson, N.C.: McFarland, 2003.

Lewis, Justin, Sut Jhally, and Michael Morgan. "The Gulf War: A Study of the Media, Public Opinion and Public Knowledge." Center for the Study of Communication, University of Massachusetts at Amherst (February 1991), www.umass.edu/~commdept/resources/gulfwar (accessed 6 August 2009).

Lindner, Andrew M. "Among the Troops: Seeing the Iraq War through Three Journalistic Vantage Points." *Social Problems* 56, no. 1 (2009): 21–48.

Lowenthal, Leo. *Literature, Popular Culture, and Society*. New York: Prentice-Hall, 1961.

Lynch, M. *Voices of the New Arab Public: Iraq, Al-Jazeera, and Middle East Politics Today*. New York: Columbia University Press, 2006.

MacEain, Enis. "Suicide Bombing as Worship." *Middle East Quarterly* 16, no. 4 (2009): 15–25.

March, James G., and Herbert A. Simon. *Organizations*. New York: John Wiley & Sons, 1958.

Marcus, J. *Surviving in the Twentieth Century: Social Philosophy from the Frankford School to the Columbia Faculty Seminars*. New Brunswick, N.J.: Transaction Publishers, 1999.

Markert, John. *Sexual Harassment: A Resource Guide for Organizations and Scholars*. Spokane, Wash.: Marquette Books, 2010.

————. "Social Eclipses and Reversion to Type: Sexual Issues Confronting Postmodern Men and Women Working in Strongly Patriarchal Societies." *Theory in Action* 2, no. 1 (2009): 86–109.

————. "Divergent Gender Messages on Spanish-Language Television in the United States: Cracks in the Edifice, Unlatching the Window of Change." *Sociological Imagination* 45, no. 1 (2009): 41–61.

————. "Superstitious Peasants: Religious Images on Spanish-Language Television in the United States." *Sociological Imagination* 43, no. 2 (2007): 21–35.

————. "The George Lopez Show: The Same Old Hispano?" *Bilingual Review*. Vol. 28, no. 2 (2007): 148–65.

————. "The Globalization of Sexual Harassment." In *Advances in Gender Research, Volume 9—Gender Realities: Local and Global*, edited by Marcia Texler Segal and Vasilikie Demos, 133–60. Amsterdam: Elsevier, 2005.

————. "Sing a Song of Drug Use-Abuse: Drug Lyrics in Popular Music—From the Sixties through the Nineties." *Sociological Inquiry*. Vol. 71, no 2 (2001): 194–220.

———. "Romance Publishing and the Production of Culture." *Poetics: International Review for the Theory of Literature* 14 (Fall 1985): 69–94.

Martel, Ned. 2005. "Turning a Critical Lens on Television News." *New York Times*, 4 February 2005, 22(E).

Martin-Munoz, Gema. 2010. "Islam's Women under Western Eyes." *OpenDemocracy*, 2002. www.opendemocracy.net (accessed 4 July 2010).

Mast, Gerald, and B. F. Kawin. *A Short History of the Movies*. New York: Macmillan, 1992.

Mathur, Piyush. "More Whitewash: The WMD Mirage." *Third World Quarterly* 27, no. 8 (2006): 1495–1507.

McAdams, Frank. *The American War Film: History and Hollywood*. Westport, Conn.: Praeger, 2002.

McCrisken, Trevor B., and Andrew Pepper. *American History and Contemporary Hollywood Film.* New Brunswick, N.J.: Rutgers University Press, 2005.

McGirk, Tim. "Collateral Damage or Civilian Massacre in Haditha?" *Time* (19 March 2006): 34–36.

McGoldrick, Dominic. *Human Rights and Religion: The Islamic Headscarf Debate in Europe*. Oxford: Hart Publishing, 2006.

McLaughlin, E. "Television Coverage of the Vietnam War and the Vietnam Veteran." 2008, www.wabirdforum.com/media (accessed 16 November 2009).

"Media Multitasking Usually Exception, Not Rule." 2008, www.marketing charts.com/television/media-multitasking (accessed 23 February 2009).

Miles, Hugh. *Al-Jazeera: The Inside Story of the Arab News Channel That Is Challenging the West*. New York: Grove Press, 2005.

Mockenhaupt, Brian. "SimCity Baghdad: A New Computer Game Lets Army Officers Practice Counterinsurgency Off the Battlefield." *Atlantic* (January–February 2010): 26–27.

Morris, Jonathan S. "Slanted Objectivity? Perceived Media Bias, Cable News Exposure, and Political Attitudes." *Social Science Quarterly* 88, no. 3 (2007): 707–28.

Neuman, W. Russel. "Patterns of Recall among Television News Viewers." *Public Opinion Quarterly* 40, no. 1 (1976): 115–23.

Newsweek Poll: Iraq. PollingReport.com, 2010, www.pollingreport.com/iraq (accessed 4 July 2010).

Nielsen Media Research 2000 Report on Television: The First 50 Years. Nielsen Media Research, A. C. Nielsen Company (2000): 1–27.

Nowell-Smith, Geoffrey "How Films Mean, or, from Aesthetics to Semiotics and Half-way Back Again." In *Reinventing Film Studies*, edited by C. Gledhill and Linda Williams, 8–17. London: Arnold, 2000.

Oberdorfer, Don. *Tet! The Turning Point in the Vietnam War.* New York: Da Capo Press, 1984.

"Our Fading Heritage: Americans Fail a Basic Test on Their History and Institutions." Wilmington, Del.: Intercollegiate Studies Institute, 2008. www .americancivicliterarcy.org (accessed 3 February 2010).

Pape, Robert A. *Dying to Win: The Strategic Logic of Suicide Terrorism.* New York: Random House, 2005.

Patai, Raphael. *The Arab Mind.* New York: Hatherleigh Press, 2002.

Patrick, Brian A., and A. Trevor Thrall. "Beyond Hegemony: Classic Propaganda Theory and Presidential Communication Strategy after the Invasion of Iraq." *Mass Communication & Society* 10, no. 1 (2007): 95–118.

Peterson, Richard A. "Six Constraints on the Production of Literary Works." *Poetics: International Review for the Theory of Literature* 14 (Fall 1985): 45–68.

———. 1982. "Five Constraints on the Production of Culture: Law, Technology, Market, Organizational Structure, and Occupational Careers." *Journal of Popular Culture* 16, no. 1 (1982): 143–53.

———. "The Production of Culture: A Prolegomenon." In *The Production of Culture,* edited by R. A. Peterson, 7–22. Beverly Hills, Calif.: Sage, 1976.

Peterson, Richard A., and Janet Kahn. "Media Preferences of Sexually Active and Inactive Youth." *Sociological Imagination* 32, no. 1 (1995): 29–43.

Pfau, Michael, Michael Haigh, Lindsay Logsdon, Christopher Perrine, James P. Baldwin, Rick E. Breitenfeldt, Joel Cesar, Dawn Dearden, Greg Kuntz, Edgar Montalvo, Dwaine Roberts, and Richard Romero. "Embedded Reporting and Occupation of Iraq: How the Embedding of Journalists Affects Television News Reports." *Journal of Broadcasting & Electronic Media* 49, no. 4 (2005): 468–87.

Pidgeon, N., R. E. Kasperson, and P. Slovic. *The Social Amplification of Risk.* Cambridge, U.K.: Cambridge University Press, 2003.

"Post September 11 Attitudes." 2001, www.people-press.org/report/144 (accessed 13 March 2009).

Postman, Neil. *Amusing Ourselves to Death.* New York: Penguin, 1985.

Postman, Neil, and Steve Powers. *How to Watch TV News.* New York: Penguin, 1992.

Pribram, E. Deidra. *Cinema & Culture: Independent Film in the United States, 1980–2001.* New York: Peter Lang, 2002.

Prichard, Robert S. "The Pentagon Is Fighting—and Winning—the Public Relations War." *USA Today* (July 2003): 11–14(A).

"Public Attitudes toward the War in Iraq: 2003–2008." 2008, www.pew research.org/pubs/770 (accessed 13 March 2009).

"Public's Priorities for 2010: Economy, Jobs, Terrorism." Pew Research, 2010, www.people-press.org/report/584/policiy-priorities-2010 (accessed 30 June 2010).

Rampton, Sheldon, and John Stauber. *Weapons of Mass Destruction: The Uses of Propaganda in Bush's War on Iraq.* New York: Tarcher/Penguin, 2003.

Ravitch, Diane. *What Do Our 17-Year-Olds Know?* New York: Harper and Row, 1987.

Richelson, Jeffrey. "Iraq and Weapons of Mass Destruction." *National Security Archive Electronic Briefing Book No. 80,* 2004, www.gwu.edu/nsarchiv/NSAEBB/NSAEBB80 (accessed 9 September 2009).

Ridge, G. "Embedded: The Media at War in Iraq." *Military Review* 84, no. 1 (January–February 2004): 74–75.

Rising-Moore, Carl, and Becky Oberg. *Freedom Underground: Protesting the War in America.* New York: Chamberlain Brothers/Penguin, 2004.

Ritter, Scott. *Iraq Confidential: The Untold Story of America's Intelligence Conspiracy.* New York: I. B. Tauris, 2005.

Ritzer, George, and Douglas J. Goodman. *Sociological Theory,* 6th ed. New York: McGraw Hill, 2004.

Riverbend. *Baghdad Burning: Girl Blog from Iraq.* New York: Feminist Press, 2005.

Robb, David L. *Operation Hollywood: How the Pentagon Shapes and Censors the Movies.* Amherst, N.Y.: Prometheus Books, 2004.

Roberts, Donald F., and Ulla G. Foehr. "Trends in Media Use." *The Future of Children* 18, no. 1 (2008): 11–37.

Roscoe, Jane, and Craig Hight. *Faking It: Mock-documentary and the Subversion of Factuality.* Manchester: Manchester University Press, 2001.

Rosenstein, Aviva W., and August E. Grant. "Reconceptualizing the Role of Habit: A New Model of Television Audience Activity." *Journal of Broadcasting & Electronic Media* 41, no. 3 (1997): 324–44.

Rushing, Josh. *Mission Al Jazeera: Build a Bridge, Seek the Truth, Change the World.* New York: Palgrave Macmillian, 2007.

Russell, Charles, and Bowman Miller. "Profile of a Terrorist." In *Perspectives on Terrorism,* edited by Lawrence Zelic Freedman and Yonah Alexander, 45–60. Wilmington, Del.: Scholarly Resources, 1983.

Sageman, Marc. *Understanding Terror Networks.* Philadelphia: University of Pennsylvania Press, 2004.

Schmitz, D. F. *The Tet Offensive: Politics, War, and Public Opinion.* Lanham, Md.: Rowman & Littlefield, 2005.

Schuman, Howard, and Willard L. Rodgers. "Cohorts, Chronology, and Collective Memory." *Public Opinion Quarterly* 68, no. 2 (2004): 217–54.

Shaw, Tony. *Hollywood's Cold War.* Amherst: University of Massachusetts Press, 2007.

Simendinger, Alexis. "In Credible Standing." *National Journal* 35, no. 23 (2003): 1782.

Simon, Herbert A. *Administrative Behavior*, 3rd ed. New York: Free Press, 1973.

Slone, Michelle. "Responses to Media Coverage of Terrorism." *Journal of Conflict Resolution* 44, no. 4 (2000): 508–22.

Speckhard, Anne. "The Emergence of Female Suicide Terrorists." *Studies in Conflict & Terrorism* 32, no. 11(2008): 1023–51.

Storey, John. *Cultural Theory and Popular Culture: An Introduction*, 4th ed. Athens: University of Georgia Press, 2006.

Strinati, Dominic. *An Introduction to Theories of Popular Culture.* New York: Routledge, 1995.

Swidler, Ann. "Culture in Action: Symbols and Strategies." *American Sociological Review* 51, no. 2 (1986): 273–86.

Taylor, Ella. 2006. "Sundance in Fragments: Festival's Documentaries Offer a Survey of Global Disorder." *L.A. Weekly*, 2 February 2006.

Tumber, Howard, and Jerry Palmer. *Media at War: The Iraq Crisis.* Thousand Oaks, Calif.: Sage, 2004.

Turvey, Malcolm. "Iraqis under the Occupation: A Survey of Documentaries." *October Magazine* 123 (Winter 2008): 234–41.

"USA *Today*/Gallup Poll: Afghanistan." 2010, www.pollingreport.com/afghan (accessed 29 June 2010).

van den Berg, A. "Critical Theory: Is There Still Hope?" *American Journal of Sociology* 86, no. (1980): 449–78.

Walker, James, and Robert Bellamy. *The Remote Control in the New Age of Television.* Westport, Conn.: Praeger, 1993.

Watt, Ian. *The Rise of the Novel.* London: Chatto and Windus, 1957.

Waxman, Sharon. "Sparing No One, a Journalists Account of the War." *New York Times*, 10 June 2004, 1(E).

West, Darrell M., and Marion Orr. "Managing Citizen Fears: Public Attitudes toward Urban Terrorism." Paper presented at annual American Political Science Association conference. Washington, D.C., September 2005.

Whitney, Craig R. 2005. *The WMD Mirage: Iraq's Decade of Deception and America's False Premise for War.* New York: Public Affairs, 2005.

Williams, Brain Glyn. "Mullah Omar's Missiles: A Field Report on Suicide Bombers in Afghanistan." *Middle East Policy* VX, no. 4 (2008): 26–46.

"A Year After Iraq War." 2004, www.people-press.org/report/206 (accessed 13 March 2009).

Zimmerman, Karl. "They're in the Army Now—Not Really: Most 'Embedded' Journalists Are Fish out of Water." *National Review* (21 April 2003): 31–34.

Zimmerman, Patricia R. *States of Emergency: Documentaries, Wars, Democracies*. Minneapolis: University of Minnesota Press, 2000.

INDEX

ABOUT THE AUTHOR

John Markert is an associate professor at Cumberland University, a small liberal arts college outside of Nashville, Tennessee. He earned his B.A. and M.A. in sociology from the University of South Florida and his Ph.D. in sociology from Vanderbilt where he focused on media organizations. Dr. Markert has published articles in a wide range of scholarly journals, including *Critical Sociology*, *Sociological Imagination*, *Sociological Spectrum*, *The Social Science Journal*, *Theory in Action*, and *Advances in Gender Research, Volume 9*. He recently published *The Social Impact of Sexual Harassment* (2010) with Marquette Books.